Ivor Browne

Music and Madness

For Chariji and Juno

Ivor Browne

Music and Madness

Ivor Browne

ATRIUM

First published in 2008 by Atrium
Atrium is an imprint of Cork University Press
Youngline Industrial Estate
Pouladuff Road
Togher
Cork
Ireland

Reprinted 2008

British Library Cataloguing in Publication Data
A CIP catalogue record for this book is available from the British Library.

ISBN 978-0-9552261-2-0
Printed by ColourBooks Ltd., Baldoyle, Dublin

For all Atrium books visit www.corkuniversitypress.com

Contents

Much madness is divinest sense –
To a discerning eye –
Much sense – the starkest madness –
'tis the Majority
in this, as all, prevail –
Assent – and you are sane –
Demur – you're straightway dangerous –
And handled with a chain.

Emily Dickinson
The Complete Poems of Emily Dickenson, London, 1970.

Acknowledgements

My deep appreciation goes to my patients, who, through the years, taught me so much about life and the nature of suffering towards growth. I may not remember all their names and, sometimes nowadays, maybe not even some of their faces, but I so often think of their courage and affection. Sure, where would I have been without them?

Thanks to my wife, June Levine, who told me I should be writing it all down instead of rabbiting on about it, and to my stepdaughter Diane Reid, who, from her reading of the first draft, boosted my confidence by always asking me if I had any more she could read. My stepson Michael Mesbur gave me invaluable help in producing the diagrams, for which I am hugely grateful. I should mention with gratitude Loughlin Kealy, Stella Kearns, Dr Michael Corry for the illustrations of the brain, of materialistic society and the therapeutic relationship which they made for inclusion in the book.

Thanks to Paddy Walley, Art O'Briain and Loughlin Kealy, Professor of Architecture at University College, Dublin, for helping me to restore memories of our time in The Irish Foundation for Human Development.

Thank heaven for Lucy Freeman for her advice and skilful restructuring of a draft that was all over the place. Also thanks to my editor, Maria O'Donovan, and to Sophie Watson of Cork University Press. Between them they did a mammoth job.

My heartfelt thanks to outside editors Professor Garrett O'Connor, the Dubliner who is CEO of the Betty Ford Institute in California and my beloved friend and inspiration for so many years, and to the late Professor Anthony Clare, colleague and friend in need, whose untimely death in Paris in 2007 came as such a shock. Thank you Frances Osbourne and Trish Ford for patient typing, and to Fintan O'Toole for his inspirational articles in *The Irish Times*. And thanks again to Colm Tóibín, Catriona Crowe, Noeleen Dowling and Fionnula Flanagan.

Preface

I set about writing this book because of my deep dissatisfaction with the direction which psychiatry and the treatment of mental illness has taken. There is also the wider question of the drift of western society into materialism, the mechanistic philosophy underlying this, and the growth of the free market. This trend has now reached global proportions, with transnational corporations spreading across the surface of the planet. These two processes are not unrelated, as psychiatry too is increasingly under the control of just such pharmaceutical empires.

In attempting a critique of these trends, I felt the only way I could approach it was to describe, as best I could, my own painful growth and development, during the second half of the twentieth century, as a human being trying to find if there is a meaning or purpose to our life here; then later to trace my formation as a psychiatrist, a long struggle, that I suppose could be described as a kind of psychotherapy for slow learners. Often in life we cannot see how we have got to where we are, or how we come to shape our own unique view of reality.

It is not my intention to write an autobiography or my memoirs. I do not feel that the struggles of my personal life, with its many failures and mistakes, are likely to be of much interest to anyone else, but they shaped me. Also, to write an acceptable autobiography, one needs to be a writer to make it readable, and I have no pretensions in that regard. I felt too that my children and my former wife are entitled to their privacy, as is my wife June, without whose support and constant help this book would certainly never have been written.

To begin with, I am critical of some of my father's behaviour but when I look back now all I feel is a deep sense of gratitude (while it was my mother who opened up my heart to spirituality). It was my father who gave me my appreciation of music, of literature, history and philosophy. The environment that my father created around 'the field', a field he rented, was not only a physical space but also a total way of life for me and the friends who lived in the area – a safe, alternative world. I can see that he created this alternative reality primarily to protect his own vulnerability, but he was also determined that we would have a better life than he had had growing up. In the process he gave us a wonderfully rich environment, which in modern terms was fully ecological. The only drawback was that it was difficult to emerge from this into the ordinary, everyday reality outside. I had difficulty relating to school and even to medical school later. On the positive side, I believe it gave me a different view of reality, so that I often saw things from a different perspective.

I only took up medicine to keep my parents off my back. Music was my obsession and I was determined to become a jazz musician. Fortunately, contracting tuberculosis put an end to that, as I can see now that the kind of traditional jazz I was following was really a road to nowhere. Even now I have a sense of myself as a failed musician. I had never thought of entering the Royal College of Surgeons, and only did so to keep my father calm while I got on with my dream of becoming a jazz musician. I only awoke from that dream completely during my pre-registration hospital year. It was 1955 and I was standing self-consciously in the medical staffroom of the old Richmond Hospital in front of the Abe, Professor Leonard Abrahamson, our professor of medicine. What the Abe said to me was, 'You're only fit to be an obstetrician or a psychiatrist'. Now, before he presented me with those options, I had already had a vague notion of becoming a psychiatrist. However, as music was my passion, I had never let my studies get in the way of it until, halfway through my medical course, tuberculosis ended my trumpet blowing forever.

Even after I qualified as a doctor, I had little passion for medicine; that is, until I took up psychiatry. Then, gradually, I began to accept that this was my true vocation. Fairly early on I came to realise that if a person suffering from psychiatric illness were to change for the better, this would depend on their working to bring about that change in themselves. Later, I realised that, even at its simplest, any change involves two things – work and suffering; the deeper the change to be accomplished, the greater the amount of effort, pain and suffering involved. I no longer accepted the mainstream views on psychiatric illness, but I had not yet any clear alternative.

In the early years after I was appointed Professor of Psychiatry in University College Dublin, I had to deliver a weekly lecture to the fourth-year medical class of around 120 students. I mention this because, frequently, on going in to face the entire class of students who expected a clear medical description of psychiatric illness, I found I had no scientific foundation on which to base my intuitive sense of an alternative view. I still had only a dawning awareness of the social and personal factors underlying most forms of emotional disturbance.

During my experience with Dr Joshua Bierer in the Marlborough Day Hospital in London, which I will recount later, I had realised that there were deeper layers to human personality and traumatic experience, which lay behind most psychiatric illness. Later, in the Harvard School of Public Health, I was exposed to ecological concepts and, for the first time, understood the fundamental importance of our immune system in combating pathological organisms and other threats from the environment. I had never even heard of these concepts, or the epidemiological aspects of illness, during my ordinary medical training. I had thought of mental illness as something which simply happened to us, like catching a cold, or going down with flu. For the first time I was made aware of concepts like the 'internal milieu' of Claud Bernard and physiological 'homeostasis', as described by Walter Cannon. From all this experience I gradually began to see the fundamental importance of self-management in the maintenance of our health. Of course, at the time, I had no consciousness of the nature of a 'living system' or of the importance of 'boundedness'. Yet, intuitively, I absorbed this awareness as a state of being and so, when I came upon these concepts later, I was already receptive to them.

Looking back and asking the question, what did I gain personally from all the work with the Irish Foundation for Human Development, the group conferences on 'Authority and Leadership' and the work in Derry, I think it was, for me, the clarification of the ideas that underlay all these activities in which we were involved; also the gradual realisation that, ultimately in nature, 'co-operation' is more effective than the neo-Darwinian concept of 'competitiveness'.

It was in the early 1970s that I first heard of the work of the Chilean biologists Maturana and Varella. Their theories of autopoiesis, and of the biology of cognition, were a revelation. Later came Prigogene's concept of 'self-organisation', which, together with the concept of 'autopoiesis', for the first time gave a clear definition of what it is to be 'alive'. I now had a glimpse of an entirely different view of the nature of living creatures, as distinct from the reductionist scientific paradigm, which was all I had been exposed to up to that point. I have now come to believe that the future of mental health must lie in the growth and empowerment of the person. Drugs may temporarily relieve symptoms, but ultimately only the person can realise his/her own potential.

So these are some of the questions that I attempt to address in this book. It is for the reader to judge to what extent I have been successful. The case illustrations are all true. Only the names and identifying information have been altered.

Ivor Browne
March 2008

Introduction

It was new year's eve in 1986 and there was a late lunch in Ivor Browne's house in Ranelagh in Dublin. There were only four of us at the table: June Levine, Ivor's partner, who had cooked the lunch, myself and the playwright Tom Murphy. The light was dwindling even as we sat down to eat. We were in no hurry. We were all going out later, but to different places. I cannot remember what we talked about, but I remember that the atmosphere was funny, pleasant, relaxed.

Except that the phone rang all the time. I thought at first it rang because people wanted to wish June and Ivor a happy new year, but some of the calls were long and were taken by Ivor not in the dining-room, where he was, but in the kitchen, where he had to go each time. He would return to the dining-room table looking preoccupied and weary. Sometimes, as the meal wore on, it was almost comic; he would have a bite of food in his mouth and suddenly the phone would go again and June would be careful to ensure that Ivor took the call in the kitchen and that neither of the guests went into the kitchen while he was speaking.

Eventually I asked what the problem was. June merely sighed and said that maybe they should go to India next year for the Christmas season. Ivor said nothing, but as the phone rang several more times it became impossible for him not to offer some explanation. What he said amazed me.

At that time, Ivor was Chief Psychiatrist in the then Eastern Health Board, and Professor of Psychiatry at University College Dublin. His home number was ex-directory, but those who called had, in desperation, managed to get hold of it. All of them had the same problem: a member of their family had come home for Christmas and, over the seven or eight days since their arrival, it had become increasingly apparent that they needed psychiatric care, until

1

finally it had become essential that they be committed to an institution or urgently be seen by a psychiatrist. This was why they were
calling. Some of those who rang were relatives of patients of Ivor's,
but others who called merely knew him or June socially and found
themselves helpless since the friend or relative who now needed Ivor's
assistance had come home from abroad.

Was it like this all the time, I asked? No, June and Ivor said, only
at Christmas. It is what Christmas does to people. How come, I
asked? Ivor looked at me calmly. Drink, he said. Scarce light. A return to a family or a home place with many unresolved associations.
The Christmas season is, he said, full of excitement and good cheer
at first, but once people are cooped up with their families, things
start to go wrong. Families, he added, are often not the best places
for people to be. I nodded. We continued our meal.

Before we left each other's company that day, we wished one
another a happy new year. I had, as I walked back through Dublin,
something new to think about. I had a sense that the season which
was not fully over brought with it, at times, an ambiguous silent
legacy, something insidious and mostly unmentioned, making its
way as panic and crisis in houses fully decorated for festivity. It was
something I had vaguely known and oddly felt but had never heard
formulated before so clearly as a matter of fact.

Over the next while, as I met Ivor Browne at social gatherings,
I found that he had no small talk. A few times, almost as a way of
evading the calmly searching questions he was asking me about my
own background, I changed the subject to that new year's eve meal.
I thus discovered certain interesting things about modern psychiatry
which I did not know.

In other areas of medicine there had been, I knew, great advances. In the fight against cancer, for example, early detection followed by surgery, with the use of radiotherapy and chemotherapy,
had improved things. Even in surgery itself, the arrival of dissolving
paper stitches was a great advance. In the fight against heart disease,
drugs lowering blood pressure and cholesterol, by-pass surgery and
less invasive forms of surgery had made things better for people. In
the fight against AIDS, triple therapy had made a huge difference.

But in the battle against mental illness, I discovered, advances
had been more deceptive and those in treatment had a right to be
more equivocal about them. It had seemed at one time that Prozac

might be a cure for depression, and that several drugs seemed to re-duce psychotic episodes in those suffering from schizophrenia. Even drugs like Ritalin for attention deficit disorder seemed to be work-ing, or having some beneficial effect. All this was a vast improvement on electro-convulsive therapy (ECT), or indeed on lobotomy or life-time incarceration, all of which had happened in living memory.

As I listened to Ivor Browne, and then over the next few years to others who were suffering from various types of mental illness or had sufferers amongst their friends and associates, things were, however, not so clear. The mind was not a cancer cell or a virus; it was a more delicate and mysterious organism. While many of the drugs pre-scribed by psychiatrists had been effective, they had served to mask the actual problem rather than eradicate it or alleviate it. The side ef-fects of some drugs had, in turn, caused further problems, some of them very serious. But because the drugs seemed to work, especially at first, a whole generation of psychiatrists had emerged who knew which drugs to use for which symptoms and in which doses. They had no interest in psychoanalysis and had not asked if the symptoms might have causes (just as oncologists did not ask if cancer cells had causes) which might also be looked at. Such questions in psychiatry seemed to belong to the 1960s and had, most of the time, gone the way of electric shock treatment and life-long incarceration.

I pressed Ivor to formulate all of this, as he pressed me to tell him if my parents were still alive. He pressed me further when I told him that my father had died when I was twelve, to tell him how I genuinely felt about this. I can still see him watching me, holding my gaze. I must have shrugged as I tried to explain that my father was a secondary school teacher; he died just before I was due to go to his secondary school, and I had dreaded the idea of him teaching me. So, I told Ivor, in a way when he died I was relieved.

Did you know him well, Ivor asked me. No, I said, no, there were four other children, three older than me, and he was very sick for the last four years of his life. But did you ever have a relationship with him, Ivor continued. Oh yes, I said, when I was younger, before he became sick, I used to go down to the museum he had founded in the town every day with him after school, and when I was even younger I used to go and sit at the back of his class, or write on the black-board. Suddenly, as I spoke, and as Ivor still watched me – his look was always even and open – my eyes filled up with tears. Do you realise, he asked me, that you have blocked the experience of his death, all your grief, and you are going to have to do something about it?

Over the next while we discussed the theory of this. There were certain people, Ivor said, who had lived through traumatic experiences without actually experiencing them, who had used a mechanism to block the ferocity of the trauma and gone on living, pretending that what had happened had been fine, no real problem, or had not really occurred. Strangely, he said, this could include someone's own birth – the agony and trauma of being born would lock itself into the psyche, where it would harden. It could also include grief – the loss of a loved one would be simply too unbearable and it would be stored away, held at bay, rather than really felt. It could also include rape or sexual abuse.

This blocking would work in the short term – it would make the pain easier to tolerate – but in the long term it would work like a badly built dam. The water around it would stagnate; only some would go through, the rest would build up. It would have a deforming effect on the personality. The only way for the person then to manage was by finding other ways to dam the water, but these would always be temporary. The successful way was to live the experience, to let what happened hit the psyche as if for the first time, even though it was many years later. This was one of the ways, he said, in which psychoanalysis or psychotherapy worked.

He ran a workshop in the disused Protestant church at St Brendan's in Grangegorman, Ivor said. It lasted from Friday morning until Sunday evening. He told me I should do it. It was used by his patients or by people who he felt had been disabled in one way or another by a trauma which they had not fully experienced. Sometimes they were not even aware of what the trauma was, or they had mistaken it for something else. Each time he had a vacancy, however, I managed to be away.

In May 1992, Ivor telephoned me. He suggested that, since people came to the workshop in pairs, I do a workshop with June Levine as my partner. June herself was interested in doing it and, since we knew each other and trusted each other, Ivor thought we could work together easily. I agreed to do it – it was time – and thus I found myself driving to the church early on a Friday morning not long afterwards. I was wearing loose clothes and I had not eaten anything heavy, as instructed.

The group therapy we did that morning was almost playful. After lunch we painted. For the real session we had to divide into pairs.

4

We fetched mattresses; June advised me to put ours into a corner. We arranged that I would go first; she would have her sessions on Saturday morning and Sunday morning and I would have mine now and on Saturday afternoon. I had no idea what was going to happen.

I took off my shoes and loosened my clothes, as I was told to do, and lay down on the mattress. June sat on a beanbag beside me. Twenty other pairs, maybe more, settled down as well. I closed my eyes and a soft voice, which I recognised as belonging to one of Ivor's colleagues, started to speak through a sound system. He asked us first to relax, then to breathe softly. There was soothing music in the background, and perhaps a drum sound. He spoke slowly and told us to breathe as though our breath was liquid. I did what he said. He then told us to begin to breathe faster as though our life depended on it. The music changed, the drum sound became louder. I'm not sure at what moment it happened but I suddenly moved into a different state of consciousness. I don't know if some of the crying and moaning sounds came from the PA system or from the people around me, but I think from both.

I was in terrible distress. I knew that June was there beside me and that Ivor was somewhere close by. I could ask her for a Kleenex if I needed it, or to hold my hand, or just to stay close. I knew that I could even stand up and go to the toilet if I needed to. But I had entered another world which was more urgent and real than the one I had left. I had to breathe hard, breathe like hell to stay there. It was dark in the church, but sometimes lights came on. Amid the loud music, there were heavy drum sounds and cries, babies crying, someone moaning in pain.

And I was moaning too and screaming. I was in my parents' bedroom on the morning that my father died. My mother was downstairs. It was difficult to know how much time was passing. I know that I screamed 'I cannot deal with this' over and over. I know that I screamed at the top of my voice. I know that June became worried about me and Ivor came to look at me. I would ask for Kleenex and blow my nose and, without any prompting, go back into myself and start screaming and thrashing around on the mattress.

What was happening was real; the distress was absolute. I both could and could not stop. I was back in that bedroom. An hour, two hours must have gone by. I kept blowing my nose and calming down and then starting off again. I felt the shock and the powerlessness of the grief – fierce, wild, absolute things. The realisation that he was dead would cause me to seize up on the mattress and start to scream and cry out. When Ivor came over at one stage, I thought that he was going to take me out of this ordeal – sometimes I desperately wanted to stop – but he made me turn on all fours and he held my stomach. 'Get it all up now', he said, as he pushed in my stomach muscles. He had brought a metal bowl with him and I screamed so hard I started to vomit mucus into the bowl.

And when I lay back he told me to breathe heavily again. The whole terrible pain came back. As before, I began to sob and then cry and then call out and scream, but it was worse now, this sense of pure loss, or being abandoned, of someone being torn away, of being utterly forlorn but, more than anything, of not being able to deal with it.

I do not know how much longer it went on. It could have been half an hour or more. The music changed all the time, but there were always drums and sounds of voices, with other music in the background – African or South American music. Eventually, Ivor came and said that I could rest now.

Ivor asked me if I wanted to try a drug he had mentioned – Ketamine. The effect would be different, he said. I thought he meant that it would take me further towards the distress, and felt that I should try it; since I had gone so far I should go further, see it through in some way. So I said I wanted the drug, which was injected by a nurse.

Nothing happened for a while, but then I began to laugh and I began to see beautiful colours: a dark orange which glistened at the edges, and then a luscious light blue which floated in front of me, then pink, then lemon. Then the colours, which had an extraordinary life in them, became formal arrangements, like paintings by Willem de Kooning or Sam Francis or Jackson Pollock, with the paint still wet. And slowly all this became weaker and the real world around me became more noticeable and present. The lights were coming up and the music changing. The same voice which had initiated the session now brought it to an end. I did not know how I felt.

The next day it was my turn to mind June. My job was to sit with her until she asked me to do something. Thus I had a good chance to look around. Once the fast breathing started it was like a vision of hell; everyone on the mattresses was involved in a private nightmare, as though there was a story being told to them which made them scream and cry out and then lie quietly for a while. I knew that some of the women on the mattresses had been raped and sexually abused and I knew they were trying to work this out.

The Ketamine, which not everybody took, affected different people in different ways. One woman just cried; another man wanted to hit everyone he looked at and had to be sat upon. As my second session on the mattress approached, I did not think that I could delve any further into the experience of my father's death. I thought that something new would arise, as we fetched the mattresses and rolled them out. But, as I lay down and the music started and then the breathing, it began again, but more intensely. Whereas the previous day I had been crying out for help, I was now asking to be let go and then began to make gestures as though releasing something from my mouth, crying out: 'I will let you go.'

This was almost unbearable and I signalled to June that I had had enough. When Ivor was called, however, he said that I should go on. I should start the fast breathing again. There was more, he said. So I lay back on the mattress and took deep breaths and began to listen to the sounds all around me. I went straight back into my private, hidden world and soon, very rapidly, ideas of thanking my father for life and of wanting to bless him came to me and I began to enact them over hours, rising and falling, still in the spell of the music and the breathing. And then, I was slowly brought back down.

Fifteen years later, it is difficult to make raw remarks about what happened that weekend. But it has to be said that I did not know before then that my father's death, the pure and almost unbearable grief which I had denied for so many years, was so close to me, could so quickly be summoned up. It was an extraordinary thing to learn.

Ivor has extraordinary powers of perception and sympathy, which is what makes him such a great doctor. He had noticed the unreleased pain in me as soon as he met me. I must have been carrying it around, or wearing a badly made mask to cover it. It came into the room, it seemed, as soon as I did. It would be impossible to say that after that weekend it went away altogether or anything like that, but the recognition of the problem alone came to me as an enormous relief. It might be easier to say that whatever happened helped me a lot, and lifted a burden from me; I felt both a new self-awareness, a new lightness. I have been less unhappy since then, less uneasy in the world. Maybe I should go back and do therapy again soon.

I also knew that there were people all over Ireland who had suffered similarly or much worse in childhood or early adulthood, who were suffering now from depression or addictions or had had psychotic episodes and had been declared schizophrenic. It seemed to me strange that many of these people – most of them even – had been prescribed expensive drugs but had never been offered the knowledge or the experience which I had received that weekend. Many of these patients, looked after by professional and conscientious psychiatrists, would not even have received psychotherapy or any form of psychoanalysis, except perhaps the most rudimentary.

It seemed to me that it was necessary for a debate to occur in Ireland and elsewhere about these matters, with the patients having as much to say – especially those who have been in long-term treatment – as the doctors. The debate need not be stark in its terms or shrill in its tones; it need not be one in which drugs as the sole cure for mental illness should be on one side and other systems, such as a serious exploration of the sufferer's psyche, which I had endured or enjoyed, should be on the other.

It is also essential that we hear the doctors' stories as well as the patients', that we learn about how they trained and what they learned and how they themselves have lived.

Since Ivor Browne has been a towering and powerful influential figure in Irish psychiatry over the past half century, since he has held views on the treatment of mental illness which have been dissenting and open to suggestion, and since he has lived through a period of great change but also of serious conservatism within his own profession, his story is one of the most important for us to hear. His book is a significant contribution in a campaign on which all doctors in the area of mental health are embarked – to rescue patients from darkness, to get them on their feet again. As the poet Elizabeth Bishop said when she was in the depths of terrible depression and a friend wrote to her, it was like receiving a lantern or a diviner's stick. So, too, this book, in its calm wisdom and its clear and original thinking, based on a lifetime's experience, may help both doctors and patients towards a new understanding of the human mind and how suffering can be alleviated and mental illness better understood.

COLM TÓIBÍN
Dublin, 2008

Part One

Shapings
1929–1949

1

The Beginning

I was born in the front bedroom of number 1 Sandycove Avenue East, Dublin, half an hour after midnight on 18 March 1929. I was not meant to have been born at all. As a child I regularly heard my father say, 'I'm afraid Ivor was a mistake, I don't know if I'll ever be able to educate him'. And I spent a great part of my life trying to prove that this was not so. I only found out years later why I had 'been a mistake'. Having decided, no doubt without even consulting my mother, that there should be no more children, my father introduced his chosen form of family planning: he instructed my mother to lock her door at night. He had stopped drinking when he got married, except for the odd glass, but on the night in question he had had a few drinks. When he returned home, he threw discretion to the winds and climbed through a window in her bedroom, with the result that I was conceived.

My father had me christened William Ivory. I've had a life-long difficulty with the name. It sounds innocent enough, particularly as I have always been called Ivor, and there was an early St Ivor in Wexford. But, as I was to discover, William Ivory was the name of the Cromwellian soldier who was given the lands of the Brownes at Mulrankin, confiscated after Cromwell crushed the rebellion of 1649. This was a turning point in the history of the Browne family as, until the rebellion of 1641, the Brownes and other Norman families in south Wexford had sided with the English. It was also the first time that religion entered the picture and the Brownes, being Catholic, joined the Irish and thus the rebel cause of the time.

William Ivory must have been one of the most detested men in south County Wexford; the hatred of him had lived on in folk memory in that part of Wexford right down to my father's time. Small wonder that I grew up not knowing who I was and feeling that I didn't belong. It never fails to amaze me how parents are unaware of how deeply children are affected throughout their lives by what their parents think, say and do.

When the Great War broke out in 1914, my father was working in the bank in Clonakilty, west Cork. It was there that he started to play traditional music. He used to play the mandolin at crossroads dances. But when the war came he was so disgusted with his nationalist family, because he felt he had been given less educational opportunities than his siblings, that he decided to join the British Navy. He went into the navy as an ordinary sailor and took part in the Battle of Jutland. Later he applied for a commission and became a lieutenant. He was posted out to the Mediterranean, where he spent a long time in Malta and Algeria.

When he came back after the war, this bronzed sailor made quite a stir at the head office of the National Bank on College Green in Dublin. According to my mother: 'The girls were all after him and making up to him, but I got him!' In any event he and my mother became engaged. She was Church of Ireland and he a Catholic. He was in a state of rebellion against his family, which was at least part of the reason why he married a Protestant, although he had, no doubt, fallen in love with her. He refused to be married in the Catholic Church but at the same time never had the courage to tell his father that he was marrying a Protestant.

Later, my father's brother, who was a priest, had the marriage recognised by the Catholic Church and from then on my father returned to the Church, although always with some ambivalence. He refused to sign the Ne Temere decree, which was demanded by the Church at that time. My mother was happy to do whatever he wanted, so he decided that any boys that might be born would be Catholic and any girls Church of Ireland. There was a rather strange outcome to this as far as I was concerned. Every Sunday morning my mother and my sister would head off to the Church of Ireland church on the hill above Bullock Harbour and my father, my older brother and I would go to Mass in the Catholic church in Glasthule. I must have been a dreamy child for one Sunday, to my amazement, I realised for the first time that there were women and girls in the church. I felt that there must be something terribly wrong as

I supposed that all men were Catholic and all women Protestant.

My father was pre-Freudian. By that I mean he had no awareness of the unconscious and did not know how to question his reasons for certain actions. His reason for naming me William Ivory was part of his life-long rebellion against his family, as was his marrying a Protestant. Although he did this, it did not alter his underlying conditioning in a conservative Catholic family. This showed up in his dislike and rejection of all my mother's relatives. He identified me with the Protestant side of the family and always referred to me as a Fitzmaurice, like my mother's family. I have no doubt that most of this kind of behaviour on his part was unconscious, and that he loved me as much as he did his other children. I realised how important it was for him to identify me with my mother's family when, one day, a photograph turned up of his sister, Maisie, taken when she was about twelve. She was in a long dress but looked so like me that it could have been me dressed up as a girl. The effect on my father was dramatic. I remember him staring at it dumbfounded, saying over and over again, 'I don't believe it'.

During my own analysis as a young psychiatrist, I came to understand that a lot of my father's energy went into trying to prop up his shaky self-esteem. He felt he had been treated badly by his family and suffered because of it. He deeply resented the fact that his family had not given him a third-level education, as I think he sensed that he would have been naturally suited to an academic career. He also would have liked to be a farmer and to have inherited the family lands, but instead he was relegated to the bank, which he hated. He was born into a nationalistic Catholic family, replete with priests and bishops over the generations. His younger brother, Dick, was a priest. In 1916, his older brother John was in the Irish Republican Army (IRA) and his sister Kathleen was arrested and locked up in Kilmainham Gaol with a couple of other young women for three months. On one occasion Sir Roger Casement spent a weekend in his family home in Rathronan, so it was clear that the family was deeply involved in the struggle for national independence.

The Brownes never lost the sense of being an aristocratic family. For generations they were known as the 'Gentleman Brownes'. By the nineteenth century, after 200 years of dispossession, my great-grandfather had fought his way back up again to become quite a well-off tenant farmer. By the time my father was born they had bought back Rathronan Castle, which was originally part of the lands of the Brownes prior to Cromwell, and a couple of other farms as well.

My earliest memory of my parents was that each had their own room. I remember well that when my father had gone to bed and was reading, my mother would go in and give him a kiss on the cheek. He would respond in a distracted sort of way, as if this was an unwarranted intrusion. So, from my earliest memories, there was no evidence of sexuality or a sensual relationship in our home. That was the atmosphere in which I grew up.

My mother was a warm, loving person but, because of my father's inhibited attitudes, she learned to suppress her natural tendencies. If she had been allowed to express herself she would have realised her sensual nature. In so far as I have a sensitive, gentle side, this has come from her. Unfortunately, she was so gentle that she was unable to stand up to him. But I have vivid memories of sitting on her knee and laying my head on her breast, feeling the safety, warmth and love coming from her. Both she and my father, in their different ways, lacked self-confidence in dealing with external reality and this left me fearful and anxious later in trying to face out into the world.

My father described himself as 'a man's man' and, prior to his marriage, had associated mainly with male friends. This may have been the reason why, for a long time in my youth, I was terrified to be seen with a girl. When I became aware of girls and fell in love with one called Hazel at the age of fourteen, I would have been terrified to be seen with her, or with any girl in daylight. The strange thing is, no one had ever said I shouldn't have a girlfriend. So the only thing I can think is that my fear of being seen with a girl represented a silent law, which I had absorbed from the Irish-style, inhibited, sexless atmosphere at home. And perhaps being a 'mistake' made me anxious around matters relating to the 'mistake'.

The friends we had coming to 'the field' that my father rented were both girls and boys. He transformed it into an adventure space for us. There were about twenty of us altogether and this represented almost all the young people around Sandycove at the time. As we approached adolescence most of us broke into pairs. Being far too shy to think of approaching anyone, a sister of my sister Ismay's boyfriend, whom I didn't care about at all, was selected for me. Hazel, at that time, was not a member of the group in 'the field'.

My older brother Val was different to me. When he was only about twelve years old he converted an old ship's lifeboat into a launch, put a cabin on it and installed a motorcar engine in it. He used to have lots of girlfriends and would take them out in the boat quite openly, without any diffidence at all. But then he was accepted as a Browne, was outgoing and good at sports.

Sometimes I would go to visit my father in the head office of the National Bank in College Green. When you entered the main hall there was a row of tellers. At that time all of these were men and from upper middle-class families, many of them west-British types. Because I was so tall for my age, when I approached the counter one of them would say, 'Here comes a front row forward'. My father would look crestfallen and say – 'No, he doesn't show any talent for that at all. His brother is a fine player though', and I would feel all legs and arms and want to disappear with the shame of it all.

At parties my father would often launch into one of his favourite topics, of how he hated the bank. 'I should never have been put into the bank,' he would say. 'The bank is a job for a person with no imagination or initiative, a person who's dull and only capable of doing a routine job, who has no creative ability.' Then a light would come into his eye, a dawning. I dreaded what was coming next, but to him it was as if he had never done this before and had just had a revelation, a fresh insight. He would turn to me: 'Ivor, did you never think of going into the bank?' It was as if, each time, he had at last found a solution as to what might become of me. I do not think for a moment that he had any intention of being hurtful, or had any conscious awareness of what he was saying about me. I believe each time the subject came up it was a new thought to him and he jumped at a possible solution as to what my future might hold.

I was seen as something of a problem and not the full shilling, not just by my father, but also by the group of friends who hung around 'the field'. On one occasion, my friends became so concerned at my apparent lack of contact with reality, and dreamy state, that they came as a deputation to my father saying that something should be done about me, and that they felt I should be seen by someone. Needless to say, I had no idea all this was going on and was quite oblivious to their concern. Fortunately for me, my father was too in-volved in his own struggle to maintain his sanity to do anything about it, otherwise I might have been defined as a patient and been led towards psychiatric illness.

In most ways the life we had in 'the field' was idyllic. My father paid £12 a year for it and set up all kinds of creative activities for us. We had a happy group of friends and were able to camp out there all summer, going down to swim on the rocks, with the whole world to ourselves and hardly ever a sight of a stranger. We had a rowing boat moored in Bullock Harbour for going fishing and for trips out to Dalkey Island. Our home and family life were secure and stable, with parents who dedicated their lives to us and were always there for us. And yet my memory of my childhood is one of feeling lost and miserable most of the time. I suspect one reason was that the world we had at home, in 'the field' by the sea, with the boat, and so on, was so complete that not only I but most of my friends never integrated into school, or into the world at large.

The terror has never left my memory of my first day at school, and all my life, until I retired, I hated Monday morning, when one went back out into the world again. That first Monday, when I was about five, my mother took me around the corner to a private school. To this day, I see Miss Manley, who ran the school, as a ferocious, big lady dressed in black. We were shown into an old-fashioned sitting room, which was semi-dark and forbidding. Being with my mother, I was quite happy and relaxed. When my mother and Miss Manley finished talking, my mother rose to leave and I got up to go with her. To my horror, Miss Manley grabbed me, and I was dismayed to see my mother disappearing while I was held there in terror. From that day I don't think I ever felt safe or at ease in school, either in Miss Manley's or in Blackrock College. It always felt like a foreign, hostile world to me, somewhere to escape from as soon as possible, back to the sanctuary of my world at home and in 'the field'.

This was a world of Irish history, the Normans, 1798, the British Empire, all of which my father fed to me on a daily basis. He was strongly attached to the history of Wexford and filled my head with stories of the 1798 rebellion and of our Norman ancestors, who had lost everything at the hands of Cromwell. As an indication of how deep a hold all this had on my mind, I remember on one of our Sunday walks that he took us on an unusual route up to the castle on the top of Dalkey Hill. My father had often told me that this was one of the castles that marked the boundary of the Pale, the area around Dublin controlled by the British. Apparently Dun Laoghaire County

Council were doing some repair work on it at the time. The castle was fenced off and, when we approached the fence, a workman came down and told us that we were not permitted to enter. That is what actually happened, but my memory of the event is utterly different. I can see, as clearly as if it were yesterday, Norman soldiers with their helmets, with the piece of metal down along the nose, looking at us over the battlements and aiming crossbows at us. And the man who came down to tell us to leave was dressed in Norman armour, with long, tight stockings. I can still recollect the real terror and the feeling that we were all going to be killed.

2

Rathronan

When I was a child we went every summer to the farm in County Wexford where my father was born and raised, and his ancestors before him. That's more than half a century ago now. I still remember the joy of being in direct contact with nature, with trees and fields and growing things. On that farm they produced nearly everything they needed. They had their own vegetable garden, which supplied all the vegetables, and cows, sheep, ducks and free-range hens that provided the meat, dairy produce, eggs and so on that they required. They grew their own grain. The wheat was sent to the water-powered mill less than a mile away, from which the sacks of flour were returned and stored in the granary. From this they made their bread and cakes. They had a small dairy where they separated out the cream from the milk and churned beautiful country butter. There was also an orchard with apples, pears, plums and currants from which they made jams and desserts. All this provided a fully nutritious and varied diet. This was a reasonably prosperous farm that provided for virtually all the needs of those living there. They had to buy little, just tea, clothes and a few other items. The culture was one of an extended family, with farm workers, a couple of servants, children and adults. All the relationships, human and economic, were close at hand, within a radius of a few miles. This was a world of direct, face-to-face contact with friends and neighbours, comprehensible to a child. I can still feel that sense of belonging and it helped set me up for life.

Contrast this with our present society, where the economic interconnections extend over thousands of miles, and yet where we are lucky if we even know the name of the person living next door. Everything which that farm produced was organic. This was typical of the mixed farming that was common around the country at that time. Think what a favourable position we would be in now if this were still the current form of farming here, when organic produce is at a premium and is being sought all over Europe. If we could only have managed to avoid the madness of the Common Agricultural Policy, with its total preoccupation with mechanised farming. We know now how badly this has backfired, with beef and dairy mountains that nobody knows what to do with.

Although the time we spent there was only about one month a year, and only up to when I was eleven or twelve years of age, those times in Rathronan seem to me to be a significant part of my early years and somehow to represent a deeper identity, my 'real' home, giving me a sense of historical continuity.

We would arrive at Wexford station on the train; it always seemed to be as it was getting dark. My Aunt Attle (Kathleen) would be there to meet us, with Topsie the mare harnessed to the bucket trap. Aunt Attle would bring rugs to wrap around us, as it was always cold on the long, ten-mile journey over to Bridgetown, and finally Rathronan. I remember being bored stiff as my father and his sister discussed the history and all the family connections of the farms and ruined castles we passed. How I wish now that I could hear those conversations again. My aunt was a serious local historian and, unfortunately, much of this valuable social history of Wexford died with her.

Rathronan was a beautiful house, which has now sadly fallen into ruin. There was a drive of nearly half a mile down from the main road, where the Catholic church was situated. At that crossroads there was also a shop. It was hardly a village, but yet it was something of a meeting point for the surrounding area. Cullen's shop was the old style grocery-cum-pub. One would enter into a dark atmosphere with its musty smell of grain, with big sacks lined along one side of the shop, and a wonderful world of sweets.

That crossroads was the social meeting place for all the males in the area when the day's work was done. Particularly at weekends, all the men and boys used to assemble along the banks at each side of the end of the road. They were divided into age groups: very old men, some with long beards and an air of authority; then came the middle-aged men, then the young working men and, finally, groups of young boys, all sitting in a row on both sides of the road. This was their only entertainment.

Usually we went down to Wexford by train but one summer, when I was six years old, my father decided we would take the motor-boat and go down the Grand Canal and on down the River Barrow to Waterford Harbour. When we reached the sea, we travelled around the Hook Head to Kilmore Quay, reaching Wexford and Rathronan that way. It was a tremendous adventure for us and, in that boat, a more hazardous journey than I realised. The canals were still an active mode of transport at the time, particularly for the Guinness barges, but many other goods were also shipped down the country in this way. The diesel barges were taking over but there were still a lot of horse-drawn barges working as well. They would have one horse that walked along the towpath, pulling the barge with ropes to which he was harnessed. The poor horse really had to struggle if there was a head wind, but when there was a following wind there was no means of stopping the barge when it was coming into a lock. The horse would obey the call to halt, but the boat would crash into the side walls of the lock, out of control, with a horrible crunch, the wind sweeping it along and the men on board cursing. After we entered the canal I was surprised at the number of locks we had to go through as we made our way through the city. We seemed to be travelling all day, going miles and miles, away out into the country. My first recollection of our being moored up was at the seventh lock at Bluebell, near Bally-fermot, which is now right in the centre of a major industrial estate, with 40,000 people living down the road. But at that time it was in the middle of open country and, by the time we got there, I thought we were far away from Dublin.

Once we reached the Barrow it was very difficult to navigate. Parts of the river turned into rapids and short stretches of canal had been built to get around them. The skipper of one of the diesel-driven Guinness barges offered to tow us until we got past the diffi-cult stretches. As it turned out, they towed us for over twenty miles. Ismay and I were delighted, as we were allowed to go on board the barge and even steer it with the big helm for some of the way. The whole adventure made such an impression on me that to this day, if a diesel truck passes by and I smell the fumes, I'm back on the river standing on that big barge.

Finally we reached Waterford Harbour and set out around the fa-mous Hook Lighthouse to sail to Kilmore Quay. There were dan-gerous waves and we were lucky to reach Kilmore Harbour that day.

3

The Field

To return to our life in Sandycove and 'the field', where my father grew all the vegetables, the main fertiliser he used was seaweed. Bringing that up manually from the rocks meant carrying it for thirty yards and then up almost forty steps to the lane and into 'the field'. He solved the problem by rigging up a sort of funicular system. He ran a wire from where the seaweed came ashore up to the top of the steps, then ran a pulley on the wire with a hook to which a dustbin, filled with seaweed, could be attached. This could be pulled along the wire by a rope. Several of us youngsters would be detailed to fill the dustbin with seaweed, while others would run with the rope up the lane, pulling the full dustbin up the wire to the top of the steps. Others would then unload it into a wheelbarrow and bring it into 'the field' to the vegetable plot.

Needless to say, we enjoyed the whole procedure and would work away all afternoon bringing up big loads of seaweed. When the work was completed for the day, my father would bring us all up to the local pub in Sandycove to 'splice the main-brace'. This was one of his nautical terms from the navy. When sailors in the navy carried out some special operation, they were rewarded by being given a special ration of rum. So we would go to the pub and he would order pints of plain all round. Plain porter was single X Guinness, less alcohol than the ordinary pint of today, but delicious when in the right condition. We'd have a couple of pints and then go home for tea. In this way I started drinking at the age of ten. I suppose that nowadays my father would be in trouble for encouraging children to drink.

My first visit to Dalkey Island was in a Moses basket carried by my parents. Often, when I was bigger, we went there for a picnic in the summer. If we caught mackerel on the way we would light a fire on the island and cook them. The best times were when we got a run of mackerel; often we would go out in the early morning and, if we were lucky, catch up to a hundred. To come home and fry them for breakfast was a real joy, and there were always neighbours willing to take the rest. To this day, I still like to row out there.

By chance, one day in Sandycove, we found a hole in one of the pools out at the edge of the rocks. To my surprise there was a large red crab in it, the kind that is suitable for eating. We found more than a dozen holes, a number of which had crabs in them. I made a long hook with strong wire, about a yard in length, hammered it into a wooden handle and in that way was able to pull them out. My mother showed me how to cook and dress the red crabs with breadcrumbs, salt and pepper, and then put the mixture back into the washed empty shell. When they were prepared we used to reheat them in the oven and then spread the crab on buttered toast. My father was particularly partial to dressed crabs. One day he thought that this would be nice for his lunch in the bank. He brought in a primus stove to heat the crab in its shell on a metal plate over the stove. The smell of burning shell soon wafted out of his office and all across the bank's headquarters. There was consternation among the staff, and complaints from customers, about the pungent smell, but as usual my father was completely oblivious to the crisis he was causing and didn't understand what all the fuss was about.

Although my father wasn't particularly sociable, he liked to have parties on a fairly regular basis. It was in the tradition of parties at that time for each person to do a turn, sing a song, or give a recitation. His idea of a good party was when he would provide most of the entertainment. He would play the mandolin, and sing songs with the guitar. He would then insist on my mother singing songs that he had taught her, and he would sing duets with her and get furious if she made a mistake. He also had several recitations, which were the centrepiece of his repertoire – 'Shanaghan's old Sheebin', 'A Man's Man', and others. On one occasion like this, when he had been out with my mother to a party, he had invited the assembled guests to a return party at his house the following week. On the way home on the Dalkey tram he must have sobered up and was now regretting his foolhardy invitation. As they were coming through the gate towards the house, and probably in response to my mother urging him to make the best of it, he was heard to say, 'I know, Gracie, but drink alone will cost us almost a pound.'

Still, the memories of those parties, with the songs and the music, remain for me some of the happiest times of my childhood. I remember particularly the sweetness of my mother's voice when she sang 'Silver Threads Among the Gold' or 'Plaisir d'Amour', and also my father playing jigs and reels on the mandolin. Later, when I took up the trumpet, and Ismay the piano and guitar, we used to join in the concerts.

I continued to hate going to Miss Manley's. She eventually became seriously ill and, on the day she died, all of us children were waiting outside hoping we wouldn't have to go to school that day. What was even more important, we knew that if she died we wouldn't have to go back there at all, so when the news came out that she had passed away, we all cheered. Such is the heartless nature of young children.

At first I was delighted at the prospect of going to a different school, but when I went to Willow Park, I was forced to play rugby and I hated it. I was bigger than the others in my class but more timid than any of them. Also I never seemed to have enough wind to keep up. One day my father came to a match to watch me play. I never got near the ball and was afraid to tackle or fight for the ball the few times it did come near me. The shame I felt when my togs weren't even dirty by the end of the match! On the way home my father said, 'You should be able to pick up those little fellows and throw them to the ground.' I felt like crawling under the seat of the tram in the face of his sarcasm. Not only was I bigger than the other boys in that school but I was taller than most of the masters as well. I used to be jeered at by the boys, who thought I should be able to beat up the other fellows as I was far bigger than them.

PART TWO

Music and Medicine
1949–1962

4

The Trumpet

My earliest spiritual awakening was my first Holy Communion. I felt that Jesus was inside me as the host melted in my mouth. Of course, the experience was tainted by all the guilt and nonsense about not touching the host with your teeth, the fear of it sticking to the roof of your mouth and not touching food or water from midnight the night before. Still, that experience of Communion lasted for many years; the clear, raw feeling of the morning air in the dawn and the experience of Jesus Christ being inside you afterwards.

But another opening of my heart was my introduction to jazz, and hearing the spontaneous warmth and innocence of recordings like Louis Armstrong's 'West End Blues' for the first time. I can still respond to these, even though the emotion is less intense, after more than sixty years. This was, for me, the first dawning of a personal awareness. Until then, although I was not consciously aware of it, I was in a state of deep confusion. I had a father who was an Irish Catholic but who, in the service of his rebellion against his family, had adopted a pro-British, anti-Catholic view, and a mother who was a Protestant, but innocent and self-effacing; so I did not know who I was nor where I belonged. Perhaps by making a strong identification with jazz and Afro-American culture I was identifying with a suppressed minority who also felt themselves to be outsiders. However, I did not realise this until it came up in analysis many years later.

One evening several of us were out in the boat fishing for mackerel. I was sitting in the bottom of the boat and amusing myself by imitating a trumpet, cupping my hands around my mouth. An older fellow said to me: 'You should take up the trumpet.' It was a throwaway remark but it hit me like a bolt from the blue. From that moment on I started planning and scheming as to how I could get my father to buy me a trumpet. Everything else became of secondary importance. My father was particularly thrifty and careful with money, saving every penny in the hope of being able to give us a good education. Buying me a trumpet was not one of his priorities. So the scheme I developed was to mention the idea of a trumpet and then duck out of the room while he exploded. A week or so later I would mention the idea again, and then again, until the notion got into his head. It was in this way that I wore my father down and eventually, tormented with the idea of a trumpet and unable to rid himself of it, he came to me: 'What are we going to do about this damn trumpet?' And then I knew I had him! I was twelve when, to my great delight, I got my first trumpet. From then on this occupied my every waking hour and my dreams for the future.

At that time there were a number of semi-professional musicians who used to come to our house to play jazz. From somewhere inside me came the deep conviction that I would be a musician, that some day I would be a great trumpet player like Louis Armstrong. I started to practise intensively and decided to take lessons. The place to go seemed to be the School of Music in Chatham Street, to Colonel Saurtswieg. Most of the Dublin professional trumpet players had gone to him at one time or another but they couldn't get his name right. They'd say 'I'm going up to auld Saursiwag at the technical', or 'I'm gettin' lessons from auld Sarsfield'. I used to be a bit afraid of him but he was a very good teacher and I made fairly rapid progress.

By this time I had left Willow Park and moved to the secondary school, Blackrock College. Ever since I'd left Miss Manley's my academic standard had been falling. I had started in the B stream but, since then, each year I went up a number, from first to second to third year, but down a letter. Now, at twelve, I was in the C stream and eventually when I left at fourteen I had drifted down to 3E. This class was placed upstairs, away from all the others, out of sight. I suspect this was in case the inspector from the Department of Education called, and the college hoped we wouldn't be noticed. We were a weird, mixed lot, some mentally retarded, some with personality disorders and a few, like me, who could not be bothered to learn anything because I was preoccupied with music.

It was strange. Above all else my father wanted us to have a good education and yet he took no interest in how I was getting on at Blackrock. I think he was so involved in the world he had created at home that he didn't want to know about the world outside. The authorities at Blackrock College were only interested in those who did well in one or other area, to keep up the reputation of the college. If you were good at rugby then they didn't give a damn how you did academically, and if you excelled in studies then they were sure of getting the best results in the Leaving Certificate.

In my case the only thing in which I showed any ability was the high jump. When it came to the time for the Leinster Sports, the college showed a great interest in me and supplied me with trunks and other gear for the event. I was only fourteen but I competed in both the senior and junior competition and won the junior title. I also won the senior event in the college sports the same year. But, for my part, I was so obsessed with music that I sneaked out over the toilet wall, so no one would notice, to go home and practise. As a result, I never received my Junior Leinster Sports medal.

My difficulties in school were compounded by the fact that I was so tall. Normally we think of bullying occurring when a bigger, stronger boy takes on the smaller, delicate ones, but paradoxically the reverse happened in my case. One small but very popular fellow used to bully me. He would sneak up behind me and hit me a blow when I was least expecting it and then run away, thinking he was very daring. This would give rise to great amusement among the others. I could never catch him but my real problem was, even if I had, I'd be afraid to hit him back for fear of being accused of bullying myself. He constantly teased and jeered at me and I felt there was nothing I could do. I remember being so miserable that, even though I hated schoolwork, I used to be glad to get back into the classroom just to get away from him. I'm sure he thought it was just a bit of fun but I felt wretched. It was just one more reason why I hated school so much.

My real life only existed around home and the relationship with my friends in 'the field'. I never formed any real friends in school. All I wanted to do was get away from school as quickly as possible. This made things very difficult later when I had to leave that world and go into medical school. But I wasn't the only one who found it difficult. A number of the others who were part of our group told me later that they had the same difficulty when they had to face the outside world. So, although in many ways we had a wonderful environment in 'the field' – down on the rocks, out in the boat fishing and day-dreaming on Dalkey Island – it was a closed world of fantasy, which made it difficult later to face the reality outside. The positive effect of this on me was that I've always been able to see things from a different angle, and this was perhaps the reason why I did reasonably well later.

I used to cycle to Blackrock every day, except when it was very wet. It was four miles there in the morning, four miles back at lunch time, and then back again in the afternoon, sixteen miles a day. I suppose because of day-dreaming I was nearly always late. The Dean of Studies would wait for me on the steps and I'd get four slaps with the leather or cane. This was in addition to the 'biffing' I suffered nearly every day because of fooling around or not having my home-work done. Because of the regularity of this beating, I became com-pletely immune to it and trained myself not to feel it. But I was acutely aware of how different it was for sensitive, studious lads who would very seldom get beaten. When they did, it would have a dreadful effect on them and they would be terrified. I would feel very sorry for them and was amazed that the priests seemed to have no awareness of the difference.

Another observation I made at the time was how cruel and un-aware some teachers could be. They would ask some shy, sensitive boy a simple question, or a problem in maths, and it was obvious to me that, because of his fear and confusion, he wasn't able to think. The teacher would bring him up to the board and keep roaring at him, red in the face with rage, and the poor lad would be completely blocked, unable to do anything. I was acutely aware of what was going on and of the stupidity and injustice of it, but I was far too timid at the time to do anything.

I left Blackrock College at fourteen, as I knew there was no fu-ture in my staying on there. I had missed the primary exam a cou-ple of years earlier by managing to injure myself. Now, at fourteen, having been hidden upstairs in 3E, it was clear to me that I was never going to pass the Intermediate Certificate. So I left and, as usual, my parents didn't take any action to see what was going on. After this I did nothing for a while but then, to keep my parents off my back, I agreed to go to Potters College, in Dun Laoghaire. This was mainly a secretarial college, but I took a number of ordinary subjects like English, French, maths and so on, with a view to moving on into third-level education at some stage. At this point I had no clear di-rection except my determination to become a jazz musician.

My sister Ismay was studying social science in Trinity and she brought home books on psychology. I found these interesting, I suppose mainly because they related in some way to my own identity confusion. After several years drifting on in this way, a point came where I had to make up my mind about what I was going to do. I knew there wasn't a hope in hell of my ever passing the Leaving Certificate to get into Trinity or University Colleage Dublin (UCD), so I thought I might sneak into the College of Surgeons, which had a separate entrance examination. I understood that to become a psychiatrist you first had to do a medical degree and, of the alternatives around, this seemed the least disagreeable. The entrance exam into the Royal College of Surgeons consisted of four subjects. The first time I took the exam, at the beginning of the summer of 1947, I got a little slip of paper saying 'failed in all four subjects'. As usual, my father, other than registering some disappointment, took little interest.

However, my brother Val, who by this time had returned from the war, decided something had to be done. I think he regretted that he had neglected his education and failed to get into university, so he decided the same thing wasn't going to happen to me. Although I deeply resented his interference at the time, I owe him a deep debt of gratitude for his intervention. He told me I was going to study all that summer or he would 'kick the arse off me', and he literally stood over me for several months until the autumn repeat examination when, to my amazement, I passed all four subjects.

So now I had been accepted into the College of Surgeons to commence my medical training, but, on entering the pre-medical year, I came up against the same difficulty once again. I couldn't integrate into the new environment. Also, because I was born left-handed, and had been forced by Miss Manley to write with my right hand, I've been partly dyslexic ever since and have always been slow in both reading and writing. During that year we had to attend lectures in physics, chemistry and biology, but I had such difficulty taking notes in the lectures and trying to keep up that I kept falling behind. To try to overcome this difficulty I attended grinds. Even with the help of the grinds, when the exam came I couldn't write fast enough and was only able to finish half the paper. So I failed once again in all subjects and had to repeat the year.

Although it was a further reinforcement of my sense of being a failure, I wasn't too worried at failing the pre-med as I was only seventeen years old. I made an agreement with my father that I would attend lectures and study during the day but the evenings with music were mine and not to be interfered with. I held to that arrangement for the next couple of years.

The subject we were studying that year, as well as physics and chemistry, was biology, which involved both botany and zoology. Looking back, although we studied the anatomy of dead frogs, rabbits and other creatures and also the physiology of the different organs and systems, nowhere was there any mention of the living behaviour of the animal or plant as a whole being, nor any attempt at a definition of life. The nearest they got to this was to say that living creatures were able to reproduce themselves. It was to be many years before this vital question of what it is that distinguishes living creatures became clear. The ability to reproduce does not define life, for, in order to reproduce, an animal or plant must first of all be alive. No one would doubt that a mule or jennet is alive, yet they are not capable of reproduction. It is extraordinary that this question was never even raised, nor was there any part in the whole medical curriculum where the behaviour of the whole human being was given any attention. Sadly, this is still true in many medical schools.

In any event, having repeated the year, I managed to scrape through the exams and got a place in first year. Once again, because of my slow writing, I only succeeded in answering part of each of the examination papers.

By this time we had managed to get the basis of a jazz band together, with Ismay playing banjo and guitar. I had inveigled Val into playing the clarinet and he struggled grudgingly with this for years. Looking back I can see that I was a complete tyrant in persuading people to become part of my dream. It was at this time that I met Charles Meredith, who was probably the only one, other than possibly myself, who had any real talent for music. He played the trumpet and trombone, like myself, and several other instruments. He was living in Foxrock and was the only one who went on in later years to become an established musician, playing under the pseudonym of Rock Fox.

We were rehearsing now on a regular basis in the breakfast room of the old house in Sandycove, directly under my father's bedroom, but we did not, for a long time to come, have any access to public performance. It amazes me now to think of my father's patience and tolerance, as he hated the sound of anything to do with jazz yet would go to bed with a seven-piece band blasting away directly below his bedroom. Eventually, when he couldn't stand it any longer, he would knock on the ceiling, which we felt was totally unreasonable behaviour on his part. We would get a sweeping brush and knock back up at him and continue playing, until he would get so mad that he would come rushing down the stairs and throw us out.

I was obsessed with music and would spend many hours with a muted trumpet playing along with records of King Oliver, Bessie Smith, Louis Armstrong and others, to the point where I completely identified with the black culture of America. I was lost in a dream world of life in New Orleans and Chicago as they were in the early years of the last century. Many times I would miss my lunch and go into May's record shop to listen to jazz. When I had saved up enough from my lunch money, I would buy a record. I can remember, as though it were only yesterday, the very first jazz record I bought. This was the Count Basie Quintet playing 'Lady Be Good'. It featured Lester Young on the tenor sax and was on the Parlaphone label. These were the old wax 78 discs that I played on a portable gramophone, yet this record still sounds as fresh to me as the day I bought it over fifty years ago.

At weekends, on Saturday nights, I used to sit in with the small groups of musicians who played for the dances in tennis clubs such as Sandycove or Longford Tennis Club. The music they played was the pop music of the time, the popular tunes of the late 1940s and '50s, but I used these as the basis for jazz improvisation and, because I wasn't costing them any money, I was tolerated. Because of this obsession with music I missed out on the normal teenage activities; I never learned to dance properly, although I have a natural sense of rhythm. To this day I feel a sense of loss in never having learned to dance.

Having finally passed the pre-medical examination and gained access to first year, I settled down to study and managed to pass both the first- and second-year examinations. The latter was known as the Half, that is the mid-point of the medical course, after which exposure to the world of clinical medicine began. It was during those first three years that I learned some valuable but painful lessons with regard to my own behaviour and that of others, which stood me in good stead many years later when I became a practising psychiatrist.

Being so attached to home I felt hopelessly shy and isolated. I can see now that the other students were quite ready to be friendly and to accept me, but then, feeling awkward and convinced that I was not wanted, I rejected any social advances that were made, always either returning home as soon as possible after lectures or sneaking off to listen to jazz on my own in the record shop. On several occasions, when students would ask me to come down for a cup of coffee, I would decline the offer and, of course, if you refuse such an overture, you don't get asked a second time. In this way I became more and more isolated, feeling unwanted and lonely.

This came to a head one evening when I was waiting in Westland Row station with several other students for the train to return home. I became convinced that they were talking about me and I actually called one of them aside whom I knew a little better than the others and, feeling quite distraught, asked him whether they were talking about me. He looked at me in astonishment and didn't seem to know what to say. I know I was on the verge of a paranoid state at that point and perhaps if this had continued I would have become psychotic, although it may be that I didn't have the genetic, introverted personality that would have finally pushed me over the edge. Whatever about that, it was only years afterwards, when working in psychiatry, that I understood what was happening to me at that time. Because of shyness and self-preoccupation, we isolate ourselves and reject the natural friendliness of others but then become convinced that it is they who are rejecting us. Because of this painful experience at that time, I have always had a particular empathy with the constricted world of the schizophrenic.

Another humiliating experience that I suffered at that time was related to body odour. Sitting beside students in lectures, I was convinced that many of them suffered with BO, until one day I had the awful realisation that the smell was actually coming from my own armpits. I felt utterly devastated by this realisation but it taught me a little about projection, and how easily we project our shortcomings on to others. Accusation is so often confession.

5

Medical School

Having passed the midway exam in anatomy and physiology, we were introduced to hospital for the first time. The Meath Hospital was one of the hospitals affiliated to the College of Surgeons, so I made the choice to go there. At that time, in the late 1940s, tuberculosis was rampant in Ireland and, because one of the consultants in Meath specialised in the treatment of tuberculosis, there were many cases of active tuberculosis in the hospital. Because of this the authorities in the medical school insisted that every student have a chest X-ray before becoming involved in clinical duties around the hospital.

I had only been attending clinics for a few weeks when I went for the routine X-ray. When I was summoned to report to the doctor, I reminded myself that my father had always said what a healthy outdoor life we led, so there couldn't be anything wrong. Still, it felt ominous and I avoided making any contact with the doctor for several weeks. Then one day one of the students reminded me that I'd better report back to the doctor. Finally I went to see what it was all about, only to find, to my horror, that my X-ray showed an active focus of tuberculosis in the apex of the left lung. The disease was only at an early stage but nevertheless I was devastated and, when I went home to tell my parents, my father was flabbergasted, saying: 'I don't believe it!' From then onwards neither my father nor mother ever really accepted that I had the disease. My mother used to say that I was 'threatened' with tuberculosis. What they didn't realise, of course, was that the very healthy nature of our lifestyle in Sandycove meant that I had never had any contact with tuberculosis and therefore had not built up any resistance to it, so as soon as I was exposed to the active cases in the hospital, I became infected. This was something my father simply couldn't understand, and so he refused to accept that I was sick. The consultant, Dr Brendan O'Brien, said that I would have to be on full bed rest for at least six months, which meant that I would have to miss a whole year of college.

So, a bed was made up for me on the ground floor in the breakfast room at home. Although I had no symptoms and felt perfectly healthy, I was confined to bed, only being allowed to get up to go to the toilet. At that time fresh air was considered important for those suffering from TB, so, even though it was winter, the windows and doors were opened wide, irrespective of the weather. Since many people with advanced TB were thin and emaciated, the theory which was current in those days was that it was important to have a rich diet with plenty of milk, cream, butter and so on. Hearing this, my mother set about feeding me, so that within a few months I had put on several stone in weight.

Although at the time I was deeply upset at having to miss a year of my studies and be confined to bed, looking back now I can see that it was one of the best things that could have happened to me. Having gone through the usual obsessive ruminations over sin and confession, guilt over masturbation and so on in early adolescence, prior to contracting TB, I had lost all interest in religion and considered myself an atheist. This was mainly because I was so preoccupied with music and other things that I had little time to consider questions of spirituality or the meaning of life.

However, once confined to bed I had plenty of time and I began to think about these issues. I started to read a great deal, becoming interested in Thomistic philosophy, reading Cardinal Newman and Jacques Maritain, the Confessions of St Augustine, and even having a go at the works of St Thomas Aquinas himself. As a result I once again became a devout Catholic, convinced of the truth of Christianity. I even had notions about joining one of the contemplative orders and, later, when I was up and about again, used to visit Mount St Joseph, the Cistercian Abbey in Roscrea. I became quite friendly with Father Joseph Boylan, whom I think was something of a true contemplative and mystic. I am afraid my notions of a spiritual life were rather theatrical, involving fantasies of myself wandering around peaceful gardens in the long white robes of the Cistercians.

By September I had had six months of complete bed rest and my condition steadily improved. The only drug treatment I received was Paramino Salasylic Acid (PAS), which was foul tasting. The antibiotic Streptomycin was already available but was being reserved for severe cases. So, when September came, I went for a further check-up X-ray, and Dr O'Brien said I would be able to return to my medical studies in October.

A friend came to visit the following week and brought a tape recorder – one of the early ones. This was too much to resist. I had to hear what I sounded like playing the trumpet so, sitting up, I blew happily for about an hour and felt tired but elated with the result. When I went back for the final X-ray, not only had the disease in the apex of my left lung deteriorated considerably but the apex of the right lung was also infected. The doctor was flabbergasted and could not understand how such deterioration could have happened in two weeks – there was no way I was going to admit that by playing the trumpet I had blown the TB from one lung to the other. The upshot was that I had to return to bed for a further six months and missed another year in college.

At that point I was not yet nineteen years old and was far too immature, both academically and socially, to be ready to pursue a medical career. Increasingly, I came to value solitude and the opportunity to read and study philosophy. And so the months dragged on to March or April, by which time I was allowed to get up again on a gradual basis.

At last, in 1951, after two years, I was ready to re-enter medical school. The two years of illness gave me another important piece of understanding. Having always considered myself a mistake and a potential failure, my attitude, when presented with something new, whether it was swimming, playing tennis or whatever, was: 'Oh, I wouldn't like to try that unless I was good at it.' What I failed to realise, of course, was that nobody is initially good at anything. We have to learn to fail and try again. The simple truth is that if we love what we do and keep trying then eventually we will succeed and can become good at virtually anything. Human beings have an enormous potential, most of which is seldom realised. This negative attitude is very common among those with psychiatric problems; they are afraid to try something new for fear that they may fail. I also had the attitude that, if I tried something and failed, I would leave myself open to ridicule. Therefore it was better to play safe and not expose oneself to dangerous social situations, or new activities where one might be emotionally hurt.

It was during the two years I was sick, with plenty of time to think, that it came to me that fear of failure was worse than failure itself. So, when the time came to face the world again, I said to myself, 'From now on I will try things, and expose myself to not getting them right the first time.' It was a very painful but important learning experience, for, although I did have many failures and often made a fool of myself, from then on I tried new things and stuck at them. To my surprise I gradually began to succeed, where before there was only avoidance and a feeling of failure.

When I joined the new group of students who originally had been two years behind me, I began to make friends and managed to pass the exams each year. It was during those years of sickness, too, that it had dawned on me how tied I was to home and family, so I started to make some rather desperate attempts at developing greater independence.

A friend called Stanley and I got a notion to travel across the country. We hired a pony and trap in Tipperary and decided that we would make our way across to Kerry. A third friend, who was nick-named 'The Ging', joined us. Some of the experiences we had on that journey still remain totally fresh in my memory. One day we set up camp beside a clear stream. We lit a fire and put on the bacon, cabbage and potatoes to simmer. It was a golden day, when time seemed to stand still. In between we were fishing in the river and swimming, so the day drifted by in a sense of total peace and it was actually evening by the time we sat down to eat. At that time there were relatively few tourists coming to Ireland and when we wanted potatoes, cabbage or other vegetables we simply called to a farmhouse and asked for some. There was never any question of paying for what we needed; it was taken for granted that they gave us what was required. This was true until we got to within about six miles of Killarney, even then a major tourist centre. Then everything changed. In that area there was a price tag on everything, even potatoes.

We had made no provision for anywhere to sleep and each day we had to find a suitable barn as a resting place. We learned that you have to find a barn that is reasonably full of hay and within easy access while there is still daylight or you are in trouble after dark.

Eventually we made our way to Killorglin to Puck Fair. This was the first time I had ever been to Puck Fair and it was an astonishing sight. The big puck goat had been hoisted about 100 feet up on a

stand. He was a prize specimen, with enormous horns, who was captured wild up in the mountains, and he surveyed the whole town
below, looking depressed and disgusted at the drunken behaviour of
the multitudes beneath him. At that time most of the Travellers still
had the old style of horse caravan and there were literally hundreds
of these stretched out along the road, freshly decorated and painted.
The Travelling people came from all over the country to attend Puck
Fair and it was, for them, an annual festival.

The local account of the origin of the festival was that some time
in the past, perhaps around the time of Cromwell, a goat had saved
the town by warning them of the approach of the soldiers. But the
fact that the Travellers converged from all over the country on this
one place, at this time, and celebrated their unique marriage ceremonies suggested to me that the origins of the festival were much
older, going back to pagan times. The puck raised on high probably
represented a form of ancient goat worship which was still continuing, although in a disguised and diluted form. Certainly the amount
of drinking and debauchery, during the few days that it lasted, suggested that the fair could have some relation to the god Pan.

By this time I had completely run out of money, while the other
two still had some left. As I had no money to feed myself, I decided
to try playing and singing on the street. I had a whistle and a guitar
with me, but a sow had eaten my sandals so I was bare-footed. I
started up on the main street and the other two set about making a
collection for me from passers-by. I felt somewhat diffident at first
but to my surprise no one objected and soon we had collected quite
an amount of money.

After we left Puck Fair we journeyed back to Killarney and went
up into the hills to Kate Kearney's cottage. There I had what I think
must have been a unique experience of playing the whistle for the assembled jarveys and collecting about a shilling from them. It was
probably the first time in their lives they ever thought of giving away
money rather than receiving it.

We travelled on, following the track up into the mountains as it
got steadily darker, with the rain misting down on us. Our sense of
being lost and deserted was palpable until eventually, feeling that if
we went on we would only make matters worse, we found an over-
hanging ridge of rock and placed the pony-trap against it. There we
spent the night, snatching a few hours of fitful sleep. We got going

as soon as the dawn broke and in the daylight we were able to find our way over the mountains and look down on Kenmare, with the sea stretching away to the west.

After leaving Kenmare we made our way to Cork city. On arriving there, once again I had no money and I wanted to accompany the others for a decent meal, so I decided to have another go at playing on the street. I was playing outside Roches Stores in Patrick Street when a policeman came along. I wondered if I was going to be arrested or told to move on, but as he was passing he winked and said out of the corner of his mouth: 'Give us the "Star of Munster".'

When I was in the second last year of the medical course, we finally decided that our jazz band should go public. For four weeks we took over a hall every Saturday night. Each week the crowds grew bigger, but by the third week the dancing had faded out and the crowd stood around the stage mesmerised. I remember it being said that we sounded like the early King Oliver band or the Louis Armstrong Hot Five. It was something of a triumph in my trumpeting career. However, by the end of the fourth week I found I was streaming with what seemed like a really heavy cold and several people said I had better do something about it. I kept putting it off because I could guess what the problem was and when I finally went for an X-ray it was to find that I had relapsed with tuberculosis yet again.

It was a big shock to have to acknowledge that my hopes of a career as a jazz musician would have to come to an end. In hindsight, though, it was probably the best thing that could have happened, because the kind of traditional jazz I was interested in at the time was already going nowhere. Had I continued and become a professional musician I probably would have ended up playing music I hated in some third-rate dance band.

It was at about this time that I began to develop an interest in Irish music. I can remember the exact occasion when this happened. I was driving around town with my sister and brother in his little open Morris car and, as we went down Capel Street, we suddenly came upon a traditional fiddle player. He was one of the Dunne family from Limerick, a Traveller family, all of whom were partially blind. We stopped the car to listen and I was astonished at the free, passionate sound of his playing. I said to my brother, 'He's improvising, just like a jazz musician.' Up until then my only real experience of Irish traditional music had been my father playing a few jigs and reels on the mandolin and I had never taken any interest in it, nor had I ever thought of it as being a free and creative form of musical expression. So I was really astounded to hear the rhythm and free-spirited playing of a real traditional musician. From then on I became fascinated with traditional music, and looked around to find where I could hear more of it.

Eventually I found the Pipers' Club, which was located in the old IRA building in Thomas Street. Every Saturday night musicians of all kinds turned up simply for the joy of playing with each other. It was there that I first heard Leo Rowsome on the uilleann pipes. This was an absolute revelation; I couldn't believe the complexity of the instrument or the beauty of the music it produced. It was out of this little gathering of Irish musicians, which had kept traditional music alive in Dublin, that the whole revival of Irish music spread across the country. It was some of the musicians in this club who established Comhaltas Ceoltóirí Éireann, which became a national movement for the preservation and development of traditional music, and it was from this small beginning that the first *fleadh*s were organised. The effect of these early *fleadh*s in different towns around the country was extraordinary. Prior to that, Irish music was in deep slumber and well on the way to dying. The younger generation had little or no interest in it. It is true that some families here and there along the western seaboard and in other isolated parts of the country had kept traditional music alive, but such families, where most of the members played flute, fiddle or accordion, were often considered peculiar. They would even tend to be avoided, akin to families known to be suffering from tuberculosis or mental illness. However, a small number of the faithful would gather on Saturday nights in the kitchen for a session, playing or dancing sets.

The first *fleadh* I went to was in Loughrea and it was remarkable to see the local musicians, who had the habit of keeping out of sight, join the hundreds of visiting music fans until the whole town was filled with the sound of joyous music. At that time the numbers coming to the *fleadh*s were small, made up mainly of musicians or those who loved the music, so that it was possible for people to play freely in the street or in the pubs without being overwhelmed by vast crowds of tourists.

The predicament of the uilleann pipes was even more perilous.

You could count on the fingers of your hands the number of pipers remaining around the whole country and there was no one other than Leo Rowsome and Matt Kiernan in Dublin and, to a lesser extent, the Crowley family in Cork capable of making or repairing the instruments.

One of the sadnesses of my life is that I just missed meeting Johnny Doran, the last of a whole generation of travelling pipers and had played on the streets and in houses all over Ireland. He was still alive when I first went to the Pipers' Club in Thomas Street, but shortly before this a wall had fallen on his caravan and broken his back. Fortunately, some time before this, he had been recorded by Delargy in the Folklore Commission and, by any standard, these recordings show him to have been a great piper. Johnny was welcomed in the homes of traditional musicians in every town in Ireland. He had invented a metal cup in which he placed the bottom of the chanter so that he could play standing up and it is said that, like the pied piper, he once coaxed the people of Kilrush to follow him out of the town, mesmerised by his playing. Ted Furey, the father of Finbarr and the Furey brothers, told me how he used to travel with Johnny Doran. One night, when they had camped somewhere down in County Clare, he awoke to find no sign of Johnny. Being somewhat alarmed he got up and went to look for him. After searching for some time he heard the pipes faintly in the distance and, following the sound, came upon Johnny Doran playing contentedly, surrounded by a flock of sheep.

Leo Rowsome's family had been in north County Wexford for several hundred years and there was a long relationship between his family and the Traveller families of Leinster, going back over several generations – the Cashes, Connors and Dorans, who were all related. I became very friendly with Leo Rowsome from that time, and I was fascinated by the complexity of the uilleann pipes. Seamus Ennis, whom I only met much later, used to say that it took seven years for a piper to establish what he called 'the grip', and a further seven years to make a piper.

In the hands of a skilled musician the uilleann pipes make a wonderful delicate music, with an extraordinary variety of tones and variations. Most pipes at the present time are at concert pitch, tuned to D, which is suitable for playing with other instruments such as fiddles, accordions, etc. But these make a very bright sound and are quite loud. The pipe-makers of the eighteenth and nineteenth centuries, however, frequently made what are known as flat pipes, tuned a tone or a tone and a half down to C, B or even B flat. These have a beautiful, gentle, mellow tone which brings out the true beauty of the pipes as a solo instrument.

Leo Rowsome had acquired two flat sets by the pipe-maker Harrington of Cork, a brass set and a silver set, each of which were nearly 200 years old. I was greatly taken with these and eventually persuaded Leo to sell them to me for £100, which at the time seemed to me an extravagant sum. I later handed them on to my son Ronan, who is a highly skilled piper. Each at present would probably be worth in excess of 20,000, as they are genuine antiques.

I think it was at the second *fleadh* I attended, in Ennis, County Clare, that I first met Denis Murphy, the great Kerry fiddle player from Gneevgullia. I was wandering through the streets listening to different musicians when I heard the sound of a violin coming from the front room of a hotel. There was something different about this sound that attracted me, so I went in. Here was a tall, fair man with glasses, playing solo. The sound of his playing was so soft, melodious and flowing that I stayed on and on to listen. When he stopped playing Denis introduced himself to me. He had a high-pitched, melodious Kerry accent, not unlike the sound of his violin. I didn't realise it at the time but I was being introduced to the great musical and poetic tradition of Sliabh Lucra. This district in east Kerry was the birthplace of the poets Aogán O'Rathaille and Eoghan Rua O'Suilleabháin, and the area also boasted a fine musical tradition of pipers and fiddlers. In more recent times, the great fiddle player Padhraig O'Keefe, who died as recently as 1963, taught a whole generation of younger fiddle players – Paddy Cronin, Denis Murphy and his sister Julia Clifford among them.

Denis was so friendly that evening that we became great friends and I visited him often in his home in Gneevgullia. On the first occasion I went there I had the privilege of meeting Padhraig O'Keefe; it was a unique experience to hear the two of them playing together. Denis had modelled himself so closely on his mentor that when they were playing they even wrinkled up their noses at exactly the same time. A characteristic of the fiddle playing in that area that they both displayed was that, at a certain point in a tune, one of the fiddles would drop down an octave below the other, playing a sort of bass part but with identical notes.

Unfortunately Padhraig was a heavy drinker and by the time I met him this had taken a toll on his health. He had been a teacher in his earlier years, but, because he was so often absent with the music and the drink, he retired early. The story I heard was that he was away in another town when the inspector visited his school. Someone rushed to inform Padhraig, but when he heard the news he said, 'Let him go', and he never returned to the school or to teaching again. Padhraig could write music beautifully but he had also invented his own notation for teaching his pupils. Hearing this I asked Denis to get him to write out a tune for me. After much persuasion, towards the end of the night, he wrote the slow version of 'The Blackbird' and at the top, where one would usually write *moderato* or *allegretto*, he wrote 'any time dear, slowly'. One evening, when Denis was going to confession, he met Padhraig and asked him if he would like to come with him. Padhraig's reply was typical: 'Sure I have no sin only ateing my nails and grinning.'

Denis told me that on another occasion a German visitor was very anxious that Padhraig should write out a tune for him, but the whole night went by playing music and it still hadn't been done. The next morning was a Sunday and Denis, Padhraig and others went to Mass. Denis was worried that Padhraig might slip out of the church and that any hope of getting the tune written then would be gone. Sure enough, halfway through the Mass, Padhraig left and made his way up the road. Denis followed him and asked where he was going. 'I'm going for a drink,' Padhraig said.

'Surely after all the drink last night you can't be thirsty,' said Denis.

'Thirst, is it?' Padhraig asked. 'I've a thirst that would frighten Jaysus.'

The routine at Denis' home during my visits was always the same. No matter what hour you went to bed he would wake you early in the morning with a bottle of stout and a large whiskey. It was the last thing that I wanted at that hour but Denis would stand over me while I drank it. Then, as soon as we had had breakfast, he would start playing. He was the only person I know who would literally play music all day, starting at breakfast time and going on until late at night. I don't think I have ever known anyone else with such a total love of Irish music. On one particular occasion, when Denis, as usual, had started playing after breakfast, a couple of fellows called by who were on their way to a building job. Hearing Denis, they stopped to play a tune. I don't know what happened to their work but they never got there that day; they were still playing at midnight. I never tired of listening to the soft, gentle tones of Denis making the fiddle 'sing'.

He told me that one time, years before, when his father was alive, a close relative had died, and at that time in Kerry mourning continued over a whole year, during which no one was allowed to play music. Apparently Denis' mother, Manie, strictly supervised this rule, so months went by without Denis or his father being able to play a note. He said his father was literally pining away. Then one day, when Manie was in town shopping, Denis' father said: 'You go out on the road and keep an eye out for her and I can play a tune. Then I'll go out and watch so that you can play.'

Denis spent several long periods in New York. His sole purpose in going was to work enough years to get the social security pension; then he could come home and live in relative ease on it. When I was in the States in 1960 I went to visit him. It was as if he and his wife, Julia Mary, had just arrived, although they had actually been there for three or four years at the time. Their cases were still half unpacked, lying on the floor; they were simply waiting for the moment to come when he would be entitled to the pension and they could leave for home.

There were lots of Irish musicians in New York. Some, like Denis, had come over from Ireland but others had been there for generations. Denis used to play regularly with these. One day I asked him: 'Are you not having a great time here in America?' He replied: 'Here, you have to be watching the work and the music and sure you couldn't be watching both of them.' Eventually he did serve his time and got the pension so that he was able to return to spend his last happy years in Ireland just concentrating on the music.

On one of my visits to see him he told me that, some years before, Seamus Ennis had arrived in Kerry with Dylan Thomas, the Welsh poet. They had taken Denis off with them up around the west of Ireland and out to the Aran Islands on an endless drinking and music spree. Denis said that after a couple of weeks of this he just wanted to get home. He said: 'You'd want to just get your hand on a spade.'

Some years later I went on what was to be my last visit to see Denis. I met him on the road, as he was just returning from a funeral. We threw our arms around each other and he gave me a great hug. He died shortly afterwards and I didn't have the heart to visit Gneevgullia for many years.

In the meantime, I was progressing slowly through my medical studies. It was when I was coming to my final year that I met Orla, now my former wife, who was a year or two behind me in college. Her mother was Delia Murphy, the well-known folk singer.

Prior to this I had decided that during the summer vacation, I would travel the streets of Ireland, playing the whistle and singing with the guitar. On my first trip I went into a hotel near Naas to try my hand at playing and see if I could earn some money. I had just started to play when the manager offered me half a crown to go away. Things got better after that; while I didn't make a lot of money and slept in many barns, I made enough to feed myself along the way. The following summer I went away again but this time I took my big black Labrador dog, Caesar, with me. I had taken him out collecting locally for St Vincent de Paul, with a basket on his back, and he was a great success. So I fitted him with the basket and took him down the country. This way I made considerably more money than I had on my previous journey. In Ballybunion I made nearly £5 in a couple of hours, a lot of money in those days.

On that trip too I went to Puck Fair once again. The event that year was being covered by Arthur Helliwell, who wrote a very popular column in the *Sunday People*. He was very taken when he saw me performing and decided, as well as interviewing me, to take up a collection on my behalf. He was known for the famous hat that he wore and he used this to take up the collection. He followed me around all day and at about 10 o'clock that night I was hoisted up on to a cart, where I continued to sing, with a big crowd all around us.

Later that summer, at the Galway races, I joined up with several members of the Dunne family from Limerick. We had a big coat spread out on the ground and it was covered with money by the end of the afternoon, and this we divided between us. I was in my bare feet, as usual. The next day I joined up with Delia Murphy and I put on the suit and shoes that I had in my kit bag to return to the Galway races, this time as a respectable member of the public. I was walking through the crowd when I heard one old Traveller woman saying to another: 'There's the big, hairy bugger who was up here yesterday with no shoes on him.'

Back home in Dublin, one morning, Delia Murphy wanted to go to the National Library in Kildare Street. When we were coming out, we met a fellow on the steps at the entrance who had the classic Dub appearance and accent. What I remember particularly was his big red neck, as he was wearing an open-necked shirt. I had no idea who he was. Then Delia introduced him as Brendan Behan. I had never heard of him as he wasn't as yet well known and I think most of his writing had been in Irish up until then. We went with him for a drink but I'm not too clear exactly what happened after that. I know Delia disappeared and I stayed on drinking with Brendan. We went pub-crawling all day and my abiding memory is of laughing more than I've ever laughed in my life. I can recall only fragments of the conversation. At one point he was imitating a Welsh brass band and choir doing the Our Father. Then he would describe the girls who were trained by the nuns in Sion Hill to play the Irish harp and sing in polite, refined little voices, as having a pioneer pin on their breast and wearing a chastity belt. He went on like this all day, with one story after another, until I nearly collapsed with laughter. When we were walking the streets going from one pub to another, every time we passed a painter or any other tradesman Brendan would stop for a chat. He seemed to know every tradesman in Dublin. Sometime in the afternoon we ended up in the headquarters of the Gaelic League and he was chatting away to them in Irish, with me tagging along, not understanding a word. Then finally in the evening we landed out at the cottage where Orla was staying at the time. There were a lot of rats around that place, so she kept a .22 rifle for shooting them. As soon as Brendan set eyes on the rifle he snatched hold of it and went out into the yard. We were seriously drunk by this time and he insisted on my throwing empty bottles that were lying around the yard up into the air so he could shoot at them. I was happy enough doing this for a while but eventually I got tired of it. As soon as I'd stop though, he would point the rifle at me, threatening to shoot, so I had to start throwing them up into the air again. This went on interminably, with him getting drunker and wilder all the time, until, thank God, it got too dark for him to see and he gave up. That is my last recollection of that memorable day.

All this time, when I was in Dublin, I continued to go regularly to the Pipers' Club in Thomas Street, but then a split occurred among the members of the club. Some of the organisers of Comhaltas in the club became rather officious and bureaucratic, and the musicians who liked just to come and play resented this. They decided they would go elsewhere, found a large room over an old pub on a corner halfway up Church Street and started to meet there on Wednesday nights instead.

Most of the musicians followed the rebels over to Church Street, but a few who were loyal to the old group in Thomas Street remained. Leo Rowsome was one of these. Some, like myself, went to both places. The room over the pub in Church Street was not that large and it used to be crowded with musicians every Wednesday night. There was a large statue of the Sacred Heart at one end of the room and it seemed quite an incongruous setting for traditional music. All the same, Church Street was like a creative pressure cooker. All the young musicians who afterwards formed groups that became internationally famous were crowded into this one room. Finbarr and the Furey Brothers, often accompanied by their father Ted Furey, were there; Barney McKenna, Ronnie Drew and the others who formed The Dubliners; Liam O'Flynn, Donal Lunney and Christy Moore, who became Planxty; and the first group Seán Ó Riada got together to form Ceoltóirí Chualann – Paddy Moloney, Sean Potts, Michael Tubridy and the others who later became famous as The Chieftains.

Tommy Potts, the great, eccentric Dublin fiddle player, would come regularly, when he wasn't in one of his bouts of religious fervour. At such times he would give up playing altogether for months on end. Another regular participant was Sunny Brogan, who was a wonderful button accordion player and an archetypal Dub. He was hardly five feet in height, and he would often come to within two or three inches of me and talk into my chest when he was describing some of his woes. He suffered from severe bouts of depression and had never worked a day in his life. He once got a job tending the furnaces in Dublin Zoo but, over the first weekend, he let all the fires go out so he was sacked. Tommy Potts met him one evening in the pub when he was complaining of how terribly depressed he was. He said he couldn't even swallow a mouthful of food or get down a cup of tea. In the middle of this tale of woe he lowered about a quarter of the pint of Guinness he was holding. Tommy irreverently re-marked: 'You didn't have much trouble with that one, Sunny.' Brogan was deeply insulted at the idea that depression could interfere with him drinking his pint.

The Clancy Brothers, who first popularised the old Irish come-all-yes and traditional songs in America, would also come in to Church Street whenever they were home from the States. Felix Doran, the brother of the great piper Johnny Doran, who was a scrap dealer in Manchester and was, himself, a considerable piper, would turn up whenever he was home. There were many wonderful nights of music, the climax of the night often being the old-style, *sean-nós*, dancing of Paddy Bawn. There were some gifted ballad singers from the old Dublin tradition and *sean-nós* singers from Connemara who would also show up from time to time.

6

Becoming a Doctor

By now it was 1954 and I had reached my final year in medical school. I had largely got over my social inhibitions and had made many good friends, particularly a few of the black students, who were originally of West Indian origin but came from New York – Herbie Holmes, Eric Williams and several others. I used to go to their parties and sing the blues with the guitar. They were fascinated by the fact that an Irish fellow could have got so much into the heart of the blues. I used to sing songs from Bessie Smith, Louis Armstrong, Big Bill Broonzy and others.

Prior to reaching the final exam, we had to do a period of residence in one of the maternity hospitals. Generally the time we spent in the maternity hospital was raucous, with a lot of parties and fairly heavy drinking. One night, after returning from the pub, I wanted to go to bed but a couple of friends decided that it was too early and they took the mattress off my bed and threw it down into the basement. I had a rough time trying to haul it up and get it past them into my room. In retaliation, a couple of days later, I went home to Sandycove and gathered up about fifty green crabs from the rocks and brought them into the hospital in containers. That night, when those fellows pulled back the clothes to get into their beds, they were horrified to see these creatures crawling around. What I didn't realise was that crabs can survive a long time out of the water, so they gradually made their way from the students' quarters all around the hospital, into the wards and even the labour ward. There was a desperate commotion, with nurses and mothers screaming as the poor crabs struggled slowly around the floor. The master of the hospital was called and a lot of questions were asked as to how they got there

48

but I kept a low profile and said nothing.

When I eventually came to the final exam in June I managed to pass surgery and midwifery but failed in medicine. I had a beard at the time and during the summer some of the other students advised me to shave it off. When I re-presented at Christmas in 1954, I finally got through. Afterwards someone told me that the Abe had asked: 'Who is that fellow?' and when he was told it was me without a beard he said: 'He looks better now.'

When I finally qualified in 1954, I was faced with the fact of being a doctor. Having been treated during my years as a medical student as an incompetent eejit who knew nothing, suddenly here I was, a qualified doctor. I will never forget the shock and anxiety I experienced on finding myself on duty for the first time in the casualty department, expected to make decisions and make competent diagnoses. Nurses would say: 'You're the doctor, aren't you?' Yet I didn't know any more then than I had a month before, when I was just a medical student. Luckily, the ward sister in charge of the casualty and out-patients nearly always knew what to do.

Having little interest in ordinary surgery, I opted to do my first six months in the neurosurgical unit, which was the main neurosurgical centre for the whole country. By taking my first six-month internship in this unit I not only satisfied the requirement of six months' experience in surgery, but also got a good basic grounding in neurology, which stood me in good stead later when I took up psychiatry.

The Brain Unit, as the neurosurgical complex was called, was in many ways a fascinating place to work. Adam McConnell had developed the unit over many years until it became the national centre, but, by the time I did my internship, he had retired, although he was still active and came in to visit the unit on a fairly regular basis. His protégé, Johnny Lannigan, had trained and worked with him for many years. He was the principal surgeon in the unit at that time. The other surgeon, Colin Gledhill, had come over more recently from Scotland. I worked mainly with him and I found his skill and professionalism awesome. On several occasions, when Gledhill was in the middle of a delicate operation, such as dealing with a cerebral aneurysm, McConnell would come quietly into the theatre without any gown or mask. Smoking his pipe, he would peer into the open cerebral cavity of the patient and discuss some technical point of the operation with Gledhill. In one particular instance, when he was leaning over the patient in this way, there was a drip of saliva hanging precariously from the bowl of his pipe, at any moment ready to drop into the exposed brain of the poor patient. Gledhill would be barely able to conceal his exasperation.

People with various forms of cerebral tumour and other neuro-surgical conditions came from all over the country to the unit, both adults and children. Many of these cases were tragic indeed, where the tumours were malignant and the operation to remove them was of no avail. I remember little children coming in with large cerebellar tumours and, even when one of these could be removed satisfactorily, they would nearly always return again within a few months with a recurrence as large as before. There were many patients who would come in after accidents with severe brain injury and often these would, literally, drown in their own secretions. The life-support systems and methods of keeping the airways clear and the lungs free of fluid were not as developed then as they are today, so death was a constant visitor to the unit. One of our duties as interns was to sit with dying patients as they passed away.

There was one fellow who came in suffering from Pick's Disease, a form of pre-senile dementia. He had a rare condition, which I had never seen before, known as the 'gramophone' syndrome. The moment he had an audience he would launch into two or three unbelievably dirty stories. I, and the other interns, got great amusement out of this because, when the surgeons came on their rounds, accompanied by the ward sister or the matron, this fellow would start up, 'Did you hear the one about the bishop and the nun?' Nothing could stop him regaling them with every lurid detail of one story after another, much to the intense embarrassment of the consultant and the blushes of the ward sister or matron.

The most serious recollection I have of that time was of having to assist one of the surgeons on Saturday mornings in the operating theatre. Nearly every Saturday morning one or two patients would be sent down from Grangegorman to have their brains 'chopped'. This was the major lobotomy procedure developed by Freeman and Watts, where burr holes were drilled on each side of the temples and a blunt instrument inserted to sever the frontal lobes almost completely from the rest of the brain. At that time, in 1955, there were literally hundreds of very disturbed patients, both women and men, in St Brendan's Hospital, as Grangegorman was renamed, and this operation was seen as an almost miraculous method of calming their disturbance. Indeed, it did succeed in doing this, but in the process many patients were turned into vegetables. When I think of standing there, Saturday after Saturday, assisting the surgeon as he happily whistled tunes while carrying out this drastic procedure, I feel shame and regret. But it is senseless, in retrospect, to react with such emotions of guilt, nor does it make sense to blame the surgeon, for neither of us knew any better. This was an accepted procedure at the time, recommended by supposed experts and the senior psychiatrists who ran Grangegorman.

As the years went on, the results of this terrible operation, which was carried out on thousands of patients across the western world, in the States and many European countries, became only too clear. The patient would often be discharged, supposedly cured, to be cared for at home by their poor relatives. There they showed every kind of deteriorating behaviour, often complicated by epileptic seizures, defecating on the floor and behaving like crazed animals. There was the celebrated case of a woman who was operated on in the Maudsley Hospital in London and was supposed to be their most successful cure after lobotomy. When she eventually died and a postmortem was carried out, it was found that the knife had entirely missed the brain and her subsequent improvement was presumably due to the fact that her brain had not been damaged.

On one alarming occasion a huge farmer, with a gaunt, muscular frame, who was immensely strong, was admitted to the unit, from somewhere in the depths of Kerry, with a possible brain tumour. On admission he was quiet and morose but, that night, when I arrived back to the halls of residence, there was an urgent call from the neurosurgical ward to come quickly. I, and several others, arrived at the door of the ward to find the place in a state of siege. This big fellow had become disorientated during the evening and had gone berserk. He was standing in a long nightshirt, with one of the big barium meal bottles in each hand. As soon as any of us attempted to enter the ward he would let one of these bottles fly, with a crash of glass and liquid spraying all over the place, and we hurriedly pulled the door shut for protection. We were there like this for what seemed like an age, but eventually, when I made yet another attempt to enter the ward, he let fly a heavy brass cross as I opened the door. This barely missed my head and embedded itself in the wooden panel at the side of the door. Until then I had felt afraid each time I tried to sneak the door open but, for some reason, when the cross crashed into the wall beside my head, I was suddenly overcome with rage, which was very unusual for me, and I lost all sense of fear. I rushed into the ward and charged at him, knocking him back onto his empty bed. Immediately several others came in and we were able to hold him down while we gave him an injection. I remember glancing round and seeing the terrified faces of the other patients in the ward as they cowered in their beds. The only sedation known to the staff in the unit at that time was Paraldehyde and we had to give him several injections of this horrible, smelly stuff before he finally quietened down.

I have often felt at a disadvantage in life when, faced with situations like this, I wasn't able to lose my temper and feel that surge of aggression, the 'fight/flight' reaction of the body, which would give the rush of energy to face what was happening. Instead, at such times I would generally feel drained and sick in the stomach, which leaves one in too weak a state to take effective action. To my amazement this was one time when exactly the opposite happened. Before I had time to think, I had rushed into the ward and grabbed this huge fellow, successfully getting him back onto his bed.

In the second six months of my pre-registration year I transferred to general medicine with Dr Alan Thompson. He was a very civilised man and I got on well with him. It was during that time that Leo Rowsome, the piper, was admitted with a hypertensive crisis. His blood pressure was sky high and he was on the verge of pulmonary oedema. It was vital to carry out a lumbar puncture to relieve the cerebral pressure, but the difficulty was that he was in a delirious state and was thrashing around in the bed. I had already gained considerable experience in the brain unit, carrying out spinal taps, and by that time was quite proficient, but, because of his disturbed state, it was almost impossible to hold him. I knew that, unless I succeeded, there was little hope of saving his life. I think the fact that here was one of the few remaining uilleann pipers in the country gave me that vital bit of extra motivation so that I stuck at it and eventually succeeded and relieved the pressure. The result was that he recovered and lived on for a good many years, providing the link to another generation of young pipers. Thus, with the help of a few others, this precious tradition was not lost, as the playing of the Irish harp had been a couple of centuries earlier.

With my pre-registration year coming to a close and my dream of becoming a jazz musician terminated because of TB, I had to face the future and come to some decision as to what to do next. In spite of my efforts to achieve more independence by travelling around the country singing and playing on the streets, I was still very dependent on my home in Sandycove and on my mother. I applied for a job in St Patrick's Psychiatric Hospital and was called for interview with Dr Norman Moore. I already knew him vaguely because he was Professor of Psychiatry in the College of Surgeons but, as I had shown no sign of distinction in any aspect of my medical studies up to that time, I knew I had very little chance of success. Dr Moore was very polite but told me that he had a long list of doctors applying for a post in St Patrick's and, although he didn't say it in so many words, it was clear that I was somewhere at the bottom of the list.

Having failed to get a job in psychiatry I decided to study for Membership of the Royal College of Physicians in Ireland (MRCPI). This was really only a cop-out, as the real reason for studying for the MRCPI was that I simply couldn't face leaving home to go to England. So I sat at home studying and reading. The MRCPI exam was divided into two parts and the first part was virtually a repeat of the medical curriculum, involving bacteriology, physiology, pathology and so on, with an exam in medicine also. However, the way I was going about it meant there really wasn't any chance of my passing. I used to go into the Richmond Hospital to attend medical clinics and I remember one day, when I was sitting in the consultants' staffroom, Dr Harry Counihan came in. I told him I was studying for the MRCPI and he said, 'You're wasting your time, sitting on your arse there at home. You won't get anywhere.' I didn't heed his advice and, of course, duly failed the exam in June, because I was studying at home instead of leaving home and getting a job.

7

Oxford

Having failed to obtain a job in Dublin, I had no choice but to face the prospect of emigration. I succeeded in getting a trainee psychiatric post in the Warneford Hospital in Oxford and set off in July 1956. I recall only too vividly the bitter homesickness on the journey by train from London to Oxford, looking at the track on the opposite side of the station leading towards home with tears in my eyes, longing to cross over and start the return journey. Here I was a qualified doctor, twenty-seven years of age, and I felt totally bereft, like a child facing the first day in school.

The Warneford had been a private hospital that dealt almost exclusively with the university prior to the introduction of the National Health System (NHS). At that time there was no Chair of Psychiatry in Oxford. Although by now the hospital had been incorporated into the NHS, virtually all the patients in the hospital were students or staff of the university. The other psychiatric hospital in the area, Littlemore, had traditionally been the public mental hospital for both the city and surrounding district, so not many of the ordinary townspeople came to the Warneford.

At the time the Warneford was a fairly traditional British psychiatric hospital, relying mainly on drugs, ECT and insulin coma therapy, with little emphasis on psychotherapy, what I had often heard referred to as 'good, sound, British psychiatry'. So, as far as ordinary psychiatric training went, it was pretty orthodox and not particularly innovative. The new psychoactive drugs had only recently been introduced, and there was still a fairly heavy reliance on barbiturates and concoctions like compound B, a combination of Hyacine and Morphine, for quieting excitement and disturbed behaviour. We had to take long, detailed psychiatric histories on each patient, which were then typed up by the secretaries. We also had to provide a tight case summary on the patient's discharge from hospital. In those early months I was constantly filled with anxiety that I would fail to make a diagnosis. I would feel a failure and humiliated when the consultant, with a look through the notes and a cursory assessment, would say, 'This is a case of schizophrenia' or whatever, as if it should have been obvious. It was only years later that I finally understood why. I will go into this more fully in the section on assessment and diagnosis.

What was really valuable about my year in Oxford was a shattering revelation. Because of the attitude and derived thinking in the education system in Ireland when I was growing up, I had always assumed that, if any question arose, someone in authority would give you the answer. Until I came to Oxford it had never dawned on me that one could think independently about the nature of reality, or come up with solutions oneself. But here in this hospital, I was dealing with people who, although labelled as patients, had been selected as the most brilliant academics or students from schools all over Britain and elsewhere. Their attitude seemed to be starkly different. If a question arose, they asked themselves, 'What do I think about it?' This struck me like a bolt from the blue and I began to think, 'If they can think for themselves, why can't I do the same?' From that moment on, I began to do just that, never again being willing to accept unquestioningly the views of others.

Also during my time there I was influenced by a rather unusual elderly psychoanalyst, Dr Richard Thompson, who was completely at variance with the conservative and orthodox views of the rest of the staff there. He gave me one piece of advice that I never forgot: 'Don't accept any of the current theories or belief systems in psychiatry. Keep an open mind and listen to the patients themselves. Eventually you will form your own opinion about these questions.'

Because it was my first post in psychiatry, I was very open to all that was happening around me. No answers were forthcoming during that year, or for a long time afterwards, but a number of quite unrelated experiences remain with me and I think these began to open up questions in my mind as to the true nature of psychiatric illness.

There was the distant relative of the Rothschild family who was admitted in a serious state of disarray, looking like someone who had been sleeping rough. He had fleas crawling all over him, but explained that he was doing a PhD on their behaviour and was using himself as a host for a number of different species. I don't know how genuine the story was, for he was in a very disturbed state. This presented the hospital with a real quandary as to whether to clean him up or try to accommodate him with his various colonies of fleas.

Then there was another student who had to take his university exams in the hospital because he was too anxious to join his classmates outside in the university. I had to act as invigilator as he sat there in his gown and mortarboard. Suddenly, in the middle of the examination, he went into a state of acute panic and rushed out across the fields, with me flying after him. Eventually I persuaded him to return and we got him through the examination.

I was also forced to realise during this period that some psychiatric symptomatology can have an organic basis. There was one woman who was admitted in a psychotic, almost delirious state, but on routine physical examination I found that she had a vaginal pessary that had been inserted years ago and had been forgotten. It was grossly infected and, when I removed it and we gave her an antibiotic, her psychotic state cleared up completely within a few days.

Another man in his fifties was admitted in a deeply depressed state. At that time the standard treatment for such a case was a course of ECT, but in the Warneford the practice was to do a routine Electroencephalogram (EEG) and this showed up large slow waves in the area of the frontal lobes. On neurological examination I found that he had a field defect in one eye (that is, part of his field of vision had deteriorated on one side). So we sent him to the celebrated neurologist, Richie Russell, in the Radcliffe General Hospital. His first response was to send back a report that the patient was neurologically normal. I imagine this was because he thought, 'Here are these psychiatrists wasting my time'. But when we insisted, the patient was eventually found to have a large frontal-lobe tumour. Had we given him ECT the result would have been fatal.

Then there was a young priest who was admitted because he required surgery on his penis for Phimosis (a too narrow opening, which makes it difficult to pass water). The pre-operative routine before such an operation was to give the patient oestrogens, but when he was given these he rapidly became psychotic. Nobody in the hospital, including the consultants, could make any sense of this because, of course, the belief was that psychosis is an organic, biochemically determined event. Looking back I realise now that he was a rather effeminate young man, probably latently homosexual, and that the female hormone he had been given simply tipped the balance of a shaky sexual identity. This broke down his defensive denial and thus he became psychotic.

It is important to realise that in 1956 the psychopharmacological revolution was only beginning. Largactil had only recently been discovered and was still not generally available. Most of the other psychoactive drugs had yet to appear. Because of this some of the old-style institutional syndromes were still to be seen. There was an enormous woman at the Warneford named Mrs Putnam who had been subjected to psychosurgery and must have weighed well over twenty stone. One day a little man who had been depressed for about fifteen years, staying almost continuously in his room, suddenly emerged and started to turn somersaults down the ward. He had gone spontaneously into an acute manic state. When he had finished somersaulting, he announced in a loud voice 'I need a woman. Bring me Mrs Putnam'. Then he wrote a cheque, for £1 million only, payable to the Pope. I think this was my first experience of someone in an acute manic state and I remember being astonished by his sudden, inexplicable change in behaviour.

But the person who made the deepest impression on me during that year was a little fellow who had spent many years in a closed ward in the hospital. He was said to have been one of the most brilliant students ever to come up to Oxford but had broken down within six months of his arrival. Over the years he had built up an extraordinary delusional system. By the time I met him he was probably in his early forties and had decided that he was Edward IX – that is, the authentic heir to the throne of England, which had been usurped by his sister Elizabeth. It was only years later I realised that, because he was an only child and had been brilliant all the way through school, the only way he could accommodate his failure and breakdown in the university was to create the delusion that he was a king. Nothing less than this could satisfy his need to be the centre of the world, as presumably he had been when growing up. A necessary part of maintaining his delusional system was that he should continually attempt to escape and, to this end, whenever one entered the ward, he was always standing close by the door protesting that he should be allowed to leave. He was a very gentle soul and just stood passively with his hand on the door as one entered until once again it was safely locked. But every so often someone would leave the door unattended and then he felt obliged to escape, although he had little enthusiasm for doing so. However, there was never any difficulty in apprehending him, for he would always be found reading some abstruse text, held about three inches from his eyes, as he made his way along the road to Windsor. What I found astonishing was that he could take a daily newspaper and make all sorts of connections between the different articles. In this way he was strengthening his thesis that, not only should he be ruling Britain, but that he had a central role in controlling political crises that arose in various parts of the world. For example, when it was reported in the newspaper that year, 1956, that there had seen some IRA activity, I went down one day to find our royal patient reading a Bible in Irish. On another occasion, when there was a political crisis in Japan, I found him reading chemistry in Japanese. I think there is no doubt that he was absolutely brilliant, but this was all utilised in the service of maintaining his fantasy world of being the uncrowned king of England.

Dr Thompson used to visit him on the ward almost daily, engaging him in conversation. Dr Thompson told me that, one day, when he was putting the little fellow under some pressure, the patient abruptly interrupted the discussion and said quietly: 'Look, it's taken me years to build up this internal world, please don't try to break it down.' So, beneath the delusional system that he had created, he understood quite clearly what he was doing.

On another occasion, Dr Thompson told me, 'If you want to understand psychosis, then you must build up a relationship with a schizophrenic.' There was a woman aged about fifty on one of the wards who had not spoken for many years and who lived in a completely withdrawn, isolated world, showing no emotional response whatsoever. He suggested that I should go down every day and sit with her, and try to relate to her. I did this over a period of about three months. I found it an excruciating experience and was surprised just how difficult it was to sit with someone who was completely silent, refusing to speak. I stuck it out and sat with her day after day, trying to make conversation and not knowing what else I could do. Then one day, as we sat there in silence, big tears started to roll down her face and, although she still didn't speak, she cried bitterly.

In the textbooks such a patient would be described as being

emotionally blunted, having lost the ability to feel any normal emotion, but her tears showed me that there was something fundamentally wrong with this view. Since then, I've had a number of similar
experiences with people who were apparently emotionally blunted
and I have come to realise that it is not that schizophrenics are incapable of feeling but rather that they are unable to maintain the normal boundedness between themselves and others, as they are far too
open and vulnerable to being invaded by others in their vicinity.
They are unable to control the influences in their environment and
their way of dealing with this is to take the drastic step of cutting off
all relationships with other persons. My understanding of this inner
world of the psychotic only developed gradually over the years.

Although Richard Thompson was much older than I, we became
quite close. It was he who introduced me to the late quartets of
Beethoven, some of the most magnificent music ever written, even
though Beethoven was totally deaf when he wrote them. A particular favourite of mine was the slow movement of the Quartet in A
Minor, Opus 132, which is deeply spiritual and, to me, reminiscent
of Gregorian chant. Richard was quite religious and we used to go to
early Mass every morning. I was serious about Catholicism during
that period and I remember, when receiving Communion, having
the same feeling I had had as a child. On Sunday evening we often
used to go down to Blackfriars, the Dominican Priory, to listen to the
monks singing *Compline* and the beautiful *Salve Regina*.

One evening, after dinner, I recall being subjected to a diatribe of
old-style British arrogance. A senior registrar, an Oxford graduate,
talked of how the British were superior, a master race, and eulogised
the glories of the British empire. This was one of those occasions when
I felt I couldn't stay in England another minute. Sometimes when I was
feeling homesick, I used to go up to the room of the assistant matron,
who was Irish, and sit with her to recharge my batteries. On other occasions I used to go down to visit the old colleges in Oxford; I remember New College in particular, Magdalen and others. And then there
was the beautiful, sunny day of the Oxford College boat races, with
barges on the river, students in boaters and colourful blazers – all the experience of Oxford University life and the grandeur of old England.

Towards the end of my year in Oxford I took the first part of the
DPM (Diploma of Psychological Medicine) and, when I left there in
June 1957, was formally launched on my psychiatric career.

8

St John of God's

I started work in St John of God's Psychiatric Hospital in Stillorgan, County Dublin, in the summer of 1957. St John of God was a Spanish monk who, having suffered as a mental patient, spent the rest of his life attempting to bring about more humane care for the mentally ill. The order he founded is associated with work in both mental retardation and psychiatry in many countries around the world. The hospital in Stillorgan is their main psychiatric facility in Ireland. They have also been involved in child psychiatry in a centre in Orwell Road, Dublin, for many years but their work in Ireland has mostly been with the mentally retarded in a number of centres.

At the time I took up my post as house officer, St John of God's hospital dealt only with male patients. (Some years after I left, this policy was changed and they started to admit women as well as men.) It had traditionally been a private hospital that mostly dealt with priests and brothers, but since the appointment of the medical director, Desmond McGrath, it had gradually become a more active acute hospital. Even so, during my time there, there were still a number of old priests and brothers who had been admitted over the years because of various breakdowns and sexual misdemeanours.

In addition, St John of God's had become known as a last hope for chronic alcoholics, even though it had no alcohol unit as such. In fact, Dr John Ryan (who was the consultant under whom I worked while I was there) and I wrote a paper on the detoxification of alcoholics. Partly as a result of this work, after I left they did open an alcohol unit, which has since become one of the main features of the hospital. I am sincerely grateful to John Ryan, who encouraged me to write this paper with him, because it got me started writing and publishing papers, which I continued to do over the years and without which I might never have taken an academic direction in psychiatry. Dealing with many psychiatric trainees over the years, I have noticed that, unless they start to write articles early in their careers, it is very hard to develop the habit later on and indeed many fail to do so.

There was an old priest at St John of God's who was known as Father Jim and who referred to himself as Jim. He was in a regressed schizophrenic state, spending most of his time in his room. He was very attached to one of the brothers – Brother Canice – and I think this was the first time I saw regression back to an early childhood state. Every morning he would proudly present a large turd in the bed to Brother Canice, like a child in the throes of being toilet trained. On one occasion, during the visiting hours, when a number of women were in the ward visiting their sons or husbands, he appeared out of his room clad only in his shirt and, lifting it up, announced proudly, 'Jim will piss on the ladies', to their horror and consternation. Father Jim always referred to Brother Canice as 'the auld mother'. One morning when the brother was attending to him, getting him dressed and ready for the day, Jim could be heard saying: 'Jim'll hit the auld mother' and then, in a calmer voice, 'Ah no, Jim wouldn't hit the auld mother. Jim'll hit the old mother, ah no Jim wouldn't hit the auld mother; Jim'll hit the auld mother, Jim'll hit the auld mother.' Suddenly there was a ferocious bang and Brother Canice came sailing out of the room, and was knocked almost senseless. The relationship between Father Jim and Brother Canice was never quite the same after that.

During my first year, there were a considerable number of young men admitted, most of them from the country, in a florid psychotic state, diagnosed as suffering from acute schizophrenia. We treated them with the new Phenothiazine antipsychotic drugs that were becoming available, or a combination of these with ECT. I was astonished at the way their symptoms melted away and these young fellows, who were hearing voices and having florid hallucinations with primary delusions, would become symptom-free and apparently quite normal within a few weeks. So, during the first year I was in St John of God's, I felt very optimistic that at last the answer had been found to schizophrenia. Fortunately, I stayed on there for a second year, when I saw virtually all these young men return from their family homes in the same psychotic state that they had shown on their first admission. However, the negative symptoms – lack of motivation, social withdrawal and blunted emotion – were more evident than before. In addition they now showed less response to pharmacotherapy than they had initially done and were relentlessly drifting into chronicity. This brought home to me the limitations of psychoactive drugs except in bringing temporary relief of symptoms. Once again, I was thrown back into uncertainty as to the real nature of psychiatric illness.

The other much-favoured treatment for schizophrenia at that time was deep insulin coma therapy and there was a special unit for this in the hospital. I used to dread these sessions because of the dangers involved. We worked with a small group of five or six patients at a time. They were given a sufficient dose of insulin to bring them into a deep hypoglycaemic coma. Then there was a critical period when a stomach tube had to be passed to administer a nasal feed of sufficient glucose to bring them gradually out of the coma, back to normal consciousness. I used to be haunted by the fear that the tube might go into the lungs rather than the stomach; also, if for some reason the passing of the tube and the administration of the glucose were delayed, the person might lapse into irreversible coma from which they could not be revived. This happened to one young priest to whom we administered this barbarous therapy. The psychiatric colleague working with me failed to get the tube down in time to administer the glucose. The result was that this poor fellow, although he eventually revived, suffered irreversible brain damage. I'll never forget the horror I felt seeing him over the following months until he finally passed away, crawling around naked like a crazed animal in a small pen that had been constructed to keep him under some sort of control. This was in the service of a treatment which had no therapeutic value whatsoever.

It was actually later in that same year, 1957, that Brian Ackner's brilliant study demonstrated conclusively that insulin coma therapy was no more effective than simply putting patients to sleep with barbiturates. The apparent improvement which was seen in some cases was simply due to their being taken from a large impersonal ward to a small group environment in which there was a climate of interest and hope, and where they received some human care and attention. Periodically such mechanistic interventions as this or psychosurgery have been demonstrated to be useless after hundreds or, in the case of psychosurgery, thousands of human beings have been irreparably damaged. But the lesson never seems to be taken on board that sensitive, vulnerable human beings are not machines to be tinkered and tampered with.

It was during this period that I began to have deep reservations about the efficacy of ECT and the long-term damage which can ensue from this procedure also. I was becoming increasingly uneasy about these crude forms of physical intervention; my feeling was growing that there must be a more humane way to work in psychiatry.

Another experience affected my growing uneasiness about the orthodox approach to psychiatric illness. When a new case presented for admission, the family would be ushered into one of the parlours near the entrance to the hospital. At times, the brother who was in charge of the financial arrangements would not be available and I would go in to begin the clinical assessment. I'd find myself in a room with several family members, but who was the patient? When this first happened to me I was a little taken aback. I would pick out the healthiest looking member of the family and address myself to him, only to become aware of an embarrassed silence, because I was talking to the patient. Having been caught out like this several times, I thought I had found the solution. If I picked out one of the sicker-looking members, this would not be the patient, but this didn't always work either.

It was the first real lesson I had in family psychiatry, for the truth is that, as a rule, the whole family is involved in psychiatric illness, although the main pathology may be channelled into one member. Not only is the patient as a rule not able to stand up for himself, but also the families are not competent either. This is the main reason why there has never been a satisfactory advocacy support group in psychiatry, other than the advent of Alcoholics Anonymous (AA) in the case of alcoholism. The situation is quite different in mental retardation. Here, because severe mental retardation is usually the result of either a genetic abnormality or brain damage occurring before, during or after birth, the parents are frequently competent and successful people. Hence the relatives of the mentally retarded have been highly effective and have been able to put pressure on the government by demanding financial support for the creation of more effective services.

When I was working in St John of God's I lived in the hospital and, unfortunately for the medical director, my room was directly over his office. At the time I was trying, not with great success, to learn the uilleann pipes. Whenever I had time off during the day I used to go up to my room to practise, driving the poor man nearly crazy. Once a year he used to invite a group of junior doctors to his home for dinner. When my turn for this annual event came, I went along quite happily, but the evening was an unqualified disaster. The first mishap occurred when I sat on a delicate antique chair, which cracked and disintegrated under my weight. A look of intense irritation spread over McGrath's face but he managed, barely, to restrain himself and made no comment. When we sat down to dinner there was a long, highly polished mahogany dining table with lace doilies at each place. The main dish was a chicken casserole. I was given a leg and thigh but, as I was struggling to disjoint it, it suddenly shot across the table, spraying gravy over the finely polished surface. McGrath went red in the face and bit his lip, but again managed to control himself. Then later I failed to realise that the dog was lying under my chair and at the end of the meal, when I pushed my chair back, it came down on the dog's paw. The creature gave a yelp and poor McGrath could no longer restrain himself: 'Oh you stupid clot,' he shouted. This was followed by an embarrassed silence. I have no doubt that he was as relieved as I was when the evening finally ended.

When I had been in St John of God's for over a year I went down to the All-Ireland *Fleadh Ceoil* in Mullingar. After being up late for several days, towards the end of a wonderful session of music at about 4am I coughed to clear my throat and my mouth filled with blood. I was horrified and frightened. I spat it into the toilet and hoped it was just a small blood vessel in my throat that had ruptured coughing, which, of course, was ridiculous. My capacity, like so many others, for denial in the face of something I do not want to accept never fails to amaze me. I avoided going for an X-ray for a couple of weeks, but I couldn't get rid of a persistent cold and eventually I was persuaded to do something about it.

I went to see a consultant in the Richmond Hospital and this time he advised me to come into the huts in the Whitworth section of the hospital which were reserved for people with TB. Up until then I had never had any effective treatment. Now, for the first time, I was put on Streptomycin and had a daily injection for the next year. On this occasion, like the other times when I was being treated for TB, I never felt sick and had a healthy appetite. One poor Dublin man who was slowly dying was the opposite. Unable to face most of the hospital meals, one day when I, as usual, was wolfing down my dinner, he looked at me in disgust and said: 'That fella would ate anything that would stand easy long enough.' The consultant would come to the huts on a Saturday morning for his weekly round and stop at each bed to see what evidence there was of progress. But, because this poor fellow was showing little change and slowly deteriorating, he would often walk by his bed without stopping. I was acutely aware of the unintentional cruelty of this, because here we were, all week, waiting for the one visit from the doctor, hoping to get some message of hope or improvement. I remember the sadness I felt when I saw the Dub sink down into quiet despair when the doctor did not stop at his bed. It was experiences like this, as a patient, that made me careful of the feelings of patients and aware of the need to take the time to communicate as clearly as possible, so that the person has a full understanding of his illness and a clear picture of where he stands.

Towards the end of my six months, when my X-rays showed good improvement, I was allowed up for part of the day and could go off into town. On the Sunday of the All-Ireland Hurling Final I went to Croke Park and ran into one of the Dunne family, Terry, the banjo player, who was playing and collecting money among the crowd. I invited him to come up to the huts the following week on the night before I was to leave hospital and to bring a couple of musicians with him. It was customary for someone leaving the huts to have a party and to supply a liberal amount of drink for the other patients. Terry Dunne arrived up with his banjo, his bag for collecting money attached to one end. One of the nurses came in to tell me that there were tinkers at the door who wanted to see me and she couldn't get them to go away. I had to go out and persuade her to let Terry and the others come in. We had a great night of music that went on until about 4am, with the nurses dancing sets in the middle of the ward. The next day, when the matron asked questions about the racket the night before, nobody knew anything.

The following day I packed up my stuff and prepared to leave for the last time. Although I was delighted to be getting out, I also felt sad because, having spent six months with the same small group of people, they had become real friends. This was an important learning experience for me about the nature of groups. A couple of weeks after I left, I decided to visit the unit to see my friends there, to whom I had felt, in some ways, closer than to my friends and relations outside. However, to my surprise there was a new person in my bed in the corner and I felt like a stranger. I have had this experience many times since, in weekend workshops and Tavistock-type group experiences, where intense emotional relationships develop rapidly but are closed off as quickly when one leaves.

Following my discharge from hospital, I returned to work in St John of God's for a few months, but it was now clear to me that I had nothing much further to gain there, so I was facing emigration once again. My preference would have been to go to the States, which I felt would be a more rewarding experience because of my interest in jazz. As I couldn't see any immediate prospect of being able to get there, I started searching the advertisements for jobs in Britain as the only available alternative. I was already sensing that the main developments in psychiatry were going to move in the direction of social and community mental health, so, when I came upon an ad for the post of Psychiatric Registrar in the Marlborough Day Hospital in London, I was immediately interested. To my surprise I was offered the job and in March 1959 I set off for London.

Prior to this I had asked Dermot Walsh, whom I knew well because we had done our intern year in the Richmond Hospital together, if I could have a look around Grangegorman, the main public mental hospital in Dublin. Dermot was working there at the time, so it wasn't difficult for him to arrange and I went along one winter evening as it was getting dark.

Grangegorman was divided into a male and female hospital. Most of the female hospital was on the east side of the road in the old Richmond Asylum, or Lower House as it was called, and in Unit 24, a separate unit beside the Broadstone Railway Station. This dilapidated unit had been part of the old North Dublin Workhouse. Indeed, at the beginning of the nineteenth century, the reason for the creation of the original Richmond Asylum was that there was such a build-up of pauper lunatics within the North Dublin Workhouse that something had to be done.

Even though I had already worked for more than two years in psychiatry, I remember feeling quite apprehensive at the prospect of facing the full picture of madness. But the reality was far worse than I had anticipated. Many of the wards at that time had upwards of a hundred patients in them, and some of the scenes that I witnessed that evening are burnt into my memory. Passing through a couple of day rooms in the women's hospital, there were crowds of patients all jostling each other, some of the women with their dresses pulled up over their heads and here and there a nurse, struggling amid the chaos. There was a cacophony of sound and I felt as though I was lost in some kind of hell. In another ward I passed through there was a little old lady, who could have been my own mother, who was clearly quite sane and conscious, sitting up in bed shaking with terror. Beside her was a gnome-like, demented epileptic who was trying to push a screen over on top of her. The poor woman was terrified and was, as far as I could tell, subjected to this onslaught day after day. Down in the Lower House there was a large prefabricated type of building like a giant sports arena. This had been demolished by the time I returned to Grangegorman in 1962 but at that time it served as the dining-room for female patients. When we entered it I was astonished to witness a scene of total chaos; there were shrieks and yells and the whole building was in a kind of semi-twilight. I had to duck several times to avoid being struck by a flying plate.

At that time there were approximately 2,000 patients in Grangegorman, or St Brendan's Hospital, as it had been renamed to give a more benign impression. On the male side of the hospital, in the large three-storey building which has also since been demolished, there were huge wards with beds jumbled together and day rooms with the patients crowded together similar to the women's side of the hospital. I had no way of knowing it at the time, but the reason for the chaotic state of the hospital and the terrible overcrowding was that although disturbed patients were constantly arriving in the admission units, relatively few were being discharged. So, in order to make room for the new arrivals, patients had to be transferred to the more chronic wards and, as these became overcrowded, then transferred on again. In this way, people simply got lost. Young disturbed men and women, who nowadays would either be held in the assessment unit overnight and then discharged or be admitted for a matter of days or weeks, were allowed to sink into despair in one of the chronic wards, where they then remained for years. I never forgot the horrific scenes that I witnessed on that visit and, although I was in no way conscious of it at the time, somewhere deep inside me a conviction formed that some day I would try to return and do something about the horror of this place.

There can hardly be a person in Dublin who is not aware of the existence of this mental hospital. Dublin life is replete with remarks such as, 'If you don't watch yourself you'll end up in the Gorman'. But the surprising thing is how few people living in Dublin actually know where Grangegorman is, although the hospital is nearer to the General Post Office (GPO) than St Stephen's Green. It is as if that part of the city exists on another planet. This cannot simply be a co-incidence, for the north-west area of Dublin city contains all of society's cast offs: Mountjoy Prison, Arbour Hill Prison, the Morning Star and Regina Coeli Hostels, which now occupy the old buildings that were formerly the North Dublin Workhouse, and part of Grangegorman. At the time I visited Grangegorman, the whole north-west of the city was neglected and run down, and there were only about 20,000 people living there. Since all those rejected by society – the human refuse of Dublin society – were located in this area, it was as if the existence of this part of the city had to be denied.

9

London

In March 1959 I moved to London to work in the Marlborough Day Hospital in Maida Vale, returning to Dublin in June to marry Orla. This new job brought me on a radically new kind of psychiatric experience. Dr Joshua Bierer, the medical director, was a pupil of Alfred Adler and therefore a strong protagonist of social and community psychiatry. He was by no means a slavish follower of his mentor and, indeed, it was often said of him that he was more Bierian than Adlerian. He was also a committed Zionist and, before taking up medicine as a young man, had been one of the pioneers in the early days in Israel when it was still under the control of the British, where he had helped in the formation of one of the early kibbutzim, surrounded by hostile Arabs on every side. But he then contracted tuberculosis and, because in those harsh times there was no place for anyone who was sick or weak, he was sent home. I remember, when he told me about this years later, how he cried bitterly because of what he felt was a personal disgrace. It was after this that he took up medicine and went on to become a psychiatrist.

The Marlborough Day Hospital was the first psychiatric day hospital to be established in Britain and one of the first in the world. Another was started around the same time in Canada, but it was not an innovative centre for psychotherapy like Bierer's Marlborough Day. There had also been earlier attempts to establish psychiatric day care in Russia in the 1930s, but not in the same sense as the facility in London. Bierer's Day Hospital was an attempt to set up a total psychiatric treatment centre in the community as an alternative to the mental hospital.

Bierer had managed to get hold of a fine large house, which had

69

belonged to Thomas Henry Huxley, who was associated with Charles Darwin and was one of the early pioneers of evolutionary theory. Bierer was medical director and was assisted by a second consultant psychiatrist, Dr Lee. There were two psychiatric registrars, one attached to each consultant. The other registrar worked with Dr Lee and was already there when I arrived. I was fortunate enough to obtain the post attached to Joshua Bierer. As registrars, we worked on a sessional basis, so that one or other of us was on duty at any given time.

The night hospital was located in what had been the old stables at the back of the house. When the day patients left in the late afternoon, the night hospital operated from 6pm until 9am the following morning on a five-nights-a-week basis. Both it and the day hospital were closed at the weekend. I realised then that, if facilities of this kind, with day and night cover, were to represent a full alternative to the mental hospital, they would have to provide the service on a seven-day basis. In fact, after I left Bierer did open what he called a weekend hospital.

Bierer's team was responsible for three nights – Monday, Wednesday and Friday – and on those evenings I worked from 6pm to 10pm and was on call from home throughout the night. I got time off in lieu during the day, which suited me because it meant I had three sessions during the week in which to study for the second part of the MRCPI, which I was preparing to take at that time. In the night hospital the evening sessions were devoted mainly to group therapy, and Bierer and I ran three groups per week. I also saw some patients individually on the same evenings.

The other consultant, Dr Lee, had introduced the use of the psychedelic drug Lysergic Acid Diethylamide (LSD) to the day hospital and, being impressed with some of his results, Bierer also took up this practice. Dr Lee used the drug on a fairly conservative basis, only dealing with narrowly defined neurotic patients in a one-to-one relationship.

Bierer, however, being more adventurous and feeling that there were no clear criteria for the use of LSD, tried it out with a range of more severely disturbed patients who were not otherwise making progress. A number of these were psychotic, or suffering from severe personality disorder. He also felt that giving the drug in a group setting might provide an atmosphere of security and belonging, which would enable patients to make more progress. At that time I had no idea as to what kind of patients might benefit from the use of LSD, nor what kind of context would enhance its usefulness. Indeed, although Bierer and I wrote a paper for the Royal Society of Medicine about this group therapy combined with LSD, the results were inconclusive, even though a number of patients did show a marked improvement.

The situation in the late 1950s was that Sandoz, the company that had synthesised the drug, were sending samples of LSD to various clinicians for use mainly as a research tool. It was felt at the time that, even in normal subjects, LSD produced a sort of model psychosis, and therefore might lead towards a better understanding of schizophrenia. As it turned out this idea was quite erroneous; the altered state and expansion of consciousness that LSD produces bears little relation to the clinical picture of schizophrenia.

What was extremely valuable for me personally, however, and had a profound effect on my understanding of psychiatric disorder, were the remarkable experiential changes that I saw in some of the people who were administered the drug. There was one fellow who was gay and who in his ordinary state of consciousness was very camp and militant in regard to the politics of homosexuality. To my astonishment, when he was given as little as 50 or 100 micrograms of LSD, after nearly an hour he would quite suddenly and predictably become like a small child of three or four years of age, crying bitterly for his father. I don't remember now the details of his history but I do recall that as a small child he had contracted TB and been admitted to what was then a large TB sanatorium. While there, he was interfered with sexually by some of the adult male patients in the hospital.

I also learned at that time that there was a marked difference between individuals who were administered the drug, depending on the strength of their personality. There was a Jewish patient who had been tortured in a Romanian prison but had managed to survive. When he was given LSD it had no effect whatsoever, and I was astonished to find him, even after a large dose of over 300 micrograms, sitting up in bed reading the evening newspaper.

I also got my first insight into the importance of the context in which the drug was administered. There was another fellow with a grandiose, immature personality who felt that the experiences that would emerge under LSD would be so valuable that he should be allowed to have a tape recorder by his bed to record them for posterity.

He also showed no response until I got fed up with his pretentious behaviour and removed the tape recorder. Within a short while, once his conscious control was taken away, he was crying like a baby and showing genuine emotion.

There were a number of other cases which made me question yet again the traditional view of psychiatric illness. One such was Jane, a married woman with three children who suffered from agoraphobia. This was so severe that not only could she not leave the house unaccompanied, but she would have to spend much of the day in bed because she suffered extreme anxiety and vertigo when standing up. She was brought to the day hospital each day by her mother, who then returned to the home to look after her three children. This woman was quite helpless without the constant attention and care of her mother, who appeared to be selflessly dedicated and prepared to devote all her time to looking after her incapacitated daughter and her family. With regular attendance at the day hospital, this woman's condition gradually improved, until the day came when we felt she was well enough to come to the day hospital without any help from her mother.

To my amazement, later that day I received an angry phone call from a general practitioner who had received an emergency call to visit the woman's mother. The mother had developed blisters and swellings all over her body, a severe case of angioneurotic oedema, which was almost life threatening. He wanted to know what the hell I was playing at in the treatment of her daughter that had caused this generalised eruption in the mother. I explained to him that this was an extreme stress response due to the mother losing control over her daughter, who was now becoming independent and no longer needed her. What had seemed like selfless care for her daughter and her grandchildren was actually a desperate need to keep her daughter dependent and under her control.

Another young woman, Miriam, who was in her early thirties, was brought to the day hospital by her mother in a totally helpless state. When I sat down with her to hear her story I was astonished to find that each morning her mother washed and dressed her and fed her like a baby with a spoon. But what was even more surprising was that this young woman had gone to America some years before, where she held down a highly responsible post as personal secretary to a business executive in New York. She had managed this

72

stressful job successfully for several years. She subsequently married but her husband turned out to be immature and aggressive, subjecting her to severe domestic violence. Eventually she obtained a divorce, but by this time she had lost her job and her confidence, so she felt there was no alternative but to return to England.

What I couldn't understand was how she had deteriorated from being a successful business woman to the regressed infantile state in which I first saw her. When I asked her about this she told me that, when she first came home, she was determined to maintain her independence. But she said that, whatever task arose in the ordinary running of the house, the washing, the ironing, cooking and so on, her mother competed with her to be the first to do it. She said that after two or three weeks she just gave up; then gradually her mother took over her life completely, until she reached the regressed state I have already described.

From these and similar cases I realised the extent of the struggle which is involved for all of us in separating from our parental family and developing independence. I knew this struggle already, of course, from my own experience of growing up in a family that was loving and caring but which saw itself as continuing indefinitely. With the best will in the world, my parents did not tend to foster in their children the necessary separation and growth towards independence.

I don't know if these things happen by chance, or are part of the destiny that is laid out for us, but I was fortunate indeed to have had the opportunity of working with Joshua Bierer. He was one of those rare individuals who forge a unique pathway through life, breaking all the rules. He was a pupil of Adler, and had worked with him in Vienna as a young doctor before escaping to England from the Nazis in 1938. Adler was himself a rebel and the first to break away from Freud. He had had a common-sense approach which I think gave Bierer the freedom of spirit for the unorthodox approach that he had followed relentlessly from then onwards.

Bierer's whole approach was to see a person, first and foremost, as a human being and not simply as a 'case', with a mental illness over which they had no control. I feel this was the most important lesson that I ever learned as a psychiatrist and, happening so early in my career, it shaped my path from then onwards. I can only thank God that I didn't listen to the advice given to me before I left Ireland, which was not to take a job with Bierer, because he was poorly thought of by the mainstream of British psychiatry.

When he arrived in Britain in 1938 Bierer could hardly speak any English. Kathleen Thompson, the senior occupational therapist in the Marlborough Day Hospital, had worked with him through-out most of his career. She told me that, with her help as a transla-tor, he could reach into the hearts of young, mute, withdrawn schizophrenics and had them relating and talking with him in a few hours. He believed passionately in the right of patients to take over and control their own lives and, no matter where he was, he worked relentlessly for the democratisation of relationships between patients and staff.

When he first arrived in Britain he was employed as a volunteer with no salary in Runwell Hospital, where he set up the first psy-chiatric social club, which was managed and run in the evenings by the patients themselves. As early as 1947 he took a group of chronic psychotic patients out of the mental hospital and set them up in what, I believe, was the first ever psychiatric hostel, which they ran independently and looked after themselves. This was considered madness at the time and yet he managed to make it work.

All of these pioneering efforts culminated in his setting up the Marlborough Day Hospital. The whole approach there was psycho-therapeutic: that rare phenomenon in psychiatry, a true therapeutic community. He intended that it should become, as near as possible, a complete alternative to the mental hospital. In the year that I was there I could see that he was close to succeeding. There was no ques-tion of taking only neurotic patients. Very disturbed, chronic psy-chotic patients and those with severe personality disorders were all dealt with at the Marlborough Day. Out of many hundreds of pa-tients in that year, only twenty had to be transferred to a mental hos-pital and all these emergencies occurred at the weekend, when the hospital was closed and there was no alternative.

In the night hospital, I was often put to the pin of my collar try-ing to deal with dozens of newly arrived very disturbed patients. If I complained about being left to handle everything when Joshua had to go to one of his psychiatric social clubs, he would put his arm around me and say, 'You have broad shoulders.' Still, some-how or other, we always managed. There was a wonderful Irish night sister who was the mainstay of the night hospital. She was a tower of strength when things were getting out of hand and would give me the courage to struggle on.

During the year I was there, I went twice a week to Joshua's rooms in Harley Street, where I lay on the couch to undergo psychoanalysis. This was in no sense orthodox Freudian analysis, although I did engage in free association, but Bierer was a good deal more active than a typical Freudian analyst and was not slow in coming up with interpretations. One of the insights he gave me was to point out that I had always felt I was something of an outsider, different in some way and not fully Irish. Perhaps this was partly because my mother was a Protestant and because of my father's rebellion against his Irish nationalist family, and his adoption of a pro-British stance. Bierer felt that, because of this difficulty in fitting in, I had formed an identification with jazz and oppressed black Americans, as well as other minority groups like Jews, who were considered outsiders in Ireland's dominant Catholic society. I had free-associated at length about my feelings of not being accepted by my father, then, towards the end of the analysis, I had a dream in which I murdered an elderly man and cut his body up into small pieces, which, with great effort, I washed down through the plug-hole of an ordinary wash-hand basin. When I came up with this dream, Bierer exclaimed, 'Ah! you have killed him at last.' Shortly after this he terminated the analysis and I remember feeling let down, but I think this did represent the beginning of a fundamental change of attitude towards my father. One day when I arrived at Bierer's rooms in Harley Street there was a young teenage girl who had been brought by her mother and was in a mute, totally withdrawn state. To my amazement, in less than an hour, Joshua had broken through this 'glass wall' so that the girl was talking and relating freely with him.

Joshua's whole life was dedicated to his patients and he was incapable of maintaining any boundary between his work and his private life with his wife and family. At the time I was there he was married for the second time and tensions were rising because he was seldom home. There were always patients living in the house. I remember one occasion when things had reached breaking point. He promised his wife he would take a day off to go up the river on their boat. When he finally arrived at the boat for this rare day with his wife and family, he had fifteen patients with him. Eventually this second marriage too broke down.

There is no doubt that Joshua Bierer was a larger-than-life

character. A true pioneer, he had many wonderful qualities and, in my opinion, more than anyone else was the main driving force behind the community psychiatric movement in Britain, indeed in the western world. He never received the recognition he deserved, partly because of his inability to write clearly and his difficulties with the English language. He believed that a broadly based psychotherapy was applicable to all forms of psychiatric illness and a number of the approaches he developed would now be seen as part of cognitive behaviour therapy. Of course, this was out of line with the generally accepted view of British psychiatry, which has always had a rather narrow view of the usefulness of psychotherapy. Certainly, I will always be grateful for having had the opportunity to know and work with a creative innovator like Joshua Bierer, and through him to have had a living connection with the early European psychoanalytic movement, especially with Alfred Adler who, although seldom recognised for this, laid the foundations for social and community psychiatry.

USA: Massachusetts General

For some time I had been keen to go to the States to further my psychiatric training but couldn't see any realistic way of getting there. Then, while I was in London, an advertisement appeared from the pharmaceutical company Eli Lilly offering a one-year fellowship to the United States with a stipend of $300 a month. My wife was sick of me talking about the US and asked, 'Why don't you put in an application for one of these fellowships?' I was convinced that I had no chance of success but decided to try anyway. I reckoned the adjudicators would be American, so I filled up the application form with grandiose claims of how I would return to reform and revolutionise the mental health services in Ireland. To my amazement my application was successful and I was offered a year's fellowship to go to the States to any psychiatric centre of my choosing that would offer me a position. What was an even greater surprise was to find that the judges who made the selection were Irish, not American. I wrote to a number of centres in the States and received an acceptance from several of these, including Yale and Harvard. I decided on Harvard because they offered both a post as psychiatric intern in the Massachusetts General Hospital (one of the most famous psychiatric units in the world at that time) and also an opportunity to undertake a Masters degree in Mental Health in the Harvard School of Public Health. This programme was run by Professor Gerald Caplan who was one of the leading lights in community mental health in the US at the time.

Towards the end of February 1960, I set about preparing for my departure and applied to the American Embassy in London for a visa. I should mention that my tuberculosis was still active when I went to London and I was receiving treatment with a new Eli Lilly drug for the whole of that year. At that time, if you had a history of TB and if your X-ray showed even old scars, although you had fully recovered you would not be allowed to enter the USA, so I was in a state of anxiety when I was called to the embassy expecting to have an X-ray that would inevitably show up the tuberculosis as still active in my lungs. Imagine my amazement and relief when the woman who interviewed me looked at me and said, 'You look healthy enough. We needn't bother with an X-ray for you.' But when my wife and I disembarked off the ship at New York, the immigration official asked: 'Where is your X-ray report?' When I answered that I had been told I didn't need one, he nearly had a fit. For an agonising length of time he stood there pondering what he should do. Then, presumably thinking of all the trouble it would be for him if he held me up, he waved me on. To this day I don't know how this miracle happened, because there is no way I should ever have been allowed to enter the States.

My wife and I stayed a few days in New York and, hearing that Thelonious Monk was playing at the Village Gate, I took the opportunity to experience my first live jazz on American soil. Gigi Gryce was the support band and they came on first. I thought they sounded quite good, but then, when Thelonious Monk took the stand, I knew I had arrived. With music, whether it is Irish, classical or jazz, when it's right you don't have to make any comparisons. As soon as his band played the first few notes, I knew this was it. He was a revelation. Sometimes he would bring his whole arm down on the piano keyboard in a crash that fitted perfectly. Then, when the music was really going, he would get up and do a little African dance around the piano stool before sitting down again. It was just perfect.

We took the train up to Boston to be greeted by a fierce snow-storm, just when spring should have been breaking through. Eventually we took a flat in a small street off Huntingdon Avenue called Louis Prang Street. It worked out very well and we remained there throughout our entire stay in Boston for the next two years. Louis Prang Street is a short street that leads from Huntingdon Avenue out into the Fenway Park, so we had a nice park on our doorstep. We were on the ground floor and at the back of the flat there was a sort of makeshift balcony which looked out directly at the end of the Fine Art Museum. More importantly, Louis Prang Street was only a couple of hundred yards from Harvard Medical School and the Harvard School of Public Health, where I was to undertake my course seven months later, so it meant that once September came I would be within walking distance of my work.

But for now I began work in the Massachusetts General Hospital, one of the premier general hospitals in the States, which at that time had a very prestigious department of psychiatry. Psychoanalysis was the dominant discipline in the department and all the main staff psychiatrists were themselves psychoanalysts. Professor Eric Lindemann was chairman of the department and he too was a psychoanalyst, but he was already breaking away from that tradition and was a very innovative and creative personality. He wrote the first landmark paper on unresolved grief, 'The Symptomatology and Management of Acute Grief', which was inspired by the Coconut Grove fire in Boston, in which many people perished. In the months following the fire, Lindemann observed that many friends and relatives of the victims were arriving in the accident and emergency department of the hospital manifesting various psychosomatic complaints, including hallucinations of those who had died in the fire and other symptoms that would now be recognised as the results of unresolved grief. This was long before the work of Elizabeth Kubler-Ross and others who are usually credited with having been responsible for the recognition of unresolved grief reactions.

Following on from this work, Lindemann and Gerald Caplan laid the foundations for crisis theory and the management of life crises. Lindemann was also responsible for setting up one of the first community mental health centres in the States, the Wellesley Human Relations Centre in Boston. In this way he was making a radical shift from traditional psychoanalysis. Indeed, his and Caplan's work bore more relation to the early social psychiatric concepts of Adler than to those of Freud, although they would probably not have acknowledged this.

In Massachusetts General the first person I made friends with was Dr Tom Hackett. He was an Irish-American who was one of the first of his generation to break away from psychoanalysis. He had little interest in analysis but was very active in liaison work on the general medical and surgical wards of the hospital. At that time there was a lot of dissatisfaction among the physicians and surgeons with the attitudes of the psychiatric department. When they asked for help with an acute management problem on their ward, the typical response of orthodox psychoanalysts was that the patient required long-term psychoanalysis or, if deemed unsuitable for this, should be referred to the social work department. This was not at all helpful to a physician who wanted some practical assistance in dealing with an acute crisis.

Tom Hackett's approach was much more flexible and this made him popular with the medical staff of the hospital. He was an expert in the use of hypnosis and had been strongly influenced by the work of Milton Erickson and others who developed the concepts of short-term, 'strategic' psychotherapy. He was also influenced by the work of Lindemann and Caplan, and their concepts of crisis management.

An example of Hackett's unorthodox approach was one time when he was asked to see an elderly Italian immigrant on one of the general hospital wards. This man had run a stall in the North End Italian market for many years but had recently been pushed out by some of the younger local Mafia. Not long after this he was admitted to Massachusetts General because he was becoming progressively blind, with cataracts in both eyes. At that time they used to operate on both eyes at the same time and, following the operation, the person had to keep both eyes covered. This often gave rise to severe disorientation and an acute psychosis, which later came to be known as 'black-patch' psychosis.

This is what happened to this poor old Italian. He became acutely psychotic and presented a difficult management problem. When Tom Hackett was called to see him he didn't take the usual approach of recommending anti-psychotic medication. Instead, discovering that this man had been a veteran in the Italian army in the First World War, he went out and bought a bottle of Italian wine and a take-away dish of spaghetti and meatballs. He gave this to the old man and chatted with him about his experiences in the war. The man tucked into his meal and, within a short period of time, was calm, relaxed and totally sane.

Tom Hackett and I struck up a warm friendship. He was very proud of his Irish roots and we spent a lot of time together. He worked with hypnosis and, thanks to his help, I improved my skills considerably in that area. He and I also carried out a study to assess fear of death in patients on the cardiac pacemaker which had recently been developed.

In other ways those first few months in the Massachusetts General were not a happy time for me. I felt completely lost, because the strange world of psychoanalysis was so alien to me that most of the time the psychoanalysts could have been speaking a foreign language for all I could understand. It wasn't just the working situation, but everything in America was so different. When I arrived in the States in 1960 I had never seen a supermarket or television; the motorways, the huge cars, everything was strange. How things have changed. Someone travelling now from Ireland to America would find little difference between the two countries.

On Easter Sunday 1960 our first child, Garvan, was born in the Lying-In Hospital in Harvard Medical School, just up the street from where we lived. At that time there was no question of the father being present at the birth. I first saw my son through a screen in the neo-natal unit, when a nurse held him up in her arms for me to see him. He was just a 'number' among a whole row of newly born babies. This was one of the many depersonalised experiences, which left me feeling lost and alienated. My wife developed breast abscesses and nearly died shortly afterwards and our new baby was threatened with being sent to a temporary care hostel called 'home for little wanderers'.

After a couple of months I began to feel a little more at home and to get some sense of competence in the work I was doing in the Massachusetts General. Around this time I met up with an old friend from my student days in the College of Surgeons, Willie McCourt, who had emigrated to the States prior to my arrival there. He was involved in a study concerned with sensory deprivation in Boston City Hospital at that time. He asked me if I would like to become involved, which I was happy to do. The psychiatric director of the study decided that we should investigate the effects of benzodiazapenes and antidepressants by seeing how they affected student volunteers under conditions of sensory deprivation. In fact, the rationale of the study didn't make sense, because of the large individual differences between subjects in a sensorially deprived state.

To create a situation of sensory deprivation you can either reduce all sensory input, as when a person lies in the dark in a bath filled with isotonic fluid, similar to the composition of our body fluids, or you can make the sensory input steady and constant. In either case the effect is the same, because where there is a steady input the subject ceases to react to the outside environment. An altered state of consciousness is thus induced and the internal world of experience opens up. To conduct this experiment, a volunteer student was seated in a large comfortable armchair. Cardboard sleeves were put over his arms and his hands were encased in soft gloves. Half ping-pong balls were placed over the eyes, with a steady white light bearing upon them. A white noise (that is a full frequency sound), a soft hissing sound, was fed into the ears. In this way sensory input from the outside world was cut down to a minimum as the visual, tactile, proprioceptive and sound inputs were made constant. In this situation some of the students still maintained ordinary consciousness and were unaffected, but others would drift into an altered state after ten or fifteen minutes. They had a microphone through which they could talk to us, and a number of the subjects lost all awareness of where they were and would experience marked visual and auditory hallucinations – being on tropical beaches, or in forests with snakes or other animals around them. I found this aspect of the experiment fascinating. However, it was quite impossible, given the individual differences, to know what effect, if any, the psychoactive drugs were having. To make any statement about this, one would first have to establish a baseline of individual differences in the subjects, in a drug-free setting, then add the tranquillisers and antidepressants to see what effect they had. This was not done. Nevertheless, I found being involved worthwhile because it connected with my experience with LSD and gave me the opportunity to observe the remarkable effects of sensory deprivation.

Although I was not due to start the Masters course in Harvard until September, I went to see Professor Caplan and found he was friendly and very cordial about my joining his programme. To my surprise he even said that he would be able to increase my stipend from Eli Lilly from $300 to $460 a month as soon as I started the course.

In the meantime, I had settled down less anxiously to my work in the Massachusetts General. On one occasion I spoke to one of the psychoanalysts in the department about the possible use of LSD in therapy. He turned to me haughtily and said, 'I've tried it; no good, no good,' and that was the end of the conversation.

One evening Tom Hackett said there was an invitation for both of us to go to a psychedelic party. This was at the time when Timothy Leary and Richard Alpert were still working in Harvard and were experimenting with LSD and other psychedelics. Tom, who knew them slightly, had been to one of their previous psychedelic occasions, but he hadn't liked the look of what was going on. So, instead of going to their party, we decided to take some synthetic psilocybin (the active ingredient of magic mushrooms) that he had managed to get hold of. I had no regression experiences with this substance, simply a heightened level of consciousness and acute sensory awareness. I can recall looking at one man who was present and seeing the aftershave glistening clearly on the skin of his face. Tom Hackett's wife, Ellie, who was tall and slim and had a rather long neck, turned into one of those enormous, long-necked dinosaurs. At one point during the evening I went outside, where there was a large naked tree that had not yet come into spring which seemed like a giant spidery creature bearing down on me with its long tentacles. In hindsight I have always regretted that we didn't go to the party and that I missed the opportunity to meet Tim Leary and Richard Alpert. They were dismissed from their Harvard posts shortly afterwards, so I never did get to meet them. The latter subsequently became an enlightened and famous mystic, taking the title Ram Das.

To hear live jazz was one of the most valuable experiences I had while in Boston. The Roxbury district of the city had originally been one of the main areas settled by Irish immigrants. However, by the time I was there it was gradually being taken over by blacks and the population ratio between black and white residents was roughly 50-50. There was a bar there called Connolly's, owned by a cranky little Irish-American. He had a resident black jazz trio who were not well known but were competent musicians. However, every week one or two well-known jazz musicians would come there to play for the week. These were men who had played with some of the jazz greats like Count Basie, Duke Ellington, Woody Herman and so on. Over the two years I was there I heard many of the great musicians whom I only knew from records. One week it would be Johnny Hodges and Lawrence Brown, then someone like Buck Clayton. I heard Coleman Hawkins, Flip Phillips and many others. I remember one night when the famous hard-blowing tenor saxophonist Illinois Jacquet was there. He got drunk and at one point issued out into the street playing his sax, and you could hear the sound slowly disappearing down Tremont Street. After about fifteen or twenty minutes the sound of the sax slowly re-emerged as he came back into the hall still blowing.

Normally the place was nearly empty, but on one occasion the great blues singer, Jimmy Rushing, who had sung with Count Basie for a good many years, came to Connolly's and the place was crammed to the doors. This experience confirmed for me that the blues is the real core of the black culture's relation to the music. Jimmy Rushing was enormous, he was known as Mr Five By Five. I went up to meet him and when he shook hands with me it was like holding an enormous beefsteak in your hand. I found most of the musicians friendly and approachable, but I think my favourite of them all at the time was the sax and flute player James Moody. We made friends with him and he came to our apartment for dinner. To my surprise, I discovered he was profoundly deaf and had been told that he would never be able to play music.

We also used to go fairly regularly to the Dublin Bar, where Irish musicians hung out. It was there that I met Paddy Cronin, the fine Kerry fiddle player, whom my old friend Denis Murphy had often spoken about. He had been living in Boston for many years and had raised a family there. Paddy was known for his fiery temper. One night, some of the young Irish fiddle players were teasing him, saying the Kerry way of playing was old-fashioned and out of date. Suddenly Paddy, who was normally a bit ashamed of the Kerry playing, lost his temper and shouted, 'I'll show you how I can play.' He proceeded to lift the roof off the house with Kerry music – slides, jigs and reels. I felt sad one day when I went to his house. There he was, standing up in the middle of his family, resolutely playing his fiddle, with the television blaring and the children with baseball bats and other American paraphernalia all around the room. Years later he retired and returned to Ireland.

In the Massachusetts General there was a ladies' committee, and some of the older women regularly got tickets for Symphony Hall which they seldom used. The famous Boston Symphony Orchestra was based in Symphony Hall, but it was normally very difficult to get tickets to hear them. To my delight these ladies, hearing I was interested in music, used to give us tickets for the concerts on a regular basis. During the two years I was in Boston I had the good fortune of being able to hear many concerts given by this wonderful orchestra. But there was one concert in Symphony Hall that was very different. This was the time Mahalia Jackson came to Boston. The hall was jammed with an almost entirely black audience and she gave a wonderful recital of gospel music.

11

Harvard

September arrived and I transferred to the Masters degree programme in mental health. This made my life considerably easier
because the School of Public Health was only a few hundred yards up
the road from where we lived. Also, all the other facilities of Harvard
Medical School, including the wonderful Harvard Medical Library,
were situated in the same area. The main part of the university was
several miles away across the river in Cambridge. The academic programme opened with a social evening and an introductory welcome
from the head of the university, but after that I seldom had any need
to travel over to Cambridge until the final graduation ceremony.

The Harvard School of Public Health incorporated a wide range
of disciplines. I was attached to the faculty of Public Health Practice.
Besides the division of mental health, Public Health Practice included social sciences and health, medical care, chronic diseases, etc.
The Masters programme was postgraduate and my classmates in the
mental health section were mainly psychologists and social workers,
from America and various countries overseas. These were people who
had taken time out from senior positions to undertake the course.
There were only two other psychiatrists. One was a Sikh, a colonel
in the Indian army. At that time, while there were 20,000 mental
hospital beds for a population of three million in Ireland, he told me
that in India, with a population of approximately 800 million people, there were equally about 20,000 mental hospital beds. It was
clear that in these circumstances not many people would end up in
a mental hospital in India.

The Masters course was organised in such a way that, in addition
to the specific seminars in mental health, there were some mandatory

courses such as biostatistics and a number of electives, which you could choose from the range of courses available. I chose epidemiology, anthropology and a course on the history of medicine, among others. A small Frenchman ran the course on the history of medicine. I learnt that in the fifteenth century, when changes were suggested in the medical curriculum, someone pointed out that the course was already full. One couldn't help wondering what filled a medical course to overflowing when most of what we now know had not yet been discovered.

The man who ran the course on epidemiology would take, one by one, all the main studies, such as the study of smoking in relation to cancer, and demonstrate how the methodology used could not be relied upon. This impressed me deeply and demonstrated yet again how the result of any scientific study needs to be closely scrutinised before being accepted.

Most of these electives I found enjoyable, except for biostatistics, which I found painful in the extreme. Often I would have to stay on for hours after the others had gone, struggling with long tables, at times to the point of despair. The other major difficulty I encountered was the sheer amount of information and literature we were deluged with. All of us in the mental health group, which comprised about ten students, were feeling overwhelmed by this, but I was at a particular disadvantage because of my slow reading ability. I felt so desperate that I decided to take a rapid reading course. At the beginning of the course they tested us to ascertain our current level of performance, and I was found to be reading at the level of moderate mental retardation. Being changed from left-handedness to writing with my right hand by Miss Manley had had permanent detrimental effects both on my reading and writing.

Because of the extreme pressure and stress of the course there had been several suicides among the students in previous years. Gerald Caplan had been asked to examine this situation and he came up with a highly effective piece of anticipatory guidance. At the beginning of our studies in September/October, he predicted that by January we would feel depressed and overwhelmed by the amount of material we were expected to absorb. We would feel hopeless and expect to fail miserably. Then he pointed out that, while everyone felt like this in the middle of the course, past experience had shown that by June everyone had completed the programme successfully. At the time he told us this, I think none of us paid particular attention, but by January we were feeling exactly as he had predicted. When I recalled what he had said I was immensely comforted by the fact that, since everything he had predicted so far was correct, the prediction that all of us would eventually come through would also prove to be true. From the time Caplan introduced this fairly simple strategy, there were no further suicides in the School of Public Health.

At first in the Masters course I again felt completely at sea. The concepts and the language being used by the other students, particularly those in the mental health group, were completely strange to me. For example, until I entered the School of Public Health I had never heard the word 'ecology' and had no idea what it meant. Nowadays, this is a commonplace term in everyday conversation; one reads of ecological disasters or what the ecological implications are of this or that. But in 1960 the Harvard School of Public Health was at the forefront in developing such concepts, although there was little or no awareness of such issues among the general public. This was true of many of the issues that were raised at that time in seminars and lectures. All the other students seemed quite *au fait* with what was going on and I felt like a total ignoramus. I was also amazed at the colourful expressions which Americans used.

During my academic year in Harvard in 1960, the presidential battle between John F. Kennedy and Richard Nixon was in full swing. Before this it was never thought that a Catholic, and an Irish-American to boot, could succeed in becoming president. There was so much interest that Gerald Caplan installed a special television in our seminar room, so that we could watch the debates between Kennedy and Nixon. Everyone in our group was pro-democrat, and I remember feeling proud to be Irish watching this handsome young Irish-American, who seemed like a breath of fresh air in American politics.

The main emphasis in our course was on crisis theory and crisis intervention, which Caplan was actively developing at the time. I already had some familiarity with the long-term effects of early trauma in adults from my work with Bierer in London, but the significance of life crises, if they are not dealt with appropriately at the time, was a revelation to me. Caplan's main interest was in what might be termed 'accidental crises', that is, traumatic events which might or might not happen at a given time. These could either be major catastrophes, such as earthquakes, floods and so on, which could affect

87

a whole section of society, or individual crises, like a child losing its mother at an early age, or the loss of a job, or a broken relationship, or any other sudden tragic event. Caplan defined a crisis as 'an upset in the steady state'. He said: 'A crisis is provoked when an individual, faced with an obstacle to important life goals, finds that it is, for the time being, insurmountable through the utilization of customary methods of problem solving.'[1]

Caplan always stressed that a crisis is not necessarily a negative phenomenon; it can be just as much an opportunity for personality growth and development. The outcome of a crisis therefore depends not on the nature of the crisis itself but on how it is handled and whether the person manages to deal with it effectively. Indeed, if we did not have to face the stress of life crises, we would not develop at all.

As distinct from the emphasis on 'accidental crises', the other person who made a major contribution to crisis theory was Erik Erickson. Erickson was an artist who got involved in psychoanalysis and carried out a study of child development which resulted in his book *Childhood and Society*. Erickson viewed personality development as a succession of differentiated phases, each qualitatively different from its predecessor. Between one phase and the next he described periods of disorganised behaviour, transitional periods characterised by cognitive and affective upset. He called these 'developmental crises', events such as birth, which is a crisis both for the mother and the infant, the onset of puberty and adolescence, marriage, the menopause and so on as we progress through the biological stages of life. These differ from 'accidental crises' in that they necessarily occur at a given point in development and everyone has to pass through them (see Fig. 1).

Our healthy adaptation and personality development will depend on how well we deal with these developmental phases, and indeed with those 'accidental traumas' that occur as we progress through life. A major crisis can often represent a turning point in a person's life. It is a hurdle which has to be surmounted if the person is to continue on satisfactorily through life. If a crisis can be handled successfully, then the person is usually more mature as a result. However, if it cannot be overcome, then some maladaptive pathway is likely to develop and this often signals the onset of what later becomes a formal mental illness.

The extraordinary thing is that, until I went to the States and was

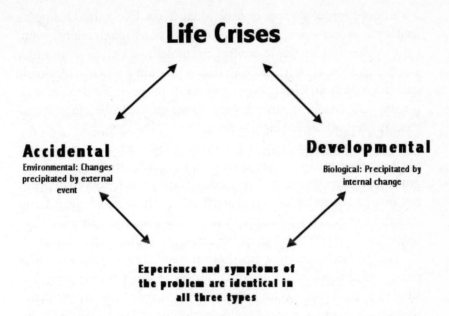

Life Crises

Accidental
Environmental: Changes
precipitated by external
event

Developmental
Biological: Precipitated by
internal change

**Experience and symptoms of
the problem are identical in
all three types**

Figure 1: The two forms of life crisis. However, as illustrated, the clincial outcome in both types is identical.

exposed to these ideas, in my previous training as a psychiatrist in Ireland and Britain there had been no awareness whatsoever of the significance of life crises. People were simply diagnosed as suffering from endogenous depression or schizophrenia with no sense of how these related to the crises or traumatic events that they had encountered, or how they had developed over time. It was as if these illnesses appeared out of the blue as the result of some genetic fault or biochemical disturbance. This was still the situation when I returned to Ireland in 1962. A mention of the very notion of 'crisis' fell on deaf ears and for a good many years afterwards I found it better just to use these concepts in my own work and not attempt to talk to other psychiatrists about them. Now, some forty years later, the idea of 'crisis intervention' is generally accepted, but its relation to the development of mental illness later is still not well understood. Indeed nowadays, in major catastrophes like the Lockerbie air disaster or a terrorist bomb explosion, there is often an exaggerated response. Droves of crisis counsellors descend on the scene at the very time when most people are in a state of shock or psychic numbness, needing rest and support and not in any sense ready to deal with the emotional effects of the traumatic experience.

Even Gerald Caplan was not fully aware of the relevance of time. Much later I realised that, when the time is right and people feel safe enough to be able to react emotionally, crisis intervention can begin and people can be helped to integrate the pain and anguish surrounding what happened. When Caplan visited Ireland about ten years later, he too spoke in a seminar of this reservation and the need to wait sensitively until the person is ready and the time is right for them to work on the traumatic experience. In the intervening years, of course, the work of Kubler-Ross and others on unresolved grief, the elucidation of post-traumatic stress disorder (PTSD) following the Vietnam War debacle, as well as the virtual epidemic of physical and sexual abuse, have all led to a much greater awareness of the importance of crisis and trauma in the genesis of emotional disorders.

Even so, psychiatric diagnosis is still treated as something unrelated to environmental adaptation or to the developmental history of the person, and past crises and traumas are often ignored. It is as if these so-called illnesses existed outside time, as some kind of rarefied independent entities, unrelated to anything but biochemical disturbance or genetic influence.

The factors affecting the outcome of a life crisis will depend on:

(1) Whether there were similar events previously in a person's life history which remained unresolved. For example, where a person is faced with the death of a loved one, was there an earlier death which was never healed? Helping a person to work through a life crisis is of key importance, because not only will the current situation be resolved, but any past traumatic events of a similar nature will also be dealt with.

(2) Family advice can be helpful or destructive, depending on whether it helps the person to fully experience what has happened or instead to deny the emotional implications of the crisis.

(3) The culture and family background out of which the person comes will also have its effect on the seriousness and outcome of a life crisis. If the person comes from a background that tends to deny the expression of emotion, this obviously will affect the person's capacity to get in touch with the emotion and feel the pain in order to resolve the situation.

Another aspect of crisis theory which was not clarified during my time in Harvard was that not all forms of crisis could be approached in the same way. There are two main forms of life crisis, which require a fundamentally different response on the part of the person involved. Firstly there is the type of crisis involved in facing an examination, tackling a new job or the struggle in late adolescence to leave one's family of origin and become independent. This kind of crisis demands action; it involves having the courage to face the situation and take the appropriate action to overcome it. The second form is one that involves hurt or loss, such as the death of someone close to us or being the victim of rape or sexual abuse. In these situations the response required is to 'feel' the pain and emotion that is appropriate to the situation and in this way resolve it (see Fig. 2).

Two Responses to Crisis

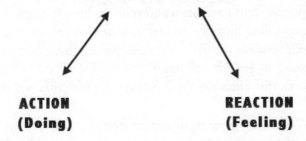

ACTION   **REACTION**
(Doing)   **(Feeling)**

Figure 2: The two contrasting types of response – action (doing) and reaction (feeling).

Again, in drawing the distinction between the two forms of 'accidental' or 'developmental' crises, associated respectively with Caplan and Erickson, an intermediate category of what I call 'socio-cultural' crises was not referred to at that time (see Fig. 1a). These are situations like facing the first day at school, doing the Leaving Certificate, or getting married. Such situations are not part of our biological development, like adolescence (in the sense that every human being has to pass through them). There are many societies that do not have a Leaving Certificate or equivalent examination, and yet, in Ireland, because of the way we have structured our society, unless this hurdle is overcome our future is severely curtailed. In this way we have institutionalised certain forms of crisis which, unless they can be successfully negotiated, are likely to have very deleterious effects, often leading to the onset of what may later

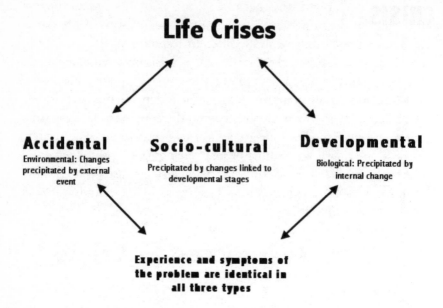

Figure 1a: Socio-cultural crisis. These are not part of our biological development but are linked to it. Unless these hurdles are overcome our future can be severely curtailed.

become a serious psychiatric illness (see Fig. 3).

There is another important point to be made here. At the time I was with Gerald Caplan, he would still have subscribed to a deterministic point of view. This is to say that, if all the influences, genetic and developmental, that went to form the personality of a person entering adolescence could be known, then it would be possible to say with certainty how that person would react. Of course, this statement was qualified, in that it is never possible to know all of these influences fully and therefore we could not make such deterministic predictions. Over the past fifty years, however, research work by the Russian chemist Prigogine and others has demonstrated unequivocally that, even if we knew all the inputs and influences acting on, for instance, an adolescent, we would still not be able to say with certainty how the situation would evolve. There is a fundamental indeterminacy in any complex system such as a teenaged human being. This is because the essential cause of how a living system will behave lies within that system itself. Although it is undoubtedly influenced

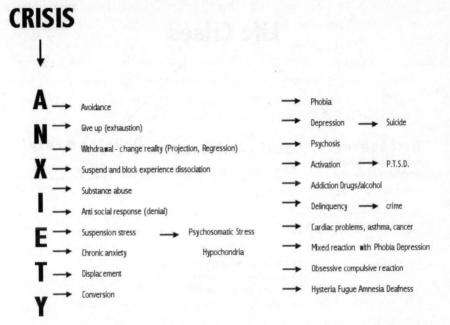

Figure 3: Where there is a maladapative response to a life crisis this may eventually result in the development of one or other of a variety of chronic psychiatric conditions.

by its past history, once it reaches a crisis point no one can say with certainty how the system will behave. This is what all the work on chaos theory in recent years has been about. (I deal with these issues more extensively in the latter part of this book.)

Developing out of the work on crisis theory, Caplan was active in setting up various forms of intervention with groups exposed to life crises. He initiated work with groups of widows and others who had suffered bereavement and people with marital and family problems, and also worked with primary care professionals such as general practitioners, social workers, lawyers, public health nurses, teachers, police and others. On his recommendation I ran a course for a group of officers from the Boston Police Department. What I think would be very valuable but unfortunately seldom happens would be for psychiatrists to spend a good part of their time in consultation with primary care professionals. Psychiatrists seldom see people at the time when an acute crisis is happening. At that stage the person is much more likely to be in touch with a general practitioner, public health nurse or other frontline professional and it may be years later, if the crisis situation has been mismanaged, that they then arrive at the psychiatrist's door. By then, the situation has probably developed into a chronic mental condition. It is my belief that if skilled intervention were available at the time of a crisis situation (or shortly afterwards), then the development of much long-term psychiatric illness could be prevented (see Fig. 3).

Unfortunately the participation of psychiatrists in this kind of preventive mental health intervention has never been developed to any extent. Central to this thinking is the need for a clearer distinction to be made between crisis intervention and psychotherapy. Crisis intervention is usually a short-term active response to help a person deal appropriately with the acute upset involved in a life crisis, while psychotherapy is a much more prolonged approach to dealing with a psychiatric illness that has already developed.

As I had had little direct experience of child psychiatry prior to going to the States, Gerald Caplan arranged for me to attend a child psychiatric clinic, on a weekly basis, under the supervision of Dr Mary Baine, an experienced child psychiatrist. The clinic was in Laurence, Massachusetts, which was about thirty miles from Boston. I continued with this throughout the two years of my stay in Boston and it provided a valuable addition to the experience I had already had in adult psychiatry.

In the final stage of the course, we had to prepare a thesis on some mental health topic of our own choosing. I took the opportunity to design a comprehensive district community mental health service. I built in a range of facilities such as day and night hospitals, an acute general hospital psychiatric unit, a therapeutic community, halfway houses, hostels and so on, thus covering all the functions of primary, secondary and tertiary care and in this way of eliminating the old-style mental hospital from the picture entirely. Although I didn't appreciate it at the time, this later formed the basis of the programme for community mental health services that I developed when I became chief psychiatrist back in Dublin. Gerald Caplan also utilised this theoretical design for a psychiatric service as a chapter in a book on community mental health which he wrote some years later, except that in his plan he retained the traditional mental hospital as one of the components.

The Masters programme was a one-year course running from

September to June. Against all my expectations, I got through with honours. Having successfully completed this, I received my Masters degree – the official title of which was Master of Science in Hygiene (Community Mental Health).

Caplan was so pleased with my work that he asked me to stay on for a second year as a senior Fellow. The main emphasis now was on acquiring research skills in the fields of preventive psychiatry and community mental health. In addition, a number of research projects were undertaken and I was fortunate to have the opportunity to participate in a couple of these. Following the completion of the course in June, Gerald Caplan arranged for me to have a three-month secondment in California. Driving across to California, with our one-year old child in the back, we took the northern route, going through Pennsylvania and on to Chicago. From Chicago we travelled west into South Dakota and the Bad Lands. What amazed me was that, once you pass Chicago, this enormous country is virtually empty until you reach California. We were two weeks on the road crossing America and finally made our way to San Francisco.

The three months spent on the west coast were really more of a vacation and an experience than a serious working assignment. We got an apartment in Berkeley, not far from the University of California campus, and I used to spend a fair bit of time in the library there. That was the terminal period of the beatniks and the centre in Haight Ashbury. I remember seeing these young women in long black dresses delivering mail and doing other simple jobs around the campus.

While we were in Berkeley I met a disc jockey who introduced me to cannabis and the lovely relaxed feeling of smoking grass while listening to jazz. He also gave me some marijuana seeds, which I brought back to Ireland to see if I could grow some plants; but that's another story. I had taken some psilocybin tablets with me, which is the active ingredient in magic mushrooms. I was surprised to find that there was no knowledge of psychedelics (other than Mescaline, which was known from the Don Juan stories and the influence of Aldous Huxley) on the west coast, so I think I may have been the first person to take a psychedelic drug out there. Remember that Timothy Leary and Richard Alpert were still working in Harvard and LSD was, as yet, generally unknown. Anyway, the disc jockey was delighted to try it and said he had never heard of it before.

My supervisors arranged a number of visits for me. I went to visit Napa State Hospital, which was one of the large mental hospitals in California at that time before Reagan closed most of them down. I also visited San Matao County, which then had a model mental health service – a community mental health centre with a small number of beds and various other community facilities, so that the whole service ran virtually independently from any input into the area of mental hospital. I have often wondered what happened to well-designed community services like this since then.

The most interesting experience I had while on the west coast was a visit to Gregory Bateson's Schizophrenia Research Unit in Palo Alto. At that time I didn't know anything about Gregory Bateson or his double-bind theory, nor about all the other innovative work that he had done over the years. I found him a most courteous English gentleman who was very willing to spend time with me. I also met Jay Haley that day, who impressed me greatly and later wrote that very fine book, *Uncommon Therapy*, on the work of Milton Erickson. The experience of hearing their views on schizophrenia was a further step for me in realising that the orthodox view of it as a largely genetic, biochemical disorder simply didn't add up.

Something I didn't realise at the time was that the only reason for Gregory Bateson, an anthropologist who was mainly interested in animal and human communication, getting involved in schizophrenia was because there were research grants available at that time to study this disorder. Nevertheless, the research which he carried out has remained a valuable contribution to the understanding of mental illness. This is true even though his theory of 'double bind' communication between members in a disturbed family has no specific relationship to schizophrenia. The sad thing is that, because this theory is not specific to schizophrenia, it has tended to be dismissed as irrelevant, when in fact it is a valuable insight into disturbed family relationships generally. It can be found in virtually any form of psychiatric disorder where the family is 'enmeshed' and has failed to free the offspring to leave and lead a separate life.

When September came and we had to return to Boston, we drove back by the southern route. I was anxious to realise a long-held ambition to visit New Orleans, with all its memories of where jazz originated. We were making good progress in that regard until we came up against Hurricane Carla. The winds were getting stronger and stronger as the hurricane moved northwards. We made it as far as

Austin, Texas, but by that time it was clear that we couldn't get any farther. In the end we had to admit defeat and make our way northwards back to Boston, threatened by tornadoes along the way.

In my second year in Boston I got involved in a research project involving engaged couples, under the direction of Rhona Rapaport, who was a senior research psychologist working with Gerald Caplan. The idea was that we would follow a small number of engaged couples through to their marriage, meeting them again when they returned from their honeymoon. Our hypothesis was that marriage would constitute something of a crisis and we wanted to see how people from different ethnic backgrounds would manage it and come through the ordeal. To my surprise they all agreed to this quite unwarranted intrusion into their private lives. Unfortunately, the study did not achieve any demonstrable result. What was a revelation to me though was the striking difference in norms of behaviour and marriage rituals between couples from different cultural backgrounds.

One of the most interesting experiences I had when working on this study was the opportunity to meet Erik Erickson. He was teaching in Harvard at the time and agreed to see us on a weekly basis as adviser to the study. Each week we would go over to Cambridge to see him in his office. I remember him as a very gentle, dignified and erudite, white-haired gentleman. He said he sometimes regretted having got involved in the theory of developmental crises because – 'now every student in Harvard is suffering from an identity crisis'.

As the end of my second year approached I was put under considerable pressure from several sources, particularly from Gerald Caplan, to stay on and work in America on a more permanent basis, but I felt a strong urge to return home, partly motivated by homesickness. Having made enquiries about job opportunities in Ireland, I got wind of a senior psychiatrist appointment to the Dublin Health Authority. I applied for this and made arrangements to return home for the interview. Having got through the interview, I returned to the States the following day and, while still there, I received news that my application for the post had been successful. We returned home to Ireland and I took up my new appointment in July 1962.

PART THREE

Dublin

1962–1963

12

St Brendan's

When I arrived in Grangegorman at the beginning of July 1962 to take up my post as Senior Administrative Medical Officer (SAMO), I didn't know what to expect. At that time there was no such thing as a consultant psychiatrist, although the SAMO title was the nearest equivalent to this. There were only four grades: Resident Medical Superintendent (RMS), SAMO, Junior Administrative Medical Officer (JAMO) and House Officer. The psychiatric staff of a public mental hospital at that time would have been considered a lower form of medical life compared to their exalted colleagues in a general hospital, or in one of the private mental hospitals such as St Patrick's or St John of God's.

Dr John Dunne was the Chief RMS in Dublin then and he lost no time in letting me know that I was the most junior of his senior psychiatrists. When I requested that I might join the staff of St Loman's Hospital in Ballyowen, he said that he thought it would be much better for me to gain some experience in Grangegorman, which he informed me was the main psychiatric centre in Ireland. I had already heard that Dr Vincent Crotty, who was in charge of St Loman's, was breaking new ground. St Loman's Hospital had been one of the new TB sanatoria established by Dr Noel Browne when he was Minister for Health but, with the decline of tuberculosis, had been turned over to psychiatry and was operating as a peripheral extension from Grangegorman, but solely for women patients. Dr Dermot Walsh had already joined Vincent Crotty and I was hoping that I too would be able to get myself transferred out there as soon as possible.

In his book, *Grangegorman*, Joe Reynolds has recorded John Dunne's official note to the chief executive officer of the Dublin

Health Authority on my taking up duty in July 1962:

> Dr Ivor Browne presented himself to take up duty as senior
> medical officer on 18th inst. He impressed me very much with
> his keenness. He has however been out of touch with mental
> hospital administration and I have decided that, before entering
> the many duties of a senior medical officer, he should spend a
> week studying the various aspects of administration, therapy,
> etc. in St Brendan's.

I realised there was nothing I could do for the present but bide my
time and accept the situation.

I have already described in some detail what Grangegorman was
like in those years but I had only seen it as a visitor. Now I had to
face the stark reality of working there day after day. What I was dismayed to find was that, not only were patients transferred from ward
to ward to make room for new people coming in, but the staff were
also constantly on the move. For the several months that I was there
I was never assigned to a ward but was always doing 'locum' for
someone else who was on holidays or sick leave. The nurses too, like
the patients, were constantly being transferred, so virtually every day
I found myself in a new location dealing with a strange group of patients and different nurses. It was quite impossible, therefore, to develop a relationship with any patient or to follow through with any
form of therapy.

The nurses worked on a day-on-day-off system, so that any instruction you gave regarding the care of a patient was seldom carried
through, as a different set of nurses came on duty the following day.
Typically what happened was that a line of patients would be pa-
raded in front of you while you went through their charts. There
was absolutely nothing you could do other than review their medication on the advice of the charge nurse, knowing that you would
be unlikely ever to see the same patient again. Even if you were assigned to the same ward again in a few weeks' time, the patients
would be likely by then to have been transferred somewhere else. As
the days and weeks went by I could feel myself sinking into a state
of despair and the sense of frustration was almost unbearable.

John Dunne held a weekly board meeting at which he saw every
patient who was considered to be possibly fit for discharge. If you

had managed, despite all the difficulties, to assist the patient towards recovery, when they came in front of John Dunne at the board he would go meticulously through their notes. Then, if he found that at some time in the past the patient had attempted suicide or shown signs of dangerous aggression, he would say, 'I think we'd better defer his discharge for some time.' The patient, whose hopes you had built up perhaps over several weeks, would collapse in despair in front of your eyes and be unlikely ever to make an effort towards recovery again. Under the Mental Treatment Act of 1945 the Resident Medical Superintendent was legally obliged to see every patient before discharge but it was evident to me that the main purpose of this was for John Dunne to ensure that no patient would be discharged who might, by suicide or some other dangerous behaviour, put his reputation at risk.

Some years prior to my joining the service, the Mental Treatment Act also stated that the RMS must personally see each patient on admission to the hospital, but one evening when John Dunne was at a show in the Gaiety Theatre, a litigious alcoholic, who happened to be a lawyer, was admitted to the hospital as an involuntary patient. Although drunk at the time, he noticed that the RMS was not present to admit him and subsequently threatened to sue both Dr Dunne and the Dublin Health Authority. Within twenty-four hours an emergency Act was passed through the Dáil which allowed patients to be seen and admitted by a senior psychiatrist by delegation from the RMS. This became known colloquially as the 'Gaiety Theatre Act' and from then onwards it was not necessary for the Medical Superintendent to see each patient personally at the time of admission. He did, however, continue to see every patient, both from St Brendan's and St Ita's (the other psychiatric hospital functioning as an extension from St Brendan's on the north side of County Dublin), prior to discharge.

When I joined the staff of St Brendan's there were some very strange doctors working there. They certainly fitted the old saying that 'the only difference between the doctors and patients in a mental hospital was that some of the patients changed'. There was one doctor who retired shortly after I arrived there who used to spend his day picking up cigarette butts left lying around the grounds by patients. There was another doctor who was a chronic alcoholic. When he was on the drink he had a patient trained who would carry bottles in a black sack and meet him at strategic points on his rounds so he could top up with alcohol. At other times, when he temporarily stopped drinking, he used to build an altar at the end of one of the wards, where he would worship on a daily basis in order to try to maintain his sobriety.

The other senior psychiatrist with whom I worked most closely was a small elderly woman, who worked conscientiously to do what she could to improve the lot of patients under her care. She was a very kind woman and had taken an elderly alcoholic patient into her home, where she looked after her devotedly. This patient was Teresa Maloney, a well-known colleague of James Connolly, a survivor of the Citizen Army days. I went up to be introduced to her one day, by which time she was virtually bedridden. I found her to be a very dignified old lady, who greeted me in a most courteous manner while she sipped her sherry.

As the weeks dragged on I made a number of attempts to obtain an interview with John Dunne to try to persuade him to let me transfer to St Loman's. When August came he sent for me to come and see him in his office. I went immediately, full of hope that he had at last relented. He greeted me with a smile and said, 'Doctor, I think a month at the seaside would be very beneficial to you to see another aspect of the work.' This was his way of telling me that I was to be sent out to St Ita's, if anything an even less desirable option than St Brendan's.

At that time there were approximately 4,000 patients between the two hospitals, a considerable proportion of whom were mentally retarded. There were, in addition, several hundred patients who had been sent out to old wooden huts in St Mary's Hospital in the Phoenix Park, and a further 200 women patients in St Loman's. No patients were admitted directly to either St Ita's or St Loman's but were transferred out to these units in order to relieve overcrowding in St Brendan's.

I heard at that time that John Dunne had put forward a plan to build a third mental hospital in the grounds of Santry Court (now a sports stadium), which the Dublin Health Authority had acquired. Myles Na gCopaleen, who wrote the famous column Cruiskeen Lawn in *The Irish Times* and was admitted to St Brendan's fairly regularly when his drinking got out of control, heard of this scheme and often used to sign his column 'Lord of Santry Court'. Few people realised what this referred to. He was announcing that, if and when this new mental hospital was built, he proposed to be its star patient.

In those days Dr Stanley Blake, who has long since passed away, was the RMS in St Ita's, which he ruled like a feudal lord. If two nurses were proposing to get married they had to present themselves to him for his permission. Prior to my time, there was actually a special railway line running from the Broadstone out to St Ita's, and patients were transferred down there by train. When patients arrived from St Brendan's, Blake had a rather novel method of diagnosis. He would review a parade of the new arrivals, selecting patients according to their strength – this one for the coal yard, another for the laundry, pig yard and so on.

Dr Blake was known for his meanness but, if a patient's health was deteriorating, he would eventually agree to them having a special diet. He had an almost uncanny sense of timing. By the time he finally agreed to a special diet, the patient was usually at death's door. One day, a patient came tottering into Occupational Therapy, white as a sheet, and said, 'He's put me on chicken!' The patient was dead within days.

I found St Ita's even more depressing than St Brendan's, with the long, sombre corridors leading to large wards full of forlorn human beings. There were old dilapidated wooden huts where the most disabled of the mentally retarded were housed. These were known as the wet and dirty wards, full of small, gnome-like creatures in long black coats sitting and standing around on floors impregnated with years of urine. Even by that time, a couple of these huts had already been vacated and knocked down. One day, when the Clerk of Works was out inspecting the site where they had been, the phone, which was still connected, rang and a doctor's voice said, 'How are all your people out there?' The Clerk of Works, being alive to the absurdity of the situation answered, 'They're all doing fine, doctor' and hung up the phone.

The RMS, at the time I was there, was a kind, gentle man who was not anxious to rock the boat or draw public attention to the state of that awful place. During the month I was there I found one patient for whom I saw some hope of improvement and I started to work with him. He made enough progress for me to be actively considering the possibility of his discharge. Then one day a nurse came to me and in a confidential tone said, 'You can't discharge him, he's the RMS' gardener.' I remained there for the month of August, but was then relieved to return to St Brendan's.

John Dunne ran St Brendan's, a huge hospital complex, with the minimum of effort. He came to the hospital pretty regularly every day but never arrived before noon. He would stay for about an hour, unless he had a discharge board to perform, and then would depart to play golf. One day a bank manager who was one of his golfing partners said to him, 'How is it, John, that, with the enormous responsibility you have running these hospitals, you are able to spend so much time on the golf course?' John Dunne replied, confidentially, 'You know if I was to spend too much time in there I'd be as bad as the rest of them.'

As autumn dragged on I became increasingly frustrated and felt that I couldn't go on working in this soul-destroying environment. I had made numerous requests to see the RMS, without success, so I decided to deposit myself outside his office from morning till night until he agreed to see me. I stayed there like that from nine in the morning until six or seven in the evening for three days, to the alarm of his secretary. Each day, when he arrived around noon, he would march past me without acknowledging my presence and would leave in the same way. I waited on in the hope he might return. On the third evening he had remained on late after his discharge board and, apparently finally becoming unnerved by the situation, he sent for me. He was angry and asked me, 'Are you holding a pistol to my head?' Shortly after this he apparently decided that it was the lesser of two evils to get rid of me and, to my delight, finally agreed to my transfer to St Loman's to join the rebel enclave.

13

St Loman's

St Loman's was like a different world. After the dirt and chaos of Grangegorman, here was a small, clean, well-run hospital with a buoyant, optimistic atmosphere. The design of the hospital was similar to that of most TB sanatoria – a long central corridor with wards opening off each side of this and, at the end, a large T-shaped ward.

The first morning I came to work at about 8.30. When I entered the doctors' sitting-room there was a young doctor already there. He looked up at me from the armchair where he was sitting, dressed in a suit and tie, and said, looking severely at his watch, 'Doctor, in this hospital we start work by 8am.' This was Dr Gerry Crowley, whom I got to know well afterwards. He had a zany sense of humour and what I didn't realise at the time was that, far from being at work early, he had been up all night drinking and hadn't seen sight nor sign of a bed. At the time he was living in the hospital, in the doctors' quarters, but one night he arrived, under the influence, in the early hours of the morning and, finding the entrance to the doctors' quarters locked, got in through a window in the nurses' home. He climbed into bed with a nurse, fully clothed, and with his boots on. He was settling down to sleep, but understandably the nurse was upset and pleaded with him to leave. Finally, when there was no sign of him moving, she told him that if he didn't go she'd have to call the matron. He replied, 'My dear, there'd never be room for the three of us.'

There were no direct admissions to the hospital at that time. It only catered for female patients transferred from St Brendan's. These were mainly acute patients, so there was a fairly rapid turnover, with a high discharge rate. Each unit had a doctor in charge who took responsibility for all the patients in that ward from the time of their admission to their discharge. One was able to work consistently with the same patients, planning a therapeutic programme for each, very different from St Brendan's. Dr Vincent Crotty, who was in charge of the hospital, was anxious that it should cater for both male and female patients and have direct admissions. Dr Dunne resisted this, but at least Crotty had managed, with pressure from the Department of Health, to negotiate their direct discharge from the hospital, so they didn't have to go through the indignity of the discharge board in St Brendan's. It was only after Dunne retired and I went back to St Brendan's that it was possible to arrange direct admissions to St Loman's.

St Loman's had only opened its doors a couple of years before I went there in 1962, so it was still in an early phase of its development. Dr Crotty was a gentle man with liberal views and under his leadership the atmosphere in the hospital was open and democratic, in stark contrast to the authoritarian ethos in St Brendan's.

One of the reasons I was successful in obtaining my transfer to St Loman's was that the department was anxious to open the first children's unit in the country for autistic children. As I had had some experience in child psychiatry, Dr Crotty asked me to take charge of this unit, which was still only in the planning stage when I arrived. I never felt that I wanted to be a child psychiatrist but, as it had enabled me to get out of St Brendan's, I was glad to accept the challenge. As it turned out, I didn't realise what I was letting myself in for. Dr Crotty had no experience with child psychiatry so, prior to my arrival he had enlisted the help and advice of the Rudolf Steiner people, who already had a couple of units for mentally retarded children in Ireland, some of whom were autistic. They had very dogmatic, doctrinaire views of how a children's unit should be designed and run, with an extremely rigid therapeutic programme, and had been handed complete control in the planning and design of the unit. So, by the time I arrived, although no children had yet been admitted, the architectural design and furnishings were already complete. These were, to say the least, unusual. There were no straight lines, the décor and decoration of the walls and ceilings were all in curves, and the tables and chairs were of unusual hexagonal and off-centre shapes and sizes. It was undoubtedly an innovative and attractive interior design, using colours believed to have specific effects in the decoration of the day rooms, bedrooms and so on. None of this was done for aesthetic reasons but emanated from the theories of Rudolf Steiner and his followers, who believed that décor would have a particular therapeutic effect in reducing disturbed behaviour.

I was quite happy with these design innovations, but unfortunately Dr Crotty had also recruited two care workers, a husband and wife, from the Rudolf Steiner organisation. It was here that my misfortune began. When the unit finally opened and children began to arrive, this couple set up an incredibly rigid and inhuman regime. The couple were insensitive in their attitude towards children. I had visited one of the Steiner institutions and found that, while their approach was rigid and doctrinaire, at least it was applied with kindness and even love, but in our new unit the situation was very different. If children refused their food they were left sitting in front of the cold plate for hours on end. The rules of the system were applied quite ruthlessly and, although it was hard to get evidence, there is no doubt that the children were subjected to physical brutality. I found the situation increasingly intolerable and went repeatedly to Dr Crotty to try to get him to see this. While I had no particular grievance against the Steiner system, as such, the couple he had employed were totally unsuitable and should never have been allowed to work with children.

Unfortunately, by this time Dr Crotty had advanced carcinoma and was rapidly going downhill. Consequently his judgement was impaired and his mind was completely closed to any criticism of the Steiner method. He simply wouldn't entertain any question of dealing with the two people he had employed, however unsuitable they were. Finally, one day, the German woman partially ripped the ear off a child she was dragging along the corridor and I felt I could no longer continue unless she was dismissed. Some time before that she had taken a cat by the tail and beaten it to death against the walls. I went to Dr Crotty and said that either they would have to go or I would. He deliberated for some time and then said, 'Then I am afraid you'll have to go.'

I was caught between a rock and a hard place. I knew that if I resigned the children would be totally at the mercy of this pair and bereft of whatever influence I was able to bring to bear on the situation. Also Dr Crotty was failing rapidly and was in no position to run the hospital without me. So I felt I had no choice but to carry on, however unbearable the situation was. In hindsight, perhaps what I should have done was simply call the police and have the woman charged, but, rightly or wrongly, I didn't want to get into open conflict with Dr Crotty when he was so near death. Looking back, it was one of the unhappiest periods of my life.

Fortunately this situation did not endure for long, as Dr Crotty became too ill to continue and had to resign. That very day I went down to the unit and told the German woman and her husband that they were fired. Everyone, the nurses and other staff, were delighted. The pair departed the next day, leaving a big notice behind them written in large letters, 'Browne's Folly'. It was a tremendous relief to be rid of them.

Some of the children in the unit were extremely disturbed and hard to handle. Once this pair were gone, however, we rapidly liberalised the regime with the help of our German psychologist, Ingo Fischer, who was working with me in the unit. He designed an innovative form of education, which attempted to find alternative ways of communicating with the children so that they might begin to learn. Their progress was very slow and tedious, but his method did bring considerable results. Unfortunately, the nurses who replaced the house parents found the work difficult and morale was low. Somehow the unit never fully recovered from the negative culture those house parents had introduced.

There was one girl of about ten years of age who was highly intelligent but unbelievably self-destructive. She used to bang her head and face against the walls continually, hour after hour. Her face was scarred, bleeding, bruised and battered. On one occasion she actually beat a hole in the wall with her head. Whenever I went to the entrance of the unit I used to feel sick to my stomach, not knowing what fresh horror would greet me when I went inside.

Then Ingo Fischer designed a machine which delivered an electric shock to the girl every time she banged her head. To our great relief, she stopped banging her head completely, as she was frightened by the electric shock she received every time she did so. At first she couldn't figure out what was happening but, as she was a highly intelligent child, she soon managed to work out that it was the machine which was doing this to her. As soon as she realised this, she went back to her old ways, banging her head as badly as ever, and the machine became useless. It was just one more example that aversive methods of treatment never really work for long.

There was another child who was so obsessive that he had his parents completely terrorised at home. If they didn't fill his cup to the exact point that he wanted he would scream all day. There were many other problems of a similar kind, which made the work very frustrating.

I realised fairly soon that these autistic children were a mixed lot: some were highly intelligent but appeared to have some neurological deficit that made it impossible for them to make sense of their surroundings. In the face of this, they withdrew into a world of obsessive rituals and only related to other human beings as inanimate objects. They seemed to have to examine everything by touch or taste. If you sat on the floor they would simply walk over you as if you were a piece of furniture. Others, while they were autistic and withdrawn, were also quite severely mentally retarded, with other evidence of brain damage.

There was occasionally a brighter aspect to the work. One little boy, who was only about two years of age when he was admitted, had been totally neglected. His mother had become mentally ill following his birth and he was left lying all day in a cot, face downwards, for months on end. In his case there was no evidence of an organic deficit and it seemed that he was simply suffering from emotional isolation. When he first came to us, if he was taken from his bed he would just lie on the floor, doubled up, with his head on the ground. Then, with love and affection, he gradually began to awaken, opening up like a flower, until he slowly learned to stand and then walk. It took many months but eventually he was running about happily and beginning to relate like a normal child.

When I was transferred to St Loman's, my wife and I were lucky enough to find a cottage for sale on the Strawberry Beds, a lovely part of Dublin on the river, just west of the Phoenix Park. Unfortunately, I had no sooner bought the place than Dr Crotty had to resign, so I had to take over the running of the hospital and move into the house on the hospital grounds. We stayed on in the hospital house until I took up the post of Chief Psychiatrist of the Eastern Health Board in 1966. It was a large, modern house with over an acre of gardens, but sadly we never got to live in the Strawberry Beds.

Settling down to work in the adult units, I had the naïve idea that if I worked hard and treated all the people coming in I would somehow get on top of the mental health problems in the hospital, whereas, of course, the faster I discharged patients, the more quickly they were replaced by others. So I found myself on a treadmill, struggling to get people out faster and faster. It took me a while to realise how stupid I was. There were always going to be more patients than I could deal with. I calmed down and worked more slowly to try to achieve a real change in people, not simply to remove symptoms. I had, as yet, no clear idea as to which patients would respond to the deeper forms of psychotherapy or to the use of LSD as a therapeutic aid, and I was still using conventional methods of therapy as well. Although I had seen some remarkable results when I was with Joshua Bierer in London, LSD was still a radical form of therapy, unheard of in Ireland at the time. I decided it would only be justifiable to try it with those patients who had failed to make any progress with more conventional methods of psychiatric treatment.

I soon found that if I gave LSD to schizophrenic patients the only effect was for them to become even more psychotic. I didn't understand at that time that, even where such patients have a traumatic history, they don't have the ego structure to be able to integrate the experiences; they simply become more fragmented. There were other cases, however, who also appeared untreatable and had been more or less given up on by the other doctors and staff. Kate who came from Finglas went about the ward all day whining and moaning in a histrionic fashion. The other psychiatrists were thoroughly fed up with her and she was generally dismissed as a malignant hysteric. She was heavily addicted to the amphetamine substitute Ritalin and was taking handfuls of these tablets every day. She had had all the conventional psychiatric medications, as well as courses of ECT, with no improvement. I decided that she couldn't really get any worse and commenced psychotherapy with the aid of LSD. All that I knew about her was that she had been admitted some time after her mother's death a couple of years before, and relations with her husband were so bad that he was pursuing a permanent separation.

She was so desperate that she was quite willing to undertake any form of therapy that I suggested. When I first gave her LSD, administering about 50 micrograms in liquid form by mouth, boosted half an hour later by an injection of Methedrine, she did not go back to the recent death of her mother. Instead she regressed to a time when she was about eight years of age. Returning home from school, she had seen a pool of blood at the roadside. Her description of this was so graphic that I could almost see the blood on the road myself. When she realised that this was where her brother had been struck by a car and died, she disappeared for three days, hiding in an old shed. As R.D. Laing described to me (personal communication), one cuts off this entire experience and then cuts off the fact that it has been cut off, so that she had no recollection of it other than the intellectual knowledge that her brother was dead. She moaned and wept bitterly all day as part of this session. We continued with further weekly treatments along these lines, gradually increasing the dose of LSD. She went through several other deaths of relatives and close friends. After each of these sessions she would weep and grieve for days on end, but gradually she became calmer and began to take a positive interest in what was happening around her. She then went through her mother's death, with an even more powerful reaction.

As she had improved so significantly, I decided to have one final session to see if there were any significant experiences remaining. To my dismay she went into the most powerful experience of all, spluttering, becoming cyanosed and suffocating. This went on all day and made me wonder if I had gone too far this time. When she came back to herself in the evening she told me that she had felt she was about two years of age and had been thrown into the sea by her brother and almost drowned. She had only been rescued when she was on the point of death. This experience came as a complete surprise to her, although she was able to confirm what had happened with relatives who were still alive.

By this time, after several months of therapy, she was so well that I decided there was no need to continue further and prepared her for discharge from hospital. She no longer required any medication and had discontinued taking the Ritalin completely. I continued to see her as an out-patient, and one day she came in and told me that neighbours and friends were saying that she and her husband were like a honeymoon couple.

Unfortunately, about seven years later, this case had a rather tragic ending. She remained happy and well for seven years, when her husband died suddenly from a massive heart attack. When I saw her again she was moaning and whining just as she had done when I first met her in hospital. I started therapy with her once again. As before

she went through the full grief reaction, crying and weeping periodically for several weeks. What I learned from this episode was that
a person faced with a similar trauma, even though fully recovered
from the earlier traumatic experience, will tend to revert to the same
old defensive behaviour, freezing the experience and inhibiting any
emotional reaction.

Mary, a middle-aged woman who lived on a housing estate in
south Dublin, had been a thorn in the side of the hospital for some
years. She periodically used to go into an angry, overactive, atypical
psychotic state. In this condition she would be quite dangerous to
her young children and those around her. On several occasions she
had been dragged into the hospital as an involuntary patient. She
was angry and difficult to manage, but with conventional anti-psychotic medication and/or ECT her symptoms would gradually improve enough for her to be discharged, only to be re-admitted again
when the next episode occurred. The staff in the hospital felt frustrated and at the end of their tether, and nobody knew what to do
with her. Each time she became psychotic she created a crisis in the
neighbourhood – one time locking herself in the bathroom with a
carving knife and threatening to cut her children's throats. On several other occasions she kidnapped young Traveller children who
were camped around the area, taking them into her house, sometimes late at night, and washing and bathing them before letting
them go. Needless to say, the parents didn't appreciate this behaviour
and had even threatened to kill her if she didn't stop.

I had already been involved on one occasion when I was on duty
and had to go out to collect her, as no one could manage to get her
into hospital. On that occasion, with the help of the GP who had
signed the temporary form, and a couple of nurses, I gave her an injection at home and then, when she went to sleep, we were able to
bring her in. Some months later there was a call to the hospital to say
that she was unmanageable, no one could do anything with her, and
she would have to be taken in again. The practice in the psychiatric
service generally, until recently, was that in such situations the pink
'temporary' form was signed by a relative and the second part was
filled in by the general practitioner, who must have seen and examined the patient. The form was then brought to the hospital, where
it was signed by the psychiatrist on duty. The patient was then legally
detained, although the psychiatrist had not even seen the patient to

ascertain whether admission was really necessary. A couple of nurses were then sent out to apprehend the patient. This situation has presumably altered now with the introduction of the new Mental Treatment Act. I never felt happy with this arrangement and when a situation like this arose I made a practice of going out with the nurses. I frequently found that, once you sat down with the supposedly mad person and chatted with them, it was often unnecessary to admit them to hospital, or at least it was possible to persuade them to come in voluntarily. On this occasion I went out to Drimnagh to find a strange scene awaiting me. Because she knew that on previous occasions when she was in the house she had been captured and given an injection, she was now sitting on a chair outside the house in her small front garden. A police car and an ambulance were already there and a crowd of neighbours had gathered to see what was happening to this 'poor woman'. She was in an agitated, angry, highly overactive state. The front door was locked and her son, who was about ten years old, was in the house. She was calling out to him, telling him to throw down photographs of her late husband, who had died more than ten years before in a building accident. Dressed in black and behaving as if he had just died, she showed these to the assembled crowd.

It was difficult to know what to do, as the crowd, seeing our arrival with nurses in white coats, were getting increasingly hostile. There was no way of talking to her, nor could we apprehend her or give her an injection with such a tense crowd of people standing around. It was a total impasse. Fortunately, after a stand-off that seemed interminable, a neighbour managed to break into the back of the house. He apparently tried to catch hold of her son, who cried out in alarm. Hearing this, she immediately ran into the house to protect him and we followed her in, and were then able to give her an injection. The crowd didn't look at all happy when she was carried out unconscious to the ambulance, but at least we managed to get her into hospital.

When I enquired locally as to what might have triggered this latest breakdown, it emerged that one of the Little Sisters of the Assumption had been killed in an accident on her motor scooter. The sisters were highly thought of in the area because they nursed poor people in their homes and solved all kinds of social problems. This sister was so popular that the convent arranged a walk-past for the people of the area, and the coffin was laid out in the local parish church. This woman went along but, when she got to the coffin, she went berserk, turned over the coffin and kicked the Reverend Mother in the shins. Needless to say, this caused a major crisis. Then, over the next couple of days she became increasingly disturbed, until the morning when we had to go out to bring her in to hospital.

Having gone through this ordeal, I decided that this time I was going to do something about her, so I started working with her with the help of LSD. Of course at that time I didn't realise that the more you push a person like this, the greater the build-up of resistance. I had no real awareness then of the importance of building a safe context within which the person feels protected enough to be able to go into the trauma and work through it.

I attempted two or three sessions with her, increasing the dose of LSD each time, but she became increasingly angry and refused to co-operate in any way. At the next session, when I gave her 300 micrograms of LSD followed by a Methedrine injection, the same thing occurred: she got intensely angry, shouting and roaring at me, threatening to sue me, the hospital and the health authority. Standing frustrated at the end of the bed, I lost my cool and shouted back at her. At that moment an extraordinary thing happened. She suddenly broke; she started to roar crying and behaved as though she was holding her husband's head in her hands. She cried and wept for hours after that, and it was clear that all the anger was only a defence against the grief which she had frozen at the time of his death and had never been able to release until that moment. From then on, as one session followed another, she became more and more calm and gentle. After a few weeks she was well enough to be discharged and, though I followed her progress for several years, she remained well and never again had a psychotic reaction.

I was still a long way from understanding all that was involved when a person faced with an overwhelming traumatic event goes into an immediate state of traumatic shock. The trauma is then suspended indefinitely and is never experienced until something activates it, perhaps years later. But at least I realised that many cases of depression, agitation and anxiety or, as in this case, an atypical psychotic reaction, arise because the person can't face going through the pain of the trauma, which has not yet been experienced. I will return to this again later.

114

Another similar example was Helen, a young woman whom I saw some years later when I had left St Loman's to take up my post as Chief Psychiatrist in St Brendan's. She too was showing symptoms of an atypical psychosis. Another psychiatrist had diagnosed her as suffering from early schizophrenia. She felt that the walls in her room were moving and changing shape, and had other symptoms of a similar kind, so that she thought she was going crazy. There was a male nurse who was a creative but rather unusual personality. He looked somewhat like King Farouk of Egypt. He was overweight, had a thin moustache, which he sometimes painted to darken it, and had a rather lecherous appearance, although he was really a big innocent at heart. With his help I had recently installed closed-circuit TV in the out-patient's department in St Brendan's, in those days a fairly primitive system. The only way we could do it at the time was to use a single bedroom at one end of the department, where we placed the camera with the patient, while at the other end of the building we had an office with the recorder and monitor. So, having adjusted the camera, one had to go to the other end of the building to see if the picture was satisfactory. In between was the out-patients department, with up to a hundred patients, waiting to see the doctors. It is necessary to explain this in order to understand what ensued with this young woman. She was unable to enlighten me as to what was causing the unusual sensory experiences she was having. I was not convinced that she was schizophrenic and, rather than have her condemned to heavy antipsychotic medication, I decided to try psychedelic therapy with LSD to see what would unfold. In order to record the experience, I gave her the LSD in the room with the TV camera. After this I waited for about an hour by her bedside but, as nothing was happening and she was still resting quietly, I went back upstairs to my office, where I had some urgent things to attend to. I gave instructions to the male nurse to keep the TV recording going in case she should show any response.

I heard nothing further until, a couple of hours later, the male nurse came up to my office looking rather dishevelled and resentful. I soon realised why! He told me that, shortly after I left, the young woman went into a violent catharsis, having activated a traumatic rape that she had been subjected to several years before. She had frozen this experience and had no recollection whatsoever of what had happened to her. When she experienced being raped, she

115

started to scream blue murder – 'Get off me, help, stop you bastard,' and so on. The nurse realised the importance of recording what was happening but, in order to do this, he would have to focus the camera in the bedroom and then run down to the other office to see what the picture was like. Then, if it wasn't focused properly, he would have to run up to the bedroom again to re-adjust the camera. Each time he opened the bedroom door, her shrieks and abuse of the rapist were clearly audible to the hundred or so patients in the waiting room. Then, when he opened the door to where the monitor was, her shrieks were clearly audible from there also. So, to the waiting patients, it seemed as if this large, lecherous-looking individual was engaged in raping two women at the same time. It was understandable that when he came up to me he was looking upset and reproachful.

This young woman, once she had activated the trauma, was able, with several more therapeutic sessions, to fully integrate the experience. Prior to her coming for therapy she had dropped out of university, as she was unable to concentrate. Now, however, she gradually made a complete recovery and was able to return to her studies and finish her degree. Certainly, this was not an ideal way to go about therapy, but, nevertheless, it was from patients like these, and others whom I had worked with in the Marlborough Day Hospital, that I gradually learned that there was more to psychiatric disturbance than identifying an illness from a cluster of symptoms and giving it a name.

There was another young person who, when I first met her, was only about fourteen years of age. Her name was Phyllis Hamilton. She had been admitted to the adult section of St Loman's because, at that time, there was no adolescent facility in the country to which she could go. I came across her one day in the recreation area of the hospital, where she was attempting to play the piano. I wondered what could have brought a beautiful young girl like this into hospital and, having made enquiries about her background, I decided to see if I could help her. Her father had sexually abused her up to the age of ten and, because of this, her behaviour had become difficult and uncontrolled, and she was sent to one of the institutions run by nuns for young wayward girls. Eventually, when they couldn't manage her, she was transferred to St Loman's.

Over the next few years she gradually worked her way through the experience of the abuse. She was very keen to take up some form of nursing and, with the help of one of the male nurses, I managed to get her taken on as an auxiliary, or cadet nurse, in St Brendan's. She was by now seventeen years old. I was very pleased with her progress. She was finding her feet, like most youngsters her age, except that she did not have the back-up of a family home. She had her own room in the hospital, was saving her wages with a view to getting outside accommodation, and could come and go as she pleased. She wanted to be a geriatric nurse and worked mainly with old people in the geriatric section of the hospital. She didn't go out much at night, but one evening another girl took her to a charity concert. It was there that she met the charismatic Father Michael Cleary, who played the guitar and sang and was generally the life and soul of the party. When her eyes fell on Michael, her life changed.

In the house where Father Cleary was living he had been taking in young adolescent girls who had nowhere to go. These were youngsters who had been discharged from institutions or who came from disturbed families and had run away from home. He apparently invited Phyllis to come and stay there as well, but she did not tell me about this until she came to me one day, in a very upset state, to tell me that she was pregnant and that Father Cleary was the father. This was their first child, who was subsequently adopted. Following this, she gave up the auxiliary nursing and continued to live with him, eventually becoming his housekeeper when he moved to Ballyfermot. From the time their relationship began she had trouble living a lie, feeling guilty, depressed and upset much of the time. But that was the price of living with the man she loved; she could not leave him and he was unable to give up being a priest. And so her life became a long saga of sadness and heartbreak. I had a part to play in that life every now and then over the years, as I will explain later.

I have often wondered if, in the beginning, I could have done anything to avoid the years of suffering for Phyllis. It was a mess that I felt would end in tears but I could not see a solution to the problem other than getting her away from Father Cleary, or getting him away from the Church, but one thing that psychiatry taught me early in my career is that you cannot tell people how to live their lives. They make choices. If they want to get better, they probably will and, if they want to create more problems for themselves, they will.

I didn't realise at that time that Phyllis' situation would become a serious problem for me personally many years later when the story of her relationship with Father Cleary broke in the press. Each person has a destiny, in which a psychiatrist or anyone else is merely a fragment. I only realised this much later, when I came to understand the nature of living systems.

14

Connemara

For a long time I'd had a dream of getting a small place in Connemara and it was while I was in St Loman's that I thought it was time to do something about it. Dr Noel Browne, who was working in St Loman's at that time, had a thatched cottage over in Connemara in an unspoilt area near Baile na hAbhann. I spoke to Noel and he said he'd look around. After a while he came back and said there was a ruined cottage in the next village, Bantrach Bán, which Micheál Thomáis, who lived next to him and who originally owned Noel's cottage, said could be purchased and rebuilt.

At Baile na hAbhann the main road turns inland towards Ros an Mhil and a small sea road goes out around the point of Galway Bay. There were two villages along that road: Cloghmore South and Bantrach Bán. Noel Browne's cottage was in the first of these villages, but away from the village itself, out on the sea where there was only one other house. This area was more isolated than most of the Gaeltacht; it was all Irish speaking and a number of the people had no English at all.

I went down to see the cottage and at first felt disappointed, as only the walls were standing and one bit of the roof. I couldn't see that much could be done with it, but Micheál Thomáis assured me that he could put the roof back on, thatch it and repair the whole building. Not feeling very convinced, I got in touch with the owner and eventually bought it for £300. Micheál Thomáis and a neighbour, Micheál Mháirín, set to work without too much delay. From then on I spent a lot of time down there, whenever I could get away, helping them but mainly watching what they were doing.

Our immediate neighbours on one side were Bridgie Gracie and

119

on the other Pádraic Ghabha and his son Seán. Every morning Bridgie would come to visit when she saw the 'puff' from us lighting the fire. It was in a sense her house, to visit by right, irrespective of who was living in it. Later, when my present wife, Juno, and I used to go down, she and Bridgie got on like a house on fire.

One day I went to visit a family in a village west of Spideal. The man of the house appeared, looking ashen and unshaven. My first thought was that someone had died. When I asked tentatively if something was wrong he told me that his wife, Cathy, was unwell. I found she was still in bed, was very depressed and hadn't been up for several days. I went in to see her and she was lying with her face to the wall, her breakfast untouched beside her. The public health nurse and the doctor had been in to see her over the past few days and she had started taking an antidepressant, with no improvement. I gradually found out from her what had happened. The lake not far from the village was protected for fishing and the bailiff who looked after this was a neighbour in the village. Her son had been seen fishing without permission and a couple of weeks previously she had been accosted by the bailiff's wife, who had reproached her about her son's behaviour. She was a very gentle woman and was completely ashamed and overwhelmed by this attack. Ever since, she had been afraid to go out. It was clear to me that, if there was no improvement, the next step would be to send her to the mental hospital in Ballinasloe, nearly a hundred miles away. Her husband told me that this had already been suggested. It so happened that I had planned to go and get some *poitín* that morning, so first I chatted with her and discussed some ways she might handle the bailiff's wife if she ran into her up the 'boreen' and then I told her I was going to get *poitín* and eventually persuaded her to come with me for the trip.

The *poitín* man lived about five miles inland on the other side of a lake and you had to row a boat over to get to his house. In due course we got to the other side and said we wanted to buy some *poitín*; he made very fine stuff. He was a fairly elderly man and had been in America for many years, involved in the bootlegging business during Prohibition, prior to coming home and setting up his *poitín* still. So he had plenty of experience in making whiskey. He made his *poitín* from barley and other traditional ingredients used in the making of Irish whiskey, so it was excellent. At the time the local Garda sergeant was his main salesman around the district.

(Unfortunately later on another *poitín* maker, who was jealous, reported him to the guards and he was closed down. This broke his heart and he gave up.)

He told us the *poitín* was buried some distance away out on the bog, so we set off. I was in my bare feet, as I always was when down in Connemara. By this time, with all the activity, the woman had cheered up considerably. As we were making our way over the bog, noticing my feet, she decided to take off her shoes and the next thing she was running across the bog laughing with joy, shouting that she hadn't felt like this since she was a child. All the depression had evaporated and she was in great form. When we got to the spot where the *poitín* was buried, we couldn't find it. He knew roughly where it was buried in big jars and we were standing around wondering what to do. As a joke I told her to say a prayer to St Anthony and, to her delight, she found she was standing on one of the kegs. After this she was fine and with a bit of guidance was able to deal with the bailiff's wife. When I visited her on my next visit to Connemara, she was going out and about the village without difficulty.

It was experiences like this which taught me how bogus is the concept of 'clinical depression'. The idea that there is a biochemically mediated form of depression which is an 'illness', quite separate from the sadness and depression which are part of the slings and arrows of ordinary life, is manifest nonsense. What current psychiatric thinking fails to understand is that, whatever biochemical disturbance may underlie depressive states, this is, itself, the result of the way we live and behave.

Towards the end of our time in Connemara, there was a golden day that June and I spent with Bridgie Gracie. It was one of those rare days in late summer when the little gardens were filled with sunlight. She took us all around, showing us who owned which pieces of land, while we spent the time picking blackberries, which she wouldn't touch. I've never forgotten those precious hours we spent with her. She died not long after that from a heart attack, worn out from a lifetime of toil, dragging buckets of water from the well.

15

The Ballyfermot Psychiatric Clinic

Shortly after I commenced work in St Loman's, I was asked by Dr Vincent Crotty to start a psychiatric clinic in the health centre in Ballyfermot. Ballyfermot, at that time, was a fairly recent housing development. Following after Crumlin, it was the next largest migration of people decanted from the tenements of central Dublin. It was developed in two phases. Lower Ballyfermot had been there for some years but the upper part had only recently opened up when I arrived to start the clinic. The development comprised a population of about 40,000, with only about twenty elderly persons in the whole area. Someone told me at the time that when some of these families, having been used to living all in one room in a tenement, arrived in Ballyfermot, they felt completely lost in the amount of space they had in the new houses. They were often found still huddled together in one room. Others were at a loss as to what to do with the bathroom, and the bath was often just filled with coal. There was one itinerant family who had made a little stairway of bricks up to the edge of the bath, which was filled to the brim with water so that the ducks they were keeping could use it as a pond.

Other than the parish church, a primary school, a technical school, a few shops and the health centre, there were virtually no facilities in the whole housing estate. A lot of families found it difficult to visit their elderly relatives back at what they still regarded as home. I think it was with this in mind that Brendan Behan referred to it as 'Bally-Far-Out'.

When I started the clinic there in 1963, there would be a long queue of people, mostly women, waiting outside my office. There were horrendous social problems of all kinds on the estate: financial difficulties, often worsened by the presence of an alcoholic husband in the home; people falling into arrears with the rent and being threatened with eviction by the corporation; too many children coming too quickly; and the problems created by moneylenders, of which there were a number in the area. Something as simple as having to borrow money to buy a First Communion dress for one of the children could land the family in a financial morass. With the exorbitant interest demanded by the moneylenders, they could never manage to pay them off and, in the meantime, other bills and commitments fell behind, so that matters went from bad to worse.

I was soon confronted by a turning point in my psychiatric career. Faced with person after person with virtually insoluble social problems, those who were depressed, anxious, overwhelmed and ready to give up, and others – such as women brutalised by alcoholic husbands – who were threatened with eviction because of rent arrears and unpaid debts, I knew I couldn't hope to deal with them all. There was a wonderful woman, Sister Frances, who was a social worker and one of the Little Sisters of the Assumption. She dealt with a myriad of these sorts of problems among her clientele, but when she came across something that was too much even for her to deal with she used to turn to me. I dreaded seeing her arriving at the door, taking off her helmet, with her motor scooter parked outside. Although I was very fond of her, if she had a problem that she was not able to deal with I knew it was going to be a truly awful mess that landed on my plate.

I was thus faced with an existential crisis. Either I would have to put my head down and simply dish out tranquillisers to all and sundry for the rest of my life and give up any attempt to relate to these people as human beings, or I would have to be quite ruthless in organising my time and take control of the situation so as not to be overwhelmed. I decided to adopt the latter approach, to set up an appointment system and only see nine or ten patients in an afternoon. In this way I would have time to listen to their stories and to establish a personal relationship, in the hope of helping them to bring about a real change in their lives. Otherwise I knew that I would be caught on a treadmill, as happens to too many psychiatrists early in their career. They then have only a couple of minutes with each patient to review medication and change the prescription from one antidepressant or tranquilliser to another.

There was one heroic woman whose story gives a clearer picture of the problems I was faced with in the clinic. At the time I knew her she was married to a bus conductor who was a hopeless alcoholic. He worked on a local bus route in Ballyfermot and I remember hearing that he and one of the drivers often used to stop the bus, leave all the passengers sitting there, go into a pub for several drinks and then return to the bus without a murmur of dissent from the people waiting to continue their journey.

When Ann first came to see me she was in a terrible plight. She told me that usually she got up to face two sets of twins under two years of age with no money, as her husband had drunk all his wages, with no milk in the house to feed the children. On one occasion when her husband had been admitted to St Patrick's Hospital to dry out from an alcoholic bout, she walked four or five miles to see him and back again. She hadn't even the money for the bus fare. When she got to the hospital she found him sitting up in bed, very pleased with himself, eating a nice pork chop dinner, while she sat there hungrily watching him, knowing she had to return to an empty house with no food for herself or her children.

Needless to say she was depressed and anxious much of the time. On one occasion she felt so bad that she went down to one of the dispensary doctors (the old dispensary system for free treatment for the poor was still current at that time). When she got to the head of the queue and entered his office, she found he was under so much pressure that he was standing up, too busy even to sit down. She looked at him, and the state he was in, and realised it would be quite hopeless to try to talk to him about her problems. So she just told him the child had a sore throat and went home, still bursting with tension. There were many instances of a similar kind she would tell me about but, as with so many other cases, one felt helpless and frustrated at being able to do so little to help.

Dr Angus O'Rourke, who was one of the private GPs serving the area, took a special interest in Ann and tried to encourage her, in spite of all her difficulties, to develop herself and break out of the quagmire she was in. He refused her request for Valium and suggested that she went back to school instead. With a lot of encouragement from both of us, she eventually built up enough confidence to decide to study for her Leaving Certificate. At that time there was no secondary school in Ballyfermot and the youngsters either dropped out after completing their time in primary school or went on to the technical college. Here there were mainly practical courses, such as apprenticeships for learning a trade, and also a number of courses for arts and crafts – dressmaking, pottery, cooking, etc. These were availed of by some of the married women in the area, although some students also went on to study for the Intermediate and Leaving Certificates.

Ann described what happened when she went to enrol and joined the queue for the Intermediate Certificate. There was another queue of women lining up to register for the arts and crafts courses, many of them her friends and neighbours. While she stood there, embarrassed, among all the young girls, the women were calling and jeering at her, 'Ann, you're in the wrong queue, what do you think you're at', and so on. With quite extraordinary courage and determination, however, she stuck it out, enduring all the ridicule until she signed up to study for her Intermediate Certificate. After a lot of struggle and heartache, she passed her exams and even went on to get a few honours in the Leaving Certificate. With continuing encouragement from Angus O'Rourke, she was actually accepted by Trinity College as a mature student to study for an arts degree. She did this, in spite of all the difficulties of trying to raise a large family and deal with an alcoholic husband.

In the years since then Ann has left all these difficulties far behind her. Her husband became sober a good many years ago, with the help of AA, and they are now back living together, contented and happy. The family are all grown up, doing well and leading their own lives. So, thank God, after all her struggles, everything has turned out well.

The same Dr O'Rourke who had helped Ann so much told me another interesting tale. He was called to attend a woman of the Traveller community (whose family had settled in one of the Corporation houses) who was in labour and on the point of delivering yet another baby. When he went upstairs he found her completely unattended, although she was just about to give birth. Angered by her plight, he went downstairs to try to find someone to help. To his consternation he found a group of men in the front parlour with a mare in the throes of delivering a foal. Looking back on this afterwards he realised that the delivery of a healthy young foal was more important to them than the arrival of yet another child.

You never knew what might happen next in the psychiatric clinic. One day, when I was particularly busy, Agnes, a depressed and apathetic middle-aged woman, came to see me. She felt she had no energy or interest in going on with the struggle of looking after her family. There was nothing in her current life to explain the state she was in so I thought I would put her under hypnosis to see what, if anything, might lie behind these symptoms. She went easily into a deep trance and, to my surprise, spontaneously went back to a time about ten years before when she had been raped. She went into a full catharsis of the experience, as if it were taking place at that moment.

When I brought her out of the trance I found, to my alarm, that she was paralysed from the waist down and could neither walk nor stand. Here was I, with nearly a dozen people in the waiting room, who had seen an apparently healthy woman walk into my office. I was on the verge of panic, faced with having to call an ambulance and have her carried out on a stretcher, but, remembering the advice of someone who had been involved in a similar situation, I put her back into a deep hypnotic trance, suggesting forcefully that when she awoke this time she would have no recollection whatsoever of the terrifying experience she had undergone ten years before. To my great relief, when she awoke, the paralysis of her legs had disappeared and she was able to walk normally again. Later I was able to bring her back to the clinic and help her, more gently, to integrate the traumatic experience, so that gradually she made a good recovery. It was experiences like this that gradually taught me that one has to hasten slowly – *festina lente* – to create a safe context within which a person is able to face a painful past.

Another very different scenario came my way. Bill, a bus conductor from Crumlin who was a gambler, turned up at the clinic because he had not only spent all his salary on horses but had gambled away money he had collected on the buses and was in serious trouble. If he did not return this money he was in danger of losing his job. As I mentioned earlier, we were interested at this time in behavioural therapy and in aversive conditioning. I decided to try the same machine that I had used in attempting to deal with the girl who was continually banging her head in the children's unit, to see if I could turn my patient away from any desire to gamble. I asked him which race had been the most exciting experience he could recall in recent times. This was the year when Arkle won the

Cheltenham Gold Cup, and he agreed that this was the race. Then, having hooked him up to the machine, which would give a painful shock at the appropriate moment, I put him under hypnosis and got him to relive the race as if he were there. To my amazement he took off like a radio commentator, watching the race from the very start. I waited until the horses had jumped the last fence and he was in a state of high excitement, then I activated the machine, which gave him an unpleasant shock. I repeated this manoeuvre over and over again on a number of occasions. Not only did he become less and less interested in gambling, but he told me that even the thought of putting a bet on a horse made him feel sick in his stomach. However, as the general experience in relation to behavioural therapy has shown, negative aversive conditioning usually only has a temporary effect. He remained free from gambling for almost a year but then gradually drifted back and was as bad as ever. I think the lesson here is that there is no solution other than the person ultimately deciding that they have to change. This is why, at the end of the day, only the approach of Alcoholics Anonymous, Gamblers Anonymous and similar therapeutic programmes seem to hold out any real hope of permanent success.

I was so frustrated with the situation in Ballyfermot that I got in touch with all the professionals in the area – the dispensary doctors, the private GPs, the social workers, the Little Sisters of the Assumption, the clergy, representatives of the Tenants Association and the voluntary agencies – to see if, by forming a network of all those involved, we could do something to ease the situation. This led eventually to the formation of the Irish Foundation for Human Development, but I will describe that story in a later chapter.

I ran St Loman's for the next few years and gradually tried to organise better services in the community, but I was increasingly frustrated by our not having control of direct admissions and the impossibility, therefore, of relating the in-patient work to the surrounding communities of Lucan, Crumlin, Ballyfermot and Clondalkin. It was impossible to get John Dunne to listen to any proposal for change in the service as a whole and the shambles represented by St Brendan's and St Ita's continued unabated. It was also frustrating only being able to deal with women, which meant that, if I felt it was necessary for a man in Ballyfermot to be admitted to hospital, he had to go into St Brendan's. Nor could he then be transferred to St

Loman's, which meant that I lost contact with him and there was no possibility of maintaining continuity of care.

To ease our frustrations Dermot Walsh (who at that time was working with me in St Loman's) and I wrote a plan for the development of services in the Dublin area. I borrowed heavily for this from the thesis I had written in Harvard; its main thrust was that the city and county of Dublin should be broken up into districts. Then psychiatric teams would be created to serve each district and related not to a hospital but to the population of the area served. The report criticised the current situation, where patients were first admitted to a private facility, whenever this could be afforded, and then, when the money ran out, were dumped into the public services.

As time went by, the retirement of John Dunne as Chief RMS began to loom on the horizon. In fact he should have gone two years earlier, when he reached the age of sixty-five, but he was anxious to stay on as long as possible and didn't actually go until 1965. Having been involved in the War of Independence, he was quite a close friend of Seán Lemass, who was Taoiseach at the time. When his official retirement date arrived, he appealed personally to Lemass and, through this means, got an extension of a further two years. As it turned out, this delay had significant consequences for my own career.

PART FOUR

Chief Psychiatrist
1965–1985

16

Chief Psychiatrist

In 1965 several posts became vacant and were advertised. Almost simultaneously, the post of superintendent of St Loman's and John Dunne's job in St Brendan's came on stream. The Department of Health had given considerable thought to the post of Chief Resident Medical Superintendent in St Brendan's and eventually decided it should be transformed into that of Chief Psychiatrist, thus not emphasising the hospital component, but nevertheless incorporating all the functions of the Chief RMS. I was particularly interested in the job of Physician Superintendent of St Loman's, as I was happy working there. In view of my relative youth (I was just approaching thirty-six years of age) and lack of experience, I didn't see myself as a serious contender for the post of Chief Psychiatrist. Nevertheless, I applied for both jobs but put my serious hopes on that in St Loman's.

I went for the interview for the post in St Loman's and was delighted to hear that I was successful. I also attended the interview for the post of Chief Psychiatrist, just for the experience, without any expectation of being successful. I brought the report that we had written thinking I would present it to the interview board to give them some idea of my views for the future development of psychiatric services. When I entered the room, I discovered that Dr Norman Moore, the Director of St Patrick's, was a member of the board. As I stood there I thought, if I were to give him a copy of this report, which effectively saw no future for private psychiatry in the Dublin area, that would be the end of any prospect I might have had of getting this job. But then I thought that I had no chance of being appointed Chief Psychiatrist anyway, so I handed over the report and carried on with the interview. I noticed that, while the others were asking me questions, Norman Moore was scrutinising the report.

To my amazement, over the next few weeks, rumours began to filter through that I had been selected for the post of Chief Psychiatrist. I simply couldn't believe it until the final confirmation came through. I always had great respect for the integrity of Norman Moore, although I didn't agree with his views on psychiatry, but this was certainly confirmation of his honesty and his genuine desire to see better psychiatric services develop, for if he had been simply protective of his private psychiatric interests all he would have had to say at the board was that I was a bit young and inexperienced and that would have been that. It's not often that one comes across such an example of unselfish honesty and concern for the welfare of patients.

When I got over the initial shock and elation of being appointed as Chief Psychiatrist, I was filled with trepidation. When I arrived in St Brendan's to take up my new post, I was faced with the enormity of the task confronting me and I wondered how I had got myself into such a position. I think there are perhaps two reasons why it happened, both of which relate to my specific personality: firstly, whenever I was faced with a challenge, if I didn't succeed, I felt a total failure and experienced an existential anxiety which drove me on; secondly, I had an unusual ability to see things from a different angle and hence to realise what alternative possibilities there might be. Perhaps this capacity to see things in a different way arose out of the fantasy world created by my maverick father, in which I was steeped during my developing years.

Whatever about that, here I was faced with the onerous task of trying to initiate some change or movement in an antiquated, appallingly overcrowded, chaotic situation. The morale among the patients and staff could hardly have been lower. The hopelessly understaffed medical personnel were almost as institutionalised as the patients. I felt that some radical initiative that would grasp the attention of the public, and of the patients and staff of the hospital, was necessary if a perception that real change was beginning was to take hold.

Fortunately a new male admission building had recently been completed, modern and functional in design, and below this, directly inside the boundary wall of the hospital, there was a new psychiatric out-patient unit. There was a large open space at this point where a new entrance to the hospital was potentially possible, but, as things stood, the forbidding boundary wall hid the new buildings. I firstly decided to knock down the high stone wall surrounding the hospital and to create a new entrance where the psychiatric out-patients building was being built. I then decided to close the gate of the present entrance, thus, without any additional capital expenditure, giving a free open access to the hospital, where the first building one encountered was a modern out-patients unit rather than a hospital ward. This grabbed the attention of the public and our patients presented no problem with the removal of the wall. However, the 'sane' people of Dublin began to vandalise the hospital and terrorise the patients, so that eventually we had to erect a railing where the wall had been.

Given the small number of doctors, and the poor state of morale in the institution, I felt the next thing to do was to try to attract young medical personnel. To this end we advertised for doctors who might be interested in a career in psychiatry. The response to this was demoralising indeed. Only five doctors applied and, of these, four had a history of either alcoholism or drug addiction. There was only one who was enthusiastic and showed promise, a young Indian doctor who had done his medical training in Dublin – Dr Joe Fernandez. He turned out to be one of the most loyal, hard-working and innovative psychiatrists I have had the good fortune to work with.

In March 1966 I put forward my first report on the proposed development of psychiatric services to the then Dublin Health Authority. The opening paragraphs of this stated:

> In Dublin, as elsewhere in this country, the emphasis has been on the treatment of patients in hospital while community services have been relatively undeveloped. In our hospitals this emphasis on hospitalisation has led to serious overcrowding in buildings which are, in the main, antiquated, with inadequate utility services, resulting, in turn, in therapeutic inactivity, a low state of morale, and an atmosphere not generally conducive to recovery. These conditions have hampered the recruitment and training of psychiatric staff, thus further aggravating the position and, over the years, have given rise to a poor public image of the psychiatric services in Dublin.
>
> The task facing us then is to develop psychiatric services

centred on the community and related to the population areas which they serve. We must make a fundamental break with the notion of the hospital with an allocation of doctors and nurses, rigidly related to the number of beds. This will involve the division of Dublin City and County into catchment areas, with a complete co-ordination of the hospital facilities with the community and domiciliary services, so that they form an integrated whole with continuity of care and treatment at every level, each area being served by its own psychiatric team.

These ideas were derived essentially from the plan already mentioned, and the Dublin Health Authority adopted the report. This plan was further developed in a second report in 1972. Each of these sectors would develop a comprehensive range of alternative facilities, including in-patient beds for acute and long-stay patients in each psychiatric sector, with continuity of care, whether in hospital or in the community, being provided by the psychiatric team serving that district. It was proposed that these community-based services should be developed as an alternative to the large, traditional mental hospital, which would gradually be phased out.

It should be pointed out that this plan was generated during the economic boom of the 1960s, known as the Lemass era. There was a mood of optimism and hope at the time. We were about to reach full employment, with jobs for everyone. At last Ireland was on the move and widespread demographic changes were taking place in society. Television was changing the mental climate, whilst the power of the Church and other conservative institutions was waning. Emigration had virtually ceased and there was even hope that a population increase was on the way, as Irish emigrants were returning home to take part in the new industrial development.

Due to all these factors there was hope that increased finance would be directed towards the development of what had, until then, always been the 'Cinderella services – psychiatry, geriatrics and mental retardation'. I was naïve enough to believe that when the authorities and public representatives enthusiastically accepted a community psychiatric plan it meant that there was a real intention to finance and implement it. I didn't realise then that institutions like mental hospitals, and prisons, do not come into existence by chance. There are processes continually at work within society that mitigate against the acceptance back into normal life of those who have already been rejected by the community. I didn't realise that mental hospitals are not something separate from the rest of society. They represent one end of a spectrum of interconnected processes, which run through every aspect of society, from the individual to the family to the wider community, from the suburban homes of the wealthy to the poorest housing estates. Mental hospitals are not places where those suffering from mental illness come to be treated and returned well again to the community. They are simply places where all those for whom society has no place are dumped to get them out of sight – the aged, the mentally retarded, the epileptic, the disturbed, and all those who lack the competence and where-withal to gain a foothold in society.

Because the capital resources didn't materialise, we were forced instead to do things piecemeal, availing of any opportunity as it arose. For this reason progress was much slower and less satisfactory than I had originally hoped. Whenever Dublin Corporation was taking over an old estate to build a new housing development, there was usually a large house that would normally be demolished. We would try to get possession of these and in this way acquired a dozen or more fine old buildings, a number of which were in quite good condition. Likewise, whenever an old school, a nursing home or an unused hospital unit became available, it was acquired for us and put to use, usually without any major capital investment, as day or residential accommodation in the service of our overall objective.

The basic idea of developing psychiatric services by sector was there from the beginning, but the facilities in each area were established quite haphazardly, rather than in an ordered way, and were often far from ideal. This is how things actually took shape. Were it not for the fact that some facilities became available to us in this way, given the failure of the government to provide the necessary financial support for new facilities, I believe that many of us would simply have lost heart and thrown in the sponge.

17

The Chair of Psychiatry

In my predecessor's time the Chair of Psychiatry in University College Dublin (UCD) was traditionally associated with the public
mental hospital. This was the only psychiatric professorship in
Dublin at the time, but psychiatry was generally perceived to be of
little importance and the students simply came to the hospital for
a few clinical demonstrations prior to graduating. Professor Tom
Murphy was Registrar of University College and he was flexing his
muscles with a view to becoming president. He and the authorities
of the university were anxious to strengthen the role of the college
versus the powerful teaching general hospitals – the Mater and St
Vincent's. In this struggle psychiatry was pivotally placed, because
the psychiatric chair was of little importance and was not sought by
either teaching hospital. However, John Dunne's retirement ushered
in a new era.

For the first time the professorship of psychiatry became important, but it was critical, if the status of the public psychiatric services were ever to change, that it should remain within the public
domain. At that time, if the relatives of any psychiatric patient could
scrape enough money together, they would have the person admitted to one of the private mental hospitals. When they ran out of
money, the patient would drift into the public facility. So we had a
ghetto service of patients who were chronic by the time they entered
it, or else were too poor to have any choice about where they went
in the first place. It was clear to me that, unless one could find some
way to change this pattern, public psychiatry was always going to remain a dumping ground.

The selection of a professor in UCD at that time was an appalling business. There was no Board of Assessors or proper interviewing procedure, such as now exists. The prospective candidate had to visit and solicit the vote of every member of the medical faculty then the Academic Council, not just in UCD but throughout the whole of the National University, in Cork, Galway and Maynooth – several hundred people. Then one had to appeal to the members of the governing body and finally the Senate of the NUI. Tom Murphy told me it was the toughest struggle for a chair in the history of the university.

Prior to my appearing on the scene, it had been generally assumed that the Medical Director of St John of God's Psychiatric Hospital would take the chair, with the support of St Vincent's Hospital, Elm Park. But then, late in the day, the Mater Hospital people realised what was happening and, not wanting the chair to go to St Vincent's, put forward their own candidate. By this time the situation was so acute that the politicians had become involved and Fianna Fáil actually put the whip on their members in the governing body and the Senate to ensure that all those with Fianna Fáil affiliations would vote for the Mater candidate. The effect of this was to divide the vote between the two teaching hospitals. With the backing of Professor Tom Murphy and the centre block of those who wanted to strengthen the position of the university vis-à-vis the hospitals, I won the day, to the surprise of everyone. I believe this was a turning point for the development of psychiatry in Ireland, because there was now a major professorial chair, the only one in the country at that stage, centred in the public service.

Having obtained the professorship of psychiatry, the way was open to negotiate with the two main private psychiatric hospitals – St Patrick's and St John of God's. St Patrick's was the oldest mental hospital in Ireland. It had been started originally by Dean Swift, who wrote in his epitaph the lines:

He gave the little wealth he had
to found a home for fools and mad
and showed with one satiric touch
no nation needed it so much.

Dr Norman Moore was the medical superintendent there at the time and, once again, as in the case of my appointment as Chief Psychiatrist, I found him open and generous, willing to put the overall development of psychiatry before the selfish interests of private practice. I think he also realised that, unless he threw his lot in with the development of the psychiatric services generally, in time the future of a purely private institution would be in doubt. Whatever about that, he accepted the principle that St Patrick's would take on responsibility for one of the new psychiatric sectors. I had managed to take over a disused TB unit in St Kevin's (later to become St James' Hospital), the large general hospital nearby, and had secured an appropriate budget to run the service. Dr Moore then took it over and arranged staffing using doctors and nurses from St Patrick's.

Having succeeded in making this arrangement with St Patrick's, I turned my attention to St John of God's Psychiatric Hospital. It so happened that a small private hospital, Cluain Mhuire, which had been run by the Mercy Order and was linked to the Mater Hospital, was not doing well and the Order was anxious to be rid of it. We arranged with them that, if the Health Authority paid off a debt of £60,000 that they had accumulated and gave an extra £20,000, making £80,000 in total, they would be willing to sell. This hospital was a three-storey building, in good condition, on four acres in an ideal location on Newtownpark Avenue near Blackrock and not too far from St John of God's. This was an amazing bargain, given the increasing value of land in that area, providing a very suitable location from which to serve the south-east area of Dublin. I put the proposition to the civil servants in the Department of Health, thinking they would jump at the opportunity, but week after week went by without a favourable response, until it looked as if the whole deal would fail. Fortunately, at the last moment the then secretary of the department finally agreed and we finalised the transaction, to my great relief. Some time later I ran into the secretary of the department at a medical function and, somewhat hypocritically, thanked him for getting the deal through. He looked at me condescendingly and said, 'I held it up as long as I could.' This facility was then handed over to St John of God's to run as a public psychiatric sector for the south-east area of Dublin.

This kind of prevarication was fairly typical of the attitude of civil servants in government departments at that time. The whole ethos was intensely conservative. It was safer to delay than to make a positive decision to take any action that might bring criticism upon the minister. Although more than half a century had elapsed since the British left the country, the Civil Service still had the character-istics of a colonial administration. When you put forward a sugges-tion, the typical response was, 'What are the British doing?' Until we joined the EU, it was as if their mental horizon didn't extend be-yond the English Channel. This was a tragedy because, had they looked to mainland Europe for inspiration as to what was happen-ing, for instance, in small countries like the Netherlands or Den-mark, these would have been far more suitable models for our needs than Britain was. Indeed, we often took on some British develop-ment at the very point where, its having failed, they were about to give it up. Throughout my whole career I can't remember the de-partment officials ever coming up with a positive suggestion for de-velopment, only reasons why something should be delayed or shouldn't be done.

In St Vincent's, Elm Park, there was a clinical teaching block which was little used. I proposed to the people in the Department of Health that, if they provided the finance, we could create a psy-chiatric unit on the ground floor, with a day hospital in the base-ment. Then we could develop a geriatric unit in a newly constructed second floor, which would also provide a walk-through to the private hospital. After the usual struggle, the department finally agreed and, as the authorities in St Vincent's couldn't come up with the finance to use the building for any other purpose, we won the day. On the north side, the Mater Hospital traditionally had a link to another private psychiatric hospital, St Vincent's, Fairview. There was no psy-chiatric unit in the Mater but, thanks to the influence of the UCD professorship, it was possible to negotiate the use of a proportion of the beds in St Vincent's, Fairview, for public psychiatric patients. These were then made available to the psychiatric team in charge of the sector for Dublin North Central. Then, in north-west Dublin, I was able to acquire two units for public psychiatric purposes in the James Connolly Memorial Hospital. This had been built as a large tuberculosis sanatorium by Dr Noel Browne when he was Minister for Health, but, when TB was no longer a major problem, it was re-developed as a general hospital for the surrounding area. In this way it was possible to provide a psychiatric unit in the general hospital for the psychiatric sector in that area.

18

Psychiatric Administration

Having been appointed Professor of Psychiatry I was faced with a personal dilemma – a parting of the ways. The way was open for me to establish a prestigious professorial unit in one of the major teaching hospitals, St Vincent's, Elm Park. This, had I availed of it, would have provided the opportunity to create a professorial unit with a high standard of practice and research, as well as opening up for me personally prospects for a lucrative private practice. I would have been able to introduce a psychotherapeutic emphasis with medical students and in the training of young psychiatrists, psychologists and other personnel. Also it would have been possible to introduce what were then new and different approaches to current psychiatric practice in Ireland.

All of this sounds eminently reasonable but, if one looks at psychiatric programmes around the world where prestigious teaching units of this kind have been established, the professorial teaching unit tends to become an elite service that caters for the 'good' patient, that is the acutely ill, those with short-term conditions with a good prognosis. These patients tend to be middle class and better educated. By contrast the 'bad' patient, usually from a poor, socially deprived background, often unemployed with poor social and work skills, is typically transferred on for care to the public service. These are more likely to be psychotic and chronic. What happens where this kind of approach is developed is that the young psychiatrist in training learns to distinguish between the 'good' and 'bad' patient. I found this to be the situation when I visited the famous Langley Porter Centre in San Francisco, and again in Athens, Greece, where there was a highly developed professorial unit and shocking conditions a few kilometres away in the enormous mental institution there, Daphne. In such circumstances, the public psychiatric sector is usually left grossly understaffed, with poorly trained psychiatric personnel and poor morale, providing sub-standard care.

The second alternative was to centre my position as Chief Psychiatrist and professor firmly in the public psychiatric service. This made it possible, with all its disappointments and shortcomings, to build up a community psychiatric framework so that the public service took on a dominant role in the development of psychiatric services. The disadvantage of following this line of development – and there is always a negative side to any decision – was that it was not possible to concentrate as much as one would have liked on the quality of psychiatric training or the standard of psychiatric practice. Hence, although a community psychiatric framework was introduced, the methods of practice and the type of training of most of those who were recruited to staff the new psychiatric districts were still in the mould of the old custodial institutional approach. The same was true of those who emerged out of the mental hospitals. Their main emphasis was on medical and pharmaceutical forms of care and treatment. I did not appreciate the full significance of this at the time. Nevertheless, if I were faced with the same decision again, I would, on balance, take the same, latter alternative.

In 1968 I was awarded a World Health Fellowship for two months and I availed of this to visit as many psychiatric centres as I could across the United States. Prior to my travelling to the United States I had discussed with Dr Norman Moore the possibility of creating a psychiatric chair in Trinity College. He was keen to see this happen and encouraged me to meet Peter Beckett, who at that time was working in a very prestigious unit in Detroit, to see if he would be interested in returning to Ireland. Peter was a cousin of the great playwright Samuel Beckett and was a highly regarded psychiatrist. Dr Moore and I both felt he would be an ideal choice as professor and that his return would greatly benefit the development of psychiatry in Ireland.

I did visit Peter Beckett, in the Lafayette Clinic in Detroit, where he was doing research into schizophrenia. To my surprise, because he already had a considerable reputation in the States, he was very open and indeed enthusiastic about the idea of returning to Ireland. On the final leg of my trip I went to visit the well thought of psychiatric unit in McGill University in Montreal. Dr Noel Walsh, a highly-qualified Irish psychiatrist, was working there at the time. I put it to him that if he were prepared to return to Dublin it might be possible to get him appointed to the new unit in St Vincent's, Elm Park, and also to create a clinical Chair of Psychiatry in my department in UCD. On my return to Ireland, Trinity College agreed to the creation of a professorship in psychiatry. In due course, Peter Beckett was appointed and he did indeed justify our hopes, making a valuable contribution to the general development of the services. Out of respect for Norman Moore, Trinity College created a second Chair of Psychiatry for the medical director of St Patrick's Hospital.

When Dr Noel Walsh returned to Ireland he was, as I had hoped, appointed as Clinical Professor of Psychiatry in UCD and as Director of the Psychiatric Unit in St Vincent's, Elm Park. Given the rivalry between the two major general hospitals affiliated to UCD, the university had to agree to the creation of a second Chair of clinical psychiatry in the Mater. This was awarded to Dr Sean Malone. Thus we finally had three chairs of psychiatry in UCD, mine as Head of Department and two clinical chairs in St Vincent's and the Mater respectively.

Following on from the dual role of my position as Chief Psychiatrist and part-time Professor of Psychiatry, both of these clinical professorships were also made part-time, given that the incumbents already had major clinical commitments. Later, the same procedure was followed in Trinity and the chair was created as a joint appointment between a clinical directorship of the sector service and the professorship in the university. The same principle was applied in Cork and Galway, where joint appointments of Clinical Director and Professor of Psychiatry attached to the teaching general hospitals was adopted. This had the advantage of basing the teaching posts firmly in the public psychiatric service. It had the disadvantage that the person appointed had, like myself, to divide their time between their teaching responsibilities and a heavy clinical and administrative commitment, leaving them insufficient time to concentrate effectively on both.

I was also anxious to set up a joint postgraduate training programme for psychiatrists. Once Peter Beckett was established back in Dublin, I approached him to see if he would be interested. I sat with him for an hour in his car outside St Patrick's and put the idea to him. After some considerable persuasion, not only did he agree but he became quite enthusiastic about the proposal. We next approached Tom Lynch, who had by this time been appointed professor of psychiatry in the College of Surgeons. He also came on side, so we worked out a proposal for unified postgraduate training. All that remained was to get agreement from the Department of Health, and funding for the project. The three of us, with Norman Moore, visited the department and, to my surprise, Norman introduced the proposal as Professor Beckett's idea. The reason for mentioning this is not that it is important whose idea it was, but this had serious implications for the future, for, from that time onwards, St Patrick's relentlessly took over the teaching programme. This might have been all right if Peter Beckett had lived, for he had trained in the States, where the main focus was on psychotherapy in the training of psychiatrists. But, once he was gone, the medical ethos and the emphasis on neurophysiology and psychopharmacology became central. This was accentuated further with the advent of the Royal College of Psychiatrists and the introduction of the Membership in Psychiatry. This view essentially treats the human being as a machine to be tinkered with, and the relationship to the person tends to get lost.

Peter Beckett was a fine human being. His only difficulty was that he was a perfectionist and so efficient that, in the Irish context, people asked more and more of him. He didn't drink or smoke, walked to work and was a model of healthy living. But, as more and more work was piled upon him, I could see he was under increasing stress. One day he just keeled over with a massive heart attack. He was a big loss to psychiatry in Ireland.

Along with Peter Beckett, I had been made a member of the board to plan the new St James' Hospital. As the planning was at an early stage I suggested that, before going any further, it would be wise to set up a research project to establish 'who needs to go to hospital' rather than being dealt with by primary care services in the community. The chairman of the board dismissed this saying, 'Oh, we've no time for that, this hospital is going to be built in the next couple of years.' Ten years later it was still not completed, and we still don't know who needs to go to hospital and who would be better dealt with in primary care.

The Health Act was introduced in 1970 and created the new health boards, with the Eastern Health Board covering not only the

Dublin area but also Wicklow and north Kildare. In preparation for the setting up of the health boards, McKinsey, the firm of consultants, were brought in to advise on how this should be done. They spent several months studying the Dublin Health Authority and the other health organisations around the country. I had many meetings with them and tried my best to convince them to bring the different strata of the health services – general practice, community care, the general hospitals (including the voluntary general hospitals) and the mental health services – together under one unified administration. They actually agreed that this would be the ideal course to pursue but made the point that in the current political circumstances it was not a practical possibility. They then went ahead and recommended a tripartite administration, general hospitals, community care (which would not include general practice) and the mental health services. Each of these three divisions of the health service was to be under the control of a separate programme manager. This unsatisfactory division of health administration was modelled on the British NHS, where it had already caused major problems in the fragmentation of services in that country. Here was a situation where most of the psychiatric services were being decentralised into the community and the attempt was being made to run down and close the large mental hospitals, yet 'community care' was under a completely separate administration. I felt at the time that this was both unnecessary and most unfortunate.

Incidentally, a rather amusing thing happened while the McKinsey consultants were conducting their research. One evening, a prominent British psychiatrist was visiting Ireland. I already had a meeting arranged with the McKinsey people, but several of my colleagues insisted that I should at least come to be introduced to this 'important' psychiatrist. I reluctantly agreed to call in to meet him on the way to my meeting. I ordered a pint of Guinness and walked over to be introduced to him but when we shook hands I accidentally tipped my pint of stout all down the front of his suit. I apologised profusely and then excused myself to go to my other meeting. I still believe this was just an unfortunate accident, but a number of my colleagues have insisted that it was my unconscious antipathy to the British establishment that was responsible.

When the McKinsey consultants had finished their work they were sufficiently impressed with me to suggest that I should be appointed programme manager over the psychiatric, geriatric and mental retardation services. Needless to say, this was not at all to the liking of the rest of the senior lay management. During the short period when I was acting as programme manager, I produced a report on the development of geriatric and psycho-geriatric services in the eastern region. I also set about rationalising the mental retardation services, which were mostly run by voluntary agencies, and had small units here and there throughout the Dublin area, often duplicating services in one area while there was nothing in another. I attempted to follow the same broad principles as in the development of psychiatric services, dividing Dublin into four quadrants, two to the north of the river and two on the south; and I applied the same thinking to the development of child psychiatric services. I then asked the different voluntary agencies to concentrate their efforts in one or other of these areas, as appropriate. On the whole they accepted my recommendations and this brought some logic into the situation. However, when it was felt that sufficient time had elapsed, I was dispatched back to my role as Chief Psychiatrist and a lay programme manager was appointed in my place.

In 1972 I presented a second report to the recently created Eastern Health Board, describing the developments in the psychiatric service over the previous six or seven years since I had taken over the role of Chief Psychiatrist. Looking back, I can see that when I was generating the basic concepts of the programme I was part of a wave of enthusiasm that was current then in the United States and Britain. My experience with Joshua Bierer and in the Harvard School of Public Health led me to the mistaken belief that there was general acceptance of the sort of optimistic vision I had for the development of a community psychiatry based on democratic human relationships. I simply didn't realise that a plan such as I envisaged could only succeed if, first of all, the psychiatric team that was to implement it had real skills and enthusiasm for the sort of psychotherapeutic relationships that could make it work, and secondly, that they were able to relate to a properly organised system of primary health care. By this I mean that broadly based groups of general practitioners with ancillary staff such as social workers, psychologists and nurses, as were being developed at that time in Canada, were organically linked to the broader aspects of community care and social welfare services. Such practices in Canada have demonstrated that they normally only have to transfer a small number of patients on to specialised medical or psychiatric services.

I should mention here that while I was involved in the development of the psychiatric programme, I had also continued my contacts with the GPs and other health professionals in the Ballyfermot area. By 1968 we had managed to get the agreement of all the doctors – both the dispensary doctors and the private practitioners in the area – to come together into four comprehensive group practices of the kind I have mentioned. All that was needed was to get the agreement and necessary financial support from the Department of Health for the scheme to go ahead. I felt that if a pilot programme in primary health care of this kind were established, and if it were successful, it could in time lead to a fundamental change in the organisation of health services in the country as a whole.

I went to the Department of Health with Dr Angus O'Rourke, one of the GPs in the area, to have a personal meeting with the then secretary of the department. He told us that the department was already working on a comprehensive reorganisation of general practice and that, therefore, there was no need to entertain a scheme such as ours. What he was talking about, although I didn't realise it at the time, was the termination of the old dispensary doctor system, replacing it by freedom of choice for people to choose their own general practitioner. After a long negotiation with the medical bodies this was decided, on a fee-for-service basis, and it eventually became law in the Health Act of 1970. Sadly, far from introducing a broadly based integrated system of primary health care, this new arrangement further fragmented the services and separated general practice from the rest of community care more than ever.

Looking back I can see it was naïve on my part to think that the secretary of the Department of Health was going to listen to a psychiatrist trying to tell him about the need for an integrated system of primary health care. Thus the opportunity to introduce a pilot scheme for a population of 40,000 in the Dublin area was lost. It is only now, after more than a quarter of a century, that the Department of Health, facing chaos in Accident and Emergency Departments across the country, is at last seriously considering the introduction of a broadly based primary health care system. With the creation of the new Health Service Executive and the appointment of a very capable and far-sighted paediatrician, Brendan

Drumm, I think there is some hope that at last something may happen. It is just possible that, if a pilot scheme of primary health care had been set up in Ballyfermot at that time and, if it had proved successful, and had been generalised across the country, we would not be facing the chaos currently arising from the over-use of general hospitals that is currently happening. Also, if such a system of integrated primary care had been established at that time, the development of community psychiatric services might have been more successful.

During the 1970s a number of factors had intervened that militated against the full implementation of the plan to decentralise psychiatric services and close down the old mental hospitals: firstly, community psychiatric development was taking place nearly ten years later than in countries like Britain, Italy, France and the United States. By the time it should really have been getting under way a prolonged recession had intervened and the first of several oil crises was already upon us. Secondly, because of the deepening recession, structural changes affecting society and the changing pattern of industrial technology, the number of unemployed was rising. Thus the modest capital input that would have enabled the alternative facilities to be provided was not forthcoming. These developments were therefore uneven and in no psychiatric sector was there a sufficient range of facilities to provide an adequate service for a catchment population. With the establishment of the Eastern Health Board in 1970, the functional area was enlarged to include Counties Wicklow and Kildare. In addition, during the period when these changes were being attempted, the population of Dublin had increased rapidly and had nearly doubled since 1960. The parallel services for adult mental retardation and the elderly remained relatively undeveloped, so that while there was a considerable reduction in the number of psychiatric patients in the two mental hospitals, the number of elderly and adult mentally retarded remained virtually unchanged. Furthermore, examination of St Brendan's revealed that we were dealing with an ageing population. The creation of large, impersonal housing estates on the periphery of Dublin for young families from the city centre to move to, thus fragmenting the extended family structure and leaving the elderly behind without support, resulted in increased pressure on the psychiatric services, particularly for the admission of these old people to hospital. There was not usually any psychiatric problem with these elderly people, it was just that they could no longer manage for themselves. Also I had, at that time, little awareness of the strength with which a living system, like the traditional mental hospital, will resist change and manifest its strong will to survive by maintaining itself as far as possible as it is. It was only years later, when I became aware of systems theory, that I realised the significance of these issues. A number of new problems were also appearing on the horizon, such as the abuse of serious drugs like heroin and cocaine, initially in the city centre and then extending out to the new housing estates, with the attendant rise in crime to support the addiction. There was also a rise in the number of homeless and an increasing problem of alcohol abuse, particularly among young people, especially young women.

By the late 1970s, because of all these factors, the mental hospital had not faded away as rapidly as I had hoped and overcrowding was becoming a serious problem once again. Also the old buildings were deteriorating. It is ironic that the financial investment that had been put into shoring them up over the past ten years would have been more than sufficient to create the full range of alternative community facilities, had the money only been spent at the right time and in the right place.

In 1978 all of this culminated in something of a public crisis. One week after I returned from my first trip to India, some junior doctors wrote a letter to the paper stating that there were rats and cockroaches in the wards. This resulted in a public outcry and for one whole week it dominated the headlines in the Dublin newspapers. Eventually Charlie Haughey, the then Minister for Health, felt it necessary to visit St Brendan's to restore public confidence. He said to me with some irritation, 'You should get off your arse and come back in here to manage this hospital.'

We were now experiencing a similar reaction to what had already happened in the US, Britain and other European countries during the 1970s. The failure to provide the infrastructure and financial resources to make community psychiatry work had led to disillusionment and a backlash against the very concept. This was the time of editorials such as 'The Ruthless Wanderer' and 'Does the Community Care?'

In Italy, following the success of Dr Franco Basaglia's community psychiatric revolution in Trieste, where he emptied and closed the mental hospital entirely, an Act was passed making it against the law to admit anyone to a mental hospital. Unfortunately, elsewhere in Italy, the community alternatives had not been developed and one saw the emergence of the *abandonati*. Elsewhere there was the same general resentment at patients being released into the community without preparation and without any suitable alternative facilities being provided for them. Ronald Reagan, as governor of California, closed large mental hospitals overnight without any preparation and large numbers of patients, unable to look after themselves, were literally pushed out onto the streets with nowhere to go.

Here in Ireland the direct intervention of Charles Haughey acted as something of a catalyst, setting a number of subsequent developments in motion. Having spent the previous years trying to develop the community services, I once again took over direct control of St Brendan's, as it had become clear that the institution was not going to fade away.

The problem of controlling the inflow of admissions into the hospital was dealt with by the creation of an assessment unit with eight beds in the out-patient department. This was operated quite separately from the admission units of the hospital. From its early beginnings in the nineteenth century the staff at Grangegorman had no effective control over admissions. Patients were signed in on an involuntary basis or signed a voluntary form and were admitted directly to the admission wards, whether they required in-patient treatment or not. Many of these could have been dealt with as out-patients or day-patients, or in community in-patient units. Whenever a new service is developed, such as a psychiatric unit in a general hospital, it tends to attract a new population, while the original clientele still tread a well-worn pathway to the old mental hospital. This is not something unique to Dublin; it has been commented upon universally in psychiatric services across the world. This is one of the reasons why community psychiatric projects have often failed.

Once the assessment unit was opened in St Brendan's, all patients who presented at the hospital were held overnight until next morning when they were either discharged or passed on to their appropriate sector service. By this means the catchment areas were now forced to undertake the work for which they were established in the first place.

For the ten years preceding the establishment of the assessment unit in April 1979, the admission rate to St Brendan's had been running at over 2,000 patients per year. In 1978 the number of direct admissions to the hospital was 2,676. By 1980, only one year later, this figure had dropped to 1,558. Needless to say, this made a significant difference to overcrowding in the hospital and allowed breathing space to carry out further reorganisation within the institution.

Another chronic problem was the influx of inappropriate groups of patients into the ordinary admission wards: the homeless, those suffering from chronic alcoholism and the elderly. A special services committee was established for dealing with the homeless under the direction of Dr Joe Fernandez. He set up a case register to follow admission patterns and the movement of those of no fixed abode around the various hostels in the city. A small in-patient unit was provided for those genuinely requiring admission, and a day centre was established in the grounds of the hospital for the homeless.

For some years we had had an alcoholic unit which I had established in St Dymphna's, the house reserved for the resident medical superintendent, where I would normally have been expected to live. Nevertheless, during the 1970s, many alcoholics, like the homeless, constituted a revolving-door population who drifted into the admission wards, often leaving again after a few days or weeks without having gained any material benefit from the experience. It was clear that to be able to dry themselves out as in-patients in many instances only served to reinforce their chronic drinking. With the establishment of the assessment centre, such patients were seldom admitted to the hospital. Having been dried out overnight or for a day or two, they were referred on to St Dymphna's, or one of the other programmes for the treatment of alcoholism. Follow-up studies indicated that the therapeutic results were significantly better than when they gained direct admission to the hospital.

Having gained some control through these measures, it was possible to empty and demolish the main building on the west side of St Brendan's. Prior to this, a two-storey wing at the end of that building had caught fire, but all the patients had got out safely. This part of the building was repaired, but it was decided not to have it reoccupied by patients. Instead it was refurbished as a nurses' training school.

When the question of demolishing the rest of the building arose, there was considerable frustration and anger among the nursing staff. Even some of the doctors who had worked for many years in the hospital were not happy with the situation, although by this time

149

the monstrous three-storey building was largely empty. Symbolically, the fate of this building represented a turning point in the continuing struggle with institutionalisation and the future of the hospital. Those of us who wanted to see its demise were greatly assisted by a patient who for years had urinated in the corner of one of the wards. This had trickled down, rotting the wood on several of the floors at this spot. We photographed this to demonstrate the poor state of the building in general. The argument was finally clinched when the maintenance staff reported that the coping-stones of the roof were subsiding and hence the building was dangerous.

Following this, a project team was established with the agreement of the Minister for Health. It was decided that all the old buildings remaining on the east side of the road, comprising the original Richmond Asylum, which were almost entirely occupied by elderly geriatric patients, should be demolished. In pursuance of this plan the next building to go was a decrepit old block known as Unit 24, which had originally been part of the North Dublin Workhouse. It was part of the folklore of St Brendan's that, during the insurrection of Easter Week 1916, several IRA men, including Kevin Barry, had sheltered there when they were on the run.

This still left the onerous task of relocating some 400 elderly persons who were still resident in the Lower House – the original Richmond Asylum. Over the next few years, with the help of an energetic young psychiatrist – Dr Angela Mohan – we managed to relocate these 400 elderly people so that the huge Lower House building too could be demolished. This meant that the oldest part of the hospital on the east side of the road was now entirely closed down. We then turned our attention to the one remaining three-storey block on the west side and eventually emptied this also, leaving only the unit for disturbed patients, the newer buildings and a couple of small units.

19

The Brendan Project

With St Brendan's end as a large mental institution in sight, it began to dawn on me that right here, in central Dublin, there was now a site of 70 acres of fine green open space, the largest open space left in the city. Even allowing that a small district unit utilising the newer buildings might remain to supply a sector service for the surrounding local population, this would still leave more than 50 acres for a possible alternative development. During the 1960s and '70s I had believed that the main role of psychiatry was to help people return to normal community life. I had not realised that any real community life, in an urban conurbation such as Dublin with a population in excess of a million people, was already largely destroyed. As we entered the 1980s there was evidence on all sides of a disintegrating society. In common with other western countries, one saw in Ireland soaring crime rates, constant vandalism and predatory behaviour, widespread abuse of drugs and alcohol and an irretrievable breakdown of family life. This, in its turn, gave rise to an alienation of whole sections of the population, such as disadvantaged young people, the chronically unemployed and those made redundant, the Travellers and much of the elderly population.

Taking these separate factors into account, it seemed obvious that the major challenge facing mental health services over the next ten years would be the large population of unemployed and alienated people and their families who were at risk of various forms of mental breakdown. It was abundantly clear that the conventional psychiatric services would have little to offer in stemming this tide. It seemed to a number of us, therefore, that it was worth giving thought to the creation of a social project based on the campus at St Brendan's as the centre of an evolving network of training and enterprise centres that were already developing throughout the inner city. St Brendan's would then have changed from being a large, custodial institution, housing the unwanted of society, to an open centre where eventually hundreds of people would come each day to become involved in some form of healthy and productive activity, in order to develop more fully as human beings. The entire project would thus be directed towards the unemployed and 'at risk' population of young people, and those not so young, in the city centre and surrounding areas.

In 1980 a beginning had already been made in this direction. A small European Economic Community (EEC) project developed by Dr Michael Corry for the resocialisation and vocational training of chronic psychiatric patients had begun on the site which was developing new approaches to the education and personal development of those who had become demotivated and alienated from society. This programme worked with people who had spent many years in hospital.

Thus it was hoped with this new project, to be named 'The Brendan Project', to create an environment where people could come to build a place and a future for themselves, a new form of 'asylum', if you like. Instead of a closed system like the old mental hospital, this would be an open system where as many as a thousand people could come each day to enrich their lives and engage in enterprising and productive activity. It was hoped that, with the Brendan Project, the old campus would come alive and turn all its unused resources into a learning centre for people at risk.

These ideas were derived from work that was already ongoing with the Irish Foundation for Human Development, which I will describe later, particularly our project in inner-city Derry. It was my hope to apply these concepts to the Brendan Project in the northwest quadrant of the inner city of Dublin, which had been run down and virtually derelict for many years. Out of the community of approximately 20,000 there were some 5,000 unemployed. The whole area consisted mainly of prisons, the mental hospital and other institutions and was in urgent need of major urban renewal.

It would primarily be a cultural undertaking: the creation of a living city celebrating the arts, music, drama and sporting activities of all kinds, not unlike the old Gaelic *tailteann*.[1] There would be some economic and commercial underpinning to create a rounded development. The hope was that it would be an urban development for the next century, built by the disadvantaged and unemployed for the disadvantaged and unemployed. There seemed little doubt that, if such a development could get off the ground, it would be capable of attracting major international interest among architects, social planners and funding organisations.

There were ongoing contacts with the European Community and the proposal was that it would participate in a 'greater European project' which was soon to start and was to be centred on the concepts of 'habilitation' and 'skills for living'. This was to include projects in Italy, Germany and northern Greece, and Ireland had also been invited to become an active participant. The Eastern Health Board had agreed to the provision of a national mental health resource centre and had contributed funding for the design of a beautiful flagship building, which was already well advanced. The project had advanced to the point where the then Minister for Health had come to St Brendan's campus to cut the first sod for the erection of this resource centre. But the project never materialised. To understand why, we have to go back to 1980. Frustrated by the lack of progress in the development of mental health services, a colleague, the psychiatrist Dr Jim Behan, and I agreed to go on the *Late Late Show* with the then Minister for Health, Dr Woods, to discuss the crisis in the mental health services. We participated in two separate shows and were able to demonstrate with a graph that the budget for general hospitals had risen steeply and actually went off the top of the chart. The expenditure on community care also showed a modest rise, while that on mental health was represented by a straight line, which, allowing for inflation, actually meant there had been a decline in the allocation of financial resources. This picture has never changed. Indeed, in recent times there have been further reductions in the proportion of the health budget devoted to mental health. Where some years ago this accounted for 10 per cent of total health spending, it has recently dropped yet again to merely 6 per cent.

Following these *Late Late* programmes there was a widespread debate across the country involving psychiatrists and others. The culmination of this was that the Department of Health set up a group of experts to study the situation and to come up with recommendations for the development of services in the future. Although up until that time I had had good relationships with the department and over the years had been frequently consulted when any questions regarding the development of mental health services arose, it was significant that on this occasion I was not asked to be a member of the planning group.

After considerable deliberation and widespread consultation with all the bodies concerned, with the exception of myself, the report, 'Planning for the Future', was finally produced in December 1984. For the first time this report fully enshrined the principles of community psychiatry. In its introductory section it had this to say:

> The main thrust of our conclusions is that the psychiatric needs of the community should be met by a comprehensive and integrated service made up of a number of treatment components and largely located in the community. A number of changes are necessary if this objective is to be achieved, in particular there must be a decided shift in the pattern of care from an institutional to a community setting, with close links between psychiatry and other community services.

Following the publication in December 1984 of 'Planning for the Future', I felt hopeful that the way was cleared for the Brendan Project to go ahead. The Eastern Health Board had accepted the project in principle, had allotted a two-acre site and had committed finance to the design of the mental health resource centre, which was to be the flagship of the project. Then, in 1985, a new programme manager for the mental health services was appointed. It soon became evident that his brief from the Department of Health was to erode my sphere of influence as far as possible. I had built up quite a comprehensive teaching and clinical unit in Garden Hill House on the St James' Hospital site, but now, because Dr Jim Behan and I were seen as a thorn in the side of the establishment, the new programme manager worked energetically to close down this unit. He couldn't get rid of me personally, but he managed to ease out the other members of the staff there, making their lives so difficult that they eventually left the health board. I had already moved back much of my activity to St Brendan's and, when Garden Hill was finally closed down, I transferred my office and teaching unit back to St Brendan's.

Next, the programme manager turned his attention to the

Brendan Project. He completely failed to understand the nature of this and thought that it was in some way preserving St Brendan's as a mental hospital. Had the project developed along the lines that I have described, it would, in a few years, have absorbed and completely closed down the remains of the old institution. He successfully lobbied the politicians and other members of the health board and eventually succeeded in getting them to pass a motion terminating the project altogether. From then onwards I no longer felt that the role of Chief Psychiatrist in planning psychiatric services was worth pursuing, as he had, in effect, taken over. Nor did I have any enthusiasm for continuing to run St Brendan's directly. Unfortunately, because of the programme manager's lack of imagination, part of the hospital remains in use and continues to deteriorate to this day, although there are now only a couple of hundred psychiatric patients left, between St Brendan's and St Ita's. After all his efforts to prevent the Brendan Project going ahead, something of what I had dreamed is finally happening. At last it has been decided to bring the Institutes of Technology, which until now have been scattered in different parts of the city, on to the site to create a proper university.

For my part, I decided to withdraw as far as possible from the administrative roles I had, perhaps mistakenly, put so much energy into over the years. I decided to concentrate my efforts on teaching and building up an innovative psychotherapeutic unit, the work of which I will describe later.

20

Leros

When the Greek government was seeking entry to the European Community in the early 1980s, rumours began to filter through that there were very unsavoury conditions in some of the Greek mental hospitals, particularly on the island of Leros. An article appeared in *Stern* magazine in Germany showing pictures of naked patients and describing the terrible conditions in the hospital there. The most senior civil servant in the Social Affairs Commission, Wolfgang Stabenow (who himself had a mentally handicapped son), and his deputy, an Irishman, Ed Fitzgibbon, went way beyond their ordinary civil service brief. They put it to the Commission that it would not be appropriate for Greece to enter the European Union unless something was done to improve the plight of mental patients in that country. Leros was not alone; conditions were also poor in a number of other hospitals, particularly in Daphne, the large mental hospital which served Athens.

Towards the end of 1983, at the request of the Greek authorities, the European Commission set up a team of experts composed of psychiatrists, health economists and a psychologist, to make recommendations for a reform programme of public mental health care in Greece. Ed Fitzgibbon specifically asked that I be one of this group, despite resistance from the Irish Department of Health, so I was appointed and was asked to take on the role of president (chairperson). The team was appointed in December 1983 and was requested to finish its work as quickly as possible because of the wish of the Greek authorities to press ahead urgently with reform proposals.

By breaking up into subgroups, we were able to travel the length and breadth of Greece and, with intensive work, completed our report by the end of March 1984. (By comparison the study group that produced 'Planning for the Future' commenced their work in October 1981 and their report was not published until December 1984. By any objective standard I feel our report is at least as comprehensive as 'Planning for the Future'. What took them over three years to complete, we accomplished in just three months.)

It appears that the island of Leros had always had an unsavoury reputation. Looking back into its history, I found a quote from Roman times which stated 'the people of Leros are bad, not one, but everyone'. In the Middle Ages it was a leper colony. Then, during the Second World War and during the civil war that followed, it was used as a detention centre for prisoners. Following this, about 3,000 chronic mental patients, many of whom were mentally retarded, were brought down there in chains on warships. The old military barracks, which the Italians had used when they took over Leros during the Second World War, was converted into a mental hospital.

Conditions in the hospital were indescribable. In some of the worst wards, the patients were naked and were hosed down by the attendant staff in the mornings. There were only two doctors in charge, who were totally demoralised, and virtually no trained nursing staff. The patients were mainly looked after by attendants recruited from the people of the island, who had little or no training of any kind. There was also evidence that patients were being subjected to both physical and sexual abuse, although this was difficult to prove.

There was a so-called children's unit, which was occupied by severely mentally retarded patients of both sexes. They may have been children when they arrived but by now most of them were adults. They were dressed in shapeless blue smocks and sat around on the floor all day, jostling each other in a totally chaotic state. I remember two of these, I think it was a man and a woman, though it was hard to tell, who held on to each other and rocked back and forth all day long; each time we visited they were there in this same state. As virtually no patients had ever been discharged, the death rate was alarming. Of the 3,000 patients who had originally been transferred to the island, the population had been almost halved by death by the time we arrived. And it continued to fall over the next few years to fewer than 1,000.

On another part of the island there was an institution for mentally retarded children which had about 300 inmates. This was the saddest place I have ever visited. Most of the children were confined to bed, some badly deformed, with little or no evidence of physiotherapy or treatment of any kind. But the image that burnt itself into my mind was that of a single toy dangling above each bed, well out of reach, where no child could ever even touch it.

To give a picture of our overall impression of the island, let me quote the following paragraph from our report:

> The problem with Leros, in fact, extends well beyond the walls of the institution and affects the whole island. The team's impression is that the use of Leros for years, perhaps even centuries, as a dumping ground for the unwanted – lepers, convicts, political exiles and now handicapped children and psychiatric patients – has led to a deterioration of the entire lifestyle and culture of the island. Here there is none of the tourist development, economic activity (like farming and fishing), or joyous atmosphere characteristic of neighbouring islands, but an accumulation of human misery. This calls for a major programme of alternative economic development for the island simultaneously with the diminution and eventual disappearance of the mental hospital.[1]

This was the first time that the European Community had allocated financial resources directly for the development of mental health services. This special aid to Greece, in the general context of vocational rehabilitation, was in line with the community policy of reintegrating the disabled into social and working life. Thus the commission proposed special measures in favour of Greece in the social field, including financial support of up to 60,000 ECU over a five-year period, to deal with this urgent priority. In March 1984 the Council of Ministers adopted the Regulation 'on exceptional financial support in favour of Greece in a social field'. The range of eligible expenditure under this special community aid covered 'construction, extension, adaptation and equipment of buildings and centres and pilot projects to establish the most efficient methods of carrying out the new programme as well as the professional training of medical, therapeutic and paramedical staff, and social workers'. This community aid covered 55 per cent of the public expenditure involved, the rest to be made up by the Greek government, and was made available in the form of grants over a five-year period.

Under the heading 'Five Year Plan for a Comprehensive Mental Health Service' our report stated the following:

1. To divide the population of Greece according to geographical regions, these to be further sub-divided into community psychiatric sectors.
2. To classify the population in hospitals by age and place of origin, and divide the in-patient population into mentally ill, including type of illness, and mentally handicapped.
3. To develop a psychiatric team for each sector, which can offer the client groups continuous care in the community, including those parts of the hospitals which remain. The emphasis of the team approach should be on continuity of care in the community in decentralised, local facilities. This differs fundamentally from the present emphasis on institutional, rather than community care.
4. To use this decentralised and unified system of care to filter the natural flow and cut off the intake into mental hospitals.

For the next five or six years the team visited Greece regularly, often several times a year. As the work progressed, change was evident throughout the length and breadth of Greece, with the opening of day hospitals, psychiatric units in general hospitals and other community facilities.

In Leros itself numbers continued to fall and agreement was reached with the Greek authorities that no further patients would be admitted to the hospital, although in spite of our efforts there was a degree of sabotage and a small number of patients did find their way into the hospital from neighbouring islands. The children's unit was closed down and a Dutch team of experienced therapists set up a project in one of the worst adult male wards, where the patients had been naked for years. They gave these patients clothes and personal space, and furniture; in short, they equipped them to live as human beings. I was astonished on our next visit to find those who had earlier been treated like animals now behaving with the human dignity that had been restored to them. This showed the staff of the hospital what was possible and was thereafter incorporated into a comprehensive training programme. By the time I handed over to others, it was clear that a fundamental change was taking place in the organisation of psychiatric services throughout Greece.

159

PART FIVE

Irish Foundation for Human Development
1968–1979

21

Starting Up

In 1968 I was awarded a World Health Fellowship to the United States. I viewed the trip as an opportunity for gaining knowledge to bring back to Ireland. In addition to visiting psychiatric facilities, I wanted to find out as much as I could about what was happening in community development. Since the Kennedy era there had been a lot of emphasis on community mental health and various kinds of self-help community projects. A number of these initiatives went under the heading of 'New Careers' and I visited several in New York, Chicago and San Francisco. I had an auspicious meeting with the organiser of one of these projects, which turned all my preconceived ideas about our work in Ballyfermot upside down. Until then I had tried to get the various health and caring professionals working more closely together to create a more useful and better co-ordinated service for the people of the area. But this was still a paternalistic approach. Although in my psychiatric work I had already realised that attempting to do things for people was useless, I had not, until now, realised that this same principal applies generally. Real change can only happen when people and communities take responsibility for themselves.

In San Francisco I met a group of mostly young black men and women (many of them former drug addicts). I can't remember what I spoke to them about but my talk was much appreciated and we got on well. This had unexpected repercussions two years later, which I will come to in due course.

The 1960s saw the emergence of a number of radical and idealistic movements, the civil rights movement with Martin Luther King in the States, Mao's disastrous cultural revolution in China, radical feminism, the hippie movement and there was widespread student unrest. In 1964 there were serious student riots in Berkeley, California. Escalating student unrest in Columbia in New York, and other universities across the States, followed this. These student disturbances coalesced and formed the backbone of the growing anti-Vietnam war demonstrations and the civil rights movement. By 1968 student unrest had spread into South America and across the western world into Europe, where it culminated in the student revolutions in Paris, London and other European cities. These winds of change affected us here in Ireland too, with the emergence of the civil rights movement in the North.

In November 1968 a radical group of students in University College Dublin calling themselves Students for Democratic Action (SDA) put forward a manifesto demanding fundamental democratic changes in the organisation of the university and in society generally. At that time UCD was still mainly located in Earlsfort Terrace. With the ever-increasing numbers of students, the pressure on this limited site was becoming intense. Early in 1969, the move to the new arts building in Belfield was mooted by the university authorities, but the library facilities on the new site were still not adequate. By March 1969, in the face of these proposed developments, the unrest among the students took a more active turn. A number of mass demonstrations were held in the great hall in Earlsfort Terrace (now the National Concert Hall). Because of my experiences in the States the year before, I too was swept along in the atmosphere of euphoria that was being generated. I went to one of the demonstrations and, along with others, made a speech supporting the students in their demands for democratic change.

Then the more radical SDA group of students occupied the administration offices; they blockaded the meeting of the academic council and would not allow the assembled professors to leave the room. The feeling of indecision and confusion among the academics was palpable. There were intense meetings of various groups of staff and students over the next few days. Proposals were drafted by the SDA and supported by the wider body of students, demanding that the authoritarian structures of the university, such as the academic council and the governing body, be swept away. These were to be replaced by a freely elected democratic structure comprising both students and staff on a roughly fifty/fifty basis.

When the main student body agreed these proposals, the occupation of the administrative block, which had continued for the previous thirty-six hours, was lifted. The governing body responded to these demands with a statement making clear that it could not hand over its authority or make such changes without legislation being formally passed through the Dáil.

Then Garret FitzGerald, who was a lecturer in the university at the time, began to manipulate the situation with the support of young members of Fine Gael. The radical demands of the SDA, which were undoubtedly unrealistic but at least were honest, were gradually compromised and replaced by watered-down proposals. These were generally more acceptable to the main body of students, who, by this time, were becoming anxious that the situation was getting out of control. Eventually, at one of the last mass demonstrations, the radical SDA students, feeling they had been betrayed, walked out of the meeting.

It was proposed that a committee should be set up to investigate what had happened and decide if disciplinary action should be taken against them. As a rebuke for the stand I and some other staff members had taken, we were appointed to this committee and, over the next few weeks, we interviewed individually a number of the radical students who were involved. Most of them were in their final year and by now were engaged in preparing to take their exams. In this way the protest movement gradually petered out as, by the following academic year, almost all of them had left the university.

During this period of unrest Don Carroll, the head of Carroll Cigarettes, who was also governor of the Bank of Ireland, was invited by one of the student bodies to give a lecture. I was asked to be chairperson of this meeting. He took the approach of an enlightened capitalist who had the welfare of society at his heart. He came, I feel, expecting to get a reasonably positive response from the students, but was attacked vociferously, his whole thesis torn apart. He was appalled and visibly shaken by this. After the meeting I spoke to him about my views on community development and the need for ordinary communities to take responsibility for themselves. He agreed, I think partly because he was hurt and confused by the negative reception he had received from the students, and said that he would be willing to help. He felt too that the Bank of Ireland would be sympathetic if such a project were put forward.

I had made friends with a number of the radical students who had been involved in the protest movement in the university. One of these, Paddy Walley, had finished his degree and had set up an organisation called Noah to try to help the homeless. Then one day he phoned me to say that he was taking the boat to England the following evening because he had been unable to get funding. I was anxious to start a community action movement in Ballyfermot but I had come to the conclusion that it was simply not possible to initiate any real change unless one had a full-time organiser. So, hearing that Paddy was about to leave Ireland, I phoned Don Carroll and put it to him that I urgently needed an organiser in Ballyfermot and here was a creative young Irishman being forced to emigrate because he could not find employment. To my amazement Don Carroll responded immediately by arranging an appointment to see Paddy himself the next day. When Paddy duly arrived in the governor's office, Don Carroll, without further ado, asked him how much he wanted as a salary. Paddy was struck dumb and had no idea what to suggest, but eventually they agreed on what the bank felt was appropriate, more than Paddy had ever expected. Paddy started work and, together with the enthusiastic participation of some of the local community leaders, we launched the first community association in Ireland. There had been a tenants' association prior to that but it was largely ineffective.

A strange parallel with my own evolution took place at the same time in San Diego in Chile. Humberto Maturana was a fairly conservative biologist working in the university there until the student revolution struck in 1968. He wrote later about how, for several weeks, all ordinary academic routine was disrupted and the students took over the university, holding spontaneous seminars and demonstrations, with the participation of numbers of the academic staff. Maturana described how his thinking was completely turned upside down and his view of the nature of biology was changed for ever. This was the beginning of his work on autopoiesis and the principle of self-organisation in living systems. His work had a major impact on my own thinking some years later.

While the community activity in Ballyfermot was continuing, something happened that nearly terminated my career. I was asked to participate in a meeting of the Logos student society in UCD on 20 November 1970. I was there to reply to a paper entitled

'Medicine, Marijuana and My Mysticism', delivered by the auditor of the society, a third-year medical student. A Jesuit, Philip McShane, who afterwards left the Order, spoke on mysticism. It was a very interesting and open discussion, and in my enthusiasm I spoke of having worked therapeutically with LSD and also of having taken it myself on three occasions. I said that, while under the influence of LSD, I could see things with far greater clarity than was normal. Perhaps unwisely, I went on to say that there seemed to be a form of hysteria about cannabis and that I thought it was wrong that people should be sent to jail for smoking it. I went on to say, 'If I want to listen to some good jazz, I can think of no better way than by getting high on grass.' There was a very enthusiastic response from the students to our discussion and I went home feeling that it had been a satisfactory and enjoyable meeting.

Next morning, which was Saturday, I had to go up to the Richmond Hospital about a patient. When I was there I heard that the then Minister for Health, Erskine Childers, was paying an official visit to the hospital that morning. As I had not been invited to be present for this official visit, I was hurrying to leave the hospital before his arrival. However, he arrived just as I was going down the first steps of the old Richmond and, looking at me severely, said in his gentle Anglo-Irish voice: 'That was a very naughty speech you made last night.' I had no idea what he was talking about but, feeling uneasy, went to the nearest newsagent to get the morning papers. Imagine my consternation on seeing the headlines in the *Irish Independent,* 'My drug trip – by UCD Professor'. And, in the *Irish Press*, 'My LSD Trip – by Ivor Browne'.

What I hadn't realised was that there had been a freelance reporter at the back of the hall at the meeting and he had taken down, word for word, what I had said. All hell broke loose. The phone never stopped ringing for the whole weekend, with journalist after journalist wanting to speak to me. It was impossible even to get time to think let alone to draft some kind of damage-limitation response. By the afternoon there were headlines on the front page of the *Evening Herald* saying, 'Dr Ivor Browne, centre of storm' and then a huge headline: 'Attack on "Drug Trip".' The article went on to say, 'A call for the immediate resignation of Dublin Health Authority's Chief Psychiatrist, Dr Ivor Browne, was made today ... The chairman of the Dublin Health Authority, Senator Dr Richard Belton, has called for a full investigation into the statements and is to take the matter up with the authority's chief executive officer.'

Another health authority member, Joseph Connolly, who was chairman of the Dublin Mental Health Board, was reported as saying that he was 'going to press for Dr Browne's removal from office'.

Throughout the weekend parents of students across the country were writing to the university demanding my resignation. The report was taken up by the Associated Press and the United Press and went all over the world. I only realised this later when I had letters from friends in Canada and Australia, the United States and several other places. Then, to my amazement, I received a telegram from the hippie group in San Francisco with whom I had got on so well when I was there in 1968. They said they were going to charter a plane and come to my assistance. Their support was the last thing I needed at the time but fortunately they didn't get around to coming.

On Sunday, having drafted a statement explaining that what I said had been taken out of context, I was invited to go on *This Week*, the news programme on RTE. This, together with statements I made to the papers and some articles that were written by others who supported my case, gradually helped the situation to calm down. Tom Murphy, the President of UCD, was very helpful and supportive, fending off complaints by parents of students, and the attack by members of the health board gradually petered out.

The whole episode made me realise what it is like for politicians and others who are at the centre of publicity of this kind. For some time I found it difficult even to go out of the house and, when I did so, I felt that everyone was looking at me. Some weeks later I had to go to a social function in the College of Surgeons. It was my first public appearance where I had to face professional colleagues. I was standing at the reception, feeling very exposed, when a voice from across the room said, 'Now you know what it feels like.' It was Paddy Hillary, who was a minister in the government at that time and later president of Ireland. Somehow that seemed to clear the atmosphere and I felt really grateful to him.

Back in Ballyfermot, once Paddy Walley got established, he addressed the situation with enormous energy and creative flair. It was soon clear that he couldn't handle the amount of activity developing on his own and it was then that the bank generously came up with two more salaries for two local young men, who were both electricians by trade. From these humble beginnings the Irish Foundation for Human Development was born, although at that time we had no name for it.

At the time we were influenced, to some extent, by information coming in of the work of Mao Tse Tung in China, where street committees were being set up in many of the towns and cities. As a result, we set up street committees in virtually every street in Ballyfermot (the terrible reality of Mao's Cultural Revolution had not filtered through at the time).

The way in which the community was organised then was that local people on the street were elected to each street committee. Representatives from each of the street committees were elected to one of a number of area committees, covering different districts of Ballyfermot. Representatives from each of these area committees were then elected to the central community association, as well as some of the professionals from the area and a couple of us from the foundation. The whole operation was financed by collections taken up from each street committee. Some of this money was kept to support the activities on the street and the remainder was passed on to the area committees. Each of these then gave some financial support to the central community association.

Enormous energy was generated for activities of various kinds all over the estate. Periodically festivals were organised at a weekend or on a bank holiday, when as many as 10,000 people were involved in all kinds of sporting activities, drama, concerts, etc., in one or other of the large open spaces which were available in the district. On one occasion we organised a concert in what had been the cinema in Ballyfermot. The Dubliners, the Furey Brothers and others performed to a tremendously enthusiastic reception by the local people. The hall was packed and there were many outside who were unable to get in. At that time Ted Furey and his family were living in the area and his sons had only recently formed their celebrated group.

All this activity in Ballyfermot was developing spontaneously, with the crucial financial support from the Bank of Ireland. This was on the basis of our personal relationship with Don Carroll, who was governor at the time. There was no formal arrangement for this work to continue on a long-term basis, nor had we any title or proper structure for the organisation that was developing. Then, a key intervention took place. I had known Paddy Lynch for some years. He had previously been chief executive of Aer Lingus and was now professor of economics in UCD. He was also a member of the board of the Allied Irish Bank, so he was highly respected among the financial elite of the city. He was a great supporter of what we were attempting to do. He told me one day that he hoped I would meet someone influential, with strong opinions on the way that charitable work by institutions such as the Bank of Ireland should be organised. This was Russell Murphy, who at that time was one of the most celebrated accountants in the city and whose views were taken very seriously in business, banking and other financial circles. When Paddy Lynch took me to see him, he was seated in a dark cavernous office, a strange figure dressed in black, and I remember thinking he looked a bit like Dracula. I was surprised that he seemed to command such respect. The view he expressed that day was that the bank, instead of giving small donations here and there to various charities, should concentrate on one significant cause that they felt was really worth supporting, and give sufficient finance to enable it to succeed. Needless to say, this was music to my ears.

In due course, Paddy Lynch spoke to Don Carroll and the members of the board of the Bank of Ireland. Given that this advice was coming from the influential Russell Murphy, they decided to accept his view and made it their official policy from then on. Some time later, at a party in Gay Byrne's house, I met Russell Murphy for a second time and once again I had the same strong impression of an almost sinister, dark, taciturn figure, and I was surprised to hear him yet again spoken of in very glowing terms. Little did I know then that this was the Russell Murphy who, when he died some years later, turned out to have defrauded a considerable number of people who had entrusted him with handling their investments of large sums of money.

In 1970 the Ballyfermot area generally had a bad name; no one going for a job would dream of giving their address as Ballyfermot. The shopping facilities were poor and there was nowhere that people could meet other than the health centre, which was not a particularly attractive venue. One of the first achievements of the new community association was to build a community centre. The community managed to raise sufficient money to erect a prefabricated building and this provided a much-needed central facility. Indeed, it was so heavily used that after a number of years the building deteriorated badly. At night-time there were dances and discos and during the day various communal activities. As Ballyfermot was a pretty tough district in those days, it was not easy to maintain order at the dances at night, but this was made possible with the help of a strange character, Dinny Boy Desmond, who came from a tough family who were said to have had connections with a ruthless, violent Dublin gang. He was certainly capable of controlling the young people, but we were often worried about some of the methods he employed to do so. In a fracas some years previously he had chewed off part of the ear of one of the people involved. One of the sanctions he used to quieten a troublemaker was to hold their head down the toilet and flush it. Apart from his capacity for aggression, I always found him a very pleasant and colourful character; he was creative and even, I believe, wrote several plays later.

Parallel to the main community development activity of the street committees which was being built up by Paddy Walley, another remarkable personality, Art O'Brian, became involved. Art, who was born and raised in Dublin, grew up in an Irish-speaking family and had taken an arts degree in economics and politics in UCD. The year before he started in UCD, he had gone to California and had spent time in Haight Ashbury, the famous centre of hippie activity. This experience had affected Art's thinking and, although he completed his degree in the university, he felt that what he was doing was totally irrelevant, so when he left he had no idea where he was heading.

Art went for an interview with Anton Trant, principal of the Ballyfermot vocational school at the time. Art had been involved in the drama society in UCD and felt that this experience could be useful in a place like Ballyfermot. To his amazement, Anton Trant told him to turn up on the following Monday and provided him with a whole studio in which to develop his ideas in creative drama with some of the backward students in the school. This turned out to be remarkably successful and Anton Trant gave him the freedom to experiment in any way that he chose. Anton Trant was himself interested in innovation in education and later became director of the curriculum development unit in Trinity College.

Although Art's work with creative drama in the vocational school was quite successful, he became increasingly convinced that, to effect real change, it would be necessary to reach these young adolescents much earlier, at the pre-school or primary school stage. He was aware of all the community activity that was going on, and so, when the new community centre was up and running, he decided to leave the vocational school and join our foundation. He set up the Community Arts Workshop which, I believe, was the first experiment in community arts in this country. Since then community arts have become well established and there is a lot of activity of this kind now around the country.

Art, with the able assistance of Roddy Day, a big strong Kerryman with a gentle personality, set up a range of activities in the community centre. For the younger children there was story-telling, creative drama and artwork. A number of the adolescents with whom he had been working in the vocational school got involved in this activity with the children and became natural leaders as the work progressed.

Roddy Day at that time was a teacher in the primary school and was wonderfully skilful in working with small children. The mothers of the children also became involved, and a club was set up for the elderly in the area. In this way people of all ages were involved.

One day I went along to the community centre to see for myself what was happening there. Soon after I arrived, nearly a hundred children burst into the centre and, without anyone seeming to organise or control them, launched into various activities. One large group rolled out a sheet of paper 30 or 40 feet in length and they all started painting at various points along the entire length of it. This looked totally chaotic and yet, after about half an hour, a complete painting emerged, as if it had been planned from the beginning. Then, at a signal, the children formed several large circular groups, each with a leader, and the story-telling began. These were some of the wildest children in the district, many from dysfunctional families, and yet the whole operation seemed extraordinarily calm and controlled, without anyone appearing to organise or supervise it in any authoritarian way.

Funding this activity was a problem at that time, as there was no official awareness of community arts or financial resources available from local authorities, as happens nowadays. Then Art heard about the Gulbenkian Foundation, which was not, at that time, supporting any projects in Ireland. He made an application to it and he and I attended a meeting with some of the senior Gulbenkian people in London in September 1973. I remember the time because, just before that meeting, I had attended as a participant my first group conference, run in Leicester in England by the Human Relations Division of the Tavistock Institute. Immediately following this, I travelled down to London for the meeting with the Gulbenkian people, where Art and I secured a sizeable grant, which sustained the activities of the Community Arts Workshop for several years.

On the evening of our stay in London we went to Ronnie Scott's jazz club, where Art Blakey was performing with his group, the Jazz Messengers. I was tremendously impressed by the solid, driving rhythm which he produced with very little of the pyrotechnics usually favoured by drummers – just solid rhythm. I remember how, when he introduced the band members, he referred to himself as Mamma Blakey's little boy.

On our return home there was a visitation by the Gulbenkian Institute. The grant we received enabled us to employ a young local woman, Mary Farrell, who eventually took over leadership of the workshop. Art had always intended making himself redundant and was anxious to see the local people run the workshop independently.

The Gulbenkian grant also made it possible to purchase a bus and this enabled Art to develop what he called 'Magical Mystery Tours'. They went on a number of occasions to the Furry Glen in the Phoenix Park and would often go on longer trips too. Professional actors were employed from the Abbey Theatre and elsewhere and these would develop a story, and in this way the event would include an element of drama. I still meet people, now middle-aged, who stop me to reminisce about Art's magical mystery tours.

The club for the old people also became very popular but here we ran into trouble with the Church, as up to now the Church had always controlled the old people's activities and it strongly resented this being taken over. The Church had serious reservations in general about community activity. In one single week, four of the different organisations that had a vested interest in the management of society – the Catholic Church, Dublin Corporation, some of the local politicians and the Department of Education – all visited the health board to complain about me personally and about the activities in Ballyfermot, hoping to close us down. However, as the health board had actually given a grant for the old people's club, they made no attempt to interfere with our work. The Church authorities became so alarmed at their loss of control over the community that the Archbishop of Dublin sent Father Michael Cleary, who I already knew because of his intimate relationship with my young patient, Phyllis Hamilton, to see what could be done to curb community development in the area. He subsequently preached sermons from the pulpit against the self-help community activity and vented his views about the evils of contraception and family planning amongst the poor women of Ballyfermot. Sadly his influence, and that of the other clergy, played a major role in the gradual deterioration of the community movement in the area.

When we began our activity in Ballyfermot, there were very few facilities. There was no garda station, no community centre and, although the Dominican nuns and De La Salle Brothers did cater in the secondary schools for students up to Leaving Certificate standard, very few actually reached this level; there was a 90 per cent drop-out rate after primary school. As a result of pressure from the five area committees and the executive committee of the Community Council, a police station was eventually provided. Then a movement was started to achieve a senior college, where the young people of Ballyfermot could complete their education up to Leaving Certificate level and beyond. This was a major struggle as there was a lot of opposition from the religious who ran the existing schools, and also from the Department of Education.

A wonderful character, Tommy Phelan, had been part of the community association from the beginning. He had been brought up in the Liberties, in one of the old tenements in Hanbury Lane. He never knew his father, and he and his mother had had a terrible struggle to survive; and in that environment he had learned to fight for his rights. He had tremendous courage. He would take on the Church, the Corporation or any of the other bureaucracies when standing up for the ordinary people. There were several other hard workers on the executive and area committees, but many of those who got involved just wanted to be part of local politics. They liked to talk but were not anxious to work, and had little stomach for standing up to opposition from the Church or others.

When the plan to provide the senior college was approved, the teachers were anxious that it should be placed close to the local schools, but Tommy and the people of the area wanted to see it located on an area known as the Harp site, where it would be in the centre of the population. The executive committee itself was split. Eventually, after a lot of negotiation and skilful manoeuvring by Tommy, he and those who had the needs of the people in their hearts, won the day and the college went ahead on the Harp site. The college was extraordinarily successful and the number of young people in Ballyfermot going on to take the Leaving Certificate and beyond grew rapidly.

Indeed the college was so successful that it went on to achieve an international reputation and its Centre for Animation Studies became one of the finest in the world. Sadly, because of this, students from all over the city and further afield applied for entry, the points system became very competitive and an elitist atmosphere took over. For this reason, nowadays very few from Ballyfermot itself are able to gain entry and the same old factors that apply elsewhere, the social split between the haves and the have-nots, has taken over here also.

After we received the grant from the Gulbenkian Foundation, one of the young leaders in the community arts workshop, Noel McFarland, set out to write a small book, *Down the Corner*, in the Dublin vernacular, to help those in the community who had difficulty learning to read. Up to then the reading books provided in the local schools were usually of English origin and bore little relation to how people actually thought or spoke in Ballyfermot. Noel's book described how a group of young kids in Ballyfermot spent their day, including robbing an orchard and other dubious activities. It was a great success in the local area and sold, house to house, over 5,000 copies. Noel himself went on to become a sub-editor on *The Irish Times*. In a similar way, a number of the leaders that Art and Paddy Walley helped to develop went on to become school principals, teachers and so on, and to lead community movements in Tallaght, Finglas and elsewhere.

By this time in 1975/6, the community activity in Ballyfermot had started to wane and negativity was beginning to surface. In my experience this can often happen in this kind of community activity. My hope originally was that, as the people of Ballyfermot began to take control of their own lives and as the community movement developed, a fresh spirit would emerge so that the old 'control' systems – the Corporation, the politicians and the Church – would fade into the background. What happened instead, however, was that the same kind of internecine political tensions, conflicts and ego-driven behaviour emerged within the community itself. The Church, feeling it was losing control over the hearts and minds of the people, worked consistently to turn the people against this dangerous, irreligious type of left-wing community activity. The spontaneous community activity and enthusiasm that was there at the beginning was replaced by bureaucratic wrangling and attempts to control any innovative activity among the ordinary people. Some of the elected members of the area committees and the community association now considered themselves to be important and to have the right to speak for the community as a whole.

Negative attitudes had become entrenched by the time that Art O'Brian returned a couple of years later from Denmark, where he had gone to study the Folk High Schools. Art and Joe Comerford decided to make a film of *Down the Corner,* but they had to go out at six o'clock in the morning to film, otherwise they would face angry demonstrations saying that they were only showing the negative face of what was increasingly felt to be a 'respectable' community.

Although the enthusiasm and idealism of the early days has waned, the street committees have faded and other problems, such as the growth of drug abuse, alcoholism and crime, have increased, all our work in Ballyfermot was not wasted. The battered old community centre, where most of the activity in the early days was concentrated, has long since disappeared, but it has been replaced by a magnificent new civic centre, which cost something in the region of 8 million to build. After a lot of negotiation, this was provided from State funds. This houses a very successful community theatre group and also a number of other activities. Perhaps what is more important, the people of Ballyfermot now have a sense of self-respect and identity from all that they have achieved, which did not exist when we began our work there. When applying for a job they are now proud to give their address as Ballyfermot, rather than giving a false address, as they did in the old days.

Because of our work in Ballyfermot the Irish Foundation was contacted to intervene in Dublin 1, the north inner city, and it was through this that I first met Loughlin Kealy, who was already heavily engaged in the area. After a spell in California and London, Loughlin had returned to the Department of Architecture and he and another architect, Gerry Mitchell, set up what they called the Urban Workshop. The concept behind this was that they, as professionals, would make their expertise available to communities to help them articulate what it was they wanted. It was at this time that Loughlin got involved in community development in the north inner city area.

The whole area was under threat, because the Dublin Transportation Study had put forward a plan to run major roads through the inner city. This would have effectively turned Dublin 1 into a traffic island and, as part of this plan, Dublin Corporation were intent on moving most of the population out of the area to peripheral housing estates. Community agitation was developing in Sheriff Street. It was then that Loughlin met Mick Rafferty, who was one of the main people resisting these dehumanising proposals and who has remained a dedicated community organiser ever since.

From 1972 to 1978, the School of Architecture was paying Loughlin's salary. When we at the community development division of the Irish Foundation became involved, we took over paying half his salary. From our experience in Ballyfermot we had realised that our efforts were still too paternalistic, still too directly involved in running the community organisation. Consequently, when we were invited to Dublin 1 in 1976, we decided to offer our expertise in planning and guidance, but to leave it to the community leaders, Mick Rafferty, Fergus McCabe and others, to manage the operation directly. Our main contribution at that time was, in collaboration with the communities themselves, to come up with a comprehensive community plan, which acted as a counter-proposal to the Corporation's road and transportation plans. Our proposal saw a radically different future for the area, with far more community housing, safe spaces for children, provision of work places, schools and so on, which would restore a living heart in that part of the city centre.

Eventually this effort did meet with some success, for a modified version of our plan was taken up by Tony Gregory, who was emerging as the people's politician for the area. Even he would probably have had little success were it not that, at the crucial moment when Charlie Haughey needed his vote to remain in control of the government, a deal was done. He insisted that his proposals for the area become official policy and thus the people of the area were saved from extinction. This was in 1982 and, as a result, more than 500 houses were built in the area, even though the life of that government was short-lived and Tony Gregory's brief period of influence fell by the wayside.

The Irish Foundation for Human Development was developing fast and three loosely defined main areas of study and action were emerging. These were concerned with: the environment and society, the essential nature of the person, and human groups and relationships between people. These functioned separately but much of their work was interrelated.

The first area of activity, under the direction of Paddy Walley, involved the exploration of the relationship between people and their environment. This involved community development work in Dublin city and the suburbs, also in Derry and in the large educational project in Mayo/Sligo supported by a grant from the EEC. It also involved an educational project in the south-west. The ethic underlying this work was the development of self-awareness and responsibility in communities as the essential basis for personal and social action.

In 1974 the Industrial Development Authority announced that it intended to locate three major capital- and labour-intensive industries in Mayo. The influx of industry represented the prospect of considerable change for the north Mayo area and it was hoped that it would provide the necessary impetus to break the long-established pattern of emigration. In January 1975 the Galway/Mayo Regional Development Organisation wanted to sponsor an action/research project that would focus on the impact of the changes brought about by industrialisation and it was decided that this project should be carried out by the Irish Foundation for Human Development.

The foundation drew up a proposal and, in 1978, established a project called 'Education for Development', embracing both community development and curriculum innovation. Its central concern was how schools could contribute to the ability of young people to be productive in the community. This concern was adopted as a pilot project within the EEC network of projects concerning the transition from school to working life. The EEC provided a sizeable financial grant to the foundation.

Loughlin Kealy became involved in Mayo at that time. As part of a wider study on industrialisation, he and Gerry Mitchell carried out a study that examined the basis for planning in the area and this was later included in the 'Education for Development' project. I myself had little to do with it other than to help in the initial stages of negotiation with the Industrial Development Association (IDA) and the other organisations concerned.

The approach and outcomes of the project were disseminated through a series of seminars and workshops. Two principal events were held: the first was a one-day meeting in Castlebar, County Mayo, for teachers from schools throughout the region and agencies concerned with employment and training. The second was a national seminar held in Dublin, with some forty contributors drawn from Ireland, Europe and the US. Lectures and workshops were presented over four days, and I also presented a paper at the seminar. The conference provided a platform for the expression of views on the future of education in Ireland. It is hard to estimate what long-term effect this project had on the local area or on the young people in the schools. There is no doubt it represented a real attempt to introduce some creative innovation and humanity into the rather rigid, exam-driven, educational system in this country, but those in the foundation had neither the management skills, educational expertise nor a clear enough vision of what they were attempting to achieve for the project to succeed completely.

In 1981, when the Mayo project was finishing up, Loughlin initiated a new creative enterprise in some of the schools in west Cork and Kerry. He worked with schools in Clonakilty, Rosscarbery and Dunmanway in west Cork and Killorglin in Kerry. Having learnt from some of the mistakes in Mayo, this endeavour was much more successful. The difference in west Cork was that Loughlin worked closely with the teachers in the schools and fitted in with the curriculum.

The second, 'person-centred', work of the foundation was under the direction of the late Dr John Cullen. He and his team developed a psychosomatic unit at St James' Hospital, where they carried out research in what has become known as psychoneuroendochrinology. They were studying physical and psychological disorders that had their origins in stress or in the living conditions of the individual.

This unit was also exploring alternative approaches to health care in the community and, in particular, it sought to develop techniques for detecting early signs of breakdown under stress. Studies were undertaken to show how a person might best care for his/her own health. This unit was integrated with the Psycho-Endocrine Unit run by Professor Austin Darragh (who is one of the finest natural physicians I have ever known), although he was not directly part of the foundation.

My main interest was in the third area of the foundation's activity, the study of interpersonal relationships and human group behaviour. Activities undertaken included education with community groups in the greater Dublin area, in the Bogside area in Derry and with various national organisations such as the Irish Farmers Association, Macra na Tuatha, and agricultural inspectors. As a follow-up to working with the latter, I was invited in 1974 to speak at their national meeting in the Department of Agriculture. I gave a paper entitled 'To Farm or not to Farm', in which I questioned the wisdom of mechanised farming and of our wholesale acceptance of the Common Agricultural Policy. I got a standing ovation at the end of my talk, I think mainly because I was saying things they dared not speak out about themselves. After this I heard on the grapevine that the word had gone out that I was never to be allowed to speak in the Department of Agriculture again.

22

The Tavistock Conferences

One of the most significant activities of the Irish Foundation for Human Development was the group conferences we organised based on the method developed by the Human Relations Division of the Tavistock Institute in London. We held several of these residential working conferences on responsibility, authority and leadership in Dublin during the 1970s.

In 1968 Garret O'Connor, who is now Chief Executive of the Betty Ford Centre but at that time was working in Johns Hopkins' Psychiatric Department in Baltimore, spoke to me about the Tavistock Group Conferences, with which he had been involved in the States. Although I sensed that this was important work, I did not want to get involved in something that sounded personally threatening, as I didn't feel I could face that at the time, so I let the opportunity pass. But in the early '70s, when the activities of the Irish Foundation were in full swing, Paddy Walley went to one of the Leicester Working Conferences of the Human Relations Division of the Tavistock Institute. When he returned full of enthusiasm, I felt I could no longer avoid getting involved, so, in September 1973, I duly attended my first working conference in Leicester. This was, to say the least, an awesome experience; it not only opened up for me a new awareness of the nature of human groups but also affected me deeply. I had little or no knowledge of the theoretical background of this method, so I was very much thrown in at the deep end.

There were about seventy people attending the conference, which continued for two weeks. In the opening session the chairs were arranged in rows, like a classroom, and there was an expectancy that some kind of talk explaining the nature of the conference would be given. The staff entered and sat in a row at the front of the room facing the members, with the director of the conference seated in the middle. In this instance the director was Pierre Turquet, who was a psychoanalyst at the Tavistock Institute in London. He was a formidable-looking individual, with an intimidating manner. He gave a short introductory talk, which none of us could make any sense of, and then asked if anyone had any questions. He and the rest of the staff sat there in silence and there was a general sense of confusion amongst the audience, nobody knowing what to do or say. After a few desultory questions on the part of some of the members, to which the staff refused to make any reply, the director and the rest of the staff of consultants got up and walked out of the room.

We all had a programme listing the time and place of each event. Each of us was assigned to a small study group of around twelve members, which continued to meet unchanged until almost the end of the conference. The room where an activity was to take place and the time, an hour and a half, were laid down exactly, but within this space and time there was no programme whatsoever. We were told that 'the primary task of the group was to study its own behaviour as it happens'.

All my life I have had great difficulty in spontaneously expressing anger, or, when I have felt that such a response was necessary, I have either failed to deal with the situation or have had to simulate an anger that I did not feel inside. So I was amazed, in this small group, to find myself expressing rage quite freely. It seems that the energy for this was coming from the group rather than from myself as an individual. I gave the poor consultant an awful time and found myself engaging in struggles for leadership, particularly among the male members of the group, in a way I would never normally entertain. Some of the women in the group seemed to be egging on a couple of the male members to fight it out to the death in their desperate struggle for leadership.

There were several other events, which had been developed by A.K. Rice and others as part of the overall methodology of the working conferences: the large group, the institutional event and, at the end of the conference, review and application groups. The large group was even more chaotic and exasperating than the small groups. In this event the entire membership of seventy people was present sitting in chairs arranged in a series of concentric circles,

James Browne, Ivor's father, on the left, playing the mandolin, outside the 'hut' in Shankill, County Dublin, where he was living before he was married.

James Browne in his British Navy uniform, with Ivor's mother Gracie, on their wedding day in February 1922.

(left) Ivor as a baby, having a bath in the garden of the family home in Sandycove, County Dublin; (right) Ivor, a little older, and happier, playing in the sunshine.

(left) Ivor on the rope swing and (right) Ivor on Prince, the pony, both at Rathronan Castle, where they holidayed each year.

Heading down the Grand Canal, left to right, Ivor (in the hat), his sister Ismay, his father (steering), his brother Val, with the punt, and his mother with a friend.

Competing in the Junior High Jump where Ivor won the Junior Medal in the Leinster Sports, June 1942.

Ivor, standing on the extreme right, a medical student in the Meath Hospital.

Ivor and his mother at Ivor's graduation as a doctor from the Royal College of Surgeons, Dublin, 1954.

Ivor (left) with Denis Murphy, the great Kerry fiddle player.

Ivor (left) in the Harvard School of Public Health with classmates.

Dr Gerald Caplin (left) Professor of Mental Health at the Harvard School of Public Health.

Ivor's graduation, Ms. (Harv.) (Masters) in Mental Health, from Harvard University, 1961.

At the doctor's house in St Loman's Psychiatric Hospital. (left to right) Ivor's daughter Tierna, Ivor, and his sons Ronan and Garvan on Conn the donkey.

Ivor's parents in latter years, on the hammock he made himself, with Caesar the labrador.

Ivor and Juno on a visit to the Taj Mahal in India during the early 1980s.

Ivor (facing) and others arriving by boat at the hospital in Leros, Greece, in the 1980s.

Leros, Greece. Originally admitted to the children's unit, these young people, of both sexes, have grown up together.

(left to right) Ivor, Jeffrey Masson (author of Assault on Truth*), with others, in Limerick when Masson came to speak in Ireland in the 1990s.*

with four consultants, two of whom usually sat close to the centre and two at the periphery. The primary task here as stated in the programme was 'to provide opportunities for members to study the behaviour of the group as it occurs'. It was here that I first became aware of the way in which energy would seem to shift from one part of the group to another, often to locate in one person, who would overflow with emotion, while others would feel drained of all feeling. Frequently one of the participants, usually a woman seated near the centre, would fill up with emotion, weeping and sobbing. At the same time several of the men, usually on the periphery, would make statements like, 'What the hell is wrong with her?' or 'What is she crying about, I don't feel anything at all.'

One experience I had in the large group, however, left me speechless with amazement and I never forgot it. I was sitting out towards the edge of the group, feeling rather bored and lifeless. Then suddenly, about five minutes before the termination of the group, I felt myself seething with rage. This was so extreme that my fists were clenched and, afterwards, I could see the marks of my nails where they had dug into my palms. My rage was directed towards the consultants and I remember saying to myself, 'I am going to hit one of those fuckers as they leave the room', but as they passed close by something prevented me from doing anything. What really surprised me was that, ten minutes later, out in the bar having a drink, I felt perfectly relaxed as I chatted to other members. I can see no possible explanation for this experience other than that I was flooded with the energy and rage of the whole group for the few moments before the event ended.

I was subjected to similar experiences in the institutional event. Here, according to the programme, the primary task 'provides opportunities to study relations between groups as they happen and in particular the problems of exercising authority on behalf of others'. The institutional event also 'involves all members of staff and concentrates on studying the relatedness between them and the members, in the context of the conference institution as a whole. Staff take part in management and consultancy roles.' For this event the entire membership assembled in the plenary room, the staff entered and the director made a short statement about the task of the event, that members were free to form groups spontaneously in any way they wished and to study the inter-relationships between them. The director and the rest of the staff then abruptly left the room.

So, seventy people were left to decide how they would form small groups. Here again, certain rooms were designated for the use of the groups formed by the members, and the overall time frame for the event was laid down. Otherwise there was a complete vacuum and freedom to do whatever we wished. Almost immediately there was a palpable feeling of panic in the room. Then someone would stand up and make a suggestion, 'I think we should break up into six groups', only to be met almost immediately by derisive cries of, 'Who the hell are you to tell us what we should do?' Every suggestion from then on was dealt with in the same way, some supporting it and others angrily dismissing it, until a sense of complete paralysis descended on the assembly. Eventually a few members would decide to take the law into their own hands and leave the room. Others would follow in dribs and drabs until what came to be known as a 'rump' group was left behind, unable to move (see Fig. 4).

I decided I would just go off on my own. By this time four or five groups had already formed in several of the rooms and I found myself walking aimlessly up and down the corridor. Then suddenly I was assailed by the most terrifying panic, feeling utterly alone, with a sense of annihilation and abandonment, realising that I might not

Figure 4: A case of the blind leading the blind.

now be accepted into any group. I am aware, in relating this, that to anyone who has not had the experience of attending one of these conferences these feelings of anxiety and terror must seem quite ridiculous, but in fact such feelings are common among those who attend. Garrett O'Connor told me that in the first conference he attended, after the institutional event plenary, he refused to leave the room. He stayed there for several days but, when he eventually emerged, he felt the same sense of terror and abandonment. Then eventually someone he already knew from outside got him into one of the groups and then he immediately felt relaxed. However, the anxiety and terror with which he was possessed when he entered was, without his realising it, projected onto another member of the group, who went to pieces and became psychotic.

What usually happens in these events is that the groups that form spontaneously are quite unable to organise themselves internally to decide on any form of concerted action, and so become increasingly chaotic. They usually remain locked in their separate rooms, even though they are quite free to send out observers, delegates or plenipotentiaries to study inter-relationships between the groups. Eventually, towards the end of the event, they usually succeed in emerging from their isolation, sending rather meaningless messages to each other, coming up with titles for the various groups and establishing some sort of relationship with each other. What is striking is the extreme preoccupation of each group with establishing its boundary and the difficulties that arise in their finding ways to cross these demarcations. Unbelievably extreme emotions of anger, fear, anxiety and even humour arise in these interchanges. A general belief emerges among the members at this stage that some form of conspiracy is at work and that all of this chaos has been arranged in some way by the staff (see Fig. 5).

In that first conference the majority of the members and myself were completely convinced of this, so I decided with a few others to plan a revolution and set up our own management team in defiance of the consultant staff. There was one fellow who bore a striking resemblance to Napoleon and, although I was the main person organising the revolution, I appointed him as chairman, with me as his deputy. On the day the revolution was to take place we had selected an empty room and had set up table and chairs, reminiscent of a scene from the French Revolution, but at the crucial moment my

Figure 5: Unbelievably extreme emotions of anger, fear, anxiety, struggles for leadership and so on arise in these interchanges.

chairman failed to turn up. At that very instant I had a flash of insight. 'This is what I always do! I set a movement going but then balk at accepting leadership and try to get someone else to take it on instead.'

This is just one example showing that what happens in these conferences is not something artificial and separate from real life, which is a complaint many participants voice when they first attend a conference. On the contrary, the design of the working conferences is such that it acts like a pressure cooker, bringing very intense emotions and primitive behaviours to the surface. But everything that happens there can be found in ordinary life, albeit in a less intense and less perceptible form.

The most lasting impression I have of those first two conferences is the way in which one loses all sense of identity. By the end of a week I hardly knew who I was. Towards the end of the second conference, which I attended about a year and a half later, I asked for an interview with the director, Pierre Turquet, to discuss the possibility of our running conferences on a similar basis in Ireland under the auspices of the Irish Foundation. Going up the stairs to his office I felt weak and fearful, like a small child, exactly the way I had felt many years ago in school when called in to face Miss Manley. This was because by the end of the conference it felt as if all my skin had been torn away, leaving me exposed and defenceless, and at the mercy of others.

In the second conference I felt freer to experiment and try out different behaviours in the various events. For example, in the small group, when the usual struggle for leadership started to emerge, instead of competing against another member who was making a bid for a leadership role I supported him. To my amazement no sooner did I do this than I felt all the confidence and energy being sucked out of me, with a complete loss of self-esteem. This was despite the fact that I had voluntarily taken the decision to let him take over.

A.K. Rice and the others developed the design for this method of studying human group behaviour from the pioneering insights of W.R. Bion. Bion, who was a Kleinian psychoanalyst, had started working with groups in the British army during the Second World War. He continued this work later when in 1948 he was asked to take on therapeutic groups by the Tavistock Clinic. From this work he developed a unique view of the ways in which groups behave, as distinct from the behaviour of the individuals who make them up. As A.K. Rice described in his book, *Learning for Leadership*:

Bion has suggested that a group always behaves simultaneously at two levels. At the manifest level a group needs to perform a specific task; at the same time it behaves as if it had made one of three discrete assumptions: to attempt to reproduce itself, to obtain security from one individual upon whom its members can depend; or to preserve itself by attacking someone or something, or by running away. He distinguished these characteristics of group life as the work group, the group met to perform its specific tasks; and the basic group, the group acting on one of the discrete assumptions. The basic group met to reproduce itself, he called that pairing; the group met to obtain security from one person, dependent, and the group met to fight or to run away, fight-flight. A basic assumption is a tacit assumption; the members of a group behave as if they were aware of it, even though it was unconscious. Not only is participation in a basic assumption unavoidable, but it involves each member sharing in the emotions to which he contributes.[1]

Speaking of any business or organisation, A.K. Rice defines the primary task as 'the task it must perform if it is to survive'. To carry out this task would, in effect, be what Bion describes as the 'work group; i.e. the group met to perform its specific task'.[2]

This is clear enough when applied to, say, a shoe factory, which must produce shoes if it is to survive, or a law school, which must produce lawyers and so on. But it is quite a different matter to say that the primary task of a group is 'to study its own behaviour in the here and now', as it happens. For, if a member of the group tries to describe what he or she thinks is happening, by the time it is described the moment has already passed. The statement is itself a behaviour of the group and is usually seen by other members as an attempt to take a leadership position. This insoluble situation, together with the fact that there is no content or discernible programme for the group to engage in, inevitably gives rise to a deep sense of frustration, creating a state of high anxiety and tension among the members.

Further, the consultant remains silent except for giving occasional interpretations as to what he thinks is happening at any given moment, so he refuses to take any leadership role, which is what the other members of the group would normally expect him to take. This increases the sense of being caught in a vacuum. The reserved manner of the staff in general, in that they refuse to fraternise and limit their comments as far as possible to interpreting the primary task, and the maintenance of a strict boundary between themselves and the members, serves to further heighten the sense of frustration.

It seems to me that the Tavistock theorists have created a catch-twenty-two situation and often deliberately behave in a rather angry, contemptuous manner, upbraiding the members for failing to address themselves adequately to the primary tasks of the conference. It is this very contradiction that constitutes the true brilliance of this method. The conference is designed to force out primitive behaviours and promote the use of defence mechanisms in order to reduce anxiety, escape ambivalence and preserve sanity. But these behaviours are also present below the surface in our interactions in ordinary society.

The strange thing is that Bion says the group behaves 'as if' it were dependent, 'as if' a pair were about to produce the solution, and 'as if' the group were preparing to fight or run away. He specifically states, 'I have not felt the need to postulate the existence of a herd instinct to account for such a phenomenon as I have witnessed in the group'. Influenced by the work of Melanie Klein, and her work on 'object relations' theory and 'projective identification', he states:

> Further investigation shows that each basic assumption contains features that correspond so closely with extremely primitive part objects that sooner or later psychotic anxiety, appertaining to these primitive relationships, is released. These anxieties, and the mechanisms peculiar to them, have been already displayed in psychoanalysis by Melanie Klein, and her descriptions tally well with the emotional states that find an outlet in mass action of the group in behaviour that seems to have coherence if it is considered to be the outcome of a basic assumption.[3]

Thus he appears to consider the basic assumption behaviours manifested by a group as pathological, always in danger of deteriorating into psychotic chaos, and hence the anxieties experienced by participants when these primitive behaviours are unleashed.

Yet the very terminology that he uses in trying to describe these 'basic assumptions', the dependency group struggling to produce a leader, the 'fight or flight' activity, or the selection of a pair by the group in an attempt to reproduce a solution, are descriptions of the survival behaviours of many groups of mammals. Much of the activity of primates such as gorillas or chimpanzees constitutes the struggle to produce a dominant leader (usually male) around which the group organises itself. The 'fight or flight' strategy evolves to deal with predators and the activity of mating serves to reproduce the next generation. But these are the natural behaviours essential for any animal group to organise itself and survive. The other main activity of gathering food could, I suppose, fit Bion's description of the work group.

These behaviours constitute the basic biological life of most mammals. In no sense can we say that the gathering of food is a more 'primary task' than the other activities; all are necessary to sustain the life of the group. So it seems that the genius of Bion in elucidating these basic assumptions is in pointing to the fact that, as human beings, we still carry, below the level of consciousness, these primitive instinctive biological behaviours. It doesn't seem useful to me to consider them as abnormal or pathological, but rather to see them as part of our fundamental nature and a reality, the existence of which we need to be aware.

At that time in 1973 I had, as yet, had no exposure to systems theory or understanding the nature of living systems, so I could make little sense of what was happening. I believe it is only now, in the light of fairly recent research in systems theory and the behaviour of living systems, that one can understand what is happening in these situations.

23

Derry

When the civil rights movement in Northern Ireland became active in 1968–9, followed by the attacks on Catholics in the Bogside and Belfast by the police and Loyalist mobs, I watched it all happening on television like everyone else. Then crowds of refugees, women and children, started arriving in Dublin and, as accommodation had to be found for them wherever possible, we had to take some of them in St Brendan's. They were housed in the nurses' home and in the alcoholic unit in St Dymphna's on the North Circular Road. At the slightest disturbance these children would rush out on to the street and start banging dustbin lids. They seemed to us quite wild. After Bloody Sunday in January 1972, when the British Embassy in Dublin was burned down, I was in the crowd at Merrion Square and, like others there feeling full of anger, I seriously considered getting on one of the buses that were being assembled to go to the North to help protect the nationalist population.

A couple of months after the massacre on Bloody Sunday, a small deputation from Derry came to Dublin to see me. The two leaders were Father Denis Bradley, who has since left the priesthood and was later Deputy Chairman of the Police Board in Northern Ireland, and Eamon Deane (a brother of the writer Seamus Deane). They had heard about the work of the Irish Foundation for Human Development in Ballyfermot and wondered if we could help them to set up something similar in the Bogside. We agreed we would see what could be done.

Towards the end of February 1972 I went to Derry to assess the situation. Up until then the civil rights movement was still struggling to maintain its campaign of peaceful demonstrations. The emergence of the Provos only came later and was an inevitable response to the continuing institutional violence of the Northern administration and the British Army. The situation in Derry was particularly difficult at that time because, following Bloody Sunday, the campaign of violence by the Provisional IRA was escalating rapidly. It was only after Bloody Sunday, and the subsequent introduction of internment that anger and despair resulted in a lot of young people joining the Provisional IRA. This is something that is generally misunderstood by commentators in the Republic.

I asked Eamon Deane and Denis Bradley if there was anyone they could think of who might take on the job of community organiser. After some consideration they suggested Paddy Doherty, who had recently returned from the West Indies. He was also known as Paddy Bogside, a name he acquired during the battle of the Bogside in 1969 when he emerged as the leader of the resistance and his house in 10 Westland Street became central headquarters of the nationalist resistance in Derry. He had gone to the West Indies following this to work in the building trade, as otherwise he would have been interned.

Prior to the commencement of the civil rights campaign Paddy had been a building foreman. Up to that point he had not seen himself as particularly radical in a political sense, although he had always been active in the community and, earlier, with the assistance of John Hume, had established the Credit Union in Derry. There was a lot of poverty then and it was virtually impossible for a Catholic to get a house or a job because of political gerrymandering by the loyalist minority. Early in their marriage Paddy and his wife Eileen lived in one room in a crowded household. They had two children and Paddy had approached the housing authority to try to get his family listed on the housing list. The official there asked how many children he had; when Paddy answered, he was told only to return to have his name listed when he had nine children. Instead of being defeated by the hopelessness of the situation, he set about buying a site. When he had that, he bought bricks week by week until he built shelter for his family and himself. This is the house where he still lives, and has lived for the past fifty years, in Westland Street in the Bogside.

Paddy is a short man, broad shouldered and built like a rock. When asked if he was interested in a job as community organiser he simply replied, 'No.' After spending two years in the West Indies he intended to set up a family business with several of his sons. Recently he reminded me that my response, when he said he intended to be a builder instead, was to say, 'Then come and build people.' When he recalled this he added, 'That bastard has hooked me in ever since.' In any event he agreed to take up the post as community organiser and I was able to obtain a salary for him from the Bank of Ireland, through the foundation, for £2,000 a year. The Bogside Community Association (BCA) was thus established, with Paddy Doherty employed by them.

By this time the IRA were active and the situation was becoming more serious. The split within the IRA had already taken place between the Provisionals and the official IRA. When I first went up there I remember seeing car-loads of both driving around the streets with guns pointing out of the windows. 'Free Derry' had been declared and there were barricades manned by armed men at all the entrance points to the Bogside so that neither the police nor the British army were able to enter the area. Paddy had some success in setting up community structures there but was soon distracted by the escalating violence and the heavy-handed behaviour of the British army. He found himself having to concentrate his efforts on protecting the community he was being paid to develop.

Tension was rising between the two IRA groups and I was asked at one point to go to a meeting in an attempt to cool the situation. The meeting was held in the Provisional IRA's Derry headquarters, which was in a house over by the gasworks. I remember Martin McGuinness was there, along with several others. There was a real danger of violence breaking out between the two groups, which could have happened except for the pressures coming from the British army and the police on the outside. After that meeting I went back to review the situation with Paddy Doherty and together we decided that, if we were to continue with our community development work, we should keep out of any direct political involvement. I think this was an important decision and we stuck to it throughout all the years we worked with the community in Derry. Had we not done so, I feel we would have got sucked into impossible situations.

By the end of July 1972, the authorities in the North felt they could no longer tolerate the existence of 'Free Derry', which had meant that a major part of the city of Derry had been removed from the United Kingdom. Consequently, there was a massive British military intervention known as 'Operation Motorman'. About 20,000 British troops, with tanks and heavy armour, invaded the Bogside to break up the barricades and do away with 'Free Derry' once and for all. They expected fierce resistance from the Provisional IRA but found that the Provisionals had crossed the border into Donegal before the army arrived.

The advent of 'Operation Motorman' ushered in a period of intense activity for Paddy Doherty and, to a lesser extent, myself, because, following this, law and order in the Bogside and Creggan area were only imposed by the army. They occupied several schools in the area and carried out many arrests, against which the ordinary people had no protection. There were guidelines laid down by the army authorities as to how the troops were to behave when making arrests, but they were often heavy-handed so, whenever Paddy learned that the troops were about to raid a house, he would go there before the army arrived. This was Paddy's chief role in the BCA. Day and night he was constantly intervening in raids and for months he got little rest or sleep. On one of these occasions the army raided the house next door to Paddy's because a number of soldiers had been shot nearby, even though the family in this house had nothing to do with the Troubles. Paddy pushed his way in because he heard the screaming and disturbance. The mother was almost prostrate in one room whilst the sergeant in charge of the raid was forcing his way into the room, shouting and swearing profusely. Paddy intervened, telling the others that their sergeant must be taken off duty as he was out of control.

A community relations officer, a major in the army, appeared and tried to calm the situation. He went in to talk to the mother, tea was ordered and the situation was settling down, when there was a rattle of gunfire and the soldiers all left abruptly. At this point Paddy asked the community relations officer, 'Do you realise all the soldiers are gone? Have you any way of contacting your base?' 'No.' 'Are you armed?' 'No. In this job we're not allowed to carry arms.' Paddy told him that he was in a dangerous situation.

In the meantime, the crowd were gathering again outside, shouting, 'There's one of the bastards still in there!' Paddy told another Derry man who was amongst the crowd, 'We have a major problem here.' He replied, 'You have a "major" problem all right. And you'll have a dead "Major", that's what you'll have.' Fortunately Paddy recog-

nised the seriousness of the situation and told the major to follow him
out the window and over the garden wall, where he brought him to the
street and pointed him in the right direction to rejoin his comrades.

People were saying there was a riot at the top of Beechwood Avenue and that some people were engaging with the army. Paddy drove
up there and was in time to see a soldier push a woman to the ground
with the butt of his rifle. She got up and rushed at the soldier before
Paddy stood between them, warning the woman that she would get
herself killed. At that moment the soldier struck Paddy on the fore-
head with the butt of the rifle. As he was losing consciousness, he
heard a sergeant say to the guy that hit him, 'You stupid bastard.
What did you do that for?' Later the colonel appeared and apologised
to him and Paddy was sent to hospital, where he had to get nine
stitches. The extraordinary irony about this whole debacle was that
when the case finally came to court Paddy, who was a pioneer and
had never taken a drink in his life, was convicted of being drunk and
disorderly. The judge said the soldier had acted appropriately.

I was in Derry on another occasion when about a hundred
British soldiers suddenly appeared in the Bogside to raid a nearby
house. Paddy rushed to the house to ensure that the soldiers were
behaving themselves and I followed him. As he pushed his way into
the house the door closed behind him and I thrust it open again.
There was a small British soldier on the other side of the door and,
with the force of my push, he shot across the room to the far wall.
Suddenly, we faced each other – he terrified of me and I equally terrified of the rifle pointing at me.

There were many contradictions during the early days of the
Troubles. Paddy had made good friends with a Church of Ireland
clergyman, Brian Smeaton, a Dublin man who had come north to do
community work on the streets. He was working on the Shankill
Road and was actually chaplain to the Ulster Defence Association
(UDA) at the time. Paddy used to go over to Belfast and even attended meetings on the Shankill Road at a time when no Catholic
would dare to venture there.

Brian Smeaton came to the Bogside on one occasion to meet
Paddy when the riots were in full swing and British army patrols
were everywhere. They were just sitting down to dinner in Paddy's
house when a young Provo rushed in with the army hot on his heels.
He lifted one of Paddy's daughters out of her chair and sat down,

pretending to eat his dinner. The soldiers burst in, pointing their rifles at the table, shouting, 'Who was the last man in?' Brian, who had a bushy beard at that time and a prominent Dublin accent, shouted in protest at this intrusion. The sergeant shouted in response, 'You, out!' They dragged him out onto the street. As soon as they were out of the room the young Provo, who also had a beard, ran out the back, over the garden wall and away. In the meantime Brian was protesting that he was a Church of Ireland clergyman working on the Shankill Road and they heard an officer shouting, 'You stupid bastards, you got the wrong man.'

One time Paddy, who was well known to the army because of his frequent interventions during their arrest operations, was talking to a community relations officer, who said, 'You know, Mr Doherty, sooner or later you'll have to come down off the fence and declare which side you're on.' Paddy looked at him and replied, 'Major, whenever I come down off the fence it can never be on your side, so just pray I stay on the fence.'

The violent campaign of the Provisional IRA in the North is always portrayed as the primary source of the Troubles there. I feel there is a deep misunderstanding about this in the rest of the world. People outside Northern Ireland assume that all Provos were psychopathic criminal types as only such people could be attracted to the IRA. The truth is that at the height of the Troubles it was young men and women who were simply appalled at the way nationalists were being treated, who joined the IRA. There had been sectarian pogroms, murders and discrimination against the Catholic population ever since the creation of the six-county state. IRA violence, regrettable though it may be, was an inevitable reaction to the primary violence of the six-county state, not the basic cause of the problem. When the peaceful civil rights movement was literally beaten into the ground by Ian Paisley and his extremist Protestant gangs, followed by vicious and brutal reprisals by the Royal Ulster Constabulary (RUC) and later the British army, culminating in internment and, ultimately, Bloody Sunday, it was inevitable that young nationalists, who saw no hope of achieving anything by peaceful means, should flock to join the IRA's ranks.

There was an amusing example of this stereotyped thinking on the part of the British. A young fellow who was 'on the run' in Donegal found it wasn't easy for him to get into Derry, so he used to jog past the British army post coming in from Donegal. It didn't seem to cross the minds of the British soldiers that a young, healthy fellow out jogging could have anything to do with the IRA.

The only occasion on which I became involved with the national- ist struggle was when another friend of ours in Derry, Mary Nelis, asked me to go to Long Kesh to visit her two sons. They were taking part in the blanket protest, where IRA prisoners remained naked, wrapped in blankets, refusing to wear prison uniforms in an attempt to regain their status as political prisoners. She felt a visit from me would help to raise their morale. Until the time they were arrested Mary Nelis was a con- servative Social Democratic and Labour Party (SDLP) supporter, but the treatment of her sons in the Maze Prison changed her political al- legiance to Sinn Féin.

I arrived at Long Kesh and battled my way through the security procedures. When I got to the public visiting room Mary's two sons were there to greet me. It was quite an extraordinary spectacle, these two young men, covered only in a blanket, their faces amazingly peaceful. They spoke to me in gentle terms about what they were trying to achieve. While I was talking quietly to the prisoners, there was a line of prison officers who presented a striking contrast to the young men on the blankets, their faces clearly stressed and full of angry resentment.

Derry, prior to the Troubles, provided the worst example of a de- pendency culture, with no sense of itself, and it was from this back- ground that Paddy Doherty emerged. He embodies, more than anyone, what this book is primarily about – being the best possible example of self-reliance and independent thinking. Perhaps I had some influence on the full realisation of these qualities, but it seems to have been something that reached to the core of his being. The work in Derry demonstrates, better than anything else, the idea that co-operation rather than competition can work. My role over the years was to try to keep the central purpose of the project on track and prevent it drifting into stagnation. Someone once said of us that 'Whenever Paddy Doherty showed signs of incipient sanity, Ivor Browne went North to drive him mad again.'

24

The Irish Conferences

In 1975 Garret O'Connor came over to Ireland from the States and I discussed with him the possibility of running working conferences here as part of the work of the Irish Foundation. The A.K. Rice Institute was the equivalent in the United States of the Human Relations division of the Tavistock in Britain. Under the auspices of these Garret had directed eighty such conferences in different parts of the States. He was enthusiastic about the idea and we decided to see if we could establish a team of consultants drawn from both the US and Britain, as well as the couple of us in Ireland who already had some experience of this method. Accordingly, he put together a team consisting of himself as director, the late Margaret Rioch, who was a well-known psychologist and researcher in the States, and Rachael Robinson, a beautiful black woman from a nursing background, who had been part of Garret O'Connor's regular team. She was the widow of the famous black baseball player Jackie Robinson. From the Tavistock we had Canon Herrick, an Anglican canon in Chelmsford Cathedral, an Australian, and a lady whose name escapes me, plus Paddy Walley and myself from Ireland.

We managed to negotiate to take the hall of Trinity College out of term time, an ideal location with a fine large room for plenary sessions and for the large group, and an adequate number of small rooms that could be designated as the space for the conference. For the first conference, with the help of Tom Hardiman and others like Paddy Lynch, with their connections in business, the civil service and trade unions, we were able to recruit a membership of approximately sixty. There were several priests and nuns, a number of higher civil servants, administrators from health boards and business men

196

and women, community workers from Ballyfermot, Derry and else-where, some of the staff of the foundation, and several from para-military organisations, both Provisionals and Official IRA. We made sure that none of the participants knew the sources from which the various members were drawn. I remember how some people were concerned when one Provisional IRA man sat throughout the entire conference with his back to the wall, staring darkly and making sure no one could approach him from behind.

In the introductory plenary I noticed that a number of the members had arrived with notebooks, pen and paper, clearly expecting to be given some form of introductory lecture. Just as I had experienced it when at-tending the Leicester conference, Garret O'Connor and the rest of us staff members entered the room and sat down in a row. Garret O'Connor delivered a short introductory talk, which clearly the audi-ence found incomprehensible, and then asked, 'What would you like to discuss?' The frustration among the participants was palpable.

As the small and large group events proceeded and the level of tension, chaos and anger among the members escalated, I found my-self experiencing considerable anxiety. I was only too acutely aware that if anything went wrong, the foundation, under whose auspices the conference was being held, would be responsible. My anxiety reached an acute stage when, in the small group where I was a con-sultant, one higher civil servant became extremely angry, saying the whole conference was a fraud and threatening to sue the foundation for seducing him into this charade under false pretences.

The way in which Garret had organised the staff team was that he and Rachael Robinson took the large group, while the remaining five of us each took one of the small study groups, with twelve mem-bers in each group, making up the total membership of sixty. Canon Herrick and the Australian, who were much more experienced than the rest of us, acted as supervisors, particularly for Paddy Walley and me. As part of this supervision Canon Herrick gave me an impor-tant insight. Having had such a struggle to achieve independence from my own family and having experienced the same problem later with many patients in my clinical practice, particularly those we re-gard as schizophrenic, I saw myself as struggling against depend-ency in all its forms. Dependency was simply bad and independence good. One day during the conference when I said this, Herrick drew me quietly aside and in his gentle way said, 'You know, you've got it all wrong. In your profession and mine we work continually in a context of dependency. If someone were not feeling in some way dependent and thus unable to manage, they would not come to seek our help in the first place. What is important is not that the person who comes to us is in a dependent state, but whether we use this dependency for growth towards independence, or whether we foster further dependence.'

One of the key things I had to learn as a member of staff was to preserve a clear boundary between the participants and myself. This is a vital aspect of the method for, as the anxiety and frustration increase, members in desperation will try every way they can to seduce you out of your role. This happened to me towards the end of the first conference, when the members had arranged a social evening and got around me to play the guitar and sing a few songs. No sooner had I succumbed than I could see the delight and derision among them, in effect saying, 'we've got him now'. I realised my mistake and withdrew as quickly as possible, but all that night I had the most dreadful nightmares and anxiety, seeing devilish faces and horrible masks jeering and mocking me. I felt I had let myself and the rest of the team down. Next morning I spoke to Garret O'Connor about what had happened and wondered whether I was fit to continue, but he just told me not to let it happen again.

One of the clearest examples of the way in which the energy of the entire group can shift on to one person, who can be literally driven mad in the process, happened at one of these conferences. David, a young biochemist, who had the typical combination of personality traits that is liable to get a person into difficulties in this situation, was a rather gentle personality with a weak ego and poor management of his boundaries. At the same time though he had a strong desire for leadership. He took on this role early in the conference, intervening with suggestions and making attempts to organise the other members in the large group and elsewhere; it was as if the entire group unconsciously saw their opportunity and for a time colluded with his desire for leadership. What they were actually doing though was transferring all their unwanted anxieties and tensions on to him. As the days went on he became visibly more disturbed and overactive until he could only be described as floridly psychotic. His mental state was such that if he behaved this way in ordinary life one would have felt he urgently required hospitalisation. This reached crisis point in the institutional event, where the task is for members to break up spontaneously into a number of small groups and then study the interaction between these. For this event the staff operate in open session so that the members can interact and negotiate with them as they see fit.

For anyone who has not had experience with this type of conference, it is hard to imagine the scene that was unfolding at this point. Four or five small groups had formed themselves and were meeting behind closed doors in several of the rooms. What was really strange was that they were uncannily quiet and there was little sign of activity or disturbance emerging from any of the rooms, even though a group could have asked for a consultant to come to help them if they so desired.

It so happened that I was called out to one of these groups, where I found them in a very laid back, apathetic state, discussing some esoteric point which seemed to make no sense whatsoever. However, for quite a while before this, and while I was there with them in the room, this same fellow, who had not joined any of the groups, was striding around the corridors shrieking at the top of his voice. I was only too aware that this was a highly dangerous situation and I was so conscious of my responsibility for the foundation if any tragedy should happen that I found it difficult to listen to what the participants in this small group were discussing. There they were, with the shrieking going on, behaving as if nothing untoward were happening, seemingly quite oblivious to the commotion going on outside. As soon as I could excuse myself, I returned in a highly anxious state to the rest of the staff to find that this man had entered the staff room and was screaming at Garret O'Connor as if in great pain. Garret, with what I can only describe as a stroke of genius, said to him, 'I am not going to deal with you as a separate person, as you seem to be carrying something important for the entire membership which they have projected into you.' To make himself heard, Garret had to shout at him: 'Go and tell all of them to take their shit back out of you.'

To my amazement he appeared to take this on board. He retreated out of the room still highly disturbed and, barging his way into each of the rooms in turn, shouted at them to take their shit back. Whether the reader will believe it or not, I can only describe what happened next. As he went from room to room each of the groups, which had up to that time been quiet, apparently apathetic and inactive, now became increasingly noisy and disturbed; shouting and wrangling erupted from each group in turn as he went from one to the other. What was even stranger was that within an hour or so, he had completely calmed down and become quite sane and rational once again.

I have never forgotten the experience of that day and it brought home to me a basic principle, not only in the management of these conferences, but in life generally. When someone becomes disturbed in this way in a working conference, it is vitally important that they are not exported out of the conference. It is the task of the director (as Garret O'Connor did so well in this instance) to hold them in the conference and to get the members to take responsibility for what they are doing. It is vital to get them to take back the energy that they have projected into that unfortunate person before the conference is terminated. However, often a deputation of the members demand that such a disturbed person be treated as a patient and hospitalised.

In a similar situation in another conference, where Eric Miller of the Tavistock was director, a group of the members came to him pleading for him to do something about a person who was in trouble, saying, 'Do you not care at all about what is happening to him?' Miller replied, 'My job here is to care for the learning.' If such a person were driven out of the conference, they could carry that disturbance with them for many months, perhaps for good. I believe that this may well be what happens in life, in families and other situations, where a person is made a scapegoat and driven mad, then exported into hospital or whatever.

In this regard I remember Canon Herrick telling me that the professional background from which the director comes will tend to determine the kind of casualty which the membership will bring forth. In an attempt to get relief from an intolerable situation, the members will inevitably try to produce a casualty. If the director is a psychiatrist, then the casualty presented will be someone going mad. If the director is a clergyman, then the casualty presented will be likely to be a cleric or a nun losing their faith. If the director is an economist or someone from a business background, then it might be a businessman that goes to the wall. Herrick also said that when he was asked to consult with a parish that was running into financial or other difficulties, he often found that the cleric in charge had got involved in an affair with his secretary. He felt this was an example of the pairing basic assumption, where the cleric had the forlorn hope of producing a solution sexually to the impending crisis.

At another conference I attended, several religious sisters took part. One of these was an elderly nun who obviously had no notion about group interaction and who found the experience quite mystifying and distasteful. From the time she entered she kept behaving as if she were at a vicar's tea party, saying things like, 'Why can't we all be nice to each other' or 'I don't know what all this fuss is about.' She happened to be a member of my small study group and there was a much younger sister in the group as well. The elderly nun continued to make the same silly platitudinous remarks until eventually I felt compelled to ask the members what they felt the group was doing to keep this woman behaving in this way. As is usual with such an 'interpretation', there were angry denials that they were doing anything to her, she was just a silly cow, etc. Then, after about ten minutes, the younger nun somewhat shamefacedly acknowledged that, when she came into the conference and saw this elderly sister, she had thought, 'She's the type of sister of the older generation who won't, or can't, adapt to new ideas.' She was referring to the changes which had come about after the Second Vatican Council. There was nothing particularly surprising about this admission but what I didn't anticipate was how the elderly nun would react. Her manner changed completely, she became serious and stopped all the denial in which she had been indulging since the conference began. When she went into the next large group session, she berated the entire assembly for the way in which they had behaved towards her. From then onwards she made serious and thoughtful contributions to the group, in marked contrast to her behaviour in the early part of the conference. This and other similar experiences made me realise that, even when we form a thought about another person without saying anything, it can still affect their behaviour and hold them in a certain role, even though as an individual they might be anxious and willing to change.

Once I gained this insight I realised that this often happens in ordinary life where a person has a valency for a certain kind of behaviour which is then activated by the powerful projection of the group. For example, someone who has an aggressive temperament may find he gets sucked in as shop steward in the union. He may then find himself locked into this role by the group and, even if he wishes to change, find it very difficult to escape. Bion took this term 'valency' from chemistry, where one element or molecule is said to be attracted to combine with another.

In becoming a member of the consultant staff in the conferences that we held in Ireland, I was naïve enough to believe that this would be less anxiety provoking than being an ordinary member. I was sadly mistaken. Being a member of the staff group is even more stressful, frustrating and disturbing than being a member. The problem of maintaining your individual boundary and sense of personal identity is far more difficult than being an ordinary participant in the conference.

I will mention just two more examples from my own experience to illustrate this point. Towards the end of one of the conferences in Trinity Hall I had to go out in the car to get a message. During that week, I had not drunk any alcohol nor had I taken medication or drugs of any kind. Yet when I drove out onto the street I felt completely exposed and seemed to have no protection from everything coming at me. Then, when I was returning to the conference, I became aware that there was no distinction between the car and myself; it felt as if all the moving parts, the wheels, the turning of the steering wheel and the engine, were all part of me. This experience was so real that, when I came to the entrance of Trinity Hall, the car came to a dead stop. I expected it to turn and drive itself in through the gate. I was absolutely shocked to find this happening and realised then that my personal boundary had dissolved completely.

Again, on the day the conference ended, I was due to attend a medical faculty meeting in the university. By this time I was consciously aware of how unbounded and over-exposed I was as a result of the intensive group experience. I decided I should go to the meeting but made arrangements to meet someone, so that I would have to leave at the end of an hour, even if the meeting was continuing. I had no sooner entered the room and sat down than I realised that this was a wise decision. I don't ever remember feeling so utterly vulnerable. It was as if I had no protection whatsoever from the energies coming at me from the other members of the faculty. What is more, I seemed to be aware of what lay beneath the surface of their personalities, the lust for power, the anger and rage against one another and all the tensions and frustrations of dissatisfied academic careers. As the meeting went on I felt a sense of real terror and lack of protection. I simply sat there unable to speak or do anything, just holding on until the hour was up.

One of the greatest pieces of nonsense in psychiatric literature, which is repeated *ad nauseam* in textbooks over the years, is the notion that schizophrenics are emotionally blunted and have lost the capacity to feel. That personal experience made me realise, once and for all, how wrong this is. Faced with the same kind of over-exposure and vulnerability that I experienced in that faculty meeting, schizophrenics have no recourse but to retreat into themselves, erecting a rigid wall around themselves for their own protection. The price they pay for this, of course, is that instead of being open, which is a natural state to all living creatures, they become closed off and increasingly unable to relate to those around them. When I went through that experience my mind drifted back to the schizophrenic woman I sat with for three months in the hospital in Oxford who seemed to be totally without feeling until the day a big tear rolled down her face.

These experiences are not unique to me or to the other individuals attending the conferences, like the young man I described, who became psychotic for a time during one of them. Nor are they something that only occurs in the unusual atmosphere of these group laboratories. They are happening, albeit in a less perceptible way, in everyday life.

After one of the Trinity Hall conferences I was approached by a Little Sister of the Assumption who had attended. She asked me if I would meet some nuns who were in charge of different convents in that Order. I sat down with a group of about seven nuns without any idea as to what they wanted to discuss. To get things started I asked them if there was any particular problem that they all felt they shared. They thought for a few moments and then agreed that a problem they shared was the difficult sister who would not adapt to the new ways introduced by the Second Vatican Council. Looking at this from the point of view of group behaviour, I asked would it solve the problem if I were to take the difficult nun out of the picture. At first there was a murmur of assent. Then, one after another, they began to look doubtful, realising of course, that this was the way in which they would have tried to solve such problems in the past. They got rid of the difficult person concerned, only to find that she was quickly replaced by another. It would have been more relevant to ask what was going on in the convent as a whole that required a difficult nun to be produced as a scapegoat?

Participants in the conference have often said to me that the insights gained in this work are dangerous. They could be used to manipulate others, without them being aware of what is happening. But what they are failing to realise is that with this new understanding comes an increased sense of responsibility, an awareness of the damage that can be done if such skills are improperly used. People like car salesmen and others, who are not consciously aware of the power of suggestion that they are using, can be much more dangerous. We are all familiar with the situation where someone decides to buy a certain make of car, say a Renault, but, following a negotiation with the salesman, ends up buying a Ford. If asked why they changed their mind they will say, 'Oh, I hadn't realised that the Ford is much better.' However, they are left with a sick, uncomfortable feeling. Later, once left to themselves, they may realise this was not really the car they wanted. This is just a simple example of what frequently happens to many of us. We allow someone who is able to use powerful suggestion to invade our boundary and project their point of view into us.

Some people are much more easily influenced in this way than others. I can think of several people I have known who, following a discussion, will decide on a course of action, but when another person suggests a different view, they change their mind and decide to do something quite different. They think they have changed in the light of new evidence but in actual fact they are allowing themselves to be taken over. This is where the awareness gained in the conference experience can be so valuable. For example, if you have difficulty managing your boundary, you can decide before going into a meeting that no matter what you feel at the time you will say something like, 'That sounds like a good idea but I'll have to think about it and I'll let you know tomorrow'. Take another example. There is a meeting and you have decided with a colleague to take an agreed approach. To your amazement, in the meeting, not only does the colleague not support you but actually speaks against what you had both agreed beforehand. It is natural to feel betrayed and let down when this happens, but this is to misunderstand. What has actually happened is that he has been taken over by group pressure and made to change his mind. He has allowed himself to be invaded and has been unable to sustain his individual viewpoint. The sad thing is that, when this happens, a person often feels committed and obliged to maintain the new position, even though in his heart he knows this is not what he really stands for. I have always felt that something like this happened to Michael Collins and the others in the Treaty negotiations. Under the pressure of the much more experienced and Machiavellian British politicians at the time, they felt they had no choice but to sign an agreement which they knew in their hearts would have disastrous consequences.

Prior to undergoing these group experiences, I had a lot of difficulty as Chief Psychiatrist with my colleagues and I often felt they were being obstructive and unreasonable. But later I realised that in the conferences most of the dynamics of what is happening are embodied in the director. Then, given that in my job I was in a leadership position, it follows that if things were not going right, the problem was probably in my behaviour rather than in that of others. I was amazed to find that once I changed my approach to accept this, most of the difficulties melted away.

This raises the whole question as to what leadership is about. When a societal group becomes too large to have face-to-face interaction, the creation of some form of leadership becomes inevitable. Once a leader emerges, the 'basic assumption' of 'dependency' in the group tends to arise. The essential function of the leader then is to ensure that the members of the society of which he is in charge take responsibility for all the positive and negative forces that exist within that group. The task is to continually resolve conflicts and contradictions among them, and to manage these within the boundary of the group. There is a paradox here, however, for looking at it in this way would suggest that the job of the leader is essentially to manage something other than him/herself. In actual fact once the leader has emerged, s/he tends to become the stage on which the conflicting forces and contradictions of the group are acted out.

The danger here is that if a whole society moves into a dependent position and personifies all of its responsibility in one individual, who is essentially no more competent or capable than any other person, it places itself in a very perilous situation. This, perhaps, was the situation with the divine king of the Incas. Once the Spaniards captured him, the whole society fell apart. Even worse was the predicament of the German people under Hitler. Once they had handed all their responsibility and initiative over to him, he was the only one who could decide anything. It was as if he were consumed by all the energy and power put into him by an entire nation, ultimately driving him mad, so that his decisions became more and more irrational. It is questionable how capable he was in the first place, but, by the time he had taken over the hearts and minds of those around him, they were virtually helpless to halt the destructive madness into which he was taking them. There is another important lesson to be learnt from the Hitler phenomenon. All of us contain both positive and negative tendencies, both good and evil. It is the task of each of us as individuals to take responsibility for all that is within us and not to try to push the unacceptable parts of ourselves on to others. The same is true of society at large. The tendency which is all too prevalent, particularly among ideological or fundamentalist groups, is to want to project out the negative and evil aspects of ourselves on to some other group. Hitler wanted to create the perfect Aryan society and to achieve this he tried to project all that was evil and dark onto the Jews, gypsies and others whom he considered to be inferior. However, in attempting to do this he gave free reign to the evil tendencies which are latent in any society to grow like a cancer within the very heart of German society itself. The same phenomenon was at work in the Spanish Inquisition, in Stalinist Russia, with Pol Pot in Cambodia and in the McCarthy era in the USA. These are some of the lessons that I feel can be learned from this unique method for studying the behaviour of human groups.

25

The Derry Youth and Community Workshop

On the suggestion of Colm Kavanagh, who had been a member of the Bogside Community Association, the foundation decided to set up the Derry Youth and Community Workshop for disadvantaged young people. The idea was to get the young people off the streets and into a learning situation.

This was the first community workshop in Northern Ireland. Our basic idea was to enable young people to grow, to develop their consciousness and creativity. Later a number of other workshops were set up around the North, but all were geared to training people, to give them trades. Later, Glenn Barr set up a workshop in the predominantly unionist Waterside, but he wouldn't allow the young people to discuss religion, sex or politics; they were simply to be trained for jobs.

Paddy Doherty applied to the authorities for a grant to set up the workshop. There was a derelict building along the Strand Road at Laurence Hill, the Foyle College, which had been set up a couple of centuries earlier by the London merchants who built the walled city of Derry to train young civil servants for the British Empire. The decision had been made by the City Council to pull it down when Paddy suggested that he take it over. The Council said it had deteriorated too much to renovate, but that didn't deter Paddy from tackling it, and the work of renovating the old building began.

In the meantime the foundation had bought a house in Clarendon Street in Derry and we had established the North-west Centre for Learning and Development. Paddy became their chief executive and under their auspices we developed the Youth and Community Workshop. The house in Clarendon Street became Paddy's headquarters now that he had left the BCA.

The arrangement which was negotiated with the authorities was that each young person would attend the workshop full time for one year. The participants were aged from sixteen to eighteen, both boys and girls, although there was a majority of boys, and were drawn from some of the toughest, out-of-control adolescents from around the city. These were young people who had dropped out or been expelled from school because they were too difficult to handle. Some had been involved in rioting and attacking the British Army with stones and petrol bombs. The majority were from the nationalist population on the West Bank, but initially a sizeable minority of Protestants also attended until Glenn Barr opened his workshop over in the Waterside.

The workshop started in 1976, and soon there were up to a hundred young people involved, of whom about twenty were Protestants. Initially the main effort centred on renovating the old Foyle College buildings, but as soon as parts of it were habitable a number of work centres were created. Most of these related to the work on the building itself, such as carpentry, woodwork, plastering, painting, bricklaying and upholstery. As more sections of the building became available, other centres, such as art, weaving, dressmaking, and jewellery design, were opened up. There was also a centre for office administration, which handled all the administrative aspects of running the workshop and where computers were gradually introduced. Later, a genealogy centre was established, which enabled people from Ireland, America and elsewhere to trace their family origins. Over the years this centre collected an amazing amount of data from the passenger lists of the famine ships and so on.

The young people were involved in the running of all these centres and could choose the one in which they would like to begin. However, because the aim was not to teach a trade as such but rather to offer a rich spectrum of work experience, each youngster had to change after one month to another centre. As a matter of principle, no distinction was made between traditionally male or female roles, so some of the boys were involved in making clothes, weaving, etc., while the girls took part in plastering, bricklaying and building work. During the year, therefore, the young people would have had experience of working in all of the different centres. When the programme was fully developed there were about fifteen tutors employed, some of whom were Protestant. Most had been unemployed but there were also some ex-prisoners who had been released from Long Kesh. Tommy Mellon was one of these. He had originally trained as a plumber but hadn't worked or slept in his own bed for eleven years so when he got out of gaol Paddy gave him a job as a tutor working with the young people. He has worked with Paddy ever since and has been a mainstay of the project.

The youngsters were very insular and most had never been far from Derry, so there were constant efforts made by Paddy and the tutors in those first years to take the youngsters from the workshops on trips into the countryside. Colm Kavanagh then took a bold initiative when he arranged for them to go to India, setting a precedent that was followed over the years by their going on trips to various parts of the world, often to work on community projects. Tommy Mellon went with the young people on several of their foreign trips to Florida, and to Soweto in South Africa, where they built houses for the people. The young people were paid a training allowance, which was considerably in excess of what they would get on the dole. The tutors too were earning considerably more than when they came off the dole.

After many months of hard work, one whole wing of the old building was fully renovated. Paddy and I agreed that we should try to achieve a high standard of excellence in the renovation of this old building. Our idea was to show the young people that they were capable of creating an environment that they would normally associate with upper- to middle-class, mainly Protestant, homes and businesses, and a far better environment than the one they were used to living in.

In 1975 we held the first of the Tavistock Group Conferences in Dublin. Paddy Doherty attended the first two of these conferences as a participant and then joined the consultant staff for the next three, the last of which was held in 1979. He was so taken with what he experienced in these conferences that, with our encouragement, he decided to apply this methodology to running the workshop, thus creating an atmosphere on the lines of a Tavistock working conference, a barely controlled democratic anarchy. Our hope was to inculcate in the young people the principles of handling authority and responsibility. The key difference here, however, was that, while a working conference lasts only for a week or two and then people return to ordinary life, Paddy managed to run the workshop in this manner, without any let-up, for more than a year. This was a unique experience and to my knowledge has never happened anywhere in the world before or since.

As the renovation of the building proceeded, one large room was turned into a sort of amphitheatre, with rows of seats running steeply up each side. This was used for debates and exercises – gatherings of the whole workshop, both of young people and tutors. Any time that 51 per cent of the total population of the workshop called for a meeting, then one would take place. Using the Tavistock method, Paddy refused to answer any direct question, so the young people and tutors had to work everything out for themselves.

One of the tutors, who had set up a well-appointed and organised workshop, decided that no one could enter without her permission because she was afraid some of the rowdy participants in the group would wreck it. This called for an angry debate in the theatre, the young people pointing out that they had done the work to establish her workshop in the first place. And so the argument went back and forth until one young boy, who had come from a very poor background and could neither read nor write, said to the tutor, 'You are controlling your workshop, not managing it.' We were astounded. This showed a highly sophisticated understanding of the nature of boundaries and the management of these in an open system. It was evidence of the amazing learning that was taking place in the workshop in terms of their handling of their independence and responsibility.

A more serious situation occurred when the British Minister for Manpower Services, Adam Butler, came down from Stormont to visit the workshop in 1981. He had heard of the innovative type of education on offer there and was anxious to see it for himself. Paddy felt that, as long as he could contain the chaos inside the workshop and not have it flow out onto the streets, he could manage to carry on. The background to this was that, prior to the minister's visit, the government had refused to give the annual increase in the training allowance that it had normally given, and the young people interpreted this as a cut in their wages. So, when the minister came, the young people took over the workshop, barricaded the gate and refused to allow him to enter. Paddy was outside the gate with the minister when all this was going on. He was trying to plead his case with the young people, saying, 'You can't keep this man out', to which they answered, 'He's fucking cut our wages'. Paddy explained that, to get their message across to the minister, they should let him in and then if they didn't like what he said or didn't like him, they could demand that he leave.

As the stand-off continued, the police were sent for and when there weren't enough of these, the army were called in, so now there were hundreds of people outside. The minister had about four body-guards, with guns underneath their jackets, and they looked terri-fied. Eventually Paddy's argument prevailed and the minister was allowed to enter. Everyone rushed up the stairs to the amphitheatre, the debate began and the minister listened. The point those attend-ing the debate made was that young people in England on this type of scheme used the money they received as pocket money. However, as one of the group pointed out, things were different in Derry: 'No-body is working in our house, my father and mother are not work-ing, my brother and sister are not working and this money is a very important part of the household budget.' The minister accepted this argument and said he would look into it. This satisfied the young people and a tense situation was resolved. At the lunch which took place afterwards in the rooms of the Honourable Irish Society, the Protestant bishop, who was sitting near the minister, was heard to say: 'You know, minister, we are trying to encourage these young people to be independent and give them enough space to grow, but then they don't always do what you would like them to do.' What he said described well the dilemma in the workshop, but also in society generally. When you give people free will and self-determination, how can you make sure nothing gets out of hand? Some time later Paddy met the minister and he asked him how he had enjoyed his day in Derry. The minister replied, 'That day in Derry is seared into my soul. I'll never forget it.'

It would be hard for anyone who didn't experience what that workshop was like to realise the level of activity, tension and barely controlled chaos that went on day after day. One day when I was there, some of the boys, in a state of rebellion, refused to take part in the normal daily activities. They were rampaging up and down the corridors and attempting to enter and smash up some of the workshops. A general meeting was called and it was decided to set up a disciplinary committee composed of a couple of the tutors and some of the youngsters. To my surprise, and alarm, I was elected, as a visiting psychiatrist, to be chairman of this committee. We assembled our committee and held a meeting in one of the rooms on the ground floor. We were to decide what measures should be taken to discipline those rebellious youngsters who were out of control, but it was hard to concentrate, or even think coherently, because of the loud banging on the floor above our heads by those rebelling upstairs. Then a large piece of the ceiling came crashing down on the table, with plaster flying in all directions. With that our disciplinary committee broke up in disorder and that was the end of our efforts to gain control of the situation. This sort of thing was going on day after day and week after week. Paddy, however, was like a rock in a storm and nothing seemed to faze him unduly or deflect him from the task he had set himself.

There was only one occasion when I remember Paddy being shaken. One morning he rang me to say that one of the young lads had set fire to the wing of the workshop, which had been renovated to a very high standard, and this was now completely burnt out. For the first time I heard a hint of despair in his voice. But, true to form, after a day or two he had recovered and they had started to rebuild.

There was concern about the poor level of literacy in the workshop; as many as 50 per cent of the youngsters were illiterate. A literacy class was set up to try to help as many as possible learn to read and write and improve their language skills, but the teacher they had couldn't handle the situation. She found that if she tried to get the youngsters to discuss anything their response would be monosyllabic. The vacancy for the post of literacy tutor was advertised and a young unemployed man called Noel, who was a deaf mute, applied for the job and Paddy decided to take him on. His intuition was that although pupils who wanted to communicate with this teacher would have to learn sign language, they would also have to think carefully about what it was they wanted to say, forcing them to construct proper sentences. So this young man was appointed as head of communications. Because the young people saw him as disabled, they had no problem in relating to him and no longer felt that they were being talked down to.

Noel formalised a system where he would write a statement on big pieces of cardboard. Thus, while the young people were learning his sign language, they were also inadvertently learning how to read.

People in the university heard about this and asked us to come and explain what was going on. Paddy sent a youngster up with Noel, who explained what he was doing in sign language. Then the seventeen-year-old verbally gave the lecture. The university audience was stunned. An expert from the department was sent to assess the needs of the young people and asked to see those who couldn't read or write. Paddy made an announcement over the internal sound system and about fifty of the young people turned up. The meeting was held in the large auditorium known as the snake pit. The expert came in and told the group that they ought to be ashamed of themselves, not being able to read and write; how could they expect to hold down a job or be able to travel; how would they know what bus to get on, and so on. To let Noel know what he was saying in sign language, several of the young people got involved in the discussion using sign language. The expert turned to Paddy. 'You didn't tell me these young people were deaf and dumb.' 'They're not,' said Paddy, 'but they're learning to read and write. It's the teacher who is deaf and he is an expert in communications.' With that the expert got up and left; he simply couldn't handle the situation.

Another approach to opening the minds of the youngsters was to run a number of exercises in the workshop to get them to understand different points of view. The most striking of these was an exercise that Paddy devised one evening while he was having a bath. He wanted them to examine the issues around Protestants and Catholics, Republican activity and the struggle with the British Army. He got all the tutors together and selected five leaders and then cleared the chairs out of the big meeting room. When the whole group were called to a meeting next morning, they entered the room to find a coffin lying on the floor, draped with the Union Jack, and a large tricolour hanging on the wall. One of the tutors had recorded a video, which was then played back through the television as if it were a news flash. This stated that a young British soldier had been killed. He had entered a house in the Bogside which was on fire to save the family inside. He had got two children out and went back to save the mother and two other children, but the building collapsed and he was killed.

The youngsters were broken up into a number of groups and a confidential statement was given to the leaders of each of the groups that they were told not to show to any of the others. The leader of the first group stood up and read his statement, which was as follows:

I am Colonel So and So, of the North Irish Horse. One of our soldiers lost his life trying to save a family. He acted as all British soldiers have acted throughout history, in the defence of people's lives, and we intend to give him a funeral with full military honours.

That group then took out the coffin and put it in the oratory, an area marked out as a small chapel. Their job was to protect the coffin. The leader of the next group stood up and read the statement he had been given:

I'm the father. My son joined the army to try to bring peace to this country and give it a decent future, so I want my son buried in the graveyard up in the Creggan.

The leader of the next group, a girl, stood up and said:

I am Gabrielle, the wife of Corporal McDaid. I met him on the Shankill Road and although he never became a Protestant he often went to church with me. I want him buried in our family grave in Belfast beside our son, who was killed by an IRA bomb.

Then the mother of the soldier stood up and said:

I bore my son and I knew him better than anybody else. He hated religion of any kind and told me that if he died he wanted to be cremated and have his ashes scattered over the fields of Ireland, which he loved.

Finally the last to stand up said:

I'm So and So of the Northern Command of the IRA and Corporal John McDaid was an undercover volunteer of ours, in spite of appearances to the contrary. We intend to give him a Republican funeral today at 2.30pm.

The television news came on again:

International experts have arrived in Derry to decide who will hold the funeral of a soldier who died while attempting to save a family trapped in a burning house. Representatives of the political parties, of the Protestant and Catholic churches, the Red Cross and Amnesty International, arrived on the scene this morning. Different people are claiming the body and it looks as if there will be serious trouble.

These roles were to be played by the various tutors. They drew lots to select a role but, following the method of the Tavistock workshops, while they were available for consultation they were not allowed to leave the big room. If the young people needed advice with their negotiations, they could approach one of the tutors playing a specific role. Interestingly, one of the tutors at that time in the workshop was Mitchel McLaughlin (the current National Chairperson of Sinn Féin) and he was given the role of a Catholic priest. He was asked if it was all right to cremate the body and he gave a surprisingly good explanation, saying that cremation is generally frowned upon by the Catholic Church but in times of crisis, whether due to plague or famine, bodies would be burned, so it could be permissible.

Although the young people were well aware that this was only an exercise, once they got involved in it it became a total reality. In their struggles to work out which group would get possession of the coffin, they went completely out of control and the exercise took on the aspect of a full-scale riot on the streets. They smashed down the timber walls of the room and some got hold of the fire extinguishers and sprayed all around them. Some of the tutors became so alarmed that they wanted Paddy to stop the exercise. Paddy explained that this battle was taking place in the middle of town every Saturday – when youngsters take on the army – but that the tutors and others generally don't care; they sit at home, watching football on television, not concerned about what happens outside. However, when the conflict is brought into the workshop, the tutors taking part have to deal with it and see it through to the end. In the meantime some of the youngsters had found dustbin lids and were rushing up and down the corridors banging them together. Some of the tutors got so frightened that they left altogether.

The whole exercise became a battle for the body, each of the groups wanting to take possession of it, even though there was, of course, no body in the coffin. They even smashed open the coffin to see if there was a body inside. It was decided that the youngsters would have to decide to end the exercise themselves. In the meantime they had called a meeting of their own, ignoring the tutors, and eventually they came up with a solution. They decided that the body would be cremated and the ashes scattered over the four provinces of Ireland, then a monument would be erected to the soldier in Donegal.

Over the next week the exercise was discussed in several meetings and Paddy was surprised how much the youngsters had learned, particularly the leaders of the groups, in realising that nothing could be solved simply by the use of violence. During the exercise a filmmaker named Armand Gatti arrived at the workshop. He was tremendously taken with what he experienced and decided to go away and try to get funding to make a film about the episode.

Armand Gatti eventually returned with finance to make the film, and the workshop was temporarily turned over for this purpose. Gatti built on the original exercise and introduced the British Army searching for a revolver that had caused the death of the soldier. He also incorporated a Spanish Armada ship which had gone aground up in Inishowen, where salvage work had been going on retrieving artefacts. All the young people, as well as the tutors, were involved in the making of the film and they travelled up to Inishowen to the strand where the salvage work on the ship had been going on. As part of the story of the film, the revolver that had shot the soldier was hidden in one of the guns that had been salvaged from the Armada ship.

Another theme in the film was the contrast between the technological centre that the British had developed in tracking the activities of the Provos, and the spontaneous information systems of the Nationalist population utilising graffiti on walls and the sides of houses. For this purpose the walls of the workshop were covered in graffiti of this kind. The film, *If Stones Could Speak*, went on limited general release, a remarkable outcome of the Derry Youth and Community Workshop.

By the time Gatti had reappeared the second time and the question of making a film arose, the work on the Old Foyle College had been completed, all to a very high standard. This was a building that had been condemned some years previously as being beyond the possibility of repair, and now it was in such beautiful condition that, when it was handed back to the City Council, it became a centre for the performing arts. More recently it has been taken over by the University of Ulster.

Realising that the use of the old Foyle College was coming to an end, Paddy and the rest of our team looked elsewhere to try to create a new dynamic. It struck me that the inner city, with its intact surrounding wall punctuated by a number of gates through which traffic could enter or leave, represented a perfect, bounded open system. About a third of all the buildings within the walls of the inner city had been destroyed as part of the IRA's bombing campaign or had fallen down through general disuse. I felt that a new energy could be introduced into the walled city, which had the potential to become a unique learning centre.

Paddy took up this challenge and started acquiring derelict sites. When the first building was fully renovated, it became the new headquarters of the Youth and Community Workshop, and all the various vocational centres were reintroduced into the new setting. In this way the bombed-out buildings on the derelict sites were rebuilt, until the whole inner city began to come to life again. There was an elderly lady who had returned to Ireland after spending many years in America who had put together something of a historical library. She donated this to the project and we incorporated it into a very fine building that had been restored, which became known as the Heritage Library. To our dismay, almost as soon as this building was restored to its full excellence, it was blown up once again by the Provos. They had intended to ambush a British Army patrol, but their explosion extended inwards instead of outwards. Paddy simply had the building reconstructed just as well as before.

Paddy then turned his attention to the larger project of building the O'Doherty castle. Prior to the walled city being built, there was an O'Doherty Castle in the lower part of the city facing the river. We decided to build a castle on the site of the original O'Doherty keep. The Derry City Council were able to acquire money from the European Union and the project went ahead. It was decided to construct a museum underneath the castle where the whole history of Derry would be depicted, including an account of the famous siege.

The culmination of all this was the visit to Derry in 1985 of about 2,000 of the O'Doherty clan from all over the world. They came from the States, South America, Australia, Great Britain and Ireland; there were also a number from the continent of Europe. A Spaniard, who was reputed to be a direct descendant of the O'Doherty chieftains, came with his brother, who was an admiral in the

Spanish navy and was believed to be the Tánaiste. A spectacular gathering led by a war piper went up to the Grenan of Eiloch and later there was the full inauguration of the O'Doherty chieftain at the crowning stone of the O'Dohertys.

With the completion of the castle and the museum, I suggested to Paddy that it would be a great idea to try to recreate the different historical periods in the museum. With his usual zeal he set about acquiring several sites up the hill from the O'Doherty castle in order to achieve this.

In addition to all this work, Paddy wanted to provide accommodation for the rehabilitation of drug addicts and alcoholics. A number of unemployed young musicians and other squatters were occupying the site which he had acquired to do this. In order to free the site for the rehabilitation of drug addicts, which has since been completed, he promised to create a music and performing arts centre for the group of hopeful young musicians in Derry. He has since done this on an alternative site and it is now a thriving creative space. Along the way we bought a disused factory in the city and the Derry Youth and Community Workshop has continued to work there up to the present. Thus the groundwork was laid for Derry to become an international centre for learning.

In recreating the historical, physical embodiment of the two traditions, nationalist and unionist, we had the underlying notion of a 'both-and', as against an 'either-or', view of society in the North. We hoped that in some way this would encourage the growth of an inclusive movement involving both communities. During the years we were attempting to achieve this, violence virtually died out in the Derry area. Perhaps this work contributed in some small way towards encouraging what later became the Peace Process. Certainly people like Mitchel McLaughlin, Martin McGuinness, and members of Sinn Féin generally, were aware of what was happening, although they didn't always approve of a movement that was outside their control.

The inner city, out of which almost all the old loyalist population had moved, was virtually a dead area, full of bombed-out buildings, but it now has hundreds of families living back in the renovated accommodation, thus encouraging other commercial and business activity to return. The inner city is now an active, thriving, living place once more.

As the board of the North-west Centre for Learning and Development was now beginning to stagnate, we gave the whole process a new lease of life by setting up the Inner City Trust. The board of this included the bishops of the Catholic Church and of the Church of Ireland, the Presbyterian Moderator, the mayor of Derry City Council and the chairman of the North-west Centre for Learning and Development. Thus this is a board above reproach, drawn from the various community leaders in Derry. All the buildings and villages that have been created now come under the auspices of the Inner City Trust and thus are owned by the people of Derry. The value of the real estate under community ownership is worth in the order of £10 million sterling and the rents from families and businesses now living and working in the inner city generate an annual income of approximately £500,000.

Ultimately it was the young people in the workshop, and those working in the various Ace Schemes (supported by Social Welfare funds and wages in the North), who provided the human energy that made the rebuilding and renovation of all the bombed-out buildings possible, and thus the recreation of Derry as a living city.

26

The Demise of the Irish Foundation

Although all its activity continued to develop throughout the early 1970s and an increasing number of community workers and professional staff had been taken on, the Irish Foundation had never been officially incorporated, nor had it any formal title. The financial resources being allocated by the Bank of Ireland were also steadily increasing, but no formal system was in place under which this relationship could be continued. In 1975 Bill Finlay had taken over from Don Carroll as governor of the bank and he was anxious that the relationship between the foundation and the bank should be set up on a proper basis. To this end, John Cullen, Paddy Walley and I had a number of meetings with Bill Finlay and other senior staff in the Bank of Ireland. These meetings went on for over a year and I wondered at the time why the situation was not being brought to a conclusion. Eventually it emerged that Bill Finlay was not prepared to finalise these arrangements until he had someone whom he felt he could trust to control the rather anarchic and chaotic ways we had of doing things. It turned out that the person he had in mind was Tom Hardiman, who was then Director General of RTÉ. Tom Hardiman is a very fine human being with total integrity. As an engineer, he is meticulous and ordered in his thinking. It is in his nature to control closely any situation in which he is involved, down to the smallest detail, and this, of course, was what Bill Finlay wanted. As the bank had committed up to £1 million to this project, he wanted to ensure that it would be properly controlled.

Don Carroll and the others were originally attracted to support our undertaking because they felt it was creative and innovative. On the other hand, the bank authorities wanted to be sure that their association with the foundation would not bring them into disrepute or into conflict with the authorities, and that their money would be well spent with proper controls. Herein lay the paradox! You cannot have creativity and innovation on the one hand and at the same time have total control.

This was all happening when much of the creative activity of the foundation was already over. Once Tom Hardiman took up his appointment as executive chairman, the foundation was officially incorporated. A board of governors was appointed that included the heads of both the main banks, the Allied Irish and the Bank of Ireland, as well as a number of other prominent people. An executive committee was formed that was comprised of the Executive Chairman, Walley, Cullen and me, and the title of the foundation was finally decided on as the Irish Foundation for Human Development. Patrick Hillary, who was president of Ireland at the time, became its patron.

Unfortunately, by the time all this was put in place we were already running into trouble. I had made a number of serious mistakes. I had taken on too many people as members of staff and, partly because of trying to deal with all my other activities in the psychiatric service, university teaching and so on, I was failing to manage their work properly. The cost of their salaries was eating up an increasingly large part of our funding. Also, a couple of years prior to the appointment of Tom Hardiman, we had decided to appoint an administrator. By this time our work in Derry had become a major part of our activity and the Troubles in the North were in full swing. He appeared conveniently on the scene just when he was needed and perhaps his real function was to keep an eye on what we were doing in the North. This may only be fanciful thinking, but in any event his participation was a disaster from the beginning. From the time he started with us he was a constant source of irritation and contributed to the negative atmosphere that was beginning to be felt among those working in the foundation. He left once Tom Hardiman took over.

There is no doubt that, in a number of ways, Tom made a positive contribution to the running of the foundation, sharpening up the management aspects of the operation, but the controlling aspect of his thinking had a dampening effect on creativity and spontaneity in the activities of the foundation. This was one factor in the downward trend of our operation from then on.

At the same time my personal life was in total disarray. My marriage had fallen apart. With my increasingly heavy work commitments, trying to manage what were, in effect, three full-time jobs, I was spending more and more time away from home, neglecting my personal and family life. By the end of 1974, having hardly spoken to each other for more than a year, my wife finally said, 'After Christmas either you go or I go.' Realising that, whatever other difficulties we had, she was a good mother to our four children, I felt that the only option open to me was to leave. In any case, three decades ago, there was little question of a father being given custody of the children.

Early in the new year of 1975, I found a miserable room on the South Circular Road near the back entrance to St Kevin's (now St James') Hospital, where my main office was situated. In fact, I didn't leave home completely at that time but returned at the weekends to ease the suddenness of the separation for the children. I remember 1975 as the loneliest year of my life.

Then, in November of that year, I attended a Gestalt Group run by Vinnie O'Connell, who was a protégé of Fritz Pearls. It was there I met June Levine. I had known her vaguely as a journalist before, but it was at the group that I came to know her personally for the first time. At one of the group sessions that weekend, when I happened to be sitting beside her, I rested my head wearily on her shoulder and felt a sense of peace that I had not known for many years.

Much later, when my former wife and I separated, I was to have appropriate visting rights, but once my wife became aware of my relationship with June, she wrongly placed blame for the break-up of our marriage on this, whereas we had separated long before. In this way she was able to turn the children against me and, although I had the legal right to see them, I couldn't force them to see me. To my dying day I shall never forget the agony I felt when, realising that I would have to leave, I went around the beds of my sleeping children to silently say goodbye to each one in turn. For a time I saw my youngest child, Dara, but, when he began to get upset in school, I felt it wasn't fair to put him under such pressure and so I stopped trying to see him also. It took me years to get over the loss of my children. It was as if they were dead and yet I knew they still existed. Every Christmas for the next five years I used to lie on the bed, unable to move or do anything. If June asked me what was wrong, I would say that I was fine. I was in a total state of denial and it was a long time before I came to accept the situation.

Early in 1976, everything seemed to close in on me. I was worn out and on the verge of collapse and finally contracted glandular fever and was admitted to St Kevin's. Although I was there for a couple of weeks, neither my former wife nor any of the children came to visit me, even though they knew nothing as yet about my developing relationship with June. Only June stood by me, and I think, were it not for her affection and support, it is unlikely I would have survived. When I was discharged I took a package tour for a week on my own in the Canary Islands. I just lay by the pool all day or swam gently and gradually began to recover.

It was later in 1976 that June and I started living together and, when the news broke publicly that I was separated and living with a well-known Jewish journalist and broadcaster, it received a very negative response from the psychiatric fraternity. This was almost thirty years ago; I heard years later that a meeting was held between the other psychiatric professors and officials of the Department of Health as to whether I was a fit person to continue in a leadership position in the psychiatric service. Although nothing was said overtly among those concerned with the foundation, in hindsight I think there is no doubt that the news had a detrimental effect on this also. The work of the foundation grumbled on for the next couple of years, but the negative atmosphere slowly deepened.

There was an inherent dilemma underlying the very nature of the foundation. The basic goal from the beginning was to try to empower and encourage others towards greater independence: individuals, human groups and communities. However, this meant that, the more successful we were in our endeavours, the less visible the foundation was, especially to our sponsors. The more that communities like Ballyfermot and the inner city became self-determining and achieved public recognition, the less evident was the role of the foundation. This was exactly what we had attempted to achieve, but, from the point of view of the bank, it gave little public recognition to them in return for the considerable financial expenditure they were incurring. There seems little doubt that these several independent influences led ultimately to the demise of the foundation.

Once the foundation was formally incorporated there had been a growing concern among members of the board about our almost total financial dependence on the Bank of Ireland. It was decided that we should attempt to fundraise in the United States and so we made contact with a fundraiser in Chicago. In 1976–7, I made several trips to the States and met a number of wealthy Irish-American businessmen in Chicago and elsewhere. We also sought the help of Fionnuala Flanagan, the well-known stage and film actress. She arranged interviews for me with some of the wealthy producers and directors around Hollywood. I did my best to explain to all these people the concept of the foundation, but I don't think I ever had what it takes to be a fundraiser, or the self-confidence to sell the idea of what we were attempting. More importantly, I didn't realise then that we were simply ahead of our time with these ideas. I don't think that many of the people I was trying to convince knew what I was talking about. Whatever it was, my attempt to raise funds in the States was a complete failure.

My old friend Paddy Doherty, through his experiences in his own work in Derry and through observing other community enterprises, developed the view that at the beginning of such an enterprise there is a stage of 'idealism', which is followed by a stage of 'institutionalisation', then a period of 'decline' and finally the organisation goes into a state of 'corruption'. That is not to say that the people working in the enterprise become corrupt, but that the original concepts and ideals of the enterprise become corrupted. Thus the organisation often ends up doing virtually the opposite to what was originally intended. It has certainly been my experience, in all the endeavours in which I have been involved, that these various stages have followed one another relentlessly. This was undoubtedly what was happening in the foundation. The early enthusiasm and anarchic creativity that was there in our early work in Ballyfermot and Derry was gradually replaced by a growing institutionalisation and, finally, by a period of decline and a general atmosphere of negativity.

In November 1978 June and I decided we would go to India to meet the spiritual leader, Ram Chandra of Sahjahanpur, in whom we had become interested. The rumblings in the psychiatric service were so ominous with all the mounting problems that I phoned the then Minister of Health, Charlie Haughey, to suggest I put off my visit. He told me to go and that if there were problems he would deal with them. The extraordinary thing is that for the whole month while we were away everything was quiet. When we got back I was expecting to face into trouble but when I asked what had been happening, people just looked at me strangely. It was as if I hadn't been away at all and everything was on hold.

Then, one week after I returned, all hell broke loose in St Brendan's hospital when some junior doctors wrote a letter to the press stating that there were rats and cockroaches in the wards. This caused a public outcry. Just as I was trying to grapple with that crisis, John Cullen and Paddy Walley decided it was time for me to be replaced as director of the foundation. Tom Hardiman felt he had no choice but to go along with their decision and, with the agreement of the board, John Cullen took over as director. The timing of the coup at the height of the crisis in St Brendan's was unfair and something of a betrayal but, although the takeover was not amicable, there was no overt conflict. From that time on the foundation gradually faded out of existence. Tom Hardiman presided over the closing down of the organisation and the dispersal of the staff and I think the Bank of Ireland were quietly pleased to be relieved of any further financial commitment. The three of us who had started the organisation drifted apart and went our separate ways. Only the activity in Derry continued, under the capable direction of Paddy Doherty. This was the one remaining part of the work of the Irish Foundation for Human Development and I was determined it should continue.

Looking back, and asking myself what I had gained personally from all the work with the Irish Foundation and the work in Derry, I think it was the clarification of the ideas that underlay all the activity in which we in the Irish Foundation were involved; and the gradual realisation that ultimately co-operation is more effective than competition.

In the early 1970s, we had heard of the work of the Chilean biologists Maturana and Varella, but at that time we still had no clear theoretical formulation on which to base our work. Their theories were, for me, a revelation, as, from them, I became aware of a whole new science of living systems (see Appendix A). For the first time I had a glimpse of an entirely different view of the nature of living creatures, as distinct from the reductionist scientific paradigm, which was all I had been exposed to up to that time. If only we had had a clearer understanding of these basic concepts at that time, what we were attempting to achieve in the foundation might have met with greater success.

PART SIX

A New Approach
1979–1994

27

Breaking the Mould

From this time onwards, I began to read everything I could regard-ing this alternative view of reality. At that time in the mid-1970s nothing had yet been written that brought together all the scientific work that was taking place in various countries on the development of a new science of life. Gradually I came to realise that what was under-stood as being scientific was a rather narrow, reductionist view, which had dominated scientific thinking in the west for some hundreds of years. The realisation came slowly that there was a quite different way of approaching reality which could be equally scientific.

As I delved further, it became clear that this dialectic was not something recent but was already evident in the early stages of philo-sophical development. One thing I have always found irritating is that western thinkers usually presume that the first real development of philosophical thought originated in ancient Greece. In recent years, however, it has become clear that the sages and mystical thinkers in both India and China had already developed highly so-phisticated philosophical insights several thousand years earlier. In-deed it seems very likely that the strange, solitary and enigmatic Heraclitus, who emerged around 500 BC, would already have been aware of these eastern influences. His concept of a transcendent prin-ciple, *logos*, governing the cosmos was that all things are in constant flux but that, at a deeper level, everything is ultimately balanced by its opposite, so that all opposites ultimately constitute a unity. These ideas were further developed by the Pythagoreans and then reached their full flowering in the thinking of Socrates and Plato.

Contemporaneously, but in sharp contrast to this, another group of philosophers put forward a starkly different view of the basis of reality, which became known as 'atomism'. This was a purely materialistic theory, which was fully developed in the fifth century BC by Leucippus and his successor Democritus. They stipulated that the physical world is constituted by an infinite number of indivisible corpuscles, which they termed atoms. This was a purely mechanistic, materialistic theory, which left no place for any cosmic intelligence or universal *logos*.

It was Aristotle who achieved a partial synthesis of these two deeply divergent views. Although, like Plato, he emphasised the importance of form or pattern, he also turned Plato's ideas upside down. He stated that a substance is not simply a unit of matter but is an intelligible structure or form embodied in matter. For him, unlike Plato, the form does not exist independently of its material embodiment. Nevertheless it is the form that gives to the substance its distinctive essence. After more than 2,000 years, it is fascinating that the four principles, or causes, postulated by Aristotle as the inter-dependent sources of all phenomena are surprisingly similar to the core perspectives which Fritjof Capra, a physicist whose work I describe later, suggests are involved in the definition of a living system: form, matter, process and meaning.

A major revolution in European thinking was made possible by the rediscovery in the twelfth and thirteenth centuries of a large body of Greek manuscripts. They became available for the first time to Copernicus (1471–1543) and others as part of the humanist revival at the beginning of the Renaissance proper. He proposed the apparent absurdity of a heliocentric model. Copernicus was convinced the earth truly moved. It was finally Galileo's discoveries, with the aid of his new telescope, which completed the victory of the new science over the medieval world.

It was at this time that the ancient Greek writings of the atomists Leuccipus and Democritus resurfaced, and this led Galileo to make the statement that was to change the western approach to science:

Scientists should restrict themselves to the essential properties of material bodies – size, shape, number, weight and motion. Only by means of an exclusively quantitative analysis could science attain certain knowledge of the world.

This statement made possible the extraordinary technological achievements which we see all around us in the world today. But as R.D. Laing pointed out: 'Galileo's programme offers us a dead world: out goes sight, sound, taste, touch, and smell and along with them have since gone aesthetic and ethical sensibility, values, quality, soul, consciousness, spirit. Experience as such is cast out of the realm of scientific discourse. Hardly anything has changed our world more during the past 400 years than Galileo's audacious programme. We had to destroy the world in theory before we could destroy it in practice.'

Francis Bacon (1561–1626) in England around the same time went even further. He is said to be the father of empirical science and stressed the importance of direct experiment. If Socrates had associated knowledge with 'virtue' in his search for wisdom, Bacon equated knowledge with 'power'. This had profound implications for the nature and purpose of science. A marked divide was now opening up between the east and the west. Where Indian and Chinese thinkers had looked inwards, the new western scientific view was to look outwards, to map and increasingly control the world of nature. This was also a strongly male, patriarchal perspective and women, to this day, have never participated in it to the same extent. It is interesting that Bacon was Attorney General for King James I, and one of his main tasks would have been to participate in the trials of witches. Thus he used words borrowed from these trials, such as how nature had to be, 'hounded in her wanderings', 'bound into service' and made our 'slave'. The aim of the scientist was to 'torture natures secrets from her'. Witches were primarily women and indeed most were practitioners of what we would nowadays think of as alternative medicine, dealing with herbs and potions derived from nature.

The shift in scientific direction brought about by Galileo and Bacon was pivotal for the influence it had on the development of western science and technology. This was brought to fruition by two further towering figures of the seventeenth century – Descartes and Newton.

In René Descartes' youth there was a sceptical crisis in French philosophy, as the old-world view was crumbling. He felt that the best way to proceed was to strip away all traditional knowledge, what he could perceive and even his own body, until he reached the one thing he could not doubt – the existence of himself as a thinker.

From this came his famous statement, '*Cogito, ergo, sum*' ('I think, therefore I am'). He decided that the essence of human nature lies in thought and thus he felt he could rebuild his philosophy of knowledge on firm foundations. This led him to the view that mind and matter were separate and fundamentally different: 'There is nothing included in the concept of body that belongs to the mind; and nothing in that of mind that belongs to the body.' This fundamental division between mind and matter has had an enormous effect on western thought and plagues medical thinking to this day. Many academics still think of their body as simply something to carry their head about. For Descartes, the material universe was a machine and nothing but a machine. There was no purpose, life, or spirituality in matter. Descartes was a brilliant mathematician and is said to be the father of analysis, i.e., that understanding is achieved by breaking things into their parts and seeing what they are made of – reductionism.

The conceptual framework created by Galileo and Descartes was completed by Isaac Newton (1643–1727). He developed a consistent mathematical formulation of the mechanistic view of nature. From the second half of the seventeenth century to the end of the nineteenth century the Newtonian, mechanistic model of the universe dominated all scientific thought. By the nineteenth century, God's creation of the world had dropped out of the picture. It was felt that it was only a matter of time until a complete scientific understanding of the entire universe would be attained. The natural sciences, as well as the humanities and social sciences, all accepted this mechanistic view as the correct understanding of reality and modelled their own theories accordingly. To this day, whenever psychologists, sociologists, or economists want to be scientific, they tend to turn to these basic concepts of Newtonian physics and base their research on them.

With the dawn of the nineteenth century and the beginnings of the Industrial Revolution, another revolution in scientific thinking was imperceptibly making its appearance. These new horizons were being opened up on several broad fronts, in both biology and physics.

The dawn of the twentieth century heralded an even greater revolution in scientific thought than that of Copernicus and Galileo in the sixteenth century. In 1905 Albert Einstein produced two papers: one dealt with the theory of relativity and the other with a new way of looking at electromagnetic radiation, which was to form the foundation of quantum theory. The material world, which had been viewed as a comfortably ticking clockwork mechanism, was now transformed into a complex of indeterminate, interweaving and inter-dependent relationships.

These new developments in physics brought about fundamental changes in our understanding of cause and effect, of time and space, of matter and objectivity, and to many scientists this came as a great shock. But this picture of evolution and change over time was moving in two opposite directions. In physics what appeared to be happening was a movement towards increasing disorder; it was this development which eventually led to the theory of the 'Big Bang'. In biology the movement was just the opposite – towards increasing order and complexity.

Ever since antiquity, natural philosophers had entertained the idea of a great chain of being. This chain, however, was conceived as a static hierarchy, starting with God at the top and descending through angels, human beings and animals to ever-lower forms of life. The number of species was fixed; it had not changed since the day of their creation.

Then Jean Baptiste Lamarck, early in the nineteenth century, introduced a dramatic change from this static view of life on earth. This was such a momentous change that, as Gregory Bateson put it, 'Lamarck, probably the greatest biologist in history, turned that ladder of explanation upside down. He was the man who said it starts with the infusoria[1] and that there were changes leading up to man. This turning of the taxonomy[2] upside down is one of the most astonishing feats that has ever happened. It was the equivalent in biology of the Copernican revolution in astronomy.' Thus it was Lamarck rather than Darwin who was the first to put forward a coherent theory of evolution. He had the remarkable intuition that all living creatures had evolved, under environmental pressure, from simpler forms. Several decades later, in 1859, Darwin published his major work, *On the Origin of Species*. He completed this monumental effort twelve years later with *The Descent of Man*.

Until the late nineteenth century, it was almost universally believed that acquired characteristics could be inherited, as had been postulated by Lamarck. Charles Darwin too took this for granted but nevertheless based his theory mainly on the concept of chance variation – that is, random mutation and natural selection. Later, following the pioneering work of the Austrian monk Gregor Mendel, the father of modern genetics, these concepts of random mutation and natural selection became the cornerstones of modern evolutionary thought. This view is summarised by geneticist Jacques Monod: 'Chance alone is at the source of every innovation, of all creation in the biosphere.' This neo-Darwinian view is based on the idea that the main evolutionary processes all took place gradually over long periods of time. Because of their dislike of any notion of purpose in nature, as time went on neo-Darwinians espoused Darwin's concept of random mutation followed by natural selection as the sole means by which all evolutionary variation proceeds.

Recent work has clearly demonstrated, however, that evolution did not proceed through continuous gradual change over time. It is simply not possible that complex structures such as eyes or wings evolved gradually, because they would have had no survival value in natural selection terms until they were fully developed.[3]

As the palaeontologist S.M. Stanley has put it:

Today the fossil record . . . is forcing us to revise this conventional view of evolution. As it turns out, myriads of species have inhabited the earth for millions of years without evolving noticeably. On the other hand major evolutionary transitions have been wrought during episodes of rapid change, when new species have quickly budded off from old ones. In short, evolution moves by fits and starts.[4]

This view of evolution is known as 'punctuated equilibria' and it indicates that the sudden transitions were caused by mechanisms other than random mutations.

It was the triumphal announcement by James D. Watson and Francis Crick in 1953 that convinced biologists not only that genes are real molecules but also that they are constituted of nothing more mysterious than deoxyribonucleic acid (DNA). This established DNA as the molecule that not only holds the secrets of life, but that also executes its cryptic instructions; it was, in short, the 'Master Molecule'.[5] In the colloquial paraphrase of the central dogma formulated by Francis Crick in 1957, 'DNA makes RNA, RNA makes protein, and proteins make us.' James Watson, the first director of the Human Genome Organisation (HUGO) set the tone: 'We used to think that our fate was in the stars. Now we know, in large measure, our fate is in our genes.'[6]

Unfortunately for this simple view, as Evelyn Keller has pointed out, 'As every molecular biologist now knows, the secrets of life have proven to be vastly more complex, and more confusing, than they had seemed in the 1960s and '70s.'[7] Furthermore, Mae-Wan Ho, the brilliant geneticist who wrote the provocative book, *Genetic Engineering: Dream or Nightmare*, says: 'The notion of an isolatable, constant gene that can be patented as an invention for all the marvellous things it can do is the greatest reductionist myth ever perpetrated . . . There is no simple, linear, one-directional instruction proceeding from the gene to RNA to protein.'[8]

In their attempt to find a way out of this dilemma, neo-Darwinians such as Richard Dawkins have proposed the existence of 'genetic programmes', but as Keller states: 'This is precisely the ambiguity that plagues the term "genetic program". Does the genetic refer to the subject or the object of the program? Are the genes the source of the program, or that upon which the program acts.'[9] What this comes down to then is, as Capra says:

> The growing realisation that the biological processes involving genes – the fidelity of DNA replication, the rate of mutations, the transcription of coping sequences, the selection of protein functions and the patterns of gene expression – are all regulated by the cellular network in which the genome is embedded. This network is highly non-linear, containing multiple feedback loops, so that patterns of genetic activity continually change in response to changing circumstance . . . The very remarkable stability and robustness of biological development means that an embryo may start from different initial stages but will nevertheless reach the same mature form that is characteristic of its species. Evidently this phenomenon is quite incompatible with genetic determinism.[10]

Recent work in the field of epigenetics strongly suggests that the conventional view, that DNA carries all our heritable information and that nothing individuals do in their lifetime will be biologically passed to their children, is incorrect. Marcus Pembrey and the Swedish researcher Lars Olov Bygren, working in isolated areas in northern Sweden, have found evidence of an environmental effect being passed down the generations. This work suggests that genes have a 'memory' and that the lives of our grandparents can directly affect us decades later, despite never having experienced these things oneself. Epigenetics proposes a control system of 'switches' that turn genes on and off – and suggests that experiences like nutrition or stress can control these switches and cause heritable effects in humans.[11] So it would seem that Lamarck's original idea of acquired characteristics is not so far off the mark as was thought following Darwin's emphasis on gradual evolutionary changes, with chance mutations honed and perfected by natural selection. As Mae-Wan Ho says:

> Lamarck's theory, on the other hand, is of transformation arising from the organism's own activities and experience of its environment during epigenesis or development. This requires a conception of the organism as an active, autonomous being, which is open to the environment. It would seem now that biological form and behaviour are emergent properties of the epigenetic network and this will only become clear when complexity theory and non-linear dynamics are applied to the new discipline of epigenetics.[12]

Finally, as Lynn Margulis states: 'Cell heredity, both nuclear and cytoplasmic, always must be considered for the entire cell, the entire organism.'[13]

So where does all this leave us? It brings me to Teilhard de Chardin and his great work, *The Human Phenomenon*. He wrote this as early as 1938, thus anticipating by a number of years the development of systemic thinking and the science of living systems. In that work he stated:

> After having allowed itself to fall too far under the spell of analysis, modern thought is finally growing accustomed to envisioning the creative evolutionary function of synthesis. There is definitely something more in the molecule than in the atom, more in the cell than in molecules, more in the social than in the individual . . . We now tend to admit that with each subsequent degree of combination, something emerges into a new order, something that cannot be reduced to the isolated elements; and, from this fact, consciousness, life and thought, are very close to acquiring the right to scientific existence.[14]

In contra-distinction to the neo-Darwinians, Teilhard de Chardin pointed to a clear direction in evolution, emphasising that it proceeds in the direction of increasing complexity with an attendant rise of consciousness. He called this the 'law of complexity-consciousness'. In this way, human beings 'pressing up against one another', were covering the planet with a web of ideas – the 'noosphere'. He referred to this again and again in the last years of his life:

> However, it may well be, perhaps, that this contradiction is a warning to our minds that we must completely reverse the way in which we see things. We still persist in regarding the physical as constituting the 'true phenomenon' in the universe, the psychic as a sort of epiphenomenon. If we really wish to unify the real, we should completely reverse the values – that is we should consider the whole of thermodynamics as an unstable and ephemeral bi-effect of the concentration on itself of what we call 'consciousness' or 'spirit'. In other words, there is no longer just one type of energy in the world; there are two different energies: one axial, increasing and irreversible and the other peripheral or tangential, constant, reversible. And these two energies are linked together in 'arrangement' but without, nevertheless, being able to either form a compound or directly to be transformed into one another, because they operate at different levels.[15]

In 1968 Ludwig von Bertalanffy first proposed a comprehensive theoretical formulation of the principles of organisation of living systems. He recognised that living creatures are open systems that cannot be described by classical thermodynamics: 'The organism is not a static system closed to the outside and always containing the identical components; it is an open system in a (quasi) steady state . . . in which material continually enters from, and leaves into, the outside environment.' By the beginning of the twentieth century Newton's world view had been replaced by two diametrically opposed views of evolutionary change – that of a living world unfolding towards increasing order and complexity, and that of a world of ever-increasing disorganisation. Ludwig von Bertalanffy could not resolve this dilemma (see Fig. 6).

It was the great achievement of Ilya Prigogine,[16] the Russian chemist, to use a new mathematics to re-evaluate the second law of

Systems Causality

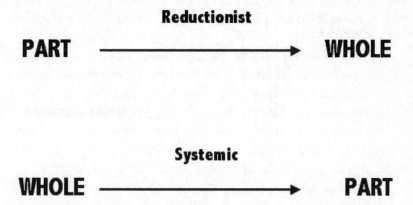

Figure 6: A new whole emerges which cannot be reduced to the isolated elements which make it up. This new reality now acts back on its constituent parts.

thermodynamics by radically rethinking traditional scientific views on order and disorder. This enabled him to resolve unambiguously the two contradictory nineteenth-century views of the universe. In his work on the characteristics of self-organising systems, Prigogine dealt with this much more systematically. He pointed out that a thermodynamically isolated system is one that neither energy nor mass can enter or leave. In actual practice the only truly isolated system possible is the universe as a whole. A thermodynamically closed system is one that energy can enter and leave but matter cannot. A well-sealed steam boiler, whose water can be heated or cooled but cannot escape, is an example of such a closed system. Most biological, psychological and social systems, however, are neither isolated nor closed. They are, instead, thermodynamically open systems. An open system is one that is capable of exchanging both energy and matter with its environment. Such open systems have always been viewed as anomalous from the point of view of classical thermodynamics.

However, when the principles underlying the second law were extended to these systems, a new set of properties emerged that were

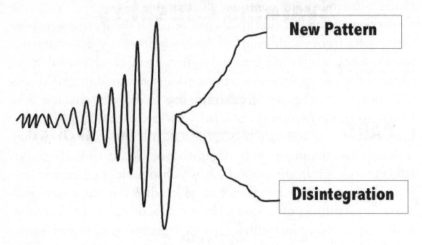

Figure 7: Self-organising systems (dissipative structures) no longer follow any deterministic pattern. As the input of energy into the system increases this gives rise to increasing turbulence which may cause a fluctuation so powerful that it destabilises the re-existing organisation – a bifurcation point.

not formerly apparent. These new properties include capacity for 'self-organisation', that is, for a spontaneous shift from a lower to a higher level of organisational complexity. Prigogine has named such self-organising systems 'dissipative structures'. He says they are capable of 'exchange entropy', since they can maintain their organisational complexity only by continually dissipating the positive entropy (more disorganisation) which they produce back into the environment. Each such locally developing system achieves an increase in structural order and complexity. It does this by ingesting, digesting and assimilating the negative entropy (greater organisation) previously possessed by the structures in its surrounding environment, and by excreting back into that environment 'waste products' that are higher in positive entropy (more disorganised) than those which were initially ingested.

In the latter half of the twentieth century, Prigogine and others were bringing about the same kind of radical change in our thinking at the macroscopic level that the quantum physicists had done during the early years of that century. In 1977 Prigogine was awarded the Nobel Prize for his work on the thermodynamics of non-equilibrium systems, but perhaps his greatest achievement was to show that such self-organising systems were characterised by change, instability and continual fluctuation.

Prigogine showed that the behaviour of a dissipative structure existing far from equilibrium no longer follows any deterministic, universal law but is unique to the system itself. He showed that, as the input of energy into such a dissipative structure is increased and as it moves further from equilibrium, it is likely to be characterised by continual fluctuation. This in turn can give rise to increasing turbulence and now and then may cause a fluctuation so powerful that it destabilises the pre-existing organisation. This is what Prigogine refers to as a 'bifurcation point', at which time it is inherently impossible to determine in advance in which direction the system will move. It may disintegrate into a chaotic state or suddenly reorganise itself into a fresh, more differentiated, higher level of organisation, which then takes on the characteristics of irreversibility (see Fig. 7).

As Prigogine himself put it, 'There is a question which has plagued us for more than a century: What significance does the evolution of a living being have in the world described by thermodynamics, a world of ever increasing disorder?' He accepts that the second law of thermodynamics is still valid, but, according to Prigogine, dissipative structures are 'islands of order in a sea of disorder, maintaining and even increasing their order at the expense of greater disorder in their environment . . . In this way order "floats in disorder", while the overall entropy keeps increasing in accordance with the second law.'

It is in this sense that Prigogine reflects that, 'Today, the world we see outside and the world we see within are converging. This convergence of two worlds is perhaps one of the important cultural events of our age.' And further: 'Our vision of nature is undergoing a radical change towards the multiple, the temporal and the complex.'

28

Definition of a Living System

Over the years, in coming to a clearer understanding of the nature of living systems, I have been searching for a definition that could equally apply to any level of 'living system', from the cell to the biosphere. The following definition seems to me to serve this purpose in a reasonably satisfactory manner:

(1) The living system contains a number of elements. From a systemic perspective one is not interested in analysing the composition of these elements any further, other than to establish their presence.
(2) These elements are involved in a dynamic process of interaction and interrelationship.
(3) The system is separated from its environment by a boundary consisting of its own elements, such as permits transactions of import and export of both energy and substance across the boundary; i.e. it is an 'open system'. It maintains and renews its own elements by its own internal processes.
(4) It continually renews itself, cells breaking down and building up tissues and organs in continual cycles of regeneration. Components of the living system are continually renewed and recycled, but the pattern of organisation remains relatively stable.
(5) The locus of control is within the system itself. This is the most essential aspect of 'self-organisation'. If the management of a living system moves outside, into the environment, then that system is becoming sick and if this continues will eventually die.
(6) Living systems show a tendency to transcend themselves. Thus they not only tend to evolve, change and adapt, but also

to reproduce themselves and thus ensure the survival and evolution of the species.

I feel the advantage of my definition is that it can apply to any level of living system, from the cell to the biosphere. Viruses are interesting in this regard, as they consist essentially of a segment of DNA or ribonucleic acid (RNA) in a protein coating and are not capable of survival for any length of time, unless they can become incorporated in a living cell. Thus they exist on the threshold between living and non-living. Of course, single-celled organisms are still the commonest form of life on this planet – bacteria of all kinds, in the soil and in the air, and plankton in the oceans. Below this level we have complex chemical systems, such as DNA or protein molecules, but these are not alive.

Fritjof Capra approached this question from a somewhat different perspective to my definition. This helps to further elucidate the core criteria of a living system: 'In a nutshell, I propose to understand autopoeisis, as defined by Maturana and Varella, as the pattern of life (i.e. the pattern of organisation of living systems); dissipative structure, as defined by Prigogine, as the structure of living systems; and cognition, as defined initially by Gregory Bateson and more fully by Maturana and Varella, as the process of life.'

KEY CRITERIA OF A LIVING SYSTEM[1]
Pattern of organisation: The configuration of relationships that determines the system's essential characteristics;
Structure: The physical; embodiment of the system's pattern of organisation;
Life process: The activity involved in the continual embodiment of the system's pattern of organisation.

As I mentioned earlier, these criteria are surprisingly close to the four principles, or causes, which Aristotle postulated as the interdependent sources of all phenomena; i.e. form, matter, process and meaning.

Gregory Bateson, in his set of essays 'Mind and Nature', regarded as a cornerstone of his work the relation of complexity to mental process. He often spoke about 'the patterns which connect'. Although he disagreed with de Chardin on certain issues, his thinking in this regard ran along parallel lines to what de Chardin called

Feedback Loop

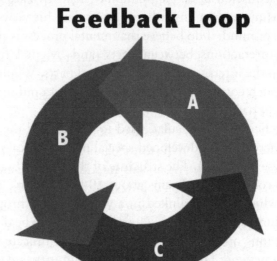

Figure 8: A Feedback Loop – a circular arrangement of causally connected elements, where the first link (input) is affected by the last (output) which results in the self-regulation of the system.

Two Forms of Feedback

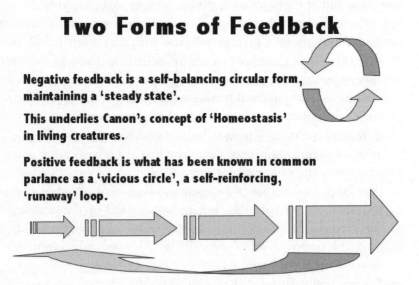

Negative feedback is a self-balancing circular form, maintaining a 'steady state'.

This underlies Canon's concept of 'Homeostasis' in living creatures.

Positive feedback is what has been known in common parlance as a 'vicious circle', a self-reinforcing, 'runaway' loop.

Figure 9: Two forms of feedback – negative and positive. Negative feedback is the way all our human physiology works.

'complexity-consciousness'. He went on to make two key statements that perhaps more than any others encapsulate his view of the essential basis of mind: 'I do believe that mental process is always a sequence of interactions between parts' and 'Mental function is imminent in the interaction of differentiated parts. Wholes are constituted by such combined interactions.' As Capra put it:

> Cyberneticists, in particular, tried to understand the brain as a neural network and developed special mathematical techniques to analyse its pattern. The structure of the human brain is enormously complex. It contains about 10 billion nerve cells (neurones) which are interlinked in a vast network through 1,000 billion junctions (synapses). The whole brain can be divided into sub-sections or sub-networks, which communicate with each other in network fashion. All this results in intricate patterns of intertwined webs, networks nesting within larger networks.[2]

A number of years before the fuller development of the theory of living systems, there was a remarkable meeting of minds in New York city, known as the Macy Conferences. These took place in 1946 when a group of highly creative people were brought together in a series of interdisciplinary dialogues to explore new ideas. What was unique about these meetings was the bringing together of two groups. The first group consisted of scientists such as Norbert Wiener, who laid the groundwork for cybernetics, and John Von Neumann, a mathematical genius who became famous as the inventor of the digital computer. The other group were from the humanities and included Gregory Bateson and Margaret Mead.

Out of these conferences came the first real clarification of cybernetics and the concept of 'feedback'. Norbert Wiener's concept of a feedback loop is that of a circular arrangement of causally connected elements, so that each element has an effect on the next, until the last feeds back the effect into the first element of the cycle. Thus the first link (input) is affected by the last (output), which results in self-regulation of the entire system (see Fig. 8).[3] As he himself put it, feedback is the 'Control of the machine on the basis of its actual performance rather than its expected performance'.

This is the way all our human physiology works (see Fig. 9). Once this question of circular feedback systems became clear, the concept of networks then developed. Networks lie at the very heart of the ecological world of living systems.

Candice Pert, the woman who discovered the endorphin receptor, has described perhaps more clearly than anyone what this means: 'A network is different from a hierarchical structure that has a ruling "station" at the top and a descending series of positions that play increasingly subsidiary roles. In a network, theoretically, you can enter at any nodal point and quickly get to any other point; all locations are equal as far as the potential to "rule" or direct the flow of information.'[4]

What Candice Pert demonstrated was that the group of macromolecules comprising sixty to seventy molecular messengers (what Francis Schmitt of Massachusetts Institute of Technology termed 'information substances') form a psychosomatic network extending throughout our entire human physiology. Because historically they were studied separately by different disciplines, this fact was not realised. As she says, 'The three classically separated areas of Neuroscience, Endocrinology and Immunology, with their various organs – the brain; the glands; and the spleen, bone marrow and lymph nodes – are actually joined to each other in a multidirectional network of communication linked by information carriers known as neuropeptides.'[5] She continues:

While much of the activity of the body according to the new information model does take place at the autonomic, unconscious level, what makes this model so different is that it can explain how it is also possible for our conscious mind to enter the network and play a deliberate part. We are all aware of the bias built into the Western ideas that the mind is totally in the head, a function of the brain. But your body is not there just to carry around your head. I believe the research findings I have described indicate that we need to start thinking about how the mind manifests itself in various parts of the body and, beyond that, how we can bring that process into consciousness . . . We know that the immune system, like the central nervous system, has memory and a capacity to learn. Thus it could be said that intelligence is located not only in the brain but in cells that are distributed throughout the body and that the traditional separation of mental processes, including emotions, from the body is no longer valid. If the mind is defined by brain-cell communication, as it has been in contemporary science, then this model of the mind can now be seen as extending naturally to the entire body. Since neuropeptides and their receptors are in the body as well we may conclude that the mind is in the body, in the same sense that the mind is in the brain, with all that that implies.[6]

From these insights she puts forward an insightful definition of the nature of mind:

What the mind is, is the flow of information as it moves among the cells, organs and systems of the body. And since one of the qualities of information flow is that it can be unconscious, occurring below the level of awareness, we see it in operation at the autonomic, or involuntary, level of our physiology. The mind as we experience it is immaterial, yet it has a physical substrate, which is both the body and the brain. It may also be said to have a non-material, non-physical substrate that has to do with the flow of that information. The mind then is that which holds the network together, often acting below our consciousness, linking and co-ordinating the major systems and their organs and cells in an intelligently orchestrated symphony of life. Thus we might refer to the whole system as a psychosomatic information network, linking psyche, which comprises all that is of an ostensibly non-material nature, such as mind, emotion, and soul, to soma, which is the material world of molecules, cells and organs. Mind and body, psyche and soma.[7]

In a similar way, at whatever level of living system or ecosystem we look, as far out as the biosphere we find this network principle involved. This is characterised by negative feedback cycles that enable the ecosystem to maintain a relatively stable condition of homeo-stasis. This is what Walter Canon referred to as the 'wisdom of the mind'.

Mae-Wan Ho sums up this view:

The stability of organisms is diametrically opposite to the stability of mechanical systems. Mechanical stability . . . is a closed, static equilibrium, maintained by the action of controllers, buffers or buttresses, which return the system to fixed or set points . . . Organic stability, on the other hand, is a state of dynamic balance that is attained in open systems far away from thermodynamic equilibrium . . . it is radically democratic, as it works by intercommunication and mutual responsiveness of all the parts, so that control is distributed throughout the system.[8]

Once the primary living system, the cell, has been formed and once it has been bounded, then this body or system can become the unit or building block of the next order system. The essential thing to understand is that while one living system may form the basic unit or building block of another, this does not mean that it is simply merged or that it loses its boundary and therefore ceases to exist as a separate entity. It remains as a system within a system. Nevertheless, it is now, as a unit, under the influence of the higher-order system. Transactions or movements of its energy or substance can then take place across its boundary, under the influence of the higher-order system. The degree to which this happens will depend on its being entrained in the higher-order system.

Having got this far, we can now discern an ascending order of living systems, each of which fulfils the essential criteria of autopoeisis and is therefore alive. The first order is the cell. This constitutes the threshold of life. Although the cell contains various complex chemicals, it is only at the level of the fully integrated cell that we can properly speak of a living system in a full autopoietic sense. The second order is the multicellular organism – an insect, a mouse, a cat, a dog or a human. The third order is the cluster of multicellular organisms – an ant heap, a beehive, a flock of birds, a shoal of fish, a primate group such as a tribe of baboons or a human community. The fourth order is the aggregation of a number of different species, such as is found in a coral reef or an African plain. The fifth order is the biosphere, the concept of the envelope surrounding planet Earth as a living, self-organising system (e.g. the Gaia theory[9] of James Lovelock).

A rather subtle paradox arises here. Although each new order of living system, once it has fully come into being, now has a controlling influence over its parts, it does not mean that it is more developed, or complex, than the lower systems of which it is formed. It is essential to realise that each new level of living system represents a fresh beginning. For example, the internal chemical complexity of a cell bears no relation to the very simple behaviour of this as a single-celled organism. In a similar way the highly complex interactions between the millions of cells internally in a dog or cat bear no relation to the quite simple behaviours of these animals as living creatures.

This disparity becomes much clearer when we turn to the social insects. Many insect societies are very ancient compared to mammals or humans; termites reach back over 400 million years and even the honey bee has been in existence for over 40 million years. Their societies are relevant to the study of human society and, in relation to their starting point, could be considered much more developed and stable than ours. They could, in a sense, be considered as adults, while we (that is, the mammalian group) are, by comparison, children. It is here that the paradox becomes most evident. The human individual as a multicellular organism is far more developed and complex than a bee, ant or termite. However, the third-order groups of human beings are, in evolutionary terms, far more recent than those of the social insects and have therefore, as living systems, not yet developed the sophistication or complex organisation of the latter.

29

Pseudo-Living Systems

When Cain beat out his brother Abel's brains,
His maker laid great cities in his soul.[1]
Robert Lowell

Wealth can be measured by the greatness of what we have
or the smallness of what we want.
François de La Rochefoucald

For the greater part of the two million years or more since human beings appeared on this planet, tribal or hunter-gatherer clusters lived in a more or less harmonious relationship with all the other living systems within the biosphere. Of course, violence and the continuous cycles of creativity and destruction were always present in nature, and human communities were no exception. Nevertheless, because of their relative powerlessness, throughout all this period human beings were not in a position to disturb or interfere with the overall balancing forces of nature, or the stability of the biosphere.

If we look back for a moment at primitive cultures, we find the primary social unit for survival and for transmission of the culture has always been a group of families. This has taken various forms at different times: the tribal settlement, the extended family, the hamlet, the village, the small market town with its hinterland. This was true also of the cluster of neighbourhoods making up great cities of the past, such as the city states of ancient Greece or Rome or the capital cities of Paris, London and Dublin, at the high point of their development, before they became overgrown, anonymous conurbations. It is not until we

Figure 10: Two corporations mating (merging).

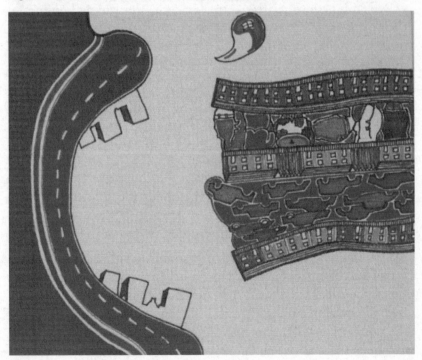

Figure 11: A corporation devouring all before it.

come to modern society and the much-lauded phenomenon of globalisation that we find the isolated nuclear family as it exists today.

These natural human settlements, even the cities of the past, developed in relation to natural resources. What they did and what they produced in order to survive and maintain themselves in existence was secondary to the main thrust — to be. Thus the celebration of life and of their being was central to their existence. What is less often recognised is that, over the same period, the age-old forms of human community — the villages and the small towns — have largely disappeared, in the west at least, or have altered their character totally as part of the giant urban conurbations that now exist. The extended family too has largely gone and even the nuclear family is now under threat. Giant corporations and organisations of all kinds have taken their place; these are primarily task-oriented enterprises concerned with doing.

Yet, because they are composed of living human beings, they will inevitably tend, as they progress and grow, to take on the characteristics of a living system. Thus we find giant corporations becoming involved in functions related to the life cycle — providing housing for their workers, crèches, swimming pools and fitness clubs, and various other social and community-like activities. In this way they take on more and more the characteristics of self-organising living systems. However, they depend ultimately on production of some kind and must satisfy the financial concerns of their shareholders. If the value of their shares on the stock exchange falls, or the cash-flow fails for even a few weeks, they can go out of existence, with the loss of thousands of jobs and all the other human activities that are the lifeblood of a living community. For this reason they can never be more than pseudo-living systems and can never embody the full definition of a genuine living system.

As I mentioned earlier a 'third-order' system of this kind, however powerful, because it is of recent origin is essentially a new beginning. Therefore, these insatiable 'blind monsters', even though they have entrained and entangled thousands of sensitive, complex human beings within them, are themselves only capable of quite primitive behaviours, similar to the dinosaurs of the ancient past. They can manifest 'fight or flight' behaviour, take over another corporation or be taken over, expand and grow or retreat and go into decline (see Fig. 10). In their pursuit of economic growth, they can destroy whole indigenous communities in developing countries; they can put an aged widow out of her tenement flat, where she has spent a whole lifetime, in order to demolish the building. Yet the human beings working in such an organisation, as individuals in their ordinary life outside, would never behave in such an insensitive fashion (see Fig. 11).

A strange twist enters the picture here in an example taken from the United States. The fathers of the American constitution were extremely concerned about protecting the ordinary American citizen from the power of unbridled corporations. Because of what had happened after the Revolution, the American fathers of the new nation went to great lengths to draw up a constitution that would place ultimate authority with the people, maintaining tight control on private corporations. Near the end of the Civil War, President Abraham Lincoln, who was deeply concerned about this issue, wrote a letter to a colonel fighting in his army:

> We may congratulate ourselves that this cruel war is nearing its end. It has cost a vast amount of treasure and blood . . . it has indeed been a trying hour for the Republic; but I see in the near future a crisis approaching that unnerves me and causes me to tremble for the safety of my country. As a result of the war, corporations have been enthroned, and an era of corruption in high places will follow, and the money power of the country will endeavour to prolong its reign by working on the prejudices of the people until all wealth is aggregated in a few hands, and the Republic is destroyed. I feel at this moment more anxiety for the safety of my country than ever before, even in the midst of war. God grant that my suspicions may prove groundless.[2]

His words were indeed prophetic. No sooner was the war over than Lincoln's fears that corporations would be 'enthroned' began to be realised – and the means of their coronation was to be the courts. A series of court cases brought by corporations with the specific intent of bending the law to their advantage saw judges granting more powers to corporations by way of generous or downright suspect interpretations of the constitution. The most notorious court decision came in 1886 when the innocuously named Santa Clara County vs Southern Pacific Railroad case was interpreted to mean that a cor-

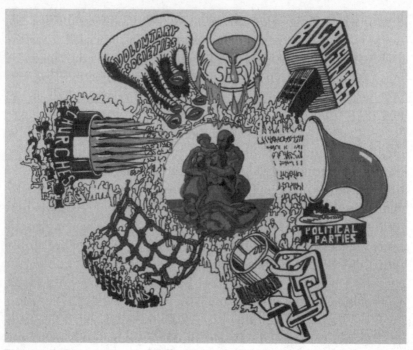

Figure 12: Organisations of different kinds actively destroying human communities and families.

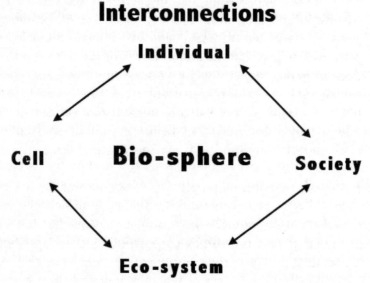

Figure 13: To be sane and healthy all the essential aspects of life must bear a clear relationship to each other – the context within which we live must be intimate enough to be understandable in human terms – our relationship to nature and to one another.

poration was a 'natural person' under the constitution. A further raft of court cases confirmed the new concept of 'corporate personhood', and corporations began to claim constitutional rights. The Supreme Court ruled that the fourteenth amendment to the constitution now gave a corporation – legally 'a person,' after all – the right not to have its 'privileges or immunities' 'abridged'. No state . . . shall 'deprive any person of life, liberty or property without due process of law'. By 1876, another US President, Rutherford Hayes, was lamenting the coming-to-pass of Lincoln's prophecy: 'This is a government of the people, by the people and for the people no longer,' he said. 'It is a government of corporations, by corporations and for corporations.'[3]

Although in the late nineteenth century there was, obviously, no knowledge of living systems theory, or recognition that a giant corporation is a form of 'pseudo-living' system, yet what happened would suggest that those involved already had this awareness. This is the real struggle which has been going on during our time as the spectre of globalisation spreads across the world in all directions; not the apparent battles between right and left, between socialism and capitalism, but the relentless transfer of power and control from the peripheral to the central, from the small to the large, from the personal to the anonymous and institutional. This is the real change that has been taking place, and it is still intensifying with every year that passes. Small private businesses amalgamate to form companies, companies merge to form transnational corporations, government departments expand to take over control of more and more areas of our personal lives, and even national, supposedly democratic, governments are superseded and become the lackeys of the transnational corporations (see Fig. 12).

The human needs we require to live a full and fruitful life are actually relatively few. The difficulty is that our economically driven society has filled us with all kinds of wants that we do not actually need nor does their acquisition, in the long run, contribute to real contentment or happiness. In order to increase production, these wants are constantly stimulated by mass advertising and hence a vicious circle is established.

The more we look deeply into ourselves and understand our physiology and the way our bodies work, the clearer it becomes that we are formed to live in a very direct relationship to nature and to each other. For us to be sane and healthy we must relate to a holistic world, so that all the essential aspects of life bear a clear relationship to one another (see Fig. 13). It is the very essence of our being as living creatures to be self-organising, and this in turn implies a reasonable degree of personal freedom and control over our lives. It follows that the context within which we need to have our being must be intimate enough to be understandable in human terms.

Moreover, when such considerations are discussed, it is almost always in relation to the needs of, and effects on, adults whose personalities are already formed. But if our fundamental need for an understandable world of human size is essential for us as adults, how much more vital and urgent is this for children?

None of us simply come into existence as adults, already formed. On the contrary, we are formed out of the matrix of relationships and environmental influences that we absorb from the moment of conception onwards. If these influences are remote, anonymous and fragmented, as is increasingly the picture in our economically driven society, then the adult who emerges will show these negative characteristics. Nor does the matter rest there, for as one generation succeeds another, this deterioration in behaviour and ethical mores will become ever more manifest.

30

Therapeutic Practice

Back in 1962 when I returned from the States and started the psychiatric clinic in Ballyfermot, I had reached an existential point. Either I would have to put my head down and just dish out tranquillisers to all and sundry, or else I would have to attempt to address the manifold social problems that were having a devastating effect on people's lives. I became convinced that, behind the presenting symptoms of anxiety, depression and so on, lay the tortured traumatic life histories of the persons concerned and the environmental problems generated by poverty and social disorganisation.

Over the years I continued to practise psychotherapy, although my main job was concerned with planning psychiatric services, but intuitively I knew that the latter activity would not make much sense unless it were continuously enlivened by a direct personal relationship with those for whom the service was intended. I also felt that I would simply die as a psychiatrist if I allowed my role as a psychotherapist to disappear.

Unfortunately, during the 1970s LSD, which I had worked with continuously since my return from the States, hit the streets and so fell into disrepute as a drug linked with abuse. As a result, all the pharmaceutical companies, particularly Sandoz, from whom I had always got my supplies, refused to manufacture it legitimately any longer. Because of this, for the next few years, although I continued to practise psychotherapy, I wasn't able to undertake the deep experiential work that I had carried on up to that time.

Then Paddy Walley, with his extraordinary ability for sensing a new direction, went to the Esalen Institute in California and met Stanislav Grof. Paddy approached me to see whether we could

255

arrange for Dr Grof to come to Ireland to run a workshop.

Stan Grof was originally from Czechoslovakia. He had trained as a psychoanalyst, even though this was forbidden by the communist authorities, then, like myself, he practised psychedelic therapy with LSD from 1957 to 1973, although this too was forbidden by the authorities. Then he managed to emigrate to the United States. There he carried out a major research project, in Baltimore, in which patients dying of cancer were treated with LSD. Following this, when he went to California, he developed a drug-free method of deep experiential therapy which achieved similar results. He developed this method by combining various procedures that have been known to tribal communities from ancient times: shamanic and aboriginal healing ceremonies, rites of passage, the practices of various ecstatic sects and the ancient mysteries of death and rebirth. All these procedures utilised various combinations of music, rhythm, dance and specific techniques involving intense breathing or withholding of breath, or more subtle methods which emphasised special awareness in relation to breathing, as practised in Zen or Tibetan Buddhism, and in certain Taoist and Christian practices.

From all these influences he developed a treatment procedure that he called 'holotropic therapy', which combines controlled breathing, evocative music and other forms of sound technology and focused bodywork. As he was not licensed to practice psychiatry or psychotherapy in the States, he utilised this method of achieving altered states of consciousness in therapeutic workshops in Esalen and elsewhere.

In about 1980 I arranged for Stan Grof and his wife Christina to hold a holotropic workshop here in Ireland. We obtained permission to run the workshop in the headquarters of the Irish Countrywomen's Association at Termonfeckin, near Drogheda. The workshop was very successful and I found it a useful learning experience, but there was an amusing side to it also. When we arrived, the ladies of the ICA greeted us with great deference and respect, obviously impressed with Dr Grof and Professor Ivor Browne. However, when the workshop got going there was a distinct change of attitude. Upwards of thirty participants attended these workshops, and once those involved moved into a state of altered consciousness, they exhibited extreme forms of emotional outburst: screaming, crying, roars of anger and so on. These were clearly audible around the house and the effect on the ladies of the ICA was quite dramatic. The respect and deference with which we were greeted initially were replaced with looks of apprehension, suspicion and fear.

The way in which these workshops are managed is that one half of the participants lie down on mattresses and go into the experience, while the others each sit with one of the participants to support them while they go through the ordeal. There was a row of large windows running down one side of the room and in one of the sessions, while I was sitting with a participant, I looked out the window and saw, to my amazement, that a complete herd of prize Friesian cows had gathered at the windows. They were looking in, astonished at the screams and cries of the human beings.

During that workshop, as a participant, I had my first experience of a 'transpersonal' state. It was towards the end of an experiential session when everything was becoming peaceful. I suddenly found myself in an entirely different sphere. I was hanging from a cross, at some time in the distant past. My arms were not stretched out horizontally, as in the usual depiction of Christ's crucifixion, but were closer to my body, at about 45 degrees, so I realised that I was hanging upside down. My hands were not fixed with nails but were held by leather or metal thongs (I could not tell which) across my palms. It was not a painful experience, as I seemed to have already died and was gazing peacefully at the world around me. The experience was absolutely clear and real at the time and I was quite shaken by it when I came back to ordinary consciousness some time later. I am describing it simply as it happened, without any attempt at interpretation. Strangely, I have always had the feeling that I had a previous life around the time of Christ.

Later Stan Grof came to Ireland again for a second workshop, which we held in St Brendan's Hospital. This too was very successful and encouraged me to get involved once again in active psychotherapy. I began to use a modified version of Grof's holotropic method, initially working with people on a one-to-one basis because I was not happy with all aspects of his way of doing things. In his workshops he usually started by giving talks describing some of the phenomena that were likely to be experienced by the participants in the sessions. He emphasised the four stages of what he termed 'basic perinatal matrices'; that is, the different stages which an infant goes through during the birth process. I was worried about this and I remember asking him whether such descriptions would influence the participants in what they would experience during the workshop. He replied quite dogmatically that it was not possible to influence what they would experience by suggestion. It has long since become evident that it is possible to suggest almost anything to someone under-going experiential or regression therapy. It is this fact, more than anything else, that has given rise to the 'False Memory Syndrome' (FMS) debacle (I will deal with this in more detail in chapter 32).

With the demise of the Irish Foundation and my diminishing role in the planning of psychiatric services, I was able to devote more time once again to psychotherapy. I continued with this work, at first on an individual basis in Garden Hill House and later with groups of patients in the old Protestant Church in St Brendan's.

This brings me to the central principle towards which all I have written so far has been leading. I have already mentioned the theory of living systems and the new scientific perspective on which this rests. Fundamental to this is the concept of 'autopoiesus' or 'self-organisation' (see Appendix A). If this is synonymous with what it is to be alive, then anything which diminishes our state of self-organisation lessens our control over and management of our health and will be a step towards sickness and, if it goes far enough, death.

Because of their reliance on a reductionist scientific epistemology, which is now more than 300 years out of date, it is simply not possible for the majority of psychiatrists to address the essential nature of psychiatric illness. There has been much talk in recent times of 'evidence-based medicine', and of properly organised 'random controlled therapeutic trials'. Psychiatric journals are full of statistical surveys and double-blind drug trials which purport to give a 'scientific' basis to modern psychiatric practice and to the biochemical causation of most psychiatric illness. Irish psychiatrist David Healy has aptly described this unfortunate development in this way:

Arguably, the term 'Evidence *Biased* Medicine' would be more appropriate. Clinical trials in psychiatry have never showed that anything worked. Penicillin eradicated a major psychiatric disease without any clinical trial to show that it worked. Chlorpromazine and antidepressants were all discovered without clinical trials. You don't need a clinical trial to show something works.[1]

I believe what lies behind these endeavours is a deep misunderstanding of the true nature of scientific research. Science is not synonymous with scientific method, which means testing the results of a scientific hypothesis as objectively as possible. True science depends, first and foremost, on the generation of creative ideas. Then, as more data comes in that supports a hypothesis, this may become a theory. It is only then that the scientific method enters the picture, to test the validity of the theory. If the ideas on which the theory is based are not sound, however, or have been bypassed by more recent scientific developments, then all the controlled trials and statistical surveys that can be applied to the question will not achieve anything.

This seems to me to be the problem with much of what passes for scientific endeavour at the present time. Scientific geniuses are few and far between and those who come up with an original idea are a rarity. Unfortunately, as scientific research has become more generalised, with the competitive publish or perish ethos, much psychiatric research has become debased, simply identified with scientific method and virtually devoid of originality.

Change is central to our existence in this material world. Humankind has changed the world out of all recognition, and yet it remains true that the only lasting positive change anyone can make is within him/herself. Change oneself and one's world changes. If you become a different person then obviously your world is different, and so are any dealings you have with it. Even at its simplest, any change involves two things – work and suffering. The deeper the change to be accomplished, the greater the amount of work, pain and suffering involved. People resist change for this very reason, even when they realise that change will have a positive benefit.

Because of mechanistic attitudes that have accompanied the enormous advances in science and technology, the western mind has fallen prey to the illusion that there is a remedy for every ill; we expect to be able to avail of these without any effort or suffering on our part. When people come to a doctor or therapist with symptoms like depression or anxiety, or simply feeling they can no longer manage, they usually come expecting the doctor to do something for them, to do something to relieve them. With the development of technological medicine during the past century, we have all been conditioned to accept the current concepts as to the nature of health and illness. The belief has grown, particularly in the west, that it is the doctor who cures. The body is seen as a machine with which something has gone wrong, and the doctor's job is to fix it by giving medicine, by operating, or whatever.

Certainly doctors can often relieve symptoms in this way and the patient may appear to have made little contribution to the change in his/her condition, but the fallacy of this view has been exposed in many areas in recent years, none more so than with the advent of AIDS. This has made it only too clear that, without the natural healing power of the body and a functioning immune system, medicine and doctors are largely helpless. Even if we take the simple example of a fracture, a surgeon only realigns the bones in approximation to each other, so that healing can take place. It is the body that heals and joins the bones together and this takes effort and work. It also involves considerable pain and suffering for the patient while the fracture is healing. There is a qualification to be made here, however. When a surgeon is dealing with parts of the body, it is quite valid for him to treat these as if they were parts of a machine, but this must always be within the context of the whole person.

Let me explain by means of a personal example. A few years ago I had to get a total knee replacement because the cartilage had virtually disappeared and the bones were rubbing against each other, causing severe pain and limitation of movement. I had already tried a variety of alternative procedures – acupuncture, deep massage, osteopaths, all to no avail. By the time I went for the operation, I could hardly walk a hundred metres. Although the installing of the artificial joint was a skilful and delicate technological operation, this was neverthless essentially no different from putting a new joint in the axle of a motor car. The operation was successful but the very next day I was told I had to start moving my leg, even though this was extremely painful. I was also informed, in no uncertain terms, that the first week of struggle to gain increasing movement of the leg, with the aid of intensive physiotherapy, was crucial. Now this is the essential point: unless I, as a 'self-organising' system, took over the responsibility for getting my leg moving, the efforts of the surgeon, no matter how expertly executed, would be to no avail. So over the next three months I had to work very hard, with expert assistance from the physiotherapists, to build the new joint into myself as a working part of my whole body. So here is the unavoidable conclusion. Once the fundamental principle that we are self-organising systems is accepted, then, ultimately, only the person himself can take responsibility for his own health, and anything that interferes with this will, in the long term, be damaging.

The necessary relationship of suffering to change becomes all the clearer when we turn to emotional problems. Because the concept of therapy, and hence of therapists, has been derived from medicine, we have tended to fall into the same error of thinking that the therapist cures the patient. When applied to psychotherapy, or for that matter to psychiatry generally, this is an erroneous notion. In dealing with psychiatric illness there is no treatment that you can apply to a person that will bring about real change in him. The person has to undertake the work himself, and this involves pain and suffering.

I should point out that there are two contrasting forms of change or learning involved here. On the one hand there is the pain involved in taking action: to learn a new skill, start a new job or take an examination. On the other hand there is the emotional work necessary to integrate an experience, such as feeling grief over the loss of someone dear or experiencing the effects of a trauma. It is important to realise that the response must be appropriate to the type of challenge facing us, whether to 'feel' or to 'act'. For example, the widow who remains dry-eyed at the funeral and who takes charge of all the practical arrangements and is often admired for bearing up wonderfully is in fact avoiding the necessary work of grieving.

Many psychiatrists seem to have missed this point entirely. They think that, by giving tranquillisers and temporarily relieving symptoms, something has been achieved, whereas in fact, no real change has taken place and sooner or later the person will slip back to where he was with a recurrence of his symptoms. The issue here is not the giving of a drug; many of the psychoactive drugs are very useful on a temporary basis. Indeed, if one is honest, no psychiatrist who deals with the full range of psychiatric disturbance could manage without them. The question is whether they are given as a treatment in themselves, or as an aid to working in relationship with the person. Often the drug is the only way of making the initial contact so that therapy can begin, when a person is so psychotic, over-anxious, or agitated and depressed that it is not possible to deal with him until he has settled down.

It is not the drug, it is the message that accompanies it that is really damaging. Typically, if a person is clinically depressed he is told that whenever he feels depression descending on him he must contact his psychiatrist and commence the appropriate medication. This is because if you believe there is such an entity as clinical depression that is biochemically determined, then there is really nothing the person himself can do to alleviate it.

Now, from a systems perspective, this is a lethal message. If self-organisation is the essence of what it is to be healthy and alive, then to deprive a person of the very quality of being in control of himself is the worst thing that could be done to him. Yet this is what is happening every day of the week in psychiatric clinics. It is because of this, more than anything else, that many people are gradually led towards a pathway of illness. Seeing themselves as ill and helpless, they move imperceptibly into a state of chronic ill health.

Before going on to discuss some of the principles underlying psychotherapy and the therapeutic relationship, I think it is essential to consider the question of diagnosis. Diagnosis is a medical concept, but in medicine it has a rather narrow focus. It is mainly concerned with the symptoms from which the patient is suffering and the elucidation of the disease process that is thought to be causing them. While I think there is some value in the elucidation of the main clinical syndromes that have been patiently separated out over the past 150 years in psychiatry, these clusters of symptoms tell one little about the cause, or the natural history, of these so-called 'disorders'. The symptoms are essentially a cross-section of the manifestations that are there now. The crucial dimension that is missing is time – that is, change over time. That is why, more and more, I question the usefulness of the major works of statistical classifications, such as the Diagnostic and Statistical Manual (DSM4) or the International Classification of Mental and Behavioural Disorders (ICD10). In recent years these have acquired an almost biblical status, with their aura of infallibility.

They have a more ominous significance, however, for, once you can name a cluster of symptoms as a disease, even though there is no pathological or laboratory evidence to support this, you have created an apparent reality. So then, if you have a specific illness due to some as yet unidentified underlying biochemical abnormality, there should be a specific remedy to deal with it. This suits the pharmaceutical industry perfectly. What we have here is a 'closed delusional system'. Unfortunately most psychiatrists have taken this great falsehood on board, thus they see no need to take the life story or traumatic history of the person into consideration, nor is there any need to see all this from a psychotherapeutic point of view.

In psychotherapy we have a much broader frame of reference and need to understand not only the nature of the problem presented, but also what kind of person it is who has the problem. The direction that therapy will take will often depend much more on the type of personality than on the presenting symptoms. So, in effect, psychotheraphy has the job of assessing the whole person. Until we get this picture clear and we come to understand this person's life, therapy cannot really begin.

Strangely enough it is very often the first glimpse we have as the person walks into the room that reveals in an instant an impression of what has gone wrong in their life. This, of course, depends on how open we are to process this impression, and also on all our previous experience. It is not a question of just looking with the eyes; but rather involves an intuitive awareness of the whole person. This is where experience is important; it may be that we saw someone ten years previously who presented a similar picture that gives the link, without even being consciously aware of the connection. But it is also being able to be intuitive, to experience through the heart. Women are generally much better at relating in this way. However, it is not enough to react emotionally; one has to learn to bring this intuitive impression into normal consciousness, so that an objective assessment can be made of it. To put it another way, this operation involves a shift from right to left brain activity.

From such intuitions we can generate hypotheses, which can then be tested by going further into the history and by a process of elimination. Unless we work in this way we can often get lost in all the details of the personal and family history and fail to find the main theme or Gestalt that is crucial to understanding what is going on in this person's life. More and more I find that people's lives manifest a theme that is essentially simple but that it often takes several weeks to elucidate.

In trying to approach this diagnostic question from a different angle, I came to the conclusion that there are two basic dimensions involved in our attempts to deal with life. These are our coping skills and our defence mechanisms. I feel that one of Freud's great achievements was his elucidation of human defence mechanisms. The difficulty I have encountered, however, is how to separate these from our ability

Personality types as a function of defence and coping skills

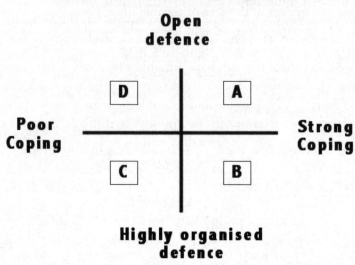

Figure 14: Personality types as a function of defence and coping skills.

to cope. One approach, developed by George Kelly, the great American psychologist, is to separate these dimensions along two axes. On one axis is depicted weak versus strong coping and, on the other, highly organised defence versus little defence organisation (see Fig. 14).

Between the two limbs of this cross, four clinical groupings emerge:

(a) The first group is of those who are reasonably healthy; they are able to cope with appropriate action or emotional response, depending on what the life challenge demands. On the other axis they show a flexible defence organisation, being open and warm without need of constricted or highly organised defences. (b) The second group is of people who are well able to cope but are rather rigid and inflexible. On the other axis they present a highly organised defence system, a constricted lifestyle that tends to avoid any situation where an open-feeling response would be indicated. These characteristics are typical of victims of trauma, and it is these patients who will tend to show the most favourable response to deep experiential psychotherapy. Their coping ability gives them the strength to fully experience whatever painful traumas their life has exposed them to. Indeed such people, far from being weaker or more vulnerable than the average, typically show enormous strength and courage in their struggle to carry on in the face of terrible life experiences.

(c) In this quadrant we find those who would generally be described as antisocial or borderline personalities. On the axis of 'defence' these too will have a highly organised defence system, but characteristically defences of a more primitive kind. Because of desertion early in life and loss of basic trust, they will test any situation or relationship by employing difficult and antisocial behaviour to see whether they will be rejected yet again. This may take the form of self-destructive or aggressive acts, and such behaviour is particularly likely to appear when unresolved traumatic experience surfaces in therapy.

On the other axis they will tend to have poor coping skills for managing life, and difficulty in concentrating or sticking at a task. They are likely to have a poor educational record and have difficulty in holding down a job. Such individuals are difficult to manage in therapy, and probably represent the most challenging patients one is likely to have to deal with. Nevertheless, it is possible to work with them if they are provided with a validating, supportive, but also disciplined environment, along the lines of a therapeutic community. With the help of such a supportive network they may gradually be able to work through their unresolved traumatic experiences, learn to trust in the context of consistent therapeutic relationships, and eventually be able to undertake rehabilitation and training to give them the coping skills for independent living.

(d) In this final quadrant are to be found those who not only have weak coping skills but also have poorly organised defences. This is because during the course of development they have failed to reach maturity, or to form an adult personality. At the deepest level they have failed to create a personal identity; nor are they able to manage their personal boundary. Within this segment will be those who fit the schizophrenic spectrum, and the more recently identified Asperger's Syndrome. There will also be found some of those with eating disorders and those suffering with chronic social phobia, panic disorder and chronic anxiety. A common characteristic of this group of patients is their childish dependency, their inability to bound themselves and their failure to achieve independence and separation from their family of origin. In such cases, even where there is a history of traumatisation, if this is activated in therapy they are unable to work with it and simply regress further into primitive psychotic defences.

Clearly this approach to diagnosis is something of an oversimplification and these four quadrants only represent a rough guide. Many patients will not fit neatly into one or other of these groups but will show a mixed picture or will shade from one quadrant to another as they proceed through life. Nevertheless, I have found this rough categorisation of personality types useful as a guide to therapy over the years and, generally, more helpful than the rigid nosological designation of mental disorders, such as in the DSM and the International Classification of Diseases.

Over the years I have come to realise that psychotherapy is best understood (and, after all, psychotherapy is the only therapy that exists in psychiatry to bring about real change in a person) as proceeding through a series of discrete phases. These tend to follow one another naturally as the person works his/her way through the therapeutic process. This is best depicted in the form of a therapeutic cycle (see Fig. 15).

One reason why it is important to depict this as a series of circular stages is that, before getting involved in the 'experiential' stages of the therapy, it is often necessary to go to the end point of the cycle and ensure that the person sets up a reasonably healthy lifestyle. What I mean by this is that they exercise – walking, swimming, going to the gym, or whatever – and also that they maintain a job, or take a training course, so that between therapeutic sessions they have some structure in their life to hold their personality together. Another reason to conceptualise this as a circular form is that, quite often, when a person has completed the circle, they will be strong enough to activate further traumatic experiences, which they were unable to face until they had dealt with the earlier traumatic work.

Having gradually worked out this circular formulation, I was surprised to find that the pioneering psychologist George Kelly had also depicted his work with clients in the form of a 'cycle of experience'. It was interesting therefore to see if the phases in his cycle showed any similarities to those that had emerged for me. Figure 16

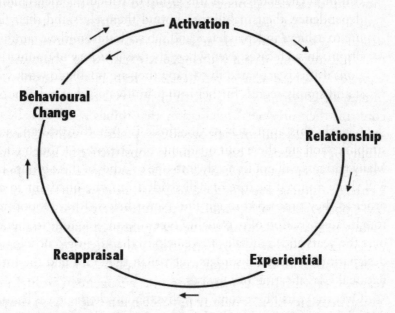

Figure 15: A Therapeutic Cycle – the different phases of the psychotherapeutic process.

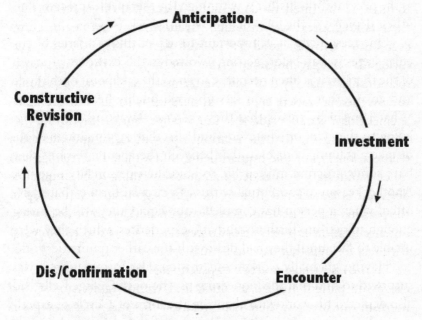

Figure 16: George Kelly's 'Cycle of Experience'.

shows his cycle of experience as compared to my therapeutic cycle and, although he uses different descriptive terms, the similarity is striking. Where I start with 'activation', he uses the term 'anticipation', his 'investment' is my 'therapeutic relationship' phase and my 'experiential' phase is his 'encounter'. My 'reappraisal' is described by him as 'dis-confirmation', by which he means that either the patient confirms their previous 'anticipation' that things will always be the same, or they disconfirm their previous experience, realising the possibility of real change. This leads to his 'constructive revision', which I describe as 'engagement in life'. The fact that, quite independently, I arrived at similar stages in the therapeutic progression suggests that these phases have some validity. This full therapeutic cycle would mainly refer to those working their way through painful traumatic experience. In other clinical situations, although the therapeutic relationship is always fundamental, other phases such as 'cognitive reappraisal' with 'dis-confirmation', or 'engagement in life' with 'constructive revision', might require the main emphasis so the person might not have to proceed fully through all stages of the therapeutic cycle.

In psychotherapy the relationship of person to person, of heart to heart, is absolutely fundamental to therapy. If this is absent then there is no context within which psychotherapy can begin. However, I think there is a good deal of confusion with regard to this. Traditionally in psychotherapy the question of the therapeutic relationship is usually dealt with in terms of transference. No doubt the psychoanalytic concept of transference is useful and the management of it is of considerable importance, but the first thing that must be stressed is that the relationship of therapist and client is a real relationship of one human being to another. The feelings and other manifestations that occur are not something to be simply understood as 'transferred' from some other significant relationship in the person's past. This undoubtedly occurs and has to be dealt with, but any relationship between two persons is also a real relationship with real feelings that have to be managed.

In the traditional practice of psychoanalysis the notion that, because the patient lies on a couch and the therapist sits behind her/him out of view, there is no relationship and what emerges is purely transference is manifest nonsense. Relationship is not simply verbal or visual, or even non-verbal, for once we are in a relationship, direct exchange of feelings and energy and also information take place (often even at a distance) whether we see each other or not. Carl Jung was once again ahead of his time in pointing this out. In 1935, in his Tavistock lectures he stated:

> In psychotherapy even if the doctor is entirely detached from the emotional content of the patient, the very fact that the patient has emotions has an effect on him. And it is a great mistake if the doctor thinks he can lift himself out of it. He cannot do more than become conscious of the fact that he is affected, if he does not see that he is too aloof and then he talks beside the point. It is even his duty to accept the emotions of the patient and to mirror them. This is the reason why I reject the idea of putting a patient on a sofa and sitting behind them. I put my patients in front of me and I talk to them as one natural human being to another, and I expose myself completely and react with no restriction.[2]

When R.D. Laing appeared on the *Late Late Show* in 1982 he recounted how, when he was training in psychiatry in Scotland, because he moved out to the front of his desk and sat directly facing the person, he was called up by his superior and told that it was inappropriate behaviour. On the same show I stated that quite independently many years ago, I myself had adopted the same idea, placing the desk against a wall so that I could sit directly facing the person I was attempting to relate with. It is only a simple thing, but talking to someone across a desk and compounding this by wearing a white coat and horn-rimmed spectacles (the typical regalia of the doctor) fundamentally alters the relationship. I know a number of psychiatrists, particularly those working in general hospitals, who continue this absurdity of wearing a white coat when there is no possible hygienic reason in psychiatry for doing so.

The story of how I came to be on the *Late Late Show* with Ronnie Laing may be of interest. When I heard that he had been invited to appear on the show I decided to go out to RTÉ to meet him before the show started. When I got there he had not yet arrived and when he did show up, he was well under the weather, having been drinking during dinner. He was supposed to be first on the show but it was felt he was too drunk to go on. Although I wasn't supposed to be there, Gay Byrne appealed to me to stay and try to sober him up.

Ulick O'Connor, who was also to be on the panel, and I worked on him for more than an hour, pouring coffee into him. By the time the last item was due to start, we felt he was sober enough to go on. It was at this point that Gay Byrne asked me to go on with him, I suppose to help him get through the show. In fact he acquitted himself well and cut through the usual superficiality of this type of programme. The first point he made was that no one would land in a mental hospital if they had a real friend. He felt that if you needed personal help, you should not go to a doctor. Doctors were technicians and had been trained out of the ability to relate in a human way. He described how when visiting the Burgholzli Hospital (where the term schizophrenia was introduced) in Switzerland recently, the doctors there were forbidden to use the intimate form of address, '*du*' or '*tu*', when speaking to patients. It was a 'them' and 'us' type of relationship. He said psychiatrists generally behaved like prison warders, keeping people in physical or chemical restraint when they ought instead to provide asylum, places of safety.

Then Ulick O'Connor, in an attempt to trap him, asked Ronnie: 'What would you do with a person like the man in Britain who, having killed two children when he escaped from Broadmoor, killed another child?' 'I'd kill him!' shouted Ronnie. 'Someone who kills – kill them! Or lock them up for life.'

Things were going fine up to this point, then Gaybo asked him:

> Knowing that you were coming on a television programme, why have you drink taken? It's perfectly obvious to people that you are under the weather, you are definitely slow and I get the whiff of alcohol off you.

Ronnie responded by saying: 'I'm speaking and behaving as I usually do, I only had one or two drinks during the day, and that's a disgusting question to ask me.'

The fact is that he had arrived very drunk and Gaybo had seen him in that condition, so it was a reasonable question to ask a person who was known for his courage and honesty throughout his career. Unfortunately, by this time Ronnie was in the late stages of alcoholism and, as is typical of alcoholics, was in a state of denial about his drinking. The fascinating thing was that, being in Ireland, with its enabling attitude towards drinking, the whole audience at this point turned on Gay Byrne for what they felt was his unforgivable attack on Laing. After some acrimonious exchanges, Gaybo announced a break, saying that Ronnie and I would be staying on for the next item, but Ronnie said he'd had enough and refused to stay.

Ronnie Laing came to Dublin on a number of occasions during this period. We had several one-day seminars with him for those of us working in the Irish Foundation. On these occasions he spoke in his usual slow way, often silent for some moments before answering a question. In one of our seminars, when the question of unresolved grief came up, he told us how one time, when he was conducting a workshop on unresolved grief, a Presbyterian clergyman said that in his opinion failure to grieve does not always require intervention and then went on to relate the following tale. He had been officiating at a funeral in the Highlands and an old man who had lost his wife was standing at the graveside stony-faced. The clergyman thought, 'I'll need to do some grief work with him later.' Then, when they were leaving the graveyard, he was walking behind this old man and overheard him saying to a friend, 'I was married to that woman for forty years and I never liked her.'

It was on Ronnie Laing's first visit to Ireland that he was invited to speak by the psychotherapy section of the Irish division of the Royal College of Psychiatrists. The meeting was to be held in St Brendan's hospital. Being Ronnie, when he heard he was to speak in a mental hospital, he insisted that any patients who wanted to come be allowed to attend. We had fixed up a sound system in the lecture theatre in the nursing school, but word had got around that he was coming and so many people turned up that we had to move the meeting down to the big hall on the ground floor. It was not possible at that stage to set up the sound system there, so there was a question whether those at the back of the hall would be able to hear. He said, 'Would all those who can't hear at the back put up their hands?' Hearing this unfortunate question, Ronnie put his finger up to his head, twisting it, indicating a nutcase. Unfortunately, the chairman saw this and got angry: 'You can hold your meeting here, but it can't be held under the auspices of the Royal College.' At that, Ronnie turned to him and told him to 'fuck off'.

Incensed at this, the chairman walked out. Some of the establishment psychiatrists, who were seated in the front row, were disgusted at Dr Laing's behaviour. Seeing this, Ronnie responded: 'Yes, you too, come on, just fuck off!' The effect of this was to cause the next few rows, whom Laing addressed in the same way, to leave. In this manner, nearly half the audience, consisting of all the more orthodox psychiatrists, left the hall, leaving only the mostly non-medical therapists remaining. Thus Ronnie Laing, with his uncanny ability for getting at the heart of things, brought to the surface a crucial division between those of us with a psychotherapeutic bent and those with an orthodox medical viewpoint. This had always been there, but was never brought out into the open. It was a remarkable achievement.

As the afternoon wore on, Ronnie, who had already taken a fair amount of alcohol at lunch, got progressively more inebriated, even producing a bottle of Glenfiddick on the stage and proceeded to drink it. The press had been supposed to come later to report on the meeting but thankfully did not arrive. As the situation was deteriorating anyway, I eventually decided to play a few tunes on the tin whistle, which greatly pleased Ronnie Laing and brought the meeting to a close.

That evening he came to our apartment in Dun Laoghaire for dinner, and afterwards we had a jazz session, he playing the piano and I doing my best to keep up with him on the guitar.

When I met Ronnie Laing for the first time some years earlier, we threw our arms around each other as if we were old friends and I was reminded of something that he wrote at the beginning of his autobiography, when he referred to 'Going around the world, meeting old friends whom I have never met before.'[3]

To return to the 'therapeutic relationship': this is a real relationship, like any other, between two human beings. But it is not simply that; it is a relationship established for a purpose, which is to help the client with their problems. Therefore, there also has to be objectivity and the relationship has to be managed. I feel there is considerable confusion about this amongst psychotherapists. When it is said that therapy should be non-directive, this is essentially correct. It is generally useless to tell a person what to do, or to do it for them.

Nevertheless, the therapy has to be managed. If the client is left to feel and behave as they have always done, they will control the therapy and there will be no change. There is an apparent paradox here. What is often misunderstood is that it is the task of the therapist to manage the context of the therapy; that is, to manage the boundary of the relationship (see Fig. 17 and Fig. 19), is to manage

Figure 17: The Therapeutic Relationship. At the commencement of the therapy the personal boundary of both the client and the therapist is intact.

the 'system' of two persons that has been established and that is now surrounded by a confidential boundary. What clients feel or do within this system is still their personal responsibility. In recent years I have found that, within this confidential boundary, the personal boundary between myself and the patient tends to dissolve and one finds oneself experiencing directly what is going on within the patient, even though they are not yet aware themselves of what this is (see Fig.18).

The therapeutic relationship then has a dual function, on the one hand to empathise and generally relate to the person as one human being to another, but on the other objectively to assess and observe what is going on in the client and in oneself as a therapist (see Fig. 19). What I mean by this is that, while it is not legitimate to tell another person what to do with their life, we have a perfect right to lay down the conditions under which we are prepared to work with them. For example, while one may not have the right or the power to get a person to stop drinking excessively, or to stop them committing suicide, one is perfectly entitled to say, 'If I am to work successfully with you in therapy, I cannot do so if you are drinking heavily, or if you are threatening to commit suicide every time the going gets rough.'

Figure 18: As the confidential boundary surrounding both develops, the personal boundary of each tends to dissolve.

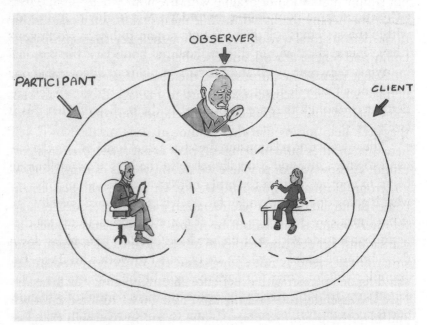

Figure 19: Dual functions of the therapist – that of 'participant' and 'observer'.

Or if you feel that, for therapy to succeed, the client should be working and not sitting at home all day brooding, or again, if you feel that they will get nowhere as long as they are living at home in a dependent state with their parents, then it is quite legitimate for you to insist that these conditions be met if therapy is to proceed. Needless to say, such conditions need to be negotiated sensitively and one often has to allow considerable time for the person to make the necessary shift in their behaviour. It is only if and when there is no movement on their part to create the conditions for therapy to progress that the decision has to be faced that, unless they can accept and make the necessary changes in behaviour, there is no point in continuing with therapy, as you are simply colluding with them to stay as they are.

This means that the statement you make is always about yourself, the conditions under which you are able to work, or not to work, with this person. The patient is perfectly entitled to refuse to go along with these conditions but then there is no basis for continuing with them in therapy. This is my understanding of what is meant by a 'therapeutic contract', and managing the context of the therapy. It is not simply a question of dealing with the hour when they are with you. Any therapy that is worthwhile means taking on a relationship to the person's total way of life, including their key relationships with family and others, at work and elsewhere.

What then is the purpose of a therapist? If a person could undertake whatever change is necessary to manage their life successfully, there would be no need for a therapist, but the very fact that they seek help means that they cannot manage on their own. It is here that another human being can play a vital role. Often in life we cannot see how we got to where we are, or what is causing things to go wrong, no matter how hard we try. Of course, the person who comes to our aid need not be a therapist; indeed, a great deal of helpful intervention is carried out by friends, relatives and self-help organisations, as I described earlier in relation to life crises. But in many situations a friend is not enough and the objectivity and understanding of a person with experience and training may be necessary. I see the essential role of a therapist as a guide, to listen creatively and help the person to map out the situation in which they find themselves; not to try to do the work for the client, but to provide the context within which they can work. Perhaps the most important thing of all is simply to provide 'hope', to let the person see that you believe change is possible and that they can do it if they are prepared to work at it.

This may not seem like much, but the giving of hope, safety and support and the management of the context within which they can work can open up areas in their life that have been hidden and cut off and this is crucial for many people if they are ever to be able to grow and become free of the burdens that they carry. Any more active interventions or therapeutic skills that we may bring to the situation are really peripheral to this central task, although they can be important in pushing forward the individual's progress towards a healthy way of life.

31

Phyllis Hamilton

The development of a therapeutic relationship brings with it responsibilities for the therapist also, as I was to learn painfully over the years. I mentioned earlier in this work when relating my experiences in St Loman's Hospital that, in my attempts to help my patient Phyllis Hamilton, I had given her a commitment that, if and when she felt she could not take the secrecy any more and needed to state publicly the lie she had been forced to live over all the years, I would vouch for the truth of what she had to say, whatever the implications for me personally.

Phyllis was barely out of childhood when she fell in love with Father Michael Cleary, but (as many a father has discovered with his daughter) I could do nothing about it. The 1960s were different times from now and, anyway, whatever I did would probably not have helped Phyllis. So I simply left the door open for her to come and see me, or call me at home if she needed to, and sadly she often did.

Situations like this tend to create repetitive crises and, whenever there was a crisis, Phyllis would come to see me. She came to see me when her first child was born and she had it adopted, and again when the second son, Ross, arrived. Eventually Michael Cleary started coming to see me, as many husbands did when their wives were not well. Phyllis felt trapped and at times she got very frustrated and depressed. We often talked about resolving the situation by him revealing his double life and facing up to marriage, but he was like two people. He wanted to be a priest and he worked hard at being a priest. He also genuinely loved Phyllis and their son Ross and was a devoted husband and father. However, when he was in his role as a priest, he seemed to be able to forget the fact that he had a family and could not face the domestic side of himself. More than once, for the sake of her own well-being, Phyllis thought she would have to separate from him.

Phyllis was strong, otherwise she could not have survived for so long, but she eventually could not go on as she was. Some time in the late 1970s she was threatening to write to the Archbishop of Dublin. I was worried about her. I thought a better course would be to get in touch with Bishop Eamonn Casey, who I had met on several occasions. I knew that he and Michael had worked in London together, and that Michael was likely to listen to him. This was before the bishop's own problems were known. Bishop Casey told me to leave it with him and he would see what he could do. He took Michael and Phyllis down to his own place for a weekend but nothing came of it, and things grumbled on as usual. Then Phyllis reached her lowest ebb to date. She came and told me that a young deacon had raped her; he had threatened to reveal the whole story about her and Father Cleary unless she let him have his way with her. Afterwards she found that she was pregnant again, this time as a result of the rape. As always, her main concern was secrecy, and she went to America and had the baby girl adopted. (Later she did go to see this fellow's bishop and told him what had happened, so justice was done and he was no longer allowed to remain in the priesthood.)

I saw Phyllis increasingly often as she got older. It was a huge crisis for her in the summer of 1992 when Annie Murphy broke the story of her relationship with Bishop Casey and that they had a son together. The news created uproar in the country and many were quick to judge Eamonn Casey. Father Cleary and Phyllis had known the bishop for years and considered him a friend. Phyllis said that Cleary felt betrayed and was hurt that Casey had never confided in him. Their son Ross was stunned by the news and Phyllis went into a state of acute anxiety.

Identifying with the bishop's dilemma, the family were devastated by the 'outing' of the Bishop and Annie Murphy. After May 1992 Phyllis never left her home through the front door again for fear that she would be photographed and be the cause of similar treatment for Father Cleary. She said that every time she switched on the television or radio they were discussing Bishop Casey and she feared that it was only a matter of time until the media discovered them. She was having trouble eating and sleeping and was getting panic attacks.

She could not look Ross' friends in the face. Things got so bad that the very mention of Bishop Casey sent her running to the bathroom.

In July, she was on the verge of a nervous breakdown and, in desperation, Father Cleary called me. When I saw her I felt that she needed to get out of the house for a few weeks for a rest. I got her into St Vincent's, Fairview, on the other side of the city, where I hoped she would not be recognised as Father Cleary's housekeeper. Eventually, she was sufficiently recovered to go home.

In the meantime we were all worried about Ross, who was showing signs of disturbance and strain. After all, the boy had never been able to speak about who his father was, and it was difficult for an adolescent to keep such a secret. After the Casey story, he had the added strain of worrying that the media would also expose Michael Cleary.

Previously Father Cleary had suffered cancer of the throat for some time but had recovered. However, it reccurred around 1993 following the crisis over Bishop Casey and he died later that year. The following April there was a function in the National Concert Hall to give the MIR Award from the Families in Need group in recognition of Father Cleary's work on behalf of his parishioners. The next morning's papers carried a quotation from a priest at the ceremony. 'An awful lot of people were upset by the rumours which sprang up after his death. We believe that a terrible wrong was done to him and we would like to honour him.'

However, at this stage Phyllis had more pressing problems. When Father Cleary died, the only money she had was her Unmarried Mother's Allowance. When the final notice for the gas, electricity and phone bills arrived she could not pay them. She had never had to worry about these things before and in a panic she eventually got in touch with Monsignor Sheehy, who made arrangements for the diocese to pay the bills. Father Cleary had written to her from his deathbed, telling her that he had left detailed instructions in the filing cabinet that, he said, she was to bring to an accountant friend of his who would advise her and look after her. There were also details of racehorses and a reference to share certificates. In the event, the contents of the filing cabinet were never found and the Church stopped paying the household bills in June 1995.

Meanwhile, in January 1994, what Phyllis feared most happened. *Phoenix* magazine published the story of Father Michael Cleary being a father. Because of the accurate details in the piece,

Phyllis knew that someone close had betrayed them. There followed statements from Father Cleary's celebrity friends and family that the story could not possibly be true. Archbishop Desmond Connell sent a letter to the priests of the diocese, which stated:

> Recent reports concerning the late Father Michael Cleary will have caused pain, anger and embarrassment to priests and people in the diocese and throughout Ireland.
>
> My policy in responding to these reports has been guided by my concern both for the good name of Father Cleary and for those closely affected by the reports. I want you and your parishioners to know of my concern for you at this time.
>
> I am confident that with God's help this ordeal can renew and deepen our sense of solidarity and of what it means in today's world to be together, the disciples of Christ.[1]

Phyllis and Ross were abandoned by almost everyone who knew them. Cleary's relatives wanted her to deny that Michael was Ross' father. Because of the way they were treated, especially by the Church authorities, Phyllis finally decided to make public the details of her relationship with the priest. It was thirty years since she had met Father Cleary, longer since she had become my patient and now she asked me to speak up for her and tell the world that she was not a liar. The year was 1995. I had retired in 1994.

I knew that I would have to do this for her. However, I was aware that all hell would break loose when I did. First, I studied the ethical guide published by the Medical Council in an effort to think through the dilemma and be sure of what I was about to do. I tried to think as clearly as I could about where my ethical duty lay, but in my heart I knew that it must be to the living patient; whatever I said was not going to affect Father Cleary. My view was that the dire need of Phyllis, her mental health and the needs of her son, Ross, had to override the situation of confidentiality in regard to Cleary. I received the following letter from Phyllis:

> Dear Ivor,
> I officially authorise you, as my doctor, to speak publicly about your professional knowledge of my life and relationship with Father Michael Cleary. I have made the decision, as you know,

to finally speak out about this matter because of the way myself and Ross have been treated since Father's death. It has also had a dreadful effect on my son as you know and I fear that if I did not do something then Ross would ultimately suffer. I feel that there is no option open to me and I am putting myself in the firing line for a lot of serious criticism and innuendo. I am fully aware of the risks you are running by deciding to defend me in the face of my detractors. Your courage in agreeing to enter the fray is something I deeply appreciate and shall never forget.

Yours truly, Phyl Hamilton

My media interviews caused the anticipated uproar. The spokesman for the Catholic hierarchy, the Bishop of Athenry, Dr Thomas Flynn, told the radio programme, *Morning Ireland*: 'At first sight he is a credible witness, but Mr Browne, as the doctor of the woman making the allegation, could not be seen as objective.' A priest in Wicklow decried me from his pulpit, and wrote in his parish newsletter that I was a 'hit and run merchant'. Whatever about reluctantly hitting, I never ran; but even after my 'trial', and later when Father Cleary's DNA proved that he was indeed Ross' father, I did not receive an apology from the holy man.

In August 1995, the news that I was to be called before the Medical Council came in an article in the *Irish Catholic*, where Brian Lea, an administrater in the Council, was quoted as saying: 'There is a body of opinion in psychiatry which believes that our duty of confidentiality encompasses not only the patient but anyone involved in the case.' Eventually three allegations were made against me by the Council itself. The charges I faced before the Fitness to Practice Committee in 1996 stated that I 'had committed a serious breach of ethical standards by disclosing information given to me in confidence; failed to act in the best interest of my patient; acted in a manner derogatory to the reputation of the medical profession'.

It was now October and my situation had been thoroughly discussed in the media and everywhere else. Even some old friends thought I should not have supported Phyllis and that what I said on her behalf was untrue. Professor Patricia Casey of University College Dublin, successor to the post I had held for over forty years before retirement, chaired the meeting. The committee proposed to call two witnesses, Dr Teresa Iglesias, senior lecturer in philosophy and medical ethics at UCD, and Dr Michael McGuinness, a consultant psychiatrist with the Eastern Health Board. However, since Dr McGuinness had been one of the first to complain to the Medical Council about my support of Phyllis, alleging that my behaviour was contrary to the principles of medical confidentiality, at the behest of my counsel he was not accepted as an expert witness.

The remaining witness for the Council was Dr Iglesias. She spoke of the importance of preserving confidentiality in the doctor/patient relationship and said that that duty extended to information received from a third party in the course of that relationship. But she also accepted that there were times when the doctor's duty to the health of the patient could come into conflict with the duty to keep confidential information received from a third party. She seemed to suggest that each of these duties was the primary one: 'The primary duty is to his patient and caring for the patient, but he has an equally primary duty not to harm the third party.' This was the only evidence against me and it amounted to no more than the fact that my decision had been a complex and difficult one to make. Dr Iglesias said that she could not say, in my case, whether the judgement I made was correct or not.

My witnesses were Phyllis Hamilton, her son Ross and the late Professor Anthony Clare, Professor of Psychiatry at Trinity College Dublin and director of St Patrick's Hospital. Professor Clare volunteered to go to the hearing for me and, since we were neither close colleagues nor close friends, I will always be grateful to him for his sense of justice in coming forward. He told the committee that he and I would stand on very different terrain on modern psychiatry, so even in our professional sympathies we were cool rather than warm, but that he would have no doubt about my professional integrity or serious purpose in the practice of my profession. He said that: 'Implicit in all the major statements I have seen on medical ethics and confidentiality is the belief and concept that the primary duty a doctor has is to his or her patient.' However, the central issue in the case was: 'What happens when there is a conflict between duties of confidentiality on the one hand to a patient and on the other hand to third parties?'

He said he personally had never in twenty-five years been in a situation where the conflict was quite as hard as that which faced me. He was asked if a doctor in such a dilemma could do any more than consult the ethical guidelines, consider the issue of principle and then make an honest decision. Clare answered, 'I don't believe there is anything more a doctor can do as long as those things are done.'

I told the committee that I thought that I had been proved right in the sense that the media coverage and the pressure from the relatives of Michael Cleary all waned from the time I spoke out; and nobody had seriously questioned the validity of Phyllis' statements after that. If I had kept silent it would have had a deleterious affect on Phyllis and Ross, and my clinical judgement at the time was that Ross was at risk of suicide.

Ross spoke about my visiting him and his mother in Wicklow before I made the statement, to which he was happy to give his blessing. 'We needed those people to see the truth,' said Ross. 'Dr Ivor Browne, with all those letters after his name, would give that credibility. There were credible people saying "No way is it true", and there were bald, harsh lies. And Ivor came in and said simply "This is true", and that is what we needed.'

For Ross, my statement to the media meant giving him a freedom he had never known. 'Actually, for the first time,' he told the committee, 'it has given to me the pride to say "Yes he is my father". I was still calling him Father Cleary, even after I had done the story. After that I was more able to say "my father", and regard him as my father, not just the guy who helped with my conception.'

Phyllis told her story to the committee as I have told it above. She said of our doctor/patient relationship: 'If I did not have that link with someone outside the secret, I think I would have gone mad.'

And that is the story of how I came, after my retirement, to be censured and admonished by the Medical Council after forty years of blemish-free service as a psychiatrist. I suppose I could be admonished again for calling it a storm in a teacup. However, compared to what Phyllis suffered for falling in love with the wrong man, it was nothing; and nothing too to what her son Ross went through.

When the dust settled, Ross was proven by DNA testing to be Father Cleary's son, but by then the media had moved on and the fact was virtually ignored. Phyllis Hamilton is dead now; I was with her on the day she died of cancer and I also attended her funeral. I am glad that Phyllis and Ross were not left to the mercy of someone who might have refused to verify their story. As for me, I would do it all again.

32

The Frozen Present

B ecause of the emphasis traditionally placed in psychotherapy on the effects of past experiences and assembling detailed accounts of early childhood and development, I think we frequently fall into the error of believing we are dealing with 'the past'. Actually, we are always involved with the 'now': the 'frozen present', what is stored in our memories, in our bodies, our attitudes and behaviour. Even if we broaden the question to include concepts like Jung's collective unconscious, or karmic influences, we are still effectively concerned with these as they manifest themselves in the present.

One of the reasons why people have so much difficulty in accepting a concept like the collective unconscious, or karmic transmission, is the question of how and where this can exist. Is it transmitted in the genetic code? This seems unlikely. The work of British biologist Rupert Sheldrake throws some light on this: 'The concept of morphogenetic fields is now widely accepted by developmental biologists and is used to explain how your arms and legs, for instance, have different shapes in spite of the fact that they contain the same genes and proteins. The problem is no one knows what morphogenetic fields are or how they work.' Rupert Sheldrake believes, 'they are new kinds of fields for which I have proposed the term morphic fields . . . Morphic fields are not fixed but evolve. They have a kind of built-in memory. This memory depends on the process of Morphic resonance, the influence of like upon like through space and time.'[1] Sheldrake's concept that, as individuals and as a species, we are surrounded by morphic fields, and that much of the learning and information that is passed on from generation to generation may be stored in these fields, could for the first time provide some understanding of this problem.

Professor Gary Schwartz, who works in Arizona, has pointed out that in any communication between two things, A and B, a network comes into being and a 'feed-back' loop is created. A memory of the relationship is formed and 'emergent properties' arise. In this way permanent storage of information can occur, and this can circulate indefinitely. It is not in something or out of something but circulates between both. This storage of information outside the brain happens in all kinds of situations, for example, between one person and another, between the heart and the brain, between cells and atoms, between a substance and the fluid in which it is dissolved. (This may, for the first time, provide a scientific rationale for how homeopathy can work. Sceptics say that by the time full dilution has taken place, nothing of the original substance remains in the fluid in which it was dissolved and therefore the remedy can have no effect. But if a 'feed-back' loop between the substance and the fluid has been established, then the potion could be effective.)

This hypothesis may also provide an explanation of how heart and, more specifically, heart-lung transplant patients, can experience memories belonging to the donor. Reports of such patients experiencing dreams, and the likes and dislikes of the donor are being reported with increasing frequency around the world.[2]

Finally I return once again to the fundamental principle that it is the person himself who has to undertake the work if he is to bring about any real change in his life. I feel it is essential to emphasise this point, as it is the aspect most likely to be missed by psychiatrists and psychotherapists. As I have said, any change and any new learning involves some pain, but if what we are attempting to change is ourselves, our deepest personality, this can involve a lot of suffering. If the person you are dealing with is not prepared to suffer then, to put it bluntly, you can have all the skills and training available and be the most experienced therapist, but you will be absolutely helpless to do anything to help him.

Traumas which happened to us years ago may be cut off as a sort of 'frozen present', but they are still in us now and, when activated, will be experienced as happening in the present. Whatever we are attempting to change, it is what is there now that we have to work with.

The experiential stage of therapy will have its main application in those with unresolved traumatic experience. It will have less relevance for those with poor ego development, who have failed to establish a personal identity, are immature and stuck in dependent family relationships.

In the old Protestant church in St Brendan's we were able to work with twelve to fifteen patients at the same time. We ran the sessions on a weekly basis, although any given patient usually only came once a fortnight to give them time to integrate the experience. We used a modified form of Grof's method, selecting the aspects we felt were most useful. For patients who were unable to get into the traumatic experience in this way, we could inject Ketamine, which, apart from being a legitimate anaesthetic, is also a powerful hallucinogenic agent. Whereas Stan Grof was only permitted to run workshops in the States, in Dublin we treated very disturbed patients on a regular basis until I retired. During that time we emptied the equivalent of two wards, most of them disturbed patients who had failed to make any progress with orthodox psychiatric care. Each patient had their own personal therapist who worked with them between sessions to help them to integrate the traumatic experiences which arose in the work in the church.

As I continued with this therapy over the years, I became more and more unhappy with the explanation of the central role of repression in this work. The usual explanation of what is happening was summed up in Freud's own words in 1924 when he wrote, 'The theory of repression is the corner stone of our understanding of the neurosis.'[3]

It became increasingly clear that the integration of experiences is a process, taking place over time, involving both neurophysiological and somatic work. To put this in its simplest form, when an event takes place in the external world we may not fully experience it as it happens. We undoubtedly register it and take an impression of the raw experience as it is taking place, otherwise the event would no longer exist within us once it has happened. But integration fails to progress beyond this point. This is why experiences of this kind if they are activated many years later are experienced as happening 'now', in the present. They do not present like ordinary memory as the recall of something from the distant past. For this reason they are not only true but are accurate as to detail, which is quite often irrelevant to the traumatic experience itself.

This simple awareness that experiencing something is a process that takes place within us, over time, seems to have been largely overlooked. This is all the more strange because we know that if something disturbing happens to us – say, an unpleasant argument with someone on a Friday afternoon – we may find ourselves going over and over it during the weekend, unable to escape the unpleasant feeling attached to it or to resolve the problem. However, having slept on it, with the benefit of dreaming for a couple of nights, we wake up on Monday morning no longer troubled. This is so, even though we may have had no further communication with the person involved. This to me is evidence that some work has been going on, at a deeper level inside us, during these couple of days. The experience is now integrated, is turning into memory, and is moving from something still in the present, something unsettling and current, into the past.

It has long been recognised that when a living creature is faced with a threat to its physical integrity it responds to the challenge with a 'fight or flight' response. Back in 1929, Walter Canon described this physiological response. He also described the phenomenon of 'homeostasis', when the threat has been dealt with in one way or another and the physiology returns to its more or less steady state.[5] He did not, however, draw attention to an equally ancient strategy for survival that is seen in many species. In situations where defensive or evasive action is not possible, it appears that an organism has at its disposal the capacity, when faced with an overwhelming threat, to 'freeze' or 'play dead'. This involves the operation of a primitive, biological, adaptive response which acts at the level of the primitive brain (outside conscious awareness or control). This reaction is utilised by many animals where neither 'fight' nor 'flight' is possible: the deer that freezes in the bushes when under threat, the spider that, when you touch it with your finger, curls into a ball and plays dead. It is also seen in a number of animals, such as the hedgehog, for which this form of inhibition, or freezing, is its main and indeed its only means of defence. The phenomenon has even been described as far down the evolutionary scale as the amoeba, by the biologists Max Hartmann and Ludwig Rumler. In a series of experiments, they exposed amoebae to a variety of stimuli. Depending on the quantity and quality of these stimuli, the amoeba reacted in one of two ways. Either it sought these stimuli (moved towards them) or avoided them and assumed a spherical shape – 'played dead'. So it is clear that this is a basic capacity in living organisms, which in many instances must have enabled the animal to survive, otherwise it would have been eliminated by natural selection.[4]

It is not unreasonable to assume that this 'freeze response' will also be present in some form in human beings. But, in a similar way to other survival mechanisms in lower animals, this capacity, while present in human beings, appears to have been modified to serve a somewhat different purpose in modern conditions. Instead of being a way of avoiding external danger, it is now mainly utilised to deal with the threat of internal destabilisation. Whenever we are faced with an overwhelming experience that we sense to be potentially disintegrative, we have the ability to freeze and to suspend the experience in an unassimilated, inchoate form. It would seem that the potentially disintegrative effect of the external threat is signalled by the initial surge of emotion. Our biological structure seems to be able to specify in advance that to experience the threatening encounter fully would destroy or disintegrate the core organisation of the brain (see Fig. 20).

Modern human beings have retained, to a surprising extent, the bodily constitution, physiological responses and emotional drives that we inherited from our Stone-Age ancestors. What is even more surprising is that a vital part of the human brain belongs

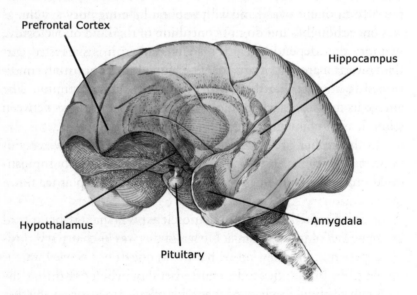

Figure 20: The main structures of the medial temporal lobe, covered by the neocortex.

to an earlier lineage, namely that of the reptiles and mammals. While these inner regions, loosely called the tempero-limbic system, have been somewhat overshadowed by the development of the neocortex, they are not to be outdone, as they not only harbour the instinctual and emotional drives but maintain all the vital survival functions of the body. In a sense, the neocortex sits astride the primitive brain like a rider on a horse and tries to direct it with fragile reins. Remarkably, most of the time this partnership works well enough, considering the rider's inexperience, but in a sizeable minority of situations, given the marked change in modern human conditions, this uneasy partnership runs into difficulties.

Most research into memory has been carried out in an attempt to better understand Alzheimer's disease and other forms of dementia. One crucial aspect which is missing from current research into memory is the question of whether we have the capacity to block this memory-processing system. This is likely to occur when a person is subjected to an overwhelming traumatic experience which they are not capable of integrating at that time.

This capacity to suspend the integration of an experience would seem to involve the medial temporal lobe system. The amygdala nuclei may have an important role in this regard. The amygdala are not a component of the medial temporal lobe memory system, as was once thought, and do not contribute to the kind of declarative memory that depends on this system. Rather, it is suggested that the amygdala are important for other functions concerning conditioned fear and the attachment of affect to neural stimuli. The amygdala may also have a broader role in establishing links between stimuli, as in making associations among sensory modalities.

In this regard Professor Richard Davidson at the University of Wisconsin, who has established some of the latest highly sophisticated imaging technology for studying the brain, has pointed out:

A decade ago the dogma in neuroscience was that the brain contained all of its neurones at birth and this was unchanged by life's experience. We now know that this is not true. The new watchword in brain science is 'neuroplasticity'; the notion that the brain continually changes as a result of our experience – whether through fresh connections or through the generation of utterly new neurons . . . One of the most exciting discoveries of the last few years is that certain areas of the brain – the frontal lobes, the amydgala, and the hypocampus, change in response to experience. They are the parts of the brain dramatically affected by the emotional environment in which we are raised and by repeated experience. The amygdala nuclei play a key role in the circuitry that activates emotion; particularly fear, while the hypocampus is essential for our appreciation of the context of events. The prefrontal cortex, on the other hand, is critical for regulating emotions – the left prefrontal cortex enhances positive emotions, while the right prefrontal area tends to increase negative or destructive emotions.[5]

In identifying these emotional connections of the amygdala complex we are perhaps getting closer to a possible site for the blocking mechanism that is activated when a person is faced with an overwhelming traumatic experience (see Fig. 21). Let us summarise then the essential aspects of this hypothesis:

(1) The integration of experience into the self is a process happening over time. This involves neurophysiological and somatic

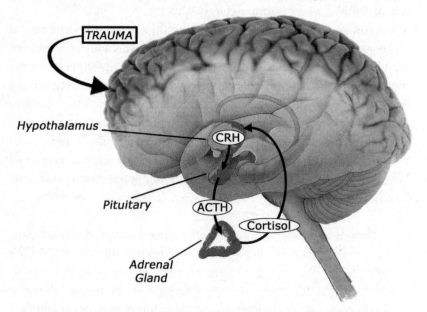

Figure 21: The hypothalmic pituitary adrenal axis (HPA), illustrating the negative feedback system from the peripheral organs back to the brain.

work. The amount of work that is involved depends on the seriousness of the external challenge.

(2) When a person is subjected to a serious trauma, an immediate, non-conscious, biological mechanism may be invoked, which will suspend the experience, either partly or completely, blocking further integration into long-term memory.

(3) The degree to which an event is traumatic depends not only on the seriousness of the event, but also on the internal set of the individual at the time this occurs. The traumatic event therefore is the meeting point of the external happening and all the learned past of the individual up to that time, including whether there have been previous insults or experiences of a similar kind that were frozen or suspended.

(4) It is now as if a piece of the external world is within the person but not part of them. This internalised 'stressor' now exists, outside time, in a potentially unstable state. A person retains these subsidiaries in an unorganised or inchoate form, some of which may be represented somatically as well as centrally. This biological failure to integrate the trauma may leave the person unable to identify the threatening experience consciously – it is as if it had never happened.

(5) In situations such as this where an experience is frozen, it may well be held in that state for years or even a lifetime. Where an earlier traumatic experience has been suspended, later events of this kind will also be blocked, thus building up increasing pressure, until 'activation' occurs.

(6) If activated later by some life event, the experience breaks through and causes flashbacks. This triggers painful emotional responses (symptoms). As with the original event, the individual once again tries to suspend the experience, but now only partially successfully.

This sequence of events then gives rise to the full-blown syndrome of post-traumatic stress disorder (see Fig. 22).

When I stated that this capacity to freeze and suspend a traumatic experience has been largely overlooked, there has been one notable exception. When my paper, 'Psychological Trauma or Unexperienced Experience', was published in *Revision* in 1990, I received a letter shortly afterwards from someone in Arizona who

agreed with my thesis and said that he had come to a similar conclusion in his work. Stupidly I mislaid his letter and was unable to
reply. It was only about ten years later that I came across the book
Waking the Tiger, and, on reading about the author, realised that
Peter Levine was the man who had written to me all those years before. His description at the beginning of the book of a cheetah pursuing an impala is a beautiful example of the way the freeze
mechanism operates:

> At the moment of contact (or just before), the young impala falls
> to the ground, surrendering to its impending death. Yet, it may
> be uninjured. The stone-still animal is not pretending to be dead,
> it has instinctively entered an altered state of consciousness
> shared by all mammals when death appears imminent.[6]

In his work Dr Levine lays great stress on somatic experiencing
and rightly emphasises the importance of establishing a safe, comfortable and supportive context as a prerequisite to the person opening up the traumatic experience. The only aspect with which I might
take issue is that he seems to consider that it is relatively unimpor-
tant for the person involved to get a clearer picture of what happened to him at the time the traumatic experience occurred. I have
found that for many people the situation remains not fully resolved
unless they can get to the full story of what happened to them. Otherwise it is comforting to find that someone else has come to a similar conclusion to my own.

The fact remains that it is hard to understand why, in the light
of all the recent advances in understanding how our neurophysiology operates, these ideas are not already accepted. There appear to
be two main reasons why this simple phenomenon of everyday experience has been largely overlooked. The first reason involves certain historical factors that surrounded the early work of Sigmund
Freud and Pierre Janet (now just over a hundred years ago), for it
was they who first clearly drew attention to the whole issue of traumatic neurosis. The second reason has simply to do with the way in
which we use language.

In recent times there has been renewed interest in the work of
Pierre Janet. Freud and Janet were contemporaries. Freud (born
1826) was three years older but Janet, who died in 1947, outlived

him by almost eight years. Although they never met they were well aware of each other's work and in the early years the general direction of their work was very similar.[7] Indeed, each of them paid tribute to the work of the other. In a letter to Fliess, Freud stated: 'Our work on hysteria has at last received proper recognition from Janet in Paris.' And Janet praised the work of Breuer and Freud: 'We are glad to find that several authors, particularly M.M. Breuer and Freud, have recently verified our interpretation, already somewhat old, of subconscious fixed ideas with hystericals.'[8]

Freud went to Paris in October 1885 and stayed until February 1886 to study under Charcot, the great French neurologist. In 1914 Freud wrote: 'Influenced by Charcot's use of the traumatic origin of hysteria, one was readily inclined to accept as true and etiologically significant the statements made by patients in which they ascribe their symptoms to passive sexual experience in the first years of childhood – to put it bluntly, to seduction.'[9]

While he was in Paris, Freud used to go down to the morgue. He would also have been familiar with the issue of sexual assaults on children, which was a topic for active discussion at that time. In 1857 a professor of legal medicine at the University of Paris, Ambroise Auguste Tardieu, published his *Etude Medico Legale* (a medico-legal study of assaults on decency). This report drew attention for the first time to the frequency of sexual assaults on children, mostly young girls. In France, during the years 1858 to 1869, there were 9,125 persons accused of rape or attempted rape of children. The vast majority of the cases that Tardieu described were between the ages of four and twelve, and almost all of them were girls. Tardieu was a medical specialist, not a psychiatrist, and he offered no implication as to the psychological effects of such trauma, but he had no doubt about the authenticity of these assaults on children.

This was 150 years ago, yet within thirty years his successors, Alfred Fournier and P.C. Brouardel, who was Dean of the Faculty of Medicine during the period when Freud was in Paris, took a starkly different view, casting serious doubt on the reliability of reports of sexual abuse of children. Fournier wrote a paper in 1880, 'Simulation of Sexual Attacks on Young Children', and in 1883 Brouardel published 'The Causes of Error in Expert Opinion with respect to Sexual Assaults'. This is what Brouardel had to say:

Hysteria plays a considerable role in the genesis of these false accusations, either because of the genital hallucinations which stem from the great neurosis or because hysterics do not hesitate to invent mendacious stories with the sole purpose of attracting attention to themselves and to make themselves interesting.[10]

This debate, which is all too similar to the debate that has been going on in recent years, was the subject of heated discussion at the very time when Freud was in Paris. When Freud later had a change of heart about sexual abuse, he would have been familiar with the views of Fournier and Brouardel.

When Freud returned to Vienna he joined forces with Joseph Breuer and they began serious work on the traumatic origin of neurosis. Freud's great contribution, in his early work, was to stress the importance of affect (to which Janet had paid little attention) and to the role of catharsis in the treatment of hysteria. Hysteria at that time was the diagnosis covering most of the manifestations we would now consider as post-traumatic stress disorder. Breuer and Freud were convinced that this condition could be the result of traumatic experiences: 'Hysterics suffer mainly from reminiscences.'[11] They also stated that these 'memories' were 'found to be astonishingly intact and to possess remarkable sensory force and when they returned, they acted with all the effective strength of new experience'.[12] They saw not only the importance of the cognitive aspect but also of the affective component which was associated with it.

We found to our great surprise . . . that each individual's hysterical symptom immediately and permanently disappeared when we had succeeded in bringing clearly to light the memory of the event by which it was provoked and in arousing its accompanying affect, and when the patient had described that event in the greatest possible detail and had put the affect into words. Recollection without affect almost invariably produces no result.[13]

The other great contribution which Freud made, and the issue on which he parted company with Breuer, was to point to the importance of sexual abuse and incest in the early years in the genesis of hysteria. Unfortunately, he went too far and insisted that,

'Whatever case and whatever symptom we take as our point of departure, in the end we infallibly come to the field of sexual experience.'[14] In this way he was hoist by his own petard, and he prepared the way for the difficulties in which he soon found himself. Nevertheless recent history has proved him right in bringing to light the frequency of sexual abuse in childhood and how damaging the psychological consequences of this can be. In his classic paper, 'The Aetiology of Hysteria', Freud stated:

> If you submit my assertion that the aetiology of hysteria lies in sexual life to the strictest examination, you will find that it is supported by the fact that in some eighteen cases of hysteria I have been able to discover this connection in every single symptom, and where the circumstances allowed, to confirm it by therapeutic success.[15]

Even earlier, in March 1896, in the French journal *Revue Neurologique*, Freud said:

> In none of these cases was an event of the kind found above (seduction in childhood) missing. It was represented either by a brutal assault committed by an adult or by a seduction less rapid and less repulsive but reaching the same conclusion.[16]

What puzzled me for many years was the fact that in little more than a year Freud apparently underwent a complete change of heart. Ernest Jones, in his biography of Freud, described dramatically what happened:

> Up to the spring of 1897 Freud still held firmly to his conviction of the reality of child traumas, so strong was Charcot's teaching on traumatic experiences and so surely did the analysis of the patients' association reproduce them. At that time doubts began to creep in although he made no mention of them in the records of progress that he was regularly sending to his friend Fliess. Then quite suddenly he decided to confide in him 'The great secret of something, which in the past few months has gradually dawned on me.' It was the awful truth that most – not all – of the seductions in childhood which his patients had revealed and on

which he had built his whole theory of hysteria, never occurred.[17]

In 1914, in 'The History of the Psychoanalytic Movement', Freud explained further:

When this ideology broke down under the weight of its own improbability and contradiction in definitely ascertainable circumstances, the result at first was helpless bewilderment. Analysis had led back to these infantile sexual traumas by the right path and yet they were not true. The firm ground of reality was gone. At that time I would gladly have given up the whole work just as my esteemed predecessor Breuer had done when he made his unwelcome discovery. Perhaps I persevered only because I no longer had any choice and could not then begin at anything else . . . if hysterical subjects trace back their symptoms to traumas that are fictitious, then the new fact which emerges is precisely that they create such scenes in fantasy and this cyclical reality requires to be taken into account alongside practical reality. This reflection was soon followed by the discovery that these fantasies were intended to cover up the autoerotic activity in the first years of childhood, to embellish it and raise it to a higher plane and now, from behind the fantasies, the whole range of a child's sexual life came to light.[18]

But what puzzled me on reading this was where was the new evidence to explain this change of heart? He gave no evidence to explain why he had completely reversed his position, had changed real events of childhood into fantasies, and had blurred the distinction between these. When I was working in London with Joshua Bierer in 1959 and was first introduced to the study of the possible therapeutic uses of LSD, I witnessed patients powerfully experiencing traumatic events that had taken place many years before as if they were happening at that moment. Later, in the United States, when I laid hands on Freud's early papers (written in the years between 1893 and 1896) I was astonished to find him describing virtually identical scenes that his patients underwent in the process of analysis. I was left with the question to which I could find no answer for many years: why did he change his mind?

Then in 1985 Jeffrey Masson's book, *The Assault on Truth*,

appeared. The circumstances surrounding Freud's abandonment of the 'seduction theory' were described in detail by Masson when he released the hidden correspondence of Freud to Fliess. Masson had been appointed by Anna Freud to look after the Freudian archive but when he published this correspondence, which threatened the very foundations of psychoanalysis, he was quickly dismissed for letting the cat out of the bag.

In April 1896 Freud presented his paper 'The Aetiology of Hysteria' to the Society for Psychology and Neurology in Vienna, and he described to Fleiss what happened: 'A lecture on the aetiology of hysteria at the Psychiatric Society met with an icy reception from the asses and, from Kraft-Ebbing, the strange comment "it sounds like a scientific fairytale" – and this after one has demonstrated to them the solution to a more than a 1,000-year-old problem, a "source of the Nile".' A month later, on 4 May 1896 he wrote, 'I am as isolated as you could wish me to be, and a void is forming around me.'[19]

This, coupled with the debacle surrounding the operation by Fliess in February 1895 on Freud's patient Emma Echstein following which, some time later, she almost died from a massive haemorrhage (for a full account of what happened see Masson's *The Assault on Truth*) resulted, little more than a year later, in his deserting his whole position on the reality of child sexual abuse. Thus, what had been a life-threatening complication of a botched operation was changed in one masterly stroke to fantasy bleeding, out of her longing for Freud himself. In this way, inadvertently and I am sure unconsciously, he found the means to rehabilitate himself in the eyes of his medical colleagues, so that he, a Jew, could once again find himself accepted amongst the conservative medical establishment of Catholic Vienna. I believe that Masson was quite correct (although he has been vilified from all sides by psychoanalysts and others) in seeing this change in position on Freud's part when he blurred the distinction between reality and fantasy as pivotal. I am convinced that psychoanalysis, and psychotherapy in general, has remained in a state of confusion because of this to the present day.

The development of psychoanalysis and its widespread popularity virtually eclipsed the work of Pierre Janet so that, when he died in 1947, his death was hardly even reported in the media. Nevertheless Janet, with the emphasis he placed on traumatic antecedents, dissociation and what he called the retraction of the field of personal consciousness, offered a model of psychological trauma that remains valid today. Janet was originally a philosopher, but he was so impressed with Charcot's work that he took a medical degree and later worked for a number of years in Charcot's department in the Salpetriere Hospital in Paris. Janet's first major work, *L'Automatisme Psychologique*, predated the first writings of Breuer and Freud in 1895 by several years. In that work he developed the concept of dissociation (desaggregation), which had originally been introduced in the 1850s by Jacque Moreau.[20]

In a later book entitled *Psychological Healing*, under the heading 'Unassimilated Happenings', he described the effects of psychological trauma as follows:

All the patients seem to have had the evolution of their lives checked: they are 'attached' upon an obstacle that they cannot get beyond. The happening we describe as traumatic has been brought about by a situation to which the individual ought to react . . . what characterises these 'attached' patients is that they have not succeeded in liquidating the difficult situation . . . Strictly speaking then, one who retains a fixed idea of a happening cannot be said to have a 'memory' of the happening. It is only for convenience that we speak of it as a 'traumatic memory'. The subject is often incapable of making, with regard to the event, the recital which we speak of as a memory; and yet he remains confronted by a difficult situation in which he has not been able to play a satisfactory part, one to which his adaptation has been imperfect.[21]

Here, although he is using rather different language, he says it is only for convenience that we speak of a 'traumatic memory'. This, together with the title of the passage, 'Unassimilated Happenings', is clearly related to the concept of an unintegrated experience.

When one combines the contributions of Pierre Janet and the early work of Freud, it is extraordinary how close they were to the view of the 'frozen present' that is presented here. Had they our present understanding of neurophysiology, of the functions of the primitive brain with all its somatic interconnections, it seems likely that one or other of them would have reached a similar conclusion. It is hard to realise now that, at the time when Freud and Janet were working, not even the commonplace peripheral hormones, such as oestrogen or adrenaline, had yet been identified. It is understandable, therefore, that Freud had to invent a psychological language, especially the concept of repression, which has generated such confusion in our efforts to understand the effects of psychological trauma.

In a world full of horrendous suffering and trauma it was only in the closing years of the twentieth century that the realisation that psychological trauma could lead to enduring consequences was finally accepted. The essential characteristics of what is now recognised as post-traumatic stress disorder were described by the American psychoanalyst, Abram Kardiner, as far back as the Second World War, and constituted what he called a 'physioneurosis'.[22] Yet it was only with the publication of the American *Diagnostic and Statistical Manual* (DSM3) that this syndrome was finally enshrined in an official psychiatric classification. This definition was framed largely around the experiences of the Vietnam War and it was as a result of this catastrophic experience that the syndrome finally gained popular acceptance.

The importance of childhood trauma leading to chronic PTSD in adult life is now recognised. Much of the confusion relating to this centres on the concept of repression. Because of the failure to understand the painful effort and time involved in the integration of traumatic experience, the assumption had been made, since the time of Freud, that everything which happened to us automatically passed into memory. The problem here is that in all the descriptions of natural disasters, accidents, sexual abuse, rape and so on, we repeatedly find the supposed traumatic memories described as being repressed and then re-experienced or re-lived. The fundamental error here is in the prefix 're', and in the notion of repressed memory. Once we use the words in this way, we are already making the assumption that the traumatic event has been fully experienced and is now integrated. It is this misunderstanding that has given rise to the tangled confusion surrounding the so-called 'false memory syndrome', which has been so damaging both to patients and their families.

For generations the abuse of women and children of both sexes, both physical and sexual, which was carried out mainly by men, was a dark secret. It was only through the struggles of the feminist movement and the courage of some paediatricians, a few psychiatrists and more recently the victims themselves that finally, over the past thirty or forty years, this abuse, and the extent of it, has been brought out into the light of day. Until then there was a culture of silence within families and elsewhere, which meant that victims had nowhere to turn. And because, in order to survive, they had to freeze the traumatic experiences and then dissociate, they usually knew little or nothing of what had happened to them. These experiences were hidden as a frozen present, unless they were activated years later by some similar event. Even then, because the post-traumatic symptoms from which they suffered were likely to be dismissed or misdiagnosed, they were still not heard. Also, because they had spent a lifetime building up defences to keep these experiences at bay, they were only too ready to disavow them if they were met with scepticism or ridicule: 'if it did happen, it happened years ago, forget about it and get on with your life!'

Unfortunately, when the silence was finally broken, this brought in its train a number of over-enthusiastic therapists, counsellors and others. Because those who have been traumatised and abused tend to present with a wide range of symptoms, these therapists saw abuse lurking below the surface in many situations where in fact no such abuse had actually occurred. They actively suggested this to patients and, particularly with the use of methods such as hypnosis, or peer pressure in fundamentalist therapeutic groups, highly suggestible subjects complied with the production of pseudo-memories. Thus innocent parents and others were wrongly accused and the wheel turned full circle, giving rise to organised groups of parents and others attempting to protect themselves from such false accusations.

Since this debate, a number of studies have shown the dynamic nature of long-term memory. These studies have demonstrated convincingly that both children and adults can and do distort past memories and, if subjected to suggestive influence, can invent occurrences that have never happened or that happened to someone else. There is now ample evidence demonstrating the dynamic nature of long-term memory. It was Sir Frederic Bartlett who said as far back as 1932:

> Some widely held views have to be completely discarded and none more completely than that which treats recall as the re-excitement in some way of fixed and changeless traces . . . [remembering is] an imaginative reconstruction or construction built out of the relation of our attitude towards a whole mass of

organised past reactions or experience.[23]

The psychologist Endel Tulving has also described this misconception:

> One of the most widely held, but wrong, beliefs, that people have about memory is that memories exist, somewhere in the brain, like books exist in a library, or packages of soap on the supermarket shelves, and that memory is equivalent to somehow retrieving them. The whole concept of repression is built on this misconception.[24]

It is now clear from much recent research that when a formed memory of this kind is retrieved, it is reassembled from a number of inputs all over the brain, from various times in the past, and therefore is essentially a new creation. It is therefore quite unreliable as a factual record of the past. Hence, if what we are dealing with is simply repressed memory, it will be quite impossible to distinguish between a true recollection and a fantasy recall. This is the argument put forward in questioning the reliability of traumatic experiences retrieved by means of regression or experiential methods. Further, because long-term memory is essentially a new creation, this will in turn go down to the primitive brain to be processed. If this is of a threatening nature it may well fire the emotional system. Therefore the fact that a pseudo-memory gives rise to a strong emotional reaction does not constitute reliable proof that this is a genuine experience.

From what I have said, however, it will be understood that this conceals a crucial misunderstanding of the nature of unresolved traumatic experience. The experiences we are dealing with in this instance are not long-term memories, nor indeed memories in the accepted sense at all, but the suspended frozen present; that is, experiences that have never been integrated into memory proper, and therefore have not yet been experienced.

In my unit we went back over approximately 180 cases who came to us because they had suffered traumatic experiences in the past, mainly sexual and/or physical abuse, or loss of significant others during childhood. Having carried out a review of these cases, we found they broke down as follows:

True	110
False Memory Syndrome	6
Unclear	53
Dropped Out	11
Total	180

Because we were operating a diagnostic assessment and only taking on those who satisfied certain diagnostic criteria, the traumatic history turned out to be correct in the large majority. This was so in that either there was corroboration from parents, siblings, other relatives or neighbours who were aware of what was going on at the time, or the abusive experience had already been activated by some more recent event, so that they were presenting for therapy with partially clear recollections and flashbacks of what had happened to them many years before.

To illustrate the sort of confirmation we have had from relatives in almost a third of our cases, I will outline here a typical example. A couple presented with marital disharmony, but it was soon clear that the dissatisfactions of the husband were out of proportion and were not explainable in terms of the marital interaction. They clearly related to problems in the man's own personality. It was decided with his agreement to undertake some deep experiential work to see if there were factors in his early life of which he was unaware. From the very first experiential session he went into a deep altered state and seemed to be trapped in some way and struggling to free himself. He continued in this way for about twelve sessions, always struggling to get free. Then in the next session, having started in the usual way, he began to suffocate, turning black in the face and causing me considerable alarm. He came to, however, and, when the session terminated, he said that he had experienced being trapped and unable to breathe; he felt he was approximately six months old.

It so happened that his parents were still alive and he was going to visit them that weekend in County Donegal. When he asked his mother about what he had experienced at first she was very defensive and angry, refusing to talk about it; then she broke down and told him what had happened. They were small farmers and when the patient was a baby they had no one to mind him when they were out working in the fields, so they used to strap him into his cot. One day when he was about seven months old they came back to the house and found him twisted up in the blankets. He was suffocating, black in the face, and almost died.

Once he went through this death-threatening experience over several sessions, with some more work, he rapidly recovered and the original marital disharmony, which had brought them to me in the first place, was easily resolved.

As the table shows, there were a small number who fitted the picture of FMS. These differed from the other cases in that their behaviour in experiential sessions was atypical. They usually presented with their story by heart. There was also a number about whom we remained unclear, in spite of all our efforts to reach a conclusion, as to the validity of their story, and finally a few who dropped out of therapy early on before any decision could be reached as to the nature of their problems.

With traumatic events, several factors combine to determine whether the initial shock and freezing that occurs is maintained indefinitely or is followed gradually by a full integration into long-term memory. Where there is alcoholism, marital conflict, or simply a family with little trust, warmth or security and the open expression of emotion is discouraged, then freezing is likely to supervene. Obviously worse, of course, is the situation where physical or sexual abuse is occurring within the family itself, perpetrated by a father or near relative.

To illustrate the situation where the simple expression of emotion is discouraged let me cite the following case. A young man in his early thirties presented with a hem-paresis (paralysis of the arm) following the death of his father, to whom he was very close. This man had a strong resolute personality and had coped for years with an alcoholic wife and a very painful, difficult domestic situation. In therapy, having been put into regression under hypnosis, he went spontaneously not to the death of his father as expected, but to a day at the seaside with his mother and siblings when he was nine years of age. Word was brought to them that his older brother, who was swimming in another part of the beach, had drowned. In the commotion the mother got the children into a taxi to go to tell the father, who worked in the nearby town. On the way this patient burst into tears, whereupon his mother turned on him and shouted 'Stop that crying! You'll upset your father.' The little boy stopped crying instantly and from that moment onwards had no recollection of the entire event (other than being intellectually aware that his brother was dead), until it was revealed under hypnosis many years later.

The freezing of an experience can take several forms, from a complete blocking of the entire experience, in both its cognitive and emotional aspects, to a partial suspension of the event. Where there is a complete suspension, the person goes into a frozen state of psychic numbing, so that there is an inhibition of all activity as well as feeling. A different kind of response is seen where, after a first rush of emotion, there is a complete inhibition of all feeling, but not of action. This leaves the person free to take whatever measures are necessary for survival. For example, a young woman awoke on the tenth floor of a hotel to find the whole building shaking in an earthquake. She got out of bed, quickly dressed herself and remembered quite specifically feeling no fear while she ran downstairs out of the building to safety. A few hours later, after it was all over, she went into a state of shock and experienced extreme panic, with her whole body shaking.

But, short of actual survival, it is also an essential device to enable individuals to deal with the practical problems that arise following a tragedy. For example, a woman whose husband dies suddenly may have to make arrangements for a funeral, deal with business problems, the question of a will, inheritance and so on, before being in a position to start grieving. Thus, for practical reasons, this denial of emotion can be an important adaptive response and, in many instances, after a few weeks or months, when the time is right the person will spontaneously, or with therapeutic help, do the emotional work necessary for full integration of the experience.

For a significant minority, however, this does not happen and then the inhibition remains indefinitely, or until some similar situation occurs, perhaps many years later, that activates the traumatic experience. R.D. Laing described this situation eloquently when he said that, not only is the experience 'cut off' and not available to consciousness, but the fact that it is cut off is itself 'cut off', so that the individual now has no awareness that the traumatic event ever took place.[25]

In the more recent edition of the DSM (DSM4), the distinction between acute, chronic and delayed onset PTSD is now accepted but there is no clear explanation as to why the appearance of symptoms can be delayed for many years. Also in the comprehensive list of symptoms there is no distinction made as to the different times when these occur. It is now well established that a long period, often of many years, may ensue following a traumatic event before the emergence of the acute symptoms of PTSD. During this phase people may appear to be going on with a reasonably normal way of life, although they are liable to recurrent episodes of depression and may show the characteristic constricted life-pattern. They typically show an acute sensitivity as to what situations to avoid, yet they will often have no knowledge as to why they are avoiding these places or situations.

Most of the people who presented to our psychotherapy unit were already manifesting the acute symptoms of PTSD and, for a long time, I thought they had been suffering like this since the original trauma. Then one woman presented for treatment who had been horribly sexually abused for most of her life, but she only came forward when it was discovered, coincidentally, that two of her children were being sexually abused by another relative. Prior to this she had no awareness of all that had happened to her. It was the shock of finding out about her children that activated her own acute post-traumatic symptomatology.

On realising this we went back over all our cases and found, to our surprise, that in almost every instance, where the original trauma had occurred many years before, they had not manifested any of the acute symptoms of PTSD at the time, apart from the constricted life-pattern and depression. In virtually every case something happened that activated the inhibited experience, so that the cases then presented with the acute symptoms of PTSD. The cause of this activation may be another trauma of a similar kind. For example, a woman who was sexually abused as a child may in adult life be raped; or a person who lost his or her mother in infancy may, years later, suffer another loss of someone close; and these events activate the earlier traumatic experience. But the activation need not result from a further serious traumatic episode. It can be something as simple as watching a television programme about sexual abuse, or simply the first night in the marriage bed. Such activating events may, for the vast majority of human beings, be entirely normal and not in any way distressing, but because, for this person, they touch the sensitive frozen experience, the effect may be catastrophic and unleash the full-blown symptomatology of PTSD that has lain dormant up to that moment (see Fig. 22).

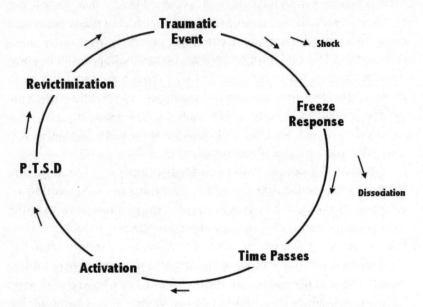

Figure 22: The Cycle of Experience involved in the full-blown syndrome of Post Traumatic Stress Disorder.

A thirty-four-year-old man presented to our service with a three-month history of increasing irritability, social withdrawal and depression. This was associated with intrusive recollections of an episode of sexual assault at the age of fourteen by his adoptive father. He had no previous psychiatric history and had been happily married for thirteen years with two children. He described being well until the visit of an old school friend three months previously. During the visit his friend used a pet name to address him which had only been used before by his adoptive father. From this point he described worsening symptomatology culminating in his seeking psychiatric help. On interview at this point he was aware of only one incident of sexual abuse. He commenced therapy and in a short time an extensive, rather sadistic history of physical and sexual abuse by the same person emerged, extending back to early childhood.

Interestingly, this concept of activation is something that Freud was aware of in his early work. In his paper 'The Aetiology of Hysteria', he states:

Let us take the instance of a young girl who blames herself most

frightfully for having allowed a boy to stroke her hand in secret and who from that time on has been overtaken by neurosis . . . Analysis shows you that the touching of her hand
reminded her of another, similar touching which had happened
very early in her childhood and had formed part of a less innocent whole, so that her self-reproaches were actually reproaches
about that old occasion . . . One has an impression indeed, that
with hysterical patients it is as if all their old experiences . . .
had retained their effective power as if such people were incapable of disposing of their psychical stimuli . . . you must not
forget that in hysterical people when there is a present day pre-
cipitating cause, the old experiences come into operation in the
form of unconscious memories.[26]

The activation of frozen experience is of great significance, for it
explains why so many cases of chronic traumatic neurosis only present for treatment in adult life. Once activation has taken place, the
individual is then in a dysfunctional state. They will now be experiencing the full-blown state of PTSD and unable, on the one hand,
to maintain the freeze and full inhibition of the experience which
they had done until now in order to cope, while on the other hand
being unable to experience fully and integrate the blocked-off traumatic experience of many years earlier,

Going back over our records, we found that the majority of patients who came to us had already been attending psychiatrists because of a diagnosis of clinical depression often complicated by
psychosomatic symptoms or substance abuse. Unfortunately what
they were offered was usually medication or, when this proved un-
successful, ECT. Such medication may bring about some temporary
relief, but then, inevitably, the depressive episodes will reoccur, with
all the usual sequelae of relapse, recurrent hospitalisation, self-muti-
lation and attempted suicide.

When a person is subjected to the same traumatic experience
again and again, as, for example, where there is incestuous abuse
within the family that continues at regular intervals for many years,
not only is there a freezing of the traumatic experience but the child
is faced with an impossible situation. Dissociation is then likely to supervene, with a splitting of the personality. As one subject described
it, the 'good little girl', that is the visible personality, continues with

relatively normal behaviour, attending school and so on, while the 'bad little girl' goes on being subjected to abuse, often feeling herself to be responsible for what is happening. In this way the two aspects of the personality continue to learn and develop quite separately, one visible and available to consciousness while the other remains hidden and is only likely to appear when activated. Such dissociation is very common in traumatic neurosis (see Fig. 22). Very rarely this may spontaneously give rise to the phenomenon of multiple personality. There is ample evidence, however, that the majority of these are iatrogenic, that is, the result of active suggestion by enthusiastic therapists who believe this to be a common clinical reality.

When in 1992 I realised that my retirement age was approaching in a couple of years' time, I went to the then programme manager of the Eastern Health Board and told him that it was time to decide whether the psychotherapy unit that I had established should continue to operate after I was gone. Up to that time we had been working on a rather *ad hoc* basis, with no supportive infrastructure. If someone was disturbed and upset after a session, there was no alternative but to return them to the ward from which they had come. There, if they became emotionally disturbed during the night, they were liable to be removed to in a single room and heavily sedated, thus defeating the whole purpose of what we were attempting to achieve. I put a proposal to the programme manager that a national trauma unit should be established, which would continue with the intensive experiential work we had been doing. This unit would then be able to accept referrals from other psychiatric services and health boards around the country.

A very fine young Irish psychiatrist, Dr Kevin O'Neill, had trained with me and had all the skill and experience necessary to run the unit and continue with our research after I was gone (he has since emigrated to Canada). The programme manager quite properly said that he was not in a position to make such a decision but he agreed to set up a committee of senior psychiatrists to examine my proposal. The committee decided that in order to evaluate this proposal properly it would be necessary to study the work that had already been undertaken in our unit, and to assess the outcome of the psychotherapy treatment programme. A psychiatrist was appointed to carry out this study. The committee were so impressed with the results that they strongly recommended that the work should continue and be further developed along the lines I had proposed.

The date of my retirement duly arrived in March 1994 but, as nothing had been done to implement this recommendation, I decided to hang on, on a sessional basis, for a further year in the hope that there would be some positive development. By the end of that year it was clear to me that the programme manager had no intention of seeing this work continue. The simple fact is that a unit of this kind causes a lot of disturbance and disruption in the smooth running of a hospital such as St Brendan's. In my experience the administrators of a health board are not primarily interested in the therapeutic outcome and welfare of the patients. Rather, they are concerned with running a service that is financially economical and causes them as little trouble and disruption as possible. I apologise if this sounds somewhat cynical but it has been my experience over the years of the way such bureaucratic organisations function.

33

Rebels and Reappraisals

Perhaps the greatest contribution Freud made was his ability to create rebels. I doubt if his orthodox followers would regard this as a contribution, but almost all the early innovations and developments in psychotherapy were introduced by psychoanalysts who rebelled and left the fold of orthodox psychoanalysis. This showed the tremendous creative energy and potential that Freud set in motion. The first real break came with the departure of three of Freud's early disciples. Alfred Adler was the first to leave and his initiatives led to many of the developments in social, group and community psychiatry. Next came Carl Jung, with a wide range of theoretical and therapeutic innovations; he coined the term 'analytical psychology' as a loose heading within which to continue his tentative explorations. Then there was Otto Rank, who was the first to stress the importance of trauma, particularly that associated with birth; in this way, he anticipated the developments which were to come later in traumatic neurosis, unresolved grief and post-traumatic stress disorder. Further developments followed, such as psychosynthesis, associated with Assagioli, Gestalt with Fritz Pearls, and the pioneering work of Melanie Klein on early development, object relations theory and projective identification; next came Lindemann's work on unresolved grief, which was developed more fully by Kubler Ross. From this developed Lindemann and Gerald Caplan's work on crisis theory and crisis intervention. Developments then took place in existential psychotherapy through the work of Irvin Yalom, Rollo May and others. Virtually all these innovators were psychoanalysts.

Since those early days many different forms of experiential psychotherapy have been developing, most of these outside the fold of

310

formal psychiatry: Stan Grof's 'holotropic therapy', the 'somatic experiencing' of Peter Levine, 'hacomi', 'psychodrama', Shapiro's 'eye movement desensitisation', process oriented psychotherapy of Mendel, hypnoanalysis and so on. Working through a different channel came Wilhelm Reich with his somatic concepts, which opened the way for all the somatic therapies that have developed since – bioenergetics, Rolfing, cranio-sacral, the Alexander technique, acupuncture, acupressure, homeopathy and a number of others.

The common factor in all these more recent therapeutic approaches is that they can produce an altered state of consciousness. Once this is achieved, the frozen experiences will tend to surface spontaneously and, with guidance and support, the person will work progressively through these, gradually transforming them into long-term memory. These experiences will then no longer cause further emotional disturbance. It is of the greatest importance that, in the use of any of these therapeutic interventions, they are carried out with the absolute minimum of suggestion, in this way avoiding any question of producing pseudo-memories.

Because of the confusion in regard to the concept of 'repression', and the failure to understand the nature of 'unassimilated happenings', most psychiatrists have set their face against any form of experiential therapy involving regression. An official statement of the Royal College of Psychiatrists under the title, 'Recommendations for Good Practice and Implications for Training,' stated the following:

> Psychiatrists are advised to avoid engaging in any 'memory recovery techniques', which are based upon the expectation of past sexual abuse of which the patient has no memory. Such 'memory recovery techniques' may include drug-mediated interviews, hypnosis, regression therapies, guided imagery, 'body memories', literal dream interpretation and journalling. There is no evidence that the use of consciousness-altering techniques, such as drug-mediated interviews or hypnosis can reveal or accurately elaborate factual information about any past experiences, including sexual abuse.[1]

This statement is quite simply untrue. First of all these methods are not 'memory recovery techniques', they are ways of integrating unresolved traumatic experiences which have been frozen and turning them into ordinary long-term memory, by enabling the person to fully experience the trauma. I have used most of these methods over the years with hundreds of patients, generally finding satisfactory results, provided the person is prepared to undertake the painful work. In many cases I was able to help the person achieve a complete recovery, where they had previously been under psychiatric care for years without any improvement and were often misdiagnosed as suffering from bipolar or clinical depression.

Many patients fitting the general picture of post-traumatic stress can appear to be stuck, so that they continue to be subjected to the same kind of traumatic experience, over and over again. For example, where there has been sexual abuse early in childhood, one finds the person being abused by others in adolescence and then often subjected to rape or other kinds of sexual abuse again and again in adult life. In a similar way one may find a repetitive pattern of loss or illness running through a person's life. In all these instances it is as if the individual lives out a theme, which the external world continually plays back to them. This phenomenon is usually explained as arising from the early learning and personality formation, which then tends to attract the same kind of traumatic insult later and evokes a reciprocal response in those who carry a complementary tendency: for example, the daughters of alcoholics who in adult life will be attracted by, and are attractive to, alcoholics, whom they often end up marrying. A similar situation of mutuality has been noted in battered wives, who attract those who will brutalise them.

There is little doubt that this represents part of the explanation for such fixed behaviour and repetitive traumatisation. But when one carefully examines the life history of such individuals it becomes apparent that there is more to it than this. In a sizeable minority of the patients I have dealt with over the years, I have found traumatic incidents happening that could conceivably be due to coincidence but, when these occur over and over again, the odds against their happening by chance are well nigh inconceivable. It was this phenomenon that Carl Jung, in his subtle way, adverted to in his essays on 'synchronicity'. He commented on the way the external world seemed to match the internal preoccupation of the person concerned.

The ancient yogic philosophy of 'karmic transmission' would represent another possible explanation for these strange repetitive interactions. Stanislav Grof has drawn attention to these obscure linkages, which he refers to as 'co-ex systems', and points out that the theme usually extends into the transpersonal area. He cites those who have experiences that are evidently not from their present life, but yet have all the immediacy and vividness of real experiences. In my work too I have frequently found the subject spontaneously going into an experience that is not from their present lifetime and that they experience as an episode from a former life. I will illustrate this with just two examples among many in the course of my work with traumatised subjects.

A young rock musician, having dealt with some personal issues from his own life, found himself quite spontaneously going into an experience where he was lying on the road dying from what he felt was the plague. After the session he told me that he felt this was some time in the twelfth or thirteenth century; that he was a doctor who had been trying to help others, who were also dying around him, but had contracted the disease himself. The strange thing is that after this first session in which this episode occurred, he developed a pain running in a diagonal direction across his chest. This pain persisted the whole week until the next session, when he again went through the same painful experience. Again the pain persisted all week and I was getting worried that his heart might be affected. Then in the third session, when he was again lying on the road, a carriage in which he felt there were wealthy people who were afraid of contracting the plague drove over him, the wheel crossing his chest on the exact line where he had had the pain. After this experience the pain permanently disappeared. The only connection to his present life was that he had always felt he should have been a doctor.

The second example is of a man who had suffered depression for nearly twenty years, with no relief from conventional medication of various kinds or ECT. He was so incapacitated that, after many hospitalisations, he had separated from his wife and family and was living in a hostel when I took him on for therapy. He had suffered severe physical abuse during his life and had also had tetanus when he was ten years old. His parents were English and, although he was brought up in this country, he had no Irish antecedents. When he had dealt with the experience of tetanus and the physical abuse in his present life, he went spontaneously into a transpersonal experience at the time of the 1798 rebellion in Wexford. He was one of the

313

rebels, named Murt, and was involved in a skirmish, in which he was captured. In the next session, he was tortured by the yeomen with crude implements made by a blacksmith. The flesh was torn off his head and he was otherwise mutilated until he died. The strange thing is that, growing up in Crumlin on the south side of Dublin where, at that time, there were a couple of blacksmiths still working, he had been terrified as a child to go near them. Once he lived through these experiences, his depression permanently lifted and he was restored to his wife and family.

Whatever position one may take in regard to such experiences, I have often found that it is only when the person has fully experienced one or more of these transpersonal episodes that they are able to take a new direction in life. They are then no longer subjected to the same kind of traumatic insult again and again. I have never taken any ideological position in regard to these occurrences; I have simply dealt with them as with any other experience.

In 1995, shortly after I retired from the job of Chief Psychiatrist, Dr Brian Weiss' book, *Many Lives, Many Masters*,[2] was published on this side of the Atlantic. I didn't get to read it until several years afterwards. When I did I was surprised to find how similar his clinical examples of past-life experience were to those that had come up spontaneously in my work. He has gone on to develop this work much more systematically than I did, however, and in a more recent book, *Through Time into Healing*,[3] he sheds new light on the extraordinary healing potential of past-life therapy. He showed how he uses regression to past lifetimes to provide a breakthrough into healing mind, body and soul. This work also helps us to realise that death is not the final word; as I had already realised, it is only a transition to a wider reality. It clarifies once again that the doorways to healing and wholeness are inside each of us.

Further evidence to support this view has come more recently from the work of Professor Gary Schwartz, who has been carrying out systematic double-blind and triple-blind studies with experienced mediums. He has demonstrated that connections with some of those who have already died are statistically significant. He has pointed out that neuroscientists study brain function in three main ways:

Correlation studies: relating visual experience to EEG readings and seeing the correlation between these.

Stimulation studies: where areas of the brain are stimulated with electrodes (e.g. in the occipital area one evokes visual experiences).

Ablation studies: where an area of the cortex is damaged in animals, or in the case of humans where there is injury to the brain (e.g. if the occipital area is damaged there will be blind spots).

From these three types of study two hypotheses arise:

(1) One can conclude from these studies that consciousness is created in the brain. If the brain is the creator of consciousness, then, when one is brain-dead, consciousness should disappear. The logic here is that if you knock out the transistors in a television set, this proves that the programmes originate in the set. However, we know that the television signal is not created by the television set; it is an antenna receiver.

(2) The second hypothesis is that the brain itself is an antenna receiver.

Correlation, stimulation and ablation studies are consistent with either hypothesis. The only way to determine which of these is correct is to apply additional research methods. Research with mediums is a critical way of testing this, as Schwartz has been showing in his work with mediums.[4] The second way is to study 'near-death' experiences.

Some people report a near-death experience (NDE) after a life-threatening crisis. This can occur in many circumstances: cardiac arrest in myocardial infarction, shock after loss of blood, septic or anaphylactic shock, electrocution, coma resulting from traumatic brain damage, intracerebral haemorrhage, attempted suicide, near-drowning or asphyxia.

Identical experiences to NDE, those involving fear of death, where death seems unavoidable, have been reported, such as mountaineering accidents, serious traffic accidents or shipwreck. The effects of near-death experiences are similar worldwide, across all cultures and times. People who have had an NDE are psychologically healthy and do not differ from controls with respect to age, sex, ethnic origin or religion. A patient's transformational processes after an NDE encompass life-changing insight, heightened intuition, disappearance of fear of death, and also specific elements such as out-of-body experience, pleasant feelings and seeing a tunnel of light, deceased relatives, or a complete life review.

Most studies have been retrospective and very selective with respect to patients. In these studies about 45 per cent of adults and up to 85 per cent of children were estimated to have had an NDE. These showed varying definitions of the phenomenon and inadequate methods of research. More recently a number of prospective studies – Dutch, English and American – have been carried out. They defined clinical death as a period of unconsciousness caused by insufficient blood supply to the brain because of inadequate blood circulation, breathing or both. If, in this situation, cardiopulmonary resuscitation is not started within 5–10 minutes, irreparable damage is done to the brain and the patient will die. The results show that medical factors cannot account for the occurrence of NDE: although all patients have been clinically dead, most did not have NDE. Furthermore, the seriousness of the crisis was not related to occurrence or depth of the experience. If purely physiological factors resulting from cerebral anoxia cause NDE, most of the patients should have had this experience. Patients' medication was also unrelated to the frequency of NDE. Psychological factors are unlikely to be important, as fear was not associated with NDE. In these studies only 18 to 20 per cent of patients had a near-death experience, and of these only 12 per cent had a core NDE. The process of change after NDE tends to take several years to consolidate. Furthermore, the long-lasting transformational effects of an experience that lasts for only a few minutes of cardiac arrest is a surprising and unexpected finding.[5] This considerably strengthens the second hypothesis that the brain is mainly an antenna receiver. These two approaches demonstrate pretty convincingly that consciousness does exist outside the brain and even continues after death.

Persons who have been traumatised or abused over many years will typically, for most of their lives, have a strongly negative self-image. They think they are only fit to be treated badly, because they are bad. They may have self-destructive tendencies, either to mutilate themselves or attempt suicide. When they first present for therapy they are usually unaware of much of their traumatic history and major areas of their personality may be dissociated, so they do not know why they have all these negative feelings about themselves. It is only as they work through the painful experiences that these dissociated areas become accessible and they can begin to take responsibility for all that they are. When there is a long history of abuse dating back to childhood, they may have become abusive to others when in the dissociated state, yet they are unable to take responsibility for this. It is only as the experiential phase nears completion that they are able to begin to take responsibility for the dissociated dimensions of their personality, and to integrate these for the first time. Then a reappraisal of their situation becomes possible. They can then disconfirm their previous anticipation that things will always be the same, realising for the first time the possibility of real change. They can now begin to see that it was not that they were bad or worthless, but that anyone who was subjected to such brutal traumatic experience would have felt the same way.

The abuser, particularly if it was the father, who had until then perhaps even been idealised, can now be seen for the weak, pathetic creature that he was. In this way, if not forgiveness, at least reconciliation and acceptance become possible. It is a question of altering their relation to, and their attitude towards, what took place, so that they are able to free themselves from it, and to take command of and responsibility for their feelings and behaviour from now onwards.

If we take the view that not only is a person a living system but that this applies to the family also, the family can be seen as a living system in its own right, with its own separate life and existence. Where there is a block in the person's family of origin, what we typically find is that there is not only a secret which cannot be allowed to see the light of day, but also a myth. The myth is that if these things were ever to be spoken of, somebody would break down or be destroyed. This is unlikely to have any basis in reality now, whatever may have been the situation in the past. The thing to do then is to bring as many members of the family as are available together face to face with the patient, to attempt to open up any secrets and, if possible, get an admission of the truth. Usually if the secret can be brought out into the light of day, not only is it a validation for the patient, but it is a general relief to all concerned. This can apply not only in cases where there has been physical or sexual trauma, but in other situations such as the loss of a baby, a miscarriage, or loss of a parent or other close relative, perhaps by suicide, in the patient's early years. It may even have happened in a previous generation. In any of these circumstances, where the event is denied by the parents and hence by the family as a whole, the patient may unwittingly take on the role of scapegoat and guardian of the secret.

In tackling such a situation it is obviously most satisfactory when the truth can be brought out and accepted by all. But, even where other members of the family refuse to acknowledge what took place, it can still be beneficial to the patient. If other family members refuse to be involved, they can still be faced openly with the truth, or one can even write an account of it and send it to them.

Thus reappraisal is quite different from the experiential mode. It takes place to a greater extent in ordinary consciousness and is essentially a 'cognitive' phase. Just as during the experiential phase there is a movement of the traumatic experience from the present into the past, there is now a movement of the person and of their view of themselves from being fixated on the past to a state of 'living' in the present.

There are several other approaches to psychotherapy which do not derive from Freud and psychoanalysis. The pioneering work of the famous Russian physiologist Pavlov on conditioned reflexes gave the impetus for the development of what became known as 'behaviour therapy' and the clinical applications of this were developed by Wolpe, Skinner and others. Initially the philosophical concepts underlying this approach were very narrow and materialistic, viewing human beings as little more than a sophisticated hierarchy of conditioned reflexes; mind was considered a redundant concept. Nevertheless, some of the methods which were developed by behaviourists have proved to be useful for the treatment of certain conditions, such as phobias or obsessive-compulsive neurosis. So, even though the theoretical concepts of the early behaviourists were over-simplified and don't stand up to critical examination, their emphasis on the fact that true insight only exists when there is a real change in behaviour has been a valuable contribution.

When this over-simplified view of what constitutes a human being broke down, as was inevitable, then some deeper concept of the nature of human reality had to be introduced. The realisation that we don't simply respond to life situations in terms of conditioned responses led to the development of what has become known as cognitive therapy. Although he would have rejected the idea that he was a cognitive therapist, it was George Kelly who laid the theoretical groundwork for cognitive therapy. He developed the theory of constructivism, i.e. that we construct and build up our personalities as we develop. Aaron Beck, who has popularised and developed the concept, studied with Kelly, and I believe it was from Kelly's insights that he developed his practical therapeutic methods.

We have found that, even when patients have fully worked through all their traumatic experience and have completed the task of reappraisal, full recovery does not take place until they have moved the locus of control into themselves and have taken over personal direction of their life. Only when they engage with life on a quite new basis, trying out new social behaviours and undertaking activities which until then had spelt danger and had to be strenuously avoided, can one speak of full recovery and true insight.

In my view it is quite incorrect to consider these different approaches to psychotherapy as separate forms of treatment. The notion that there is such a creature as a behaviour therapist or a cognitive therapist is ludicrous. These different forms of therapy should be considered as phases in a therapeutic cycle, to be brought in at the appropriate stage in therapy to suit the needs of the patient at that time. The tragedy of psychiatry and psychotherapy in its present stage of development is that the form of therapy offered to the patient is more likely to be that which the therapist espouses and is trained in than that which the patient actually needs.

The different forms of psychotherapy that have been mentioned so far assume that the client has achieved a reasonably adult status. An individual may be seriously emotionally disturbed, may have been severely traumatised and may have developed maladaptive attitudes and ways of behaving that constantly land him in trouble but, by definition, if he is available for, and capable of, benefiting from psychotherapy, he will have achieved sufficient adult status to manage his life in some sort of way.

What has not been addressed is the problem of those who, for whatever reason, fail to develop and reach adulthood, fail even to integrate a separate self and achieve a personal identity. These include many of those who are diagnosed as suffering from schizophrenia, eating disorders, chronic phobias and so on. Undoubtedly in such persons there may be a genetic influence, like any unusual personalities, more sensitive or introverted perhaps than others. It may also be that there is evidence of perinatal problems, giving rise to some form of minimal brain damage. But it still remains true that the final common path in such cases is of a person who has failed to reach maturity.

I am thinking of all those who have failed to separate from their family of origin and who, although biologically adult, are still functioning like children in the family setting and are incapable of managing their own lives. These are the people who, when they break down, are said by psychiatrists to be suffering from a 'biological' mental illness and hence are not amenable to psychotherapy. It is even said that pyschotherapy may be damaging to them. The illness is thought to be due primarily to biochemical disturbance, which is at least partially genetically determined, and hence can only be treated pharmacologically or, where this is not successful, with physical interventions such as ECT.

That this view is said to be biological is a strange contradiction, for the essence of biology is the adaptation of living creatures to their environment, which is essentially dynamic. Because such psychiatrists are still caught in a reductionist epistemology and are unaware of the self-organising nature of a living being, they see whatever evidence there is of biochemical disturbance as primary; that is, it is that which causes the illness. They seem unable to ask the question: is it the developmental failure and the behaviour of the person that is causing the biochemical imbalance?

If you think about it, in a situation like this, all that drugs can do is to reduce the fantasies, grandiose delusions and hallucinations that the person has created to make life bearable. No drug can teach you what you need to know to manage life, or to have a personal identity. This is why anti-psychotics have been shown to have little effect on the negative symptoms of schizophrenia, which, of course, are due to a basic failure of self-organisation, with a consequent lack of motivation and self-management.

I feel that this so-called biological thesis is accepted because the wrong questions are being asked. This is something that Einstein and the quantum physicists had to come to terms with in the early years of the last century. For the first time they had to take into account the scientist himself and the way in which the question was being asked. If we ask what is the causal relationship of genetics to schizophrenia, we are already biasing the results of our research. The genetic influence may merely relate to the personality type, for example, a more sensitive or introverted type of person. There may be no direct relationship to schizophrenia, as such.

The psychiatric view of what constitutes psychotherapy is too narrow. What is required here is a broad educational and habilitative strategy. It is not a question so much of helping the person to re-shape a development that has been damaged but rather helping them to reach adult independence in the first place. It is not that they have grown up in a twisted way but rather that they have failed to reach maturity at all. Needless to say, the earlier such a programme can be undertaken after the first psychotic break, the better its chance of meeting with real success. Indeed, if the person could be identified in the pre-psychotic phase, the prognosis would be even better. This is where genetic research in helping to identify those at risk may be of benefit in the future.

So, I feel that the sort of therapeutic interventions that could be of help to bring about real change and to give such individuals a foothold towards health would be something along the following lines: firstly, the establishment of a personal therapeutic relationship. This is fundamental to any therapeutic endeavour; secondly, where there is a lot of psychotic symptomatology and fixed delusional thinking, it may be necessary to give one of the newer anti-psychotic medications, such as Olanzapine, on a temporary basis, to enable contact to be established and a therapeutic relationship to develop; thirdly, this would clear the way for a therapeutic education pro-gramme in which the patient participates, to help him understand the nature of psychotic thinking, of illness behaviour and psychotic symptoms such as hallucinations and delusions.

What is involved here is an understanding of the way we per-ceive the world and the nature of the mind. When we perceive some-thing in the outside world, the light or sound waves, or other sensory modalities, enter through the eyes or ears. But then this is converted into electro-chemical activity passing along nerves. At each synapse this turns into chemical messages, until it eventually reaches the oc-cipital or temporal lobe and so on. So it is now electro-chemical en-ergy, and essentially no different from all the internal electro-chemical activity coming from other areas in the brain and body. It is now a far cry from the actual reality we have been ob-serving in the outside world.

We could conceivably be constructed in such a way that we could read this information inside ourselves in the brain, as on a radar screen. But the miracle of our perception is that we project this picture into the outside world to exactly where it originated. Thus we actually hallucinate the world around us. For example, although the eye is said to be a sensory organ, it has been shown that there are as many nerves running to the eye (efferents) from the occipital lobe as there are sensory fibres (afferents) coming in. In this way, the world we perceive outside is a projection of our own inner experience, which we locate exactly where the sensory input originated. It is not pathological, therefore, to hallucinate; we are hallucinating the world like this all the time.

What then happens when someone becomes psychotic? Here there appears to be a failure to differentiate mental activity that is initiated by a sensory stimulus from outside from that which originates from our own thoughts internally. When we fail to recognise our own thoughts, we will do what we do naturally and project these thoughts, hearing or seeing them as if they were coming from outside. And, of course, this doesn't just apply to those who are mentally disturbed, but it happens regularly in post-operative patients following anaesthesia, or where someone is toxic with a high temperature. It happens too when people are undergoing interrogation or are subjected to various forms of sensory deprivation. Indeed, in these situations people often experience vivid visual hallucinations, which are uncommon in schizophrenia. Because, as George Kelly said, human beings are natural scientists, unless we can help those who are psychotic to understand how this can happen, it is natural that they should take what the voices are telling them seriously.

Of course, this is the very problem that all of us face in the process of development: to learn to recognise what originates within us from that which is initiated from outside; also, to learn to separate self from non-self and, particularly during adolescence, to form a personal identity.

I believe it would be quite possible in this way to help those who have become psychotic, whether through developmental failure or whether drug-induced, to understand these essential facts about the way our perception works and something of the nature of mind. It would then become more difficult for them to deceive themselves and to buy into the addictive nature of delusional activity. This kind of therapeutic education, combined with other modalities of therapy, could be a useful tool in helping those who have failed to reach adult maturity and those who have had a psychotic breakdown to become more independent and self-managing; and so to give a message of hope that with work and effort there is no reason why they need continue on a pathway of illness; that they have within themselves resources to become mentally healthy and develop adult independence. The fourth therapeutic intervention I would propose is to help them to undertake the work of separation from their family of origin, in which many of them are trapped, including therapy for the family where appropriate, thus to enable them to move from a child to an adult position, from dependence to a reasonable level of independence.

In applying such ideas to the central social system that is the family I am not simply returning to the old debate about sick families or schizophrenegenic parents. Undoubtedly, some of these families could be described as sick, but that is not the issue. What I am speaking about is something much simpler. The question is whether it can be considered normal or healthy for any of us who have reached our adult years to return to live in our parental home, when inevitably the relationship will tend to return to that of parent–child. (For many of us it is difficult and frustrating even to return home for a few days at Christmas.)

The feedback cycles in the family vary across the various stages of that family. For example, it is now clear that what has been termed 'institutionalisation' does not only happen in large, custodial mental hospitals or similar institutions. The worst instances of institutionalisation I have come across have been persons incarcerated within their own families – for example, young schizophrenics and others presenting to psychiatry for the first time. What the mental hospital usually does is simply complete the process of institutionalisation initiated by the family. If we look at what institutionalisation actually is, a state of dependency, not being in charge of one's own life and destiny, it is clear that in this state everything is controlled and managed by others. It is in essence a state of learned helplessness. Once this is understood, it is obvious that it can happen anywhere, indeed particularly in the family where all of us begin life as babies in a helpless state. It is when the natural drive to mature, to become independent and self-directing, is frustrated and the person grows into adolescence and adulthood without achieving the wherewithal for independence that the true picture of institutionalisation becomes apparent.

When such a person is required by the demands of society to

strike out on their own, they frequently have what in ordinary parlance is termed a 'nervous breakdown'. Some psychiatrists will insist that there is nothing unusual or traumatic affecting the person at this time, only the ordinary stresses of life which we all have to face. Therefore the breakdown must be due to some primary biochemical abnormality. What they fail to see is that for a person who has not developed the essential skills for living to enable them to manage adult life, and who is essentially still a child, to have to face the ordinary stresses of independent living can be an absolutely devastating trauma. For such a person, unable to manage their personal boundary, the impact of ordinary living and relationships can be terrifying. So they have no choice but to retreat into themselves, creating a fantasy world, involving false self-esteem, which psychiatrists then diagnose as a schizophrenic illness.

The fifth and last point to make is that, as already mentioned, the current psychiatric view of what constitutes psychotherapy is too narrow. What is required here is a broad educational and habilitative strategy. Many of these patients will have wide-ranging deficits in social behaviour and vocational skills. This necessitates involving the full spectrum of rehabilitation and vocational training resources which exist, for the development of skills for living, if they are to reach any degree of reasonable independence for life. This implies that a full therapeutic programme for such patients will be likely to extend over several years. But it is important to realise that these later stages are not likely to involve hospitalisation or a major strain on health service resources. They can be undertaken with hostel care and the resources provided by the state under social welfare and vocational training. It should be further emphasised that, if this rehabilitative task is not undertaken, then such patients are likely to be a millstone around the neck of the psychiatric service, causing management and economic problems far in excess of that which their numbers would suggest.

It is interesting by comparison to look at services for the mentally retarded. Here, there is usually no doubt about the brain damage, resulting from genetic or organic deficit. Because, as a rule, nothing much can be done about the underlying disability, these services have, for many years now, geared themselves up to provide a sophisticated, educational and developmental approach, involving the whole educational infrastructure of teachers, remedial work, physiotherapy and so on. Also, they usually have access to their clientele from early childhood onwards. With this input, many who are quite severely handicapped achieve a near normal potential. But, if we turn to the psychiatric services, this educational infrastructure is almost entirely absent. Further, the first psychotic breakdown usually occurs in late adolescence or early adulthood. Hence, if you were to have an effective remedial therapeutic programme, with a broadly based educational input, you would need an even more high-powered, sophisticated educational infrastructure to speed up the whole process of arrested development. Full recovery then would only happen if the person were to engage with life on a quite new basis. It is this move, from a rigidly defended narrow way of life to a much more flexible set of attitudes and behaviours, including the taking on of full personal autonomy, that would permit one to talk in terms of recovery or cure.

It goes without saying that for such an approach to be successful would presuppose the existence of therapeutic communities, to provide asylum and a supportive context in which such a programme could be initiated.

Looking back over the years, I ask myself the question, what could I have done differently? I think, in addition to following the same broad plan to develop community psychiatric services, I should also have concentrated the available resources in one psychiatric district initially and personally established a demonstration unit: a facility that would have had a psychotherapeutic, person-centred approach, with a small number of overnight beds (along the lines of Joshua Bierer's Marlborough Day Hospital). In addition, this should ideally have been supported by the development of some form of therapeutic community, that is a small in-patient facility where restitutive learning could have begun. If this had proved successful it might then have been possible to replicate it in other areas.

What should be stressed, however, is that the need for such therapeutic communities as the basis for a 'person-centred' approach is even greater today than it was then, and there is still no sign of such a development in this country. Thus, unless there is a real change in the psychotherapeutic training of psychiatrists and in their methods of working, I see psychiatry moving further and further into a blind alley, with almost total dependence on psychopharmacological interventions. This reductionist approach has the seeds of its own destruction within it, given the increasing evidence of damaging side effects with the long-term use of these medications.

There is nothing particularly new or unique about the approach I am suggesting. As early as 1927 Harry Stack Sullivan spoke of the importance of psychotherapeutic intervention in dealing with psychosis and he stressed the relevance of engaging with the person as early as possible: 'The psychiatrist sees too many end states and deals professionally with too few of the pre-psychotic . . . we should lay great stress on the prompt investigation of failing adjustment, rather than, as is so often the case, wait and see what happens.'

I saw an interesting example of the value of such early intervention recently. I was asked to see a young sixteen-year-old girl by a friend of the family who had heard about her problem and asked me to intervene. As a psychiatrist I have seldom had the opportunity to see someone in the early stages of a breakdown. They have usually already been to a GP who has referred them on to a psychiatrist, who then admits them to hospital. Thus they are usually already heavily medicated and quite chronic by the time one hears about them. In this instance the family had recently moved to another part of the country and the girl, who was a gentle sensitive child, had changed to a new school. She was happy about the change but was trying too hard to make friends and succeed in the new environment. Her parents then went for a long weekend to London and by the time they returned she had become floridly psychotic.

What I did not realise at the time was that her parents had already taken her to a GP, who had referred her on to a psychiatrist. The psychiatrist said she was one of the sickest girls she had ever seen and that she should be hospitalised immediately. Had this happened, she would then have been heavily medicated and almost certainly retained for several weeks or months, by which time she would have found it difficult to integrate back into school, as, with the side effects of medication, she would have been seen as peculiar and a misfit. By that time she would have been well on the way to becoming a chronic schizophrenic. I have seen this outcome so many times in the past. What in fact happened was that they told the psychiatrist they had already made an appointment to see me and brought her to me instead.

When I saw her she resembled one of the old-fashioned pictures of hebephrenic schizophrenia; she was laughing one minute and crying the next, clearly hallucinating, feeling she could influence the outside world, the weather and so on, and also feeling that what was happening outside was controlling her. I prescribed a moderate dose of one of the new anti-psychotics, Olanzapine, for one week and asked her parents, as soon as she showed some improvement, to ground her with a programme of swimming, walking and healthy living. When I saw her a week later she was together enough to reduce the medication and, within two weeks of my first seeing her, she was back in school and the medication could be discontinued. The principal of the school arranged for a couple of girls to befriend her and she was soon able to get involved again in sports, to form social relationships and engage in other normal activities. She has had no further difficulties.

The point I want to make is that there was nothing remarkable in what I did other than to interrupt the process quickly and reintegrate her back into normal life.

It is my belief that the full picture of schizophrenia is, to a considerable degree, iatrogenic; that is, it is partially created by the psychiatric intervention itself, establishing a pathway of illness behaviour extending over weeks or months, with heavy medication and institutionalisation. Thus the young person loses connection with ordinary living at a critical time and finds it difficult to reintegrate back into society. It is only then that the full picture of the illness we call schizophrenia supervenes.

In the 1970s Silvano Arieti, in his work *Interpretation of Schizophrenia*,[6] was aware of this difficulty and provided a humanising influence with his emphasis on interpersonal relationships, at a time when most of the care was custodial and pessimistic. He also went on to introduce a cognitive dimension to the understanding of, and psychotherapeutic approach towards, psychotic patients. Since then there has been growing evidence of a revival of interest in psychotherapeutic interventions – with Loren Mosher in California and Patrick McGorry in Australia, amongst others. More recently there have been significant psychotherapeutic developments in Finland, with their integrated model of need-adapted care. This approach has since spread to other Scandinavian countries. In these various projects the results have been on the whole superior to the usual psycho-pharmacologic-based therapies, yet little or no notice is being paid to these innovative efforts by most psychiatrists, who continue to behave as if there were no alternative to their so-called biological mind-set.

Part Seven

Spirituality and the Growth of Love
1994–

34

India

'Philosophy is a subject, not based on reason but based on intuition. It starts not from doubt as most of the western philosphers hold, but from wonder.'[1]

Ram Chandra

When I visited India for the first time towards the end of 1978, I was leaving a difficult situation behind me. Trouble seemed to be brewing on all sides. The Irish Foundation was on the verge of collapsing and the psychiatric service, because of the delay in providing the alternatives to the mental hospital, was in a state of increasing disarray. Because of this I was doubtful about the wisdom of travelling at all. So I rang Charles Haughey, who was Minister for Health at the time, to say perhaps it would be better if we cancelled our trip. He told me to go to India and he would take care of any difficulty which might arise while I was away.

So Juno and I set off, hoping to meet a holy man, Ram Chandra, whom we had heard about. Looking back now I think it was the greatest privilege of my life to have the good fortune to meet such a man. When we arrived in Shajahanpur, an out-of-the-way backward town in northern India, and had worked our way through the dirt and chaos of the streets of the city, it was a great relief to arrive at the home of this holy man. Babuji was the pet name by which Ram Chandra was known. Behind the big iron gate was a clean, spacious courtyard, with a well and pump in the centre. In contrast to the noise of the streets we had just struggled through, the atmosphere of the whole place was quiet and serene. Babuji was sitting in his chair with people around him. I remember he just glanced up briefly when we arrived, but otherwise remained absorbed in himself, apparently oblivious to everything else.

I was somewhat disappointed at the first sight of this small, insignificant-looking man but then, when we sat down facing him, I had the strange feeling of having arrived 'home', and I felt as though I never wanted to leave again. When it was time for us to go, he instructed that the car be brought around and that we be driven to the ashram. He said it was dangerous on the roads at night because of Dacoits. When we were departing he came down to the gate to see us off. This was our first experience of his scrupulous civility and the importance he placed on proper etiquette and service to others.

After the group meditation next morning, we were called to his cottage to sit for a personal meditation with him. When we entered I remember noticing that he was holding a single rose that he had covered with his kurta and every now and then he smelt it through the cotton, as if the direct scent were too strong for him. 'Start meditation,' he instructed us. After some time I became aware of an overpowering scent, as if the room were filled with banks of flowers. When he told us, 'That's all', and I opened my eyes, to my surprise there were no flowers in the room, except his single rose. On another occasion around this time, I remember seeing him in the meditation hall, after a group meditation, bathed in light. But none of this made much impression on me at the time; I must then have been so closed off from my heart.

On one of our visits to his house, because I felt it impossible to say anything, any talk seeming irrelevant, Juno asked him whether he could help me with some of the problems that I was facing at the time with regard to my separation from and loss of contact with my children. Babuji usually sat in a reverie but, when asked a direct question, he would come right out of himself and focus intently. He said, 'I don't know the circumstances of your life. What I would say to you is, "do your duty".'

I felt so disappointed. Here was this great spiritual master and this was all the advice he could give me. But the strange thing is, for a good many years after that, I was astonished to find that every time a question came up and I was faced with alternatives, the exhortation 'Do your duty' echoed in my mind and I knew the course of action I had to follow. And, of course, it was almost always the very thing

I didn't want to do or to face up to.

Unfortunately, there came a time, years later, when I did not follow this advice. I got myself involved in a stupid affair and let my mind be taken over, losing the run of myself for a time. I let both the master and Juno down, nearly breaking her heart; she, who has always been so faithful and good to me. She probably should have gone her own way at the time but she stayed with me and eventually forgave me, which is more than I deserved. Looking back now I deeply regret that I didn't have the sense and character to remember Babuji's admonition when the test came. Now, with the benefit of hindsight, I am amazed at the wisdom and power of those three little words. I think it was only very gradually, over the years, that this emphasis on 'duty' was replaced by 'love' as a guide for behaviour.

Babuji was lovable, childlike and humble. One day as I watched Mallan, the small woman with the wizened face who had looked after him for so many years, preparing his hookah, I said to Babuji, 'She must be very old.' He explained that she was nearly eighty, but then added with pride, like a child, 'I am eighty-one.'

We met Babuji several times over the next few years. Once we brought him a present of a magnifying glass, which had a light in it that shone on whatever it was focused upon. For about half an hour he sat on the floor examining everything with the glass, exactly as a small child would do. Here was a person who, in a super-conscious state, could deal with concepts beyond philosophy or higher physics and who literally had power over life and death. However, at a human level, he was as innocent and curious as a small child. He used to say, 'Spirituality begins where religion ends, and realisation begins where spirituality ends.' And Chariji, Babuji's successor, further elucidated this saying: 'God is simple and therefore the means to reach him must also be simple.'

During his last visit to Paris in August 1982, after which he went home to die, Babuji was unable to rise from his bed. On a couple of occasions he came into the hall looking very feeble but, nevertheless, standing up quite straight. Three times he stumbled on his way and my heart ached as he struggled along.

'This is terrible,' I thought. 'It's like Christ on his way to Calvary.'

We were staying in the same building as Babuji, in the room directly above his. Juno was sick and unable to leave her bed all week, in sympathy with Babuji. Within a day or two everyone seemed to disappear and I felt totally isolated and became quite paranoid, convinced that no one wanted to have anything to do with me. At this same time all the big wigs were strutting about politicking and deciding how they would run things after Babuji was gone, except for Chaiji, who simply devoted his time to caring for the old man with love.

My negative feelings worsened until, before dawn on the fourth day, I woke up in a state of utter despair. I felt that the meditation system was corrupt and useless. But what could I go back to? That morning I reached the lowest point of despair in my life. Then, on the last day, everyone started to emerge and it felt as if a great black cloud were lifting. That night we had a concert with people singing, dancing and playing music. Much later it became clear to me that Babuji, though so sick and on the verge of death, had been carrying out 'deep cleansing' on more than a thousand people. And it struck me how pathetically limited was my life's work in psychotherapy compared to the extraordinary power and capacity of a spiritual master of such calibre.

I referred earlier, when discussing psychosis, to Rupert Sheldrake's view that our minds are not confined within our brains but extend out all around us. Now, recalling my experience of the way Babuji worked, I realise that I already knew this to be true. By the use of divine transmission, which he termed *pranahuti* (meaning the process of yogic transmission derived from *prana* meaning 'life' and *ahuti* meaning 'offering'), he not only showed that the mind can extend outwards from the body but was able to control this power to influence others by subtle suggestion.

My final memory of Babuji is of the afternoon when he was leaving France for the last time. He came out into the sunshine to sit with us for a little while before being driven away. He was perfectly dressed in a European suit, gleaming from head to toe, like a child on his First Communion day. The usual circle of people around him stood back a little, as if too diffident to come close. And then, a little boy, perhaps four years of age, came and stood in front of Babuji. He had platinum blonde hair, fair skin and blue eyes, contrasting beautifully with Babuji's dark eyes and brown skin. The two of them stared intently at each other for what seemed a timeless moment, a small boy wholly absorbed and Babuji's eyes full of love. That scene is alive still for me to this day. Then Babuji was taken away in a car and I never saw him again.

The Sahaj Marg system simply means 'natural path'. It is a modified form of *raja* yoga simplified to suit the lifestyle of modern human beings, a system of spiritual training based on a heart-centred meditation. The practice is founded on the principle that God is all pervasive and therefore pervades the heart of each and every person. The goal of the practice is explicitly spiritual: attaining the ultimate goal of human existence, which is oneness with God or self. Here, an aspirant is inducted into meditation directly, bypassing the preliminary stages. The unique aspect of this system is *pranahuti*. This is defined as the utilisation of divine energy for the transformation of a human being. *Pranahuti* is the offering or transmitting of the subtlest divine current directed by the spiritual master to the heart of an *abhyasi*. This process aids in gently diverting the mind towards the ultimate. There is a major emphasis on cleaning out the impressions (samskaras) that have formed around our heart over the long struggle of evolution. Also, if you accept the proposition that we have, as human beings, had many lives, then those impressions too have to be cleared out. The view here is that, deep in the core of our heart, the spirit (soul) is pure, close to the condition it was in at the time of creation, when this universe first emerged.

In this system, and the eastern tradition generally, there is, especially for westerners, the difficult concept of *bhog* (*bhoga* or *bhogam*), which in sanskrit is literally translated as 'enjoyment', but in this context is defined as 'undergoing the effects of impressions'. This is why I have often referred to the work of experiencing as a deep principle within nature. My belief is that this principle extends far beyond the individual integration of experience.

I also feel that the concept of experience transcends this material state of embodiment and resonates out into the wider sphere of reality. If this is so, it would mean that any action or trauma that takes place in the external world would have to be experienced by someone at some time, if not in the present, than at some time in the future. Here I feel a little out of my depth, but this would seem to relate to the Judaeo-Christian concept of praying for, or suffering for, one another, as on the Day of Atonement, Yom Kippur; or the Christian idea of the mystical body, where souls are all thought to be interconnected and suffering can be shared. It also raises the question whether great incarnations like Buddha or Christ can suffer and thus experience and clean away impressions for all of us.

Some years ago I went to Israel with Chariji, Babuji's present representative and successor. When there, Chariji visited the Wailing Wall. He rested his head against the wall and seemed to be working with tremendous intensity to try to affect the situation in the Middle East. Then we went up the Via Dolorosa, where he seemed to identify with Christ; I could see the deep suffering in his face. He was obviously working with subtle suggestion for, when we first arrived, there seemed to be little interest in our visit, but by the end of the week there was a constant stream of people, both Israelis and Arabs, coming to his door asking about the meditation.

35

The Heart

'There is a light that shines beyond all things on earth,
beyond us all, beyond the heavens, beyond the highest,
the very highest heavens. This is the light that shines in our heart.'[1]
Chandogya Upanishad

When I was told in India that the heart was the real centre of our emotional life, the location where all the impressions (*samskaras*) that drive our behaviour are laid down, I thought this was simply a nice poetic and figurative way of describing things. However, I realise more and more the truth of this statement; that the heart is absolutely central. Babuji used to say:

> People generally think of the heart as made of flesh and blood only . . . This is one of the limitations in viewing the heart region in its broader sense. It is really a vast circle covering everything inner and outer. The things after the first mind all belong to the region of heart.

The remarkable thing is that research has been developing over the past thirty years demonstrating that the heart is more than simply a pump. The atrium of the heart produces a hormone, atrial natriuretic factor (ANF) that interacts with other hormones and has a controlling influence over the whole cardiovascular system, dramatically affecting every major organ in the body. It impacts on the primitive area of the brain and determines the action of the thalamus and its relationship with the pituitary gland. ANF is involved in the immune system and affects the pineal gland, regulating the production and action of melatonin.

With the identification of this atrial hormone, it becomes clear that the heart plays a key role in our emotional life, memory and learning. Indeed recent work is revealing that there are networks of neurones in the heart showing evidence of 'mind', and that the heart is the real centre of our emotions, reflecting back on the brain. It is interesting that Joseph Chilton Pearce, in his remarkable book *Evolutions End*, has described in very similar terms this centrality of the heart and how it can potentially operate at several levels. He speaks of how we have 'both a physical heart and a higher universal heart . . . just as our physical heart maintains our body, the non-localised intelligence governing the heart in turn maintains synchrony with the universal consciousness at large'. He goes on to describe how the three major stages of life are heart-centred in this sense: the development of a heart–mind synchrony, needed for physical life; a later 'post-adolescent' development, which synchronises the developed physical self and the creative process; and a final 'highest heart', which moves us beyond all physical emotional systems. Two poles of experience lie within us: our unique, individual self-generating through the brain and a universal, impersonal intelligence generating through the heart.

Joseph Chilton Pearce goes on to say that his meditation teacher once told him that 'You must develop your intellect to the highest possible extent, in order that it be a proper instrument for the intelligence of the heart, but, only the intelligence of the heart can develop intellect to its highest level.'[2]

Of course, the medical view is that emotions are really controlled by the brain, and that the heart is simply there to pump the blood! But Pearce's work describes the total unity of our being, showing that the heart is really central to this unity, the emotional driving force of our character and morality. The intellect is merely an amoral instrument to assist our understanding, but is a poor guide as to how we should behave. To open this third level, or the 'spiritual heart', is the main task of spirituality. Even in the west we speak of someone being soft-hearted, kind-hearted, or hard hearted. We say someone is heart-scalded, heartbroken, or a sweetheart, showing that this awareness of the centrality of the heart was there in the language of our forebears.

When human beings behave in deplorable ways, we often hear it described as simply 'human nature'. But when we behave in cruel, aggressive ways, this is not human nature; it is behaving distortedly, as less than we are capable of being. It is not true either to say that we are behaving like an animal, for animals do not show these excesses of depravity, because their behaviour is disciplined by nature, and they behave in a way that is natural to them. What we have failed to realise is that true human behaviour, the natural state of the human being, only exists when our spiritual nature is awakened, for we are, in essence, spiritual beings. This is the third stage of flowering of the highest heart, which unfortunately so few of us achieve.

The crucial difference from the mundane levels of biological development, or issues of therapy, is that in spirituality it is extremely difficult to make real progress simply by our own efforts. Nowadays, in discussions of this kind, it is usually arrogantly assumed that, whatever changes ought to come, these will be brought about by human endeavour, by 'ourselves alone', as individuals, and also by human society as a whole.

But if we look back over human history, a quite different view is equally tenable: that there is an ultimate source at the base of the creation of this universe and that this source was not only active at the commencement of creation but is imminent, constantly brooding over the creation as it evolves. When humanity is in serious danger of going astray and destroying the very creation of which it is the leading shoot, this source is influencing us, albeit indirectly, from time to time.

There is considerable evidence, if one is willing to look that at times of major change or upheaval, special incarnations enter the world in human form that alter in a fundamental way the direction of human evolution. Within the historical period, give or take a century or two, a remarkable group of sages manifested to enlighten mankind. They lived and taught some two millennia ago; they included Lao Tsu and his contemporary Confucius in China, the Buddha and the authors of most of the Hindu texts (although the latter were already part of an ancient aural tradition which was first written down at this time), Heraclitus the philosopher of flux in Greece, the Persian Zoroaster and the authors of the Old Testament. Christ came about five centuries later and Mohammed later still. But, even if we include Mohammed, this total period covers little more than 1,000 years. Yet these great teachers are with us still, in the meanings we attach to the spoken word and to symbolic marks on paper. They still shape the context of countless millions of lives and exhort us to live by value systems that are other than, and higher than, genetic determinism and instinct. Their living thoughts, wholly insubstantial yet marvellously potent, despite their intangibility, are ceaselessly recurring in the matrix of acts that is the context, physical and mental, of our experience of human life.

It would seem that this period around two millennia ago was a critical period of major human change, with the emergence of reflective individual consciousness. Even before de Chardin, there was no need to remind the literate individual of the centuries-old matrix of thought and belief that filled our minds, shaped our thinking and determined our behaviour. We recognised and valued it as culture. Culture is, in a sense, a property, a thing we acquire like wealth, or a personal achievement of which one might be proud. Most of the great religious systems – Buddhist, Jewish, Christian, Islamic (systems that are still with us today) – date from this period. The Hindu tradition, the roots of which are lost in the mists of the past, is much older and may be related to a much earlier civilisation, a purer and simpler period at the dawn of human awareness.

My question is, are we now on the threshold of a much greater and more fundamental period of human change, which is unique and of a different order to anything that has happened before? With the development of all kinds of telecommunications, millions of messages are swirling around the surface of the planet. It could be that we are on the verge of the biosphere becoming conscious of itself. Taking as a starting point Gregory Bateson's statement that 'mind is the aggregate of differentiating parts' and de Chardin's concept of 'complexity-consciousness', it would follow that the more complex the interactions in any living system, the more 'mind' will develop and the more conscious the system will become. In this sense, from time immemorial, consciousness has been increasing in the biosphere. De Chardin spoke of human beings 'pressing up against one another' around the globe, and the question is, as the complexity of all kinds of communication between them increases, will the biosphere begin to manifest not only consciousness but self-consciousness?

To my mind, however, if such a quantum leap is to take place, it will involve not only direct interactions between human beings but also these mediated through the communication technologies. It is just possible that, in the midst of all the chaos of human activity at present, this is the really significant change that is taking place imperceptibly in the world, below the surface of our awareness, and that some form of super-consciousness is developing in the biosphere. From this point of view it may be that all the problems of human disorganisation we see around us are a temporary phenomenon, because we are still at an early stage of development. It may even be that, when the civilisation that comes after this one destroys itself, human beings will have developed so much greater telepathic ability and other personal sensitivities that people will no longer require technological means of communication.

For several hundred years now society in the so-called First World has been transforming itself into a state of positive feedback. This had its beginnings at the time of the Renaissance, when modern science and technology started to develop, but it really took off with the advent of the Industrial Revolution and has been speeding up ever since. So we have a society that is accelerating like a runaway train. This is fast becoming a global movement affecting the whole world. Our society is now like a boat on a river, drifting towards a waterfall. All around us the rapids are getting more turbulent but most of the occupants of the boat are behaving as if life is just flowing on as it always did. I feel we are now in a position where, unless all the warning signs are heeded and we make urgent efforts to reach the shore, our civilisation is going to be carried over the edge. We are in a race against time.

But if we are not operating in isolation, as the arrogance of modern human science would have it, this would seem to be a time to look carefully deep beneath the surface of ordinary human activity to discern whether another divine incarnation in human form may have appeared amongst us. There is one critical difference to be noted about the present as compared to the period of the great incarnations of the past. At that time the great human cultures of China, India, the Middle East and South America were largely separate, and communication between them haphazard and difficult. Now, as has been constantly emphasised by de Chardin, the 'noosphere' is converging and human society is coming face to face with itself at all points of the globe. This is perhaps why, in the earlier period, there were a number of distinct incarnations, although the central teachings they brought were virtually identical. Unfortunately, each of these gave rise to a separate religious tradition, leaving us with the legacy of the divisiveness of conflicting religions, each claiming to be the purveyor of the truth.

The situation now is utterly different; there is no need for different incarnations in different parts of the world, giving rise to discordant religious voices. If a special personality has come, there is likely to be only one. The function of that incarnation would be to bring about this transformation. It is time to transcend religion and, if there is to be a new spiritual growth, to move towards a universal spirituality.

In the last pages of *The Pheonomene Humaine*, de Chardin made a prophetic statement: 'Either the entire construction of the world presented here is an empty theory. Or else somewhere around us, in one form or other, we should be able to detect some excess of personal, extra human energy perceptible to us if we look carefully and it should reveal to us the great presence.' He saw this in terms of a Christo-genesis but this too, in my view, is too limited. Christ represented an incarnation appropriate to his time. What is pressing now is a transcension; and 'where religion ends would be the beginning of spirituality'. As de Chardin himself said, 'The day will come when we shall harness for God the energies of love. And, on that day, for the second time in the history of the world, the human being will have discovered fire.'

Perhaps the modern world has lost its awareness of the deep mystical forces that are at work below the surface of a civilisation which has gone badly astray. It is perhaps such an awareness of the extent to which this intangible web reaches the boundary of our individuality and involves us at all times in some greater unity that is resonating out across the world, and moving imperceptibly towards a global but truly human society. Nor are the boundaries of this larger unity impermeable. Beyond each boundary there is a greater unity, until the whole noosphere is enclosed. Beyond that last boundary is the mystery.

Afterword

It is now a quarter of a century since I began meditation under the Sahaj Marg system. I still meditate every day and, increasingly, I am aware of the divine as a background throughout the day. Quite often at night when I lie with Juno, resting her lovely head on my chest, it is as if our hearts intertwine and we become as one person. It is at times like this that I feel we are floating in the great ocean of the divine, joined by love to the absolute.

Since I started meditation I have found, to my surprise, that although it is not the main purpose of spiritual practice, my practice of psychotherapy has been transformed. I find that I often experience and understand things in the very first interview with a client, which would have taken weeks or months to achieve formerly. The more the ego is cleared out, the more sensitive you become and the more available you are to be of service to the person you are dealing with. I now see psychotherapy more and more as rough work to remove gross impressions. This prepares the way for a subtler cleaning, and for further spiritual development. Of course, not everyone is willing to continue further on this path and that is their right. But it remains true that the only really deep change is when this further step is undertaken.

Looking back over the years, it is clear to me that everything I attempted to do was premature. This is true in both my attempts to change the direction of mental health in this country, and what we were seeking to achieve in the Irish Foundation for human development. Perhaps I was just naïve and hopelessly over optimistic, or perhaps it is of some value to attempt to bring about change, even if it is too soon; that it may in some way prepare the ground for what is to come, or point the way so that these things can happen later.

I often wonder where I am now. I seem to live mostly in the

present and am peaceful and content just to be here, to listen to birds, watch animals and be part of nature. I live with Juno in Ranelagh, a place that still has something of the atmosphere of a village, even though it is now part of central Dublin. My brother and sister are still alive; she has been living in Newfoundland now for more than fifty years, so I don't see her very often. I still practice as a psycho-therapist and hold a clinic once a week, just to keep my hand in and keep up to date with what other psychiatrists are doing.

I still love music but I find, increasingly, that I am drawn towards quiet, peaceful pieces, whether it be the old Irish slow airs or the slow movements of Beethoven's late quartets, Schubert's quintet in C, or Bach's Goldberg Variations. Some of the old New Orleans jazz and blues music sounds as fresh as ever, even after sixty years, but much of what was produced then and since I can no longer listen to. Real creative genius is very rare, like Jelly Roll Morton, Louis Armstrong, Duke Ellington, Count Basie, Charlie Parker, Miles Davis or John Coltrane. And the same is true of much of what is snobbishly called 'serious' music. I also find that to me much contemporary music is just highly technical noise.

In the end, perhaps the most beautiful music of all is the 'music of silence'.

Appendix A

Autopoiesis

The Chilean biologists Umberto Maturana and Francesco Varella asked the fundamental question: 'What is it to be alive? What is the essential difference between a machine and a living organism?' They arrived at a similar formulation to that of Prigogine, that the essential characteristic of life is a state of self-organisation. The term they coined for this was autopoiesis, *auto* meaning self and *poiesis* (from the Greek root poinine) meaning to do or to make, thus self-producing. According to this view, the essence of a living thing is that it actively maintains and produces itself and that its first priority is to maintain itself in existence. As Maturana puts it, 'Living systems are cognitive systems, and living, as a process, is a process of cognition. This statement is valid for all organisms, with and without a nervous system.' In contrast to this, other structures, such as machines, they term 'alopoeitic', *allo* coming from the Greek for other. This means that they do or make things other than themselves and are made by 'others' (see Fig. 23).

Central to this notion of 'self-organisation' is the concept of 'boundedness'. It is by virtue of our boundary that we can distinguish what is inside from what is outside, what is self from non-self. As Varella points out, an interesting characteristic, which follows, is that living creatures essentially relate to themselves. This is all the more true as the complexity of self-organisation increases. Speaking of the brain Maturana said, 'The activities of nerve cells do not reflect on an environment independent of the living organism and hence do not allow for the construction of an absolutely existing external world.'[1]

At the human level we find a living system that is in an enormously complex state of communication with itself and hence manifests

343

Two Types of System

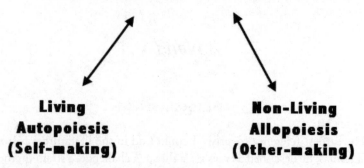

Living	Non-Living
Autopoiesis	Allopoiesis
(Self-making)	(Other-making)

Figure 23: Autopoiesis – two contrasting types of poietic system.

consciousness. What this means is that, if we ask the question 'what causes a given activity in our nervous system or any action of the whole human being?', the answer is the nervous system and the human being himself. No longer can we talk of some external input causing us to behave in a specific way. There are simply no direct correlations between the outside and the inside, between the inputs and the outputs. From this point of view, an input from the outside world can be no more than a perturbation, which meets a very complex world of internal communication busily creating its own reality. The most it can achieve is for the input to perturb the equilibrium and the state of self-coherence of the organism.

Here is the key statement of indeterminacy, that the living organism relates to the outside world only indirectly through the altering of its own state of self-coherence. Thus the organism may completely ignore the input altogether or it may readjust its state of self-organisation, with the conclusion, perhaps, that it acts in a particular manner. This has obvious implications for psychotherapy and psychotherapeutic research, since it means that studies that ask questions from the viewpoint of linear causality can only arrive at meaningless results. This is not to say that research into psychotherapy is impossible, but rather that we will have to approach it from a completely different perspective. It also means that, however useful a given psychotherapeutic method might be, it will be completely ineffective if the client refuses to undertake the work involved in carrying it through.

Notes

Chapter 10

1. The earliest reference to 'crisis' I could find in the literature was from a W. Thomas; he described a crisis as: 'a threat, a challenge, a strain on the intention, a call to new action. Yet it need not be always acute or extreme. Of course, a crisis may be so serious as to kill the organism or destroy the group, or it may result in failure or deterioration. But "crisis" as I am employing the term, is not to be regarded as habitually violent; it is simply a disturbance of habit and may be no more than an incident, a stimulation or suggestion.'

Chapter 19

1. An ancient Gaelic festival of games and other activities.

Chapter 20

1. 'Reform of Public Mental Health Care in Greece', Commission of the European Communities, Brussels, 29 March 1984.

Chapter 22

1. A.K. Rice, *Learning for Leadership – Inter-Personal and Inter-Group Relations*, Tavistock Publications, 1965.
2. W.R. Bion, *Experiences in Groups*, Tavistock Publications, 1961.
3. W.R. Bion, *Experiences in Groups*, Tavistock Publications, 1961

Chapter 27

1. Infusoria are the most primitive micro-organisms which were the first form of life and still the most common.
2. Taxonomy is a branch of biology concerned with the classification of licing organisms.
3. Darwin himself acknowledged this: 'To suppose that the eye, with all its inimitable contrivances … could have formed by natural selection, seems, I freely confess, absurd in the highest possible degree.'
4. S.M. Stanley, *Macroevolution*, Freeman, San Francisco, 1979.
5. E.F. Keller, *The Century of the Gene*, Harvard University Press, 2000.

6. James Watson, *The Double Helix*, Atheneum, New York, 1968.

7. E.F. Keller, *The Century of the Gene*, Harvard University Press, 2000, p. 55.

8. Mae-Wan Ho, *Genetic Engineering – Dream or Nightmare*, Gateway Books, UK, 1998.

9. E.F. Keller, *The Century of the Gene*, Harvard University Press, 2000, p. 55.

10. Fritjof Capra, *The Hidden Connections*, Harper Collins, 2002, pp. 151–152.

11. Marcus Pembrey, Professor of Clinical Genetics, in London.

12. Mae-Wan Ho, *Genetic Engineering – Dream or Nightmare*, Gateway Books, UK, 1998.

13. Lynn Margulis, *The Symbiotic Planet: A New Look at Evolution*, Phoenix, London, 1999, p. 29.

14. P. Teilhard de Chardin, (ed.), Sarah Appleton, *The Human Phenomenon*, Weber, Sussex Academic Press, 2003, p. 191.

15. P. Teilhard de Chardin, *Activation of L'Energie*, Harcourt, Brace, Jovanovich, San Diego, CA, 1963.

16. Prigogine worked mainly in the University of Brussels and the University of Texas.

Chapter 28

1. Fritjof Capra, *The Web of Life*, Harper Collins, 1996, p. 156.

2. Ibid, p. 82.

3. Ibid, p. 56.

4. C.B. Pert, *Molecules of Emotion*, Simon & Schuster, 1998, p. 186.

5. Ibid, p. 184.

6. Ibid, pp.186–87.

7. Ibid, p. 185.

8. Mae-Wan Ho, *Genetic Engineering – Dream or Nightmare*, Gateway Books, UK, 1998.

9. Named after the Greek earth goddess, the Gaia hypothesis is an ecological hypothesis proposing that living and non-living parts of the earth are viewed as a complex interacting system that can be thought of as a single organism. This hypothesis postulates that all living things have a regulatory effect on the Earth's environment that promotes life overall.

Chapter 29

1. *Time Magazine*.

2. A.H. Shaw Archer, *The Lincoln Encyclopaedia*, Macmillan, New York, 1950.

3. P. Kingsnorth, *One No, Many Yeses*, The Free Press, 2003, p. 285.

Chapter 30

1. David Healy, *The Antidepressant Era*, Harvard University Press, Cambridge, Mass.

2. C.G. Jung, (1935), *Analytical Psychology: Its Theory and Practice*, Routledge and Kegan Paul, 1976.

3. R.D. Laing, *Wisdom, Madness and Folly: The Making of a Psychiatrist*, Macmillan London Ltd., 1985, p. ix.

Chapter 32

1. Rupert Sheldrake, *Seven Experiments that Could Change the World*, Fourth Estate, London,1994, pp.76–77.

2. Gary Schwartz, 'Does Everything Have Memory', CD, *Memory Beyond the Brain*, V1, S.M.N.

3. S. Freud, *An Autobiographical Study*, 1924, London, Hogarth Press and the Institute of Psychoanalysis, 20: 3–70.

4. W.B. Cannon, *Bodily Changes in Pain, Hunger, Fear and Rage: An Account of Recent Researches into the Function of Emotional Excitement*, 2nd ed., Appelton-Century-Crofts, New York, 1929.

5. Richard Davidson, 'The Neuroscience of Emotion', in *Destructive Emotions*, by Daniel Goleman, Bantam Dell, London, 2004, p. 180.

6. P.A. Levine , *Waking the Tiger: Healing Trauma*, North Atlantic Books, 1997, pp. 15-16.

7. J.C. Nemiah, 'Janet Redivivus: The Centenary of L'Automatisme Psychologique', *American Journal of Psychiatry* 1989: 146: 12: 1527-1529.

8. S. Freud, *The Origins of Psycho-analysis Letters to Wilhelm Fleiss*, drafts and notes: 1887–1902, New York Basic Books, 1977.

9. S. Freud, (1914), 'History of the Psycho-analytic Movement', in *The Life and Work of Sigmund Freud*, by E. Jones, Pelican Books, London, 1964.

10. J.M. Masson, *The Assault on Truth*, Penguin Books, Middlesex, 1985.

11. S. Freud, 'Studies in Hysteria', in *Complete Psychological Works,* Vol. 18, 1893, trans. and ed. J. Strachey Hogarth Press, London, 1893.

12. Ibid.

13. Ibid.

14. S. Freud, (1886), 'The Aetiology of Hysteria', in *Complete Psychological Works*, Vol. 18, trans. and ed. J. Strachey, Hogarth Press, London, 1954.

15. Ibid.

16. S. Freud, (1896), 'Heredity and the Aetiology of Neurosis', in *Complete Psychological Works*, Vol. 3, trans. and ed. J. Strachey, Hogarth Press, London 1954b.

17. E. Jones (1964), *The Life and work of Sigmund Freud*, Pelican Books, London 1964.

18. S. Freud (1914), 'History of the Psycho-analytic Movement', in *The Life and Work of Sigmund Freud*, by E. Jones, Pelican Books, London, 1964.
19. J.M. Masson., *The Assault on Truth*, Penguin Books, Middlesex, 1985.
20. P. Janet, (1889), *L'Automatisme Psychologique*, Felix Alcan, Paris, 1973.
21. P. Janet, *Psychological Healing: Historical and Clinical Study*, Vols. 1 & 2, New York, Macmillan, 1925, under the heading, 'Unassimilated Happenings'.
22. A. Kardiner, *The Traumatic Neuroses of War*, Harper, New York, 1941.
23 F.C. Bartlett, (1932), *Remembering: A Study in Experimental and Social Psychology*, Cambridge Univeristy Press, Cambridge, 1977.
24. E. Tulving, *Organisation of Memory*, Academic Press, New York, 1972.
25. R.D. Laing, 'The Voice of Experience', in *The Tie and the Cut-off*, Penguin books Ltd., London, 1982.
26. S. Freud, (1886), 'The Aetiology of Hysteria', in *Complete Psychological Works*, Vol. 18, trans. and ed. Strachey, Hogarth Press, London, 1954.

Chapter 33

1. *Psychiatric Bulletin* (1997), 21, 663–665. These recommendations were signed by John Cox, Dean of the Royal College of Psychiatrists.
2. Brian L. Weiss, *Many Lives, Many Masters*, Piatkus Books Ltd., London, 1994.
3. Brian L. Weiss, *Through Time into Healing*, Piatkus Books Ltd., London, 1995.
4. Gary Schwartz, *The After Life Experiments*, New York, Atria Books, 2001.
5. Pin Van Lommel, 'Near Death Experiences', CD, *Memory Beyond the Brain*, V1, S.M.N.
6. S. Arieti, *Interpretation of Schizophrenia*, Robert Brunner, New York, 1955.

Chapter 34

1. Ram Chandra, 'Sahaj marg Philosophy', in *Complete Works of Ram Chandra*, Vol. 1 Shri Ram Chandra Mission, North American Publishing Committee, CA, USA, 1989, p. 297.

Chapter 35

1. Chandogya Upanishad, Penguin, 1965.
2. J.C. Pearce, *Evolution's End*, Harper Collins, New York, 1992.

Appendix A

1. H.R. Maturana and F.J. Varela,, *The Tree of Knowledge: The Biological Roots of Human Understanding*, Shambhala Publications, 1987.

Bibliography

Ackner, B., Harris, A., and Oldham, A.J., 'Insulin Treatment of Schizophrenia: A Controlled Study', *Lancet*, 1, 607, 1957.

Arieti, S., *Interpretation of Schizophrenia*, Robert Brunner, New York, 1955.

Aristotle, *The Complete Works: the Revised Oxford Translation*, Princeton University Press, 1984.

Barrington, R., *Health, Medicine and Politics – in Ireland 1900–1970*, Institute of Public administration, Dublin, 1987.

Bartlett, F.C. (1932), *Remembering: A Study in Experimental and Social Psychology*, Cambridge University Press, Cambridge, 1977.

Basaglia, F., *Psychiatry Inside Out: Selected Writings*, Columbia University Press, New York, 1987.

Bateson, G., Jackson, D.D., Haley, J., and Weakland, J., 'Towards a Theory of Schizophrenia', *Behavioural Science*, 1, 251–64, 1956.

_____, *Steps to an Ecology of Mind*, Chandler Publishing, Toronto, 1972.

_____, *Mind and Nature: A Necessary Unity*, Fontana, London, 1980.

Bertalanffy, L. von, *General Systems Theory*, Braziller, New York, 1968.

Bierer, J., and Browne, I., 'An Experiment with a Psychiatric Night Hospital', *Proceedings of the Royal Society of Medicine,* 1959.

Bion, W.R., *Experiences in Groups*, Tavistock Publications, London, 1961.

Bohm, D., *Wholeness and the Implicate Order*, Ark Paperbacks, London, 1983.

Browne, I.W., 'Psychiatry in Ireland', *American Journal of Psychiatry*, 119, 816–819, 1963.

Browne I.W., and Hackett, T.P., 'Reactions to the Threat of Immanent Death: A Study of Patients on the Cardiac Pacemaker', *Irish Journal of Medical Science*, 1963.

Browne I.W., Ryan, J.P.A., and McGrath, S.D., 'The Acute Withdrawal Phase in Alcoholism', *Lancet* 1, 959-960, 1959.

Browne, I.W., and Walsh, D., *Psychiatric Services for the Dublin Area*, 1965.

Cannon, W.B., *The Wisdom of the Body*, Norton, New York, 1932.

Caplan, G., *Principles of Preventive Psychiatry*, Tavistock Publications, London, 1964.

_____, *The Theory and Practice of Mental Health Consultation*, Basic Books, New York, 1970.

Capra, Fritjof, *The Hidden Connections*, Harper Collins, London, 2002.

_____, *The Tao of Physics*, Fontana, London, 1976.

_____, *The Turning Point*, Flamingo, London, 1983.

_____, *The Web of Life*, Harper Collins, London, 1996.

Cleary, A., The Resocialisation Project, Report on the EEC Rehabilitation Unit, St Brendan's Hospital, 1987.

Darwin, C., *The Descent of Man*, Princeton University Press, Princeton, 1981.

—, *The Origin of Species*, Mentor, London, 1958.

Davidson, Richard, 'The Neuroscience of Emotion', in *Destructive Emotions*, Daniel Goleman, Bantam Dell, London, 2004.

Dawkins R., *The Selfish Gene*, Oxford University Press, Oxford, 1976.

'Development of Psychiatric Services', Report of Chief Psychiatrist, D.H.A., March 1966.

Development of Mental Health Services, E.H.B., June 1972.

Diagnostic and Statistical Manual of Mental Disorders, fourth ed., American Psychiatric Association, Washington, DC, 1994.

Dickinson, E., *The Complete Poems of Emily Dickinson*, ed. Thomas H. Johnson, Little, Brown and Company, Boston, 1970.

Drake, S., *Galileo Studies*, University of Michigan Press, Michigan, 1970.

'Education for Development', Report on the North Mayo/Sligo Pilot Project, Irish Foundation for Human Development, November 1982.

Erikson, E.H., *Childhood and Society*, W.W. Norton, New York, 1950.

Foerster, Heinz von and Zopf, G.W., *Principles of Self-Organisation*, Pergamon, New York, 1962.

Freud, S. (1893), 'Studies in Hysteria', in *Complete Psychological Works*, Vol. 2, trans. and ed. I. Strachey, Hogarth Press, London, 1954.

(1886), 'The Aetiology of Hysteria', in *Complete Psychological Works*, Vol. 18, trans. & ed. I. Strachey, Hogarth Press, London, 1954.

_____ (1914), 'History of the Psycho-analytic Movement', in *The Life and Work of Sigmund Freud*, by E. Jones, Pelican Books, London, 1964.

Grof, S., *Beyond the Brain*, State University of New York Press, Albany, NY, 1985.

_____, *Realms of the Human Unconscious*, Viking Press, New York (1975).

Haley, J., *Uncommon Therapy: The Psychiatric Techniques of Milton H. Erickson*, W.W. Norton, New York, 1986.

Hartmann, M. & Rumler L., in *Fury on Earth: A Biography of Wilhelm Reich*, by M. Sharaf, Andre Deutsch, London, 1983.

Healy, D., *The Antidepressant Era*, Harvard University Press, Cambridge Massachusetts, 1999.

Ho, Mae-Won, *Genetic Engineering: Dream or Nightmare,* Gateway Books, UK, 1998.

Janet, P. (1889), *L'Automatisme Psychologique*, Felix Alcan, Paris, 1973.

_____ *Psychological Healing: Historical and Clinical Study*, Vols. 1 & 2, Macmillan, New York, 1925.

Jung, C.G. (1935), *Analytical Psychology: Its Theory and Practice*, Routledge and Kegan Paul, London, 1976.

_____, 'Essays on Synchronicity', in *Collected Works*, Routledge and Kegan Paul, London, 1963.

Kardiner, A., *The Traumatic Neuroses of War*, Harper, New York, 1941.

Keller, E.F., *The Century of the Gene*, Harvard University Press, Cambridge Massachusetts, 2000.

Kelly, G., *The Psychology of Personal Constructs*, W.W. Norton. New York, 1955.

Kingsnorth, P., *One No, Many Yeses*, The Free Press, Simon and Schuster, London, 2003.

Klein, M., *The Psychoanalysis of Children*, Hogarth, London, 1932.

Laing, R.D. (1960), *The Divided Self*, Penguin Books, Middlesex, 1990.

_____, *Wisdom, Madness and Folly: The Making of a Psychiatrist*, Macmillan, London, 1985.

Levine, P.A., *Waking the Tiger: Healing Trauma*, North Atlantic Books, Berkeley, 1997.

Lindemann, E., 'Symptomatology and Management of Acute Grief', *American Journal of Psychiatry,* 101, 141–48. 1944.

Lommel, P. van, 'Near Death Experiences', CD, *Memory Beyond the Brain*, Beyond the Brain V1, S.M.N.

_____, et al, 'Near Death Experiences – Survivors of Cardiac Arrest', *Lancet*, 344, 828–30, 1994.

Margulis L., *The Symbiotic Planet: A New Look at Evolution*, Phoenix, London, 1999.

Martindale, B.V., Bateman, A., Crowe, M., and Margisone, F., *Psychosis: Psychological Approaches and their Effectiveness*, Gaskell, London, 2000.

Maturana, H.R. and Varela, F.J., *The Tree of Knowledge: The Biological Roots of Human Understanding*, Shambhala Publications, 1987.

Masson, J.M., *The Assault on Truth*, Penguin Books, Middlesex, 1985.

Monod, J., *Chance and Necessity*, Collins, London, 1972.

Pearce, J.C., *Evolution's End*, Harper Collins, New York, 1992.

Pembrey, M., BBC, Science & Nature, TV and Radio follow up, 2005.

Pert, C.B., *Molecules of Emotion*, Simon & Schuster, London, 1998.

Pettit, P., *The Gentle Revolution: Crisis in the Universities*, ed. Philip Pettit, Scepter Books, Dublin, 1969.

Plato, *The Collected Dialogues*, Princeton University Press, New York, 1961.

'Planning for the Future', Report of a Study Group on the Development of Psychiatric services, Dublin, Dept. of Health, The Stationery Office, December 1984.

Prigogine, I., *From Being to Becoming: Time and Complexity in the Physical Sciences*, Freeman and Company, San Francisco, 1980.

Prigogine, I., and Stengers I., *Order Out of Chaos*, William Heinemann, London, 1984.

Ram Chandra, *Complete Works of Ram Chandra*, Ram Chandra Mission, Shahjahanpur (UP), India, 1984.

Read, J., Mosher, L.R., and Bentall R.P., *Models of Madness: Psychological, Social and Biological Approaches to Schizophrenia*, Brunner–Routledge, East Sussex, 2004.

'Report of Public Mental Health Care in Greece': Commission of the European Communities, Brussels, March 1984.

Reynolds, Joseph, Grangegorman: Psychiatric Care in Dublin since 1815, Institute of Public Administrations, 1992.

Rice, A.K., *Learning for Leadership*, Tavistock Publications, London, 1963.

Schwartz, G., *The After Life Experiments*, Atria Books, New York, 2001.

Schwartz, Gary, 'Does Everything Have Memory', CD *Memory Beyond the Brain*, Beyond the Brain V1, S.M.N.

Schwartz, Gary et al, *The Living Energy Universe*, Hamption Roads, Charlottesville, VA, 1999.

Schwartz, Gary, 'The After Life Experiments', CD, *Memory Beyond the Brain*, Beyond the Brain V1, S.M.N.

Sheldrake, R., *The Presence of the Past: Morphic Resonance and the Habits of Nature*, Collins, London, 1988.

Sheldrake, R., *Seven Experiments That Could Change the World*, Fourth Estate, London, 1995.

Squire L.R. and Zola, M.S., 'The Medial Temporal Lobe Memory System', *Science*, 253:,1380–86, 1991.

Stanley S.M., *Macroevolution*, Freeman, San Francisco.

St Augustine, *Confessions of St Augustine*, trans. by J.K. Ryan, Doubleday, Garden City, New York, 1960.

St Thomas Aquinas, *Summa Theologica*, Benziger, New York, 1947.

Sullivan, H.S., 'The Onset of Schizophrenia', *American Journal of Psychiatry*, 105, 135–139, 1927.

Tarnas, R., *The Passion of the Western World*, Pimlico, London, 1996.

Teilhard de Chardin, P., *Activation of L'Energie*, Harcourt, Brace, Jovanovich, San Diego, CA, 1963.

_____, *The Human Phenomenon*, ed. Sarah Appleton, Weber, Sussex Academic Press, Sussex, 2003.

Tulving, E., *Organisation of Memory*, Academic Press, New York, 1972.

Watson, J.D., and Crick, F., 'Structure for Deoxyribose Nucleic Acid', in *Nature*, 171, 1953.

Whelan, K., *Wexford: History and Society*, Geography Publications, Dublin, 1987.

Watson, J.D., *The Double Helix*, Atheneum, New York, 1968.

Wiener, N., *Cybernetics*, MIT Press, Boston, 1961.

Index

and pharmaceutical industry
262
Prozac 2-3
psychoactive 261
synthetic psilocybin 83, 95
tranquillisers 82, 255, 261
Drumm, Brendan 145
Dublin
community groups 178
north inner city 174-5
Dublin Corporation 134, 171, 175
Dublin Health Authority 97, 99-102,
132-3, 137, 143, 165
Dublin Mental Health Board 166
Dublin Transportation Study 175
Dubliners, The 46, 167
Dunne, Dr John 99-102, 104, 106,
127-8, 135
Dunne family 38, 44, 65

Eastern Health Board 142-4, 146,
153-4, 308-9
Echstein, Emma 297
ECT 3, 61-3
EEC 152-3, 176
Einstein, Albert 231-2, 320
Eli Lilly 77, 82
Ellington, Duke 83, 342
Ennis, County Clare 41
Ennis, Seamus 40, 43
Erickson, Erik 88, 91, 97
Erickson, Milton 80, 96
Etude Médico Légale 293
EU 156, 217
European Commission 156
European Community 156, 158
European Economic Community see
EEC
European Union see EU
Evening Herald 165
evolution 233, 236
Evolution's End 336
experiential therapy 256-8, 264-5,
310-11

false memory syndrome 258, 299,
302-3
families
disturbed 96
psychological problems at
Christmas 1-2
secrets and myths 317
therapy for 323
farm 18-20
Farrell, Mary 171
father 11-17, 21-2, 25-6, 33-4, 39, 75
father's family and ancestors 13-14, 16
fear of failure 35-6
feedback 242-3
Fernandez, Dr Joe 132
Fianna Fáil 136
field 14, 16, 21-3, 27-8
figures,
autopoiesis 344
blind leading blind 182
brain 288, 290
corporation devouring all before it 249
cycle of experience in PTSD
306
dual functions of therapist 274
extreme emotions 184
feedback loop 242
George Kelly's Cycle of Experience 267
interconnections 252
life crises 89, 91, 92, 93
organisations destroying
human communities 252
personal boundaries 274
personality types as function
of defence and coping skills
264
self-organising systems 238
systems causality 237
therapeutic relationship 273
two corporations mating
(merging) 249
two forms of feedback 242
Fine Gael 163

Institutes of Technology 155
institutionalisation 323
insulin coma therapy 62
IRA 190-5, 197
Irish Catholic 281
Irish Countrywomen's Association 256-7
Irish Farmers Association 178
Irish Foundation for Human Development 127, 152, 160-226, 271
    conferences 196-206, 209
    demise 220-6
    Dublin seminar 177
    North-west Centre for Learning and Development 207
    starting up 161-78
Irish Independent 165
Irish Press 165
Irish Times, The 102, 173
Israel 69, 334
Italy 147-8
Ivory, William 11-12

Jackson, Mahalia 84
Jacquet, Illinois 83
James Connolly Memorial Hospital 138
James I, King 230
Janet, Pierre 292-3, 297-8
jazz 25-32, 38, 75, 165, 272, 342
    heard in the USA 78, 83-4
    own band 30-1, 38
    Ronnie Scott's club 171
Jones, Ernest 295
Jung, Carl 269, 284, 310, 312

Kardiner, Abram 299
karmic transmission 312-13
Kavanagh, Colm 207, 209
Kealy, Loughlin 174-5, 176-7
Keller, Evelyn 234
Kelly, George 264, 266-8, 318-19, 322
Kennedy, John F. 87
Kerry 43, 177
Kiernan, Matt 40

Killarney 37
Kilrush 40
King, Martin Luther 161
Klein, Melanie 187, 310
Kraft-Ebbing 297
Kubler-Ross, Elizabeth 79, 90, 310

La Rochefoucauld, François de 248
Laing, R.D. 111, 230, 269
Lamarck, Jean Baptiste 232, 235
Lannigan, Johnny 49
Late Late Show 153, 269-71
L'Automatisme Psychologique 298
Lea, Brian 281
leadership 205-6
    Learning for Leadership 185
Leary, Timothy 82-3, 95
Lee, Dr 70
Lemass, Seán 128
Leros 156-9
Leucippus 229
Levine, June (second wife) 1-2, 4-7, 120-1, 222-4, 329-31, 341-2
Levine, Peter 292, 311
life crises
    figures 89, 91, 92, 93
    main forms of 91-2
    see also crisis intervention
Lincoln, President Abraham 251, 253
Lindemann, Professor Eric 79, 80, 310
Little Sisters of the Assumption 113, 123, 203-4
living systems 240-7
lobotomy 50-1
London 69-76
Long Kesh 195
Loughrea 39
Lovelock, James 246
Lowell, Robert 248
Lynch, Paddy 167-8, 196
Lynch, Tom 142

McCabe, Fergus 175
McConnell, Adam 49
McCourt, Willie 81